# LETTERS FROM THE EDITOR
## *THE NEW YORKER*'S
## HAROLD ROSS

# LETTERS FROM THE EDITOR

## *THE NEW YORKER'S*

## HAROLD ROSS

*Edited by Thomas Kunkel*

THE MODERN LIBRARY

NEW YORK

2000 Modern Library Edition

Copyright © 2000 by Thomas Kunkel

All rights reserved under International and Pan-American Copyright Conventions.
Published in the United States by Random House, Inc., New York,
and simultaneously in Canada by Random House of Canada Limited, Toronto.

Modern Library and colophon are registered trademarks of Random House, Inc.

Library of Congress Cataloging-in-Publication Data
Ross, Harold Wallace, 1892–1951.
Letters from the editor: the New Yorker's Harold Ross / edited by
Thomas Kunkel.
    p.   cm.
Includes index.
ISBN 0-375-50397-8 (acid-free paper)
1. Ross, Harold Wallace. 1892–1951 Correspondence.
2. Journalists—United States Correspondence.   3. Editors—United
States Correspondence.   4. New Yorker (New York, N.Y. : 1925)
I. Kunkel, Thomas.   II. Title.
PN4874.R615A4   2000
070.4'1'092—dc21
    [B]        99-34703

Modern Library website address: www.modernlibrary.com

Printed in the United States of America on acid-free paper

2    4    6    8    9    7    5    3

First Edition

*For Patricia Ross, who lost him too soon*

# ACKNOWLEDGMENTS

If you ever have the pleasant opportunity to spend time in the archived correspondence of James Thurber, Frank Sullivan, Rebecca West, E. B. and Katharine White, and other friends and associates of Harold Wallace Ross, something will strike you right away: It was a given on their part that Ross's own letters would one day be collected and published. They said as much, often, in their notes to one another. This was not mere tribute to Ross's status as one of the great editors of a uniquely literary age. Thurber and the others simply knew in their bones that letters so artful and funny, not to mention so revealing of the inner workings of *The New Yorker*, by rights would be passed along to a wider audience.

If the publication took several decades longer than they expected, I hope the resulting volume would have met with their approval.

One thing is certain: This book could not have happened without the support and help of a number of people—chief among them Tina Brown, former editor of *The New Yorker*, and her husband, Harry Evans, former president and publisher of Random House, who together gave it the green light several years ago. My thanks go also to *The New Yorker* for its permission to reproduce Ross's magazine-related letters, which are the bulk of this collection, and to Roger Angell and Allene White for permission to use material from, respectively, the papers of Katharine S. White and E. B. White.

Patricia Ross Honcoop, Ross's only child, not only helped bring this book about but has become a valued friend. So too have *New Yorker* staff writer Philip Hamburger and his wife, Anna, whose abiding encouragement and generosity are appreciated more than they will ever know. Thanks are also due my agent, Peter Matson, one of the last of the best; my editor at Random House, Jeanne Tift, who embraced this project with enthusiasm and understanding; and to Sono Rosenberg, whose crisp line editing saved the day on more occasions than I care to admit.

The majority of Ross's letters can be found in the *New Yorker* archives at the New York Public Library's Rare Books and Manuscripts Division, and they appear here with the library's permission. (*New Yorker* fans and Ph.D. candidates everywhere, take note: Hundreds of thousands of the magazine's manuscripts, internal memoranda, correspondence, and other documents are catalogued and open to the public there.) The library also maintains the papers of H. L. Mencken, who exchanged many wonderful letters with Ross. For their patience and unfailing good humor, I commend the library's expert staff, with special thanks going to my friend Mimi Bowling.

Other Ross letters were drawn from collections around the country. So let me acknowledge the help and permissions of: Cornell University's Kroch Library, which houses the letters of E. B. White and Frank Sullivan; Bryn Mawr College's Canaday Library, which has Katharine S. White's papers; the University of Oregon Library, which has Jane Grant's; Yale University's Beinecke Library, which has Rebecca West's correspondence and James Thurber's *New Yorker*–related material; and Boston University's Mugar Library, which keeps the Ralph Ingersoll collection. I similarly acknowledge the libraries of the University of Wyoming, Hamilton College, Harvard University, the University of Florida, New York University, Princeton University, and Syracuse University, as well as the Library of Congress, the New-York Historical Society, and the State Historical Society of Wisconsin.

Saving the best for last—thanks, Deb, for the countless ways you helped make this happen, and for everything else.

# Contents

# INTRODUCTION

Researching a biography is often compared to detective work, and certainly much sleuthing must transpire before the first word ever slips from the writer's fingertips. Even so, I find this analogy altogether too grim, not only for its criminal overtones but for its suggestion of a kind of purposeful slogging on the part of the pursuer. For most biographers there is more sheer joy in the exercise than that; it is less a life-or-death pursuit than an open-ended game of hide-and-seek. Some writers find their quarry, others never do. The serendipity is part of the fun.

As for me, I found Harold Wallace Ross in Room 328 of the New York Public Library. True, he had been dead for more than forty years. But Ross, founding editor and guiding spirit of *The New Yorker* magazine, is loudly, reprovingly alive in the tens of thousands of letters packed away in a hundred or more archival containers. Before I ever got into the magazine's archives, now kept at the library, I had formed a strong impression of Ross, one gleaned from dozens of interviews with those who knew him, from the memoirs of others, and from the sundry correspondence of his that I had unearthed in other collections. But nothing prepared me for the sheer personality that bounded from these musty gray boxes like a freed genie. In less than an hour's eavesdropping I encountered my man scolding Henry Luce, lecturing Orson Welles, baiting J. Edgar Hoover, inviting Noel Coward and Ginger Rogers to the circus, wheedling Ernest Hemingway ("Are you ever going to write any short stories again? My God"), offering to sell Harpo Marx a used car and James Cagney a used tractor, and explaining to restaurateur-to-the-stars Dave Chasen, step by step, how to smoke a turkey.

There's so much of that kind of thing in the files that one could get the impression Ross had little time to run his magazine. But of course Ross ran *The New Yorker* utterly, relentlessly, and largely in the same way he juggled his demanding social life—with a copious stream of letters, memoranda, telegrams, even scrawled notes to his staff and contributors. The editor's dispatches spill over with ideas, explanations, tips, gossip, suggestions, and occasionally apologies. He was not above haranguing or begging for material; "God damn it, *write* something!" was a familiar Rossian benediction. At other times he offered advice. "Don't waste your time and words on letters," he once said to St. Clair McKelway. "You don't get paid for them." He imparted this, naturally, in a letter.

The letters reprinted here, then, represent but a sampler of the available material, and they are intended in that vein. Which is to say they convey an honest sense of the man, his droll outlook, the way he lived an eventful but messy life, and, most important, the way he directed the magazine that remains his legacy. Ross, as the reader will see, was propelled by boundless energy and interests. He seemed to know everyone of his day worth knowing, and led an existence far larger than seems possible today.

Letter writing was at the core of that existence, as much a part of Ross as his unruly hair or the double-wide gap in his front teeth. A turn-of-the-century child of the frontier, son of an immigrant miner and a prim prairie schoolmarm, Ross was always something of a nineteenth-century figure even as he guided the twentieth century's most literate magazine. Corresponding, like smoking and swearing, was a habit Ross acquired early and never relinquished.

He was born in 1892 in Aspen, Colorado, when the place was a shabby silver-mining outpost. After silver crashed, the Rosses moved to Salt Lake City, Utah. From boyhood Harold exhibited an organic restlessness, both intellectual and physical. He devoured the stories of Jack London and the romantic exploits of war correspondents such as Richard Harding Davis, and perhaps thus inspired, he regularly ran away from home. After his sophomore year Ross quit high school to go to work for the *Salt Lake Telegram*. Then in his late teens he hit the rails as a "tramp" reporter, traveling the West working at one newspaper after another, as needed. From the San Francisco Bay area he drifted to Panama, where he worked for a time on the canal. He came back to the States by way of New Orleans and bounded into Atlanta just in time to cover the murder trial of Leo Frank. (Ross doubted Frank's guilt and wrote that his prosecution had been an affront.) He was back working in San Francisco when the United States entered the World War, and he enlisted on the spot.

In France Ross joined the staff of the army newspaper, *The Stars and Stripes*. Finally, and legitimately, he was a war correspondent, but the truth is Ross actually distinguished himself far more when he was invited to edit the weekly. For the first time in his life he realized he had a knack for managing difficult but talented people. The wartime experience likewise shaped his personal life. He grew close to staff writer Alexander Woollcott, who before the war was the drama critic for *The New York Times*, and Woollcott in turn introduced Ross to a bright and intense young woman named Jane Grant, whom Ross would marry.

This was in New York after the war, where Ross was editing veterans' magazines and had, rather by accident, helped Woollcott establish a standing luncheon that became the Algonquin Round Table. This inventive collection of friends from the media and entertainment worlds, all in their twenties and early thirties, came to symbolize for many the new youthful exuberance of postwar Manhattan. Ross and Jane enjoyed being in the middle of it all, living in what felt like a champagne bubble. Indeed, with Woollcott and another friend, they had transformed two rundown, side-by-side brownstones in the Hell's Kitchen area into an elegant cooperative, and it quickly became a nocturnal extension of the Round Table.

Professionally, however, Ross grew weary of editing stale publications for cheap, unimaginative publishers. He began to conceive a magazine of his own, one that might advance a new kind of humor, more sophisticated and wrapped in a glossy package. This, he was sure, would attract a discerning audience that top New York advertisers couldn't ignore.

Such was the genesis of *The New Yorker*. With the financial backing of Raoul Fleischmann, a card-playing acquaintance who was bored running his family's commercial bakery, Ross launched *The New Yorker* in February of 1925. After a start so shaky it was nearly fatal, the magazine caught on by dint of Ross's determination and the precocious talents of Katharine and E. B. White, James Thurber, Wolcott Gibbs, Robert Benchley, Dorothy Parker, Lois Long, Peter Arno, Helen Hokinson, and many other Ross discoveries. *The New Yorker* would flourish through the Depression and come into its own as a literary journal, a kind of world diary, during World War II. By 1950, when it turned twenty-five, Ross's "fifteen-cent comic paper" was an American icon, and its profane, eccentric proprietor acclaimed as one of the best editors in the world.

Through all those years Ross's work regimen changed little; invariably several hours a day were given over to correspondence. The ironic fact is that the man who never wrote a word (at least under his own name) for *The New Yorker* was, with the possible exception of the protean Edmund Wilson, the most prolific writer in its history.

Most of Ross's correspondence went out on *New Yorker* letterhead, of course, neatly typed by secretaries who could be as finicky about spelling and grammar as the magazine's vaunted editors. But some of his more interesting letters are those he batted out himself, late at night, in the porchlike study of his home in Stamford, Connecticut. These letters were done on flimsy beige copy paper and written in a hurry, riddled with x-outs and blithely unconcerned with misspellings, omitted words, or grammatical lapses. The lines sometimes fall off the page as the end of the paper sneaked up on him. Often at the close, to explain the disheveled condition of the foregoing, Ross would write, "No time to read over this."

Clean or shaggy, the correspondence reveals an expansive intellect and wit, and helps bury any notion that Ross was a clumsy rube whose magazine succeeded in spite of him. It is true that he was not always comfortable articulating himself out loud, especially in public, but at the typewriter Ross never flinched. His letters reveal him unvarnished, in every facet of his complicated personality. With his partner and benefactor, Fleischmann, he was typically patronizing. With Thurber he was patient. With the Whites he was natural. With H. L. Mencken he was respectful. With Rebecca West he was reflective. With his old pal Frank Sullivan he was uninhibited. Frequently he was funny—very funny. "All I know is what I read in the papers," he once wrote his friend and *New Yorker* colleague Geoffrey Hellman, "and from these I learn that George White is your wife's former husband's lawyer. He was my first wife's lawyer, and a man I bitterly resent. I am ready to gang him at any time you say." Or here is an aside to Sullivan: "If any woman was talking about me at Saratoga it was in a purely reminiscent vein." On the other hand, when taking aim at politicians or publishers or (especially) lawyers, Ross could be positively splenetic. "Long life to the legal profession!" he fired in one of many missives to his ex-wife's attorneys. "In just about ten years you boys will have this country so thoroughly tied up that it can't turn a wheel, and then everybody will just go gracefully out of business."

Elsewhere there is much generosity in the letters, as there was in the man, whether Ross was appealing to Vincent Astor for a roomier apartment for a *New Yorker* writer or soliciting a specialist's help on behalf of an afflicted niece. Mostly, a reader comes away from this material appreciating his passion, which was unbridled, and his integrity, which was complete. It was no extravagant observation when Peter De Vries said of Ross that, like Mencken and Sandburg, he proved "America's great contribution is not plastics but quarter-sawed oak."

That sentiment would have embarrassed Ross, who always deflected credit for *The New Yorker* to his staff. But he would have loved the ring of it—as he did all De Vries's lines—because the written word mattered to him. His schoolteacher mother drilled into him an appreciation for grammar and precise expression. Subsequently, Ross the grown-up read Fowler's *Modern English Usage* for pleasure and once gave an editor friend a page of commas for Christmas. He had the utmost respect for people who could build beautiful sentences, and he did everything in his power to encourage and protect them. As

E. B. White confided to Frank Sullivan, "In retrospect I am beginning to think of him as an Atlas who lacked muscle tone but who God damn well decided he was going to hold up the world anyway."

In the late thirties, when Ross was scouting for new editing talent, he interviewed a university professor but didn't think the man would abandon the comfort of academe for the rough-and-tumble of weekly deadlines. He "wanted to know what becomes of magazine editors in their old age," Ross reported to Katharine White. "Well, what does?"

Ross would never find out. A chain-smoker since his teens, Ross in the summer of 1951 learned that he had cancer. He submitted himself to the then relatively novel regimen of radiation therapy, but the cancer was intractable. He died that December, at age fifty-nine.

One sloppy winter's afternoon, after I had spent several weeks reading over Ross's letters, I walked over to the public library's annex on West Forty-third Street. A curator there pulled out another box for me. This one didn't contain letters but a few rubbery disks, rather like primitive CDs. And in fact he next brought out a phonograph-like machine and carefully mounted the disk onto it.

When he dropped the needle and flipped a switch, a thin, gravelly voice emerged. It was Ross, sounding a little like Walter Matthau, albeit in a higher, more nasal pitch, which struck me as amusing since Ross *looked* a little like Walter Matthau, too. I was euphoric, because given Ross's well-known disdain for public appearances I had begun to think I would never find that distinctive voice captured on tape, or disk, or any other medium. I sat back, turned on my tape recorder, and listened to a man dead four decades talk to me.

He was dictating letters.

# Letters from the Editor
## *The New Yorker*'s
## Harold Ross

# "WELL, HERE'S THE WAR OVER . . ."

## 1917–1924

Ross's earliest surviving letters date from his World War I service in France. Working as a reporter on the San Francisco waterfront when America entered the war, Ross signed up immediately. In Paris he joined *The Stars and Stripes*, the army newspaper, and before long found himself directing a staff that included Grantland Rice and the corpulent, flamboyant drama critic of *The New York Times*, Alexander Woollcott. Also in Paris Ross fell in love with a friend of Alec's, Jane Grant. Indeed, although the editor had always regarded eastern "dudes" with contempt, he would follow Jane and Woollcott back to Manhattan after the war. This proved a salutary decision, for it was in Jazz Age New York that Ross married Jane, learned the magazine trade, helped launch the Algonquin Round Table, went to a lot of parties, and, most important, fixed on a destiny. By the summer of 1924 he had the idea, as well as a name, for a prospective weekly magazine of his own invention. All he needed was money. Ross found his backer in Raoul Fleischmann, a social acquaintance and a bit of a gambler who considered the family business, baking bread, tedious.

———

*Ross and many fellow enlistees from California joined what became the army's 18th Engineers railway regiment. They were among the first*

*American troops to reach France, and Ross wrote the paper with this ac-
count of their Atlantic crossing.*

## TO THE *SAN FRANCISCO EXAMINER*

*[SEPTEMBER 1917]*

... It has been an uncomfortable trip. There were two thousand six
hundred troops aboard—my own regiment and another—quartered
between decks in what originally provided space for one thousand
steerage passengers. We had bunks two feet wide, six feet long and two
tiers high. The first morning all my stuff, carefully stowed under the
bunk, was under two feet of water and some of it floated off. The
whole bunch slept with their clothes on ready for a bath.

We came across the continent in seven days and went immediately
aboard this ship, a Britisher. It has been a remarkable movement of a
regiment, the first, I believe, by a British transport. We joined a convoy
train of five other vessels at a Canadian port and came across by ways
unknown to me, but obviously devious.

Three days out we were met by six chasers—one for each of us.
They are strange little craft that roll more than anything I ever saw. In
a moderate sea they seem to be under water about half the time. They
can move at thirty-five knots, however, and look like they would be
bad people for the submarines to meet up with. We slept better with
them alongside.

## TO GEORGE AND IDA ROSS

*[AUTUMN 1917]*

Dear Folks:

... There is no real news. The company is still where it has been for
a certain vague time and will be here for an equally vague time. I'm
feeling fine, eating regularly and enjoying myself. By way of comfort—mutually—may remark that I have it on rather good authority
that this railroad regiment never will get in the danger zone.

With love,

Harold

*After an unpromising stint in officer training school, Ross went AWOL and headed for Paris to join the staff of the newly formed* Stars and Stripes. *Within weeks he conceived the idea of having American troops sponsor French children orphaned or made homeless by the war, and to generate support for the campaign he again wrote the* Examiner. *He included this account of his introduction to Big Bertha, the huge gun with which the Germans shelled Paris.*

TO THE *SAN FRANCISCO EXAMINER*

*[APRIL 1918]*

. . . Last Saturday, the first day they used it, was a memorable day for me. In the first place it was my day off and I slept late in the morning. I had a programme of diversion mapped out. I was awakened by an "alerte," dressed in nothing flat, and beat it out, expecting to see a day-light air raid—and I expected there would be "some" battle.

No aeroplane in sight. I went to a large circle and, about eleven o'clock, was standing looking up in the air with my mouth open. I had heard explosions earlier, but I thought it was the alarm cannon.

I was standing with my mouth open, as I say, when WHANGO! one of the shells dropped right behind me, so close I was spun around with the concussion. My morale was shattered. I immediately retreated to a subway station and remained there two hours. I then came up and consumed a whole bottle of "morale."

TO GEORGE AND IDA ROSS

PARIS
*JULY 23, 1918*

Dear Folks:

I know there is an ink blotch on the bottom of this sheet of paper but it is the only I can find around my desk, and I would have to rummage all around the office to find any more. I got back to town yesterday morning and worked all the rest of the day and most of today, writing what I got. I just had dinner—a small steak, string beans, apple sauce and coffee. Not so bad for war. Meatless days are suspended again and one fares better at the French restaurants. In fact, since I have got out of the butter habit—I almost prefer bread without it now—and sugar habit I don't notice any restrictions on the menu. For sugar we get saccharine, and it is about as good.

I'm writing this right in the middle of our counteroffensive south of Soissons, and everybody around France is jubilant and satisfied. Don't know how much of a victory it will be for the Allies yet, but it already has put the Germans on the defensive again and is bound, at least, to have a tremendous morale effect in Germany. The Americans were in it strong, of course, and fought wonderfully—so well that I don't believe anybody will be able to fully describe it. I saw some of the soldiers as they came out of the line. They were jubilant, enthusiastic, and confident. When the American army gets going full blast it won't take long to defeat the Kaiser. . . .

Being away, I didn't get my day off as per schedule this week and am rather tired. Expect to get a week's leave pretty soon. One of the fellows has had his already and we are going to take them in turn as conditions permit. We are entitled to a leave every four months, but I have been in the army over a year now and have had none. Will spend my week at Aix-les-Bains, I think, or else Nice, and probably come back by way of Bordeaux. . . .

There haven't been any air raids in Paris for a long time and, although there were a half dozen shots from the long-range cannon a week or so ago when the Germans started their offensive, it . . . hasn't been heard from since. Will have to formally put it down as a failure, I guess. I'm going to try to get off a couple of other letters tonight, so will say goodbye.

Affectionately,
Harold

*Jeanette Cole Grant, whom everyone called Jane, was a pretty and ambitious young woman who was born on a Missouri farm but had come to France by way of New York City. Trained as a singer, she wound up on the reporting staff of* The New York Times, *where she became friends with Alexander Woollcott. They reunited in Paris, where Jane was enter-*

*taining troops and Woollcott was on* The Stars and Stripes. *Woollcott in turn introduced Ross to Jane—and he was smitten.*

TO JANE GRANT

My dear dear Miss Grant:
I hardly know how to begin a note to you, but if you would take the word of Pvt. Ross you can go to Chateau-Thierry next Monday and meet Sgt. Woollcott, Pvt. Baldridge and one Cadillac automobile and go for a tour of the battlefields ending Tuesday evening in Paris, probably. I just got back and had a wonderful trip as far as it went. Would advise you to go by all means. Further details may be obtained from the undersigned, who will be doing business despite the loss of many buttons at the usual place after noon tomorrow.
Your ardent courtier,
H. W. Ross
x x x x x x x x x x x x x x x x x x x x x
P.S. Woollcott also had button trouble.

TO GEORGE AND IDA ROSS

Dear Folks,
Well, here's the war over and little Willie a survivor, still able to sit up and take notice of what is going on. Which, I hope and suppose, will end all worrying in Salt Lake about me. There never has been cause for much but I know that you don't need much cause, though. This is the third—if I count correctly—day since the signing of the armistice. The frenzy in which Paris has been historically noting and marking the event has practically subsided. Yesterday and the day before there were thousands—hundreds of thousands, I guess—of people in the streets. Today most everybody seems to be back at work but it will probably break out tonight again. The cafes, which have been

closing at nine-thirty o'clock for nearly five years, are open in the evenings now until eleven and sometimes later. Last night at midnight I was walking a few blocks from the hotel and there was an extemporaneous dance going on at the corner of the boulevard and a side street. It was being held in the glare of the big street light, the brightest I have seen since coming to France and the brightest Parisians have seen since the war started.

The whole city is decorated with flags. The American stock, which fluctuated during the past month between notes of President Wilson, is higher than ever. In a restaurant today an old Frenchman got up and shook hands with me and (I think) would have kissed me if we hadn't had the table between us. I'm onto the kissing dodge, however, and am always elusive. During most of the two days' celebration I worked. Some of it was necessary and some wasn't, but we went right on getting out the paper just as if it amounted to something in the crush of events. I wasn't so glad for myself as I was for the fellows who have been up on the front for months under fire and in the mud and cold, which induces as high a degree of physical misery as can be imagined....

I think I told you in my last letter that young Hayes was in town. He left without seeing me. Called twice at the office. He went back to a replacement camp on his way to join his company, which was at the front. As it turns out he will get back, probably, as it goes into Germany. Haven't run across John Dodds' unit yet but know where it is. Haven't heard from Aunt Dollie or anybody else lately. Guess the mail is held up somewhere. Haven't got any sort of a notion yet as to how soon we will go back to the States. The paper probably will be kept running until most of the troops are gone and I'll be kept on it—maybe. They're talking about giving us (the Ed. staff) commissions. Haven't made up my mind whether I will accept one if they do.

With love,
Harold

TO JANE GRANT

*AMERICAN EXPEDITIONARY FORCES*
*PARIS*
*FEB 27/19*

My dear young lady:

I know that I shouldn't use a typewriter for this social correspondence, but nobody can read my writing. Anyhow look at the classy paper I found.

My service stripes are coming loose and I thought it was because you weren't thinking of me. As soon as I got your note, however, they braced up and are doing better. Albeit they do need a little policing up. Baukhage arrived this morning and told me of seeing you: You seem to have more troubles than I have, which makes me very jealous.

They have decided to continue the paper indefinitely, over the head of our recommendations, and I am resigning from my present editorial responsibility to take effect at the end of April. I'll be either a civilian or in the guard house soon.

Sgt. Bailey . . . betrayed his great secret today and embarrassingly admitted that he got a letter from you a week ago. I hate to tell on him but he also gets a letter from a girl named Nora Hansen in Clackamas, Ore. She seems to have made up her mind about him.

Anyhow, as soon as I can get hold of Ladd I'll know more than I do now. I'll use force with the [Y.M.C.A.], if necessary, but I think it will be simpler if he requests your services. I don't know whether he wants your accompanist too, or whether you want him included. What kind of a looking guy is he?

I have been to the Opera lately and sat in a box. Went with Capt. Clark, Capt. Watson, Sgt. Woollcott and other high army officials.

Winterich, Baldridge and some of the rest are very indignant about the decision to continue the paper. They feel that it can't be done.

Nora Hansen is of Swedish descent.

I haven't laughed much since you left town. Funny coincidence, isn't it?

I'm not sure what your address is, but I guess it is the same as the telegram.

With great devotion,

Ross

P.S. x x x x x x x x x x x x x x x x x

P.S. I could have waited until after seeing Ladd before writing, but I will write you again after seeing him. It gives me a chance to write to you twice. I'm clever that way.

P.S. Woollcott has sold a couple more stories and I expect to get the proceeds at a poker game soon.

P.S. I can't make up my mind about you.

P.S. My falling off party has been postponed until April 7. Found I had misfigured one day. It is going to be a success.

P.S. Caroline Singer wanted to sew my service stripe on but I wouldn't let her. I'm sentimental that way.

P.S. x x x x x x x x x x x x x x x x period

TO GEORGE AND IDA ROSS

*PARIS*
*MAY 6, 1919*

Dear Folks:

By the time you get this letter I ought to be on the ocean on my way home, and [if] it makes at least average time I'll be pretty close to the coast of the U.S.A. I am sailing from Marseilles about the middle of the month. The date is a little more certain than when I wrote my last letter. My departure will be somewhere between the 15th and the 18th, I think. Am going on a big French steamer, which carries a lot of freight but not many passengers, by way of the north coast of Africa, Gibraltar, Lisbon, Portugal, a port in Spain maybe and the Azores islands. It will take considerably longer to go that way, but the trip ought to be an extremely interesting and pleasant one. It was all arranged by an old friend of mine in the shipping business in San Francisco when I was there. I was thinking of cabling you but, inasmuch as all of the dope on myself has gone forward to you by mail thus far, I won't interrupt the logical arrival of letters with telegraphic information.

I am in civilian clothes and have been very hard to speak to for the last couple of days. Got all outfitted in Paris. Have a dark gray suit, which was finished by the time I got my discharge and, although my stock of shirts, ties, etc., isn't very large yet, I'm able to put up a pretty good appearance on the boulevard. Have bought myself a cane and am cutting a wide swath. Spent yesterday in a big park on the edge of Paris and the afternoon before that on the Champs-Elysée, sitting in the shade, until my tobacco ran out and I had to beat a retreat to the office. Last evening I went to the theater and afterward had coffee at a sidewalk cafe. The weather got summerlike, after a really miserable spring, about the same day I got my discharge, which was extremely fortuitous. Tomorrow I am going to the horse races, I think. The next two days I will devote to winding up my affairs here and after that I will pull out for southern France, where I will spend the rest of my time until the boat sails. I may visit Nice and Monte Carlo, or I may go to Biarritz on the Spanish border for a day or two. I'll probably write you once more before sailing.

I'll land in New York and as soon as I do I'll telegraph you. My intention is to start for Salt Lake as soon as I land—in less than a week, at any rate, although there is a bare possibility that I may be held up there for two or three weeks. I might have some extremely important business on hand that won't wait. It is practically certain that I'll return to the east as soon as I visit with you awhile. I may not even go to San Francisco, but will, of course, if I can. . . .

American soldiers are leaving France so fast you can't count 'em and the whole army will be out before the summer is very old, I guess. The text of the peace treaty is to be announced this evening at six o'clock and I'm going to wait around the office until I can get a look at it. I've got a couple of more letters to write so I'll say a happy goodbye with love.

Harold

*After the war Ross took a job editing the* Home Sector, *a magazine intended to be a kind of civilian extension of* The Stars and Stripes. *In 1920 Ross and Jane married, and he became editor of the* American Legion Weekly, *which had absorbed the faltering* Home Sector. *In his magazines and in other venues Ross was a passionate crusader on behalf of veterans, as demonstrated by these two letters to the editor.*

## TO *THE NEW YORK TIMES*

*NOVEMBER 13, 1920*

To the Editor:

In your issue of Nov. 11, in an editorial entitled "The Unpaid Debt," occurs this statement:

"The people of three states are paying the debt (to the soldiers) by blithely voting indiscriminate bonuses."

The inference, I take it, is that the three states referred to passed bonus referenda at the recent elections. Actually, four states—New York, New Jersey, Washington and South Dakota—voted favorably on Nov. 2 on cash bonus propositions.

The statement is, however, more than inaccurate. It is wholly misleading. It tends to leave the impression in the mind of any one unfamiliar with the progress of state bonus legislation that only three states have acted favorably on cash bonuses. As a matter of fact, the favorable action of the four states named above has swelled the number of states granting bonuses to twelve. The proportion of one to four is maintained when the ratio of the bonus states to non-bonus states is interpreted in terms of population. More than one-quarter of the nearly five million men who served in the army and navy of 1918 have received or are entitled to state bonuses, by the expression at the polls of the will of their fellow-citizens. These states are, in addition to the four named above, Massachusetts, Vermont, New Hampshire, Rhode Island, Maine, Minnesota, Wisconsin and North Dakota.

Harold W. Ross

## TO *THE NEW YORK TIMES*

*FEBRUARY 21, 1924*

To the Editor:

... I wonder if President Coolidge realizes the impression made by the statement attributed to him after the meeting. The Ex-Service

Men's Anti-Bonus League has so few ex-service members that it is in no wise qualified to speak for ex-service men. It is supported by contributions from industrial interests and it is engaging in a propaganda effort which to my mind is just as unfair as is that of the employers who are forcing their employees to write letters to their senators and representatives. In fact, I daresay some of the same men are concerned in carrying out both schemes, for the idea behind the propaganda largely emanates from one selfish and wealthy group.

I think the President should be opposed also to the propaganda which has emanated from the office of Mr. Mellon, Secretary of the Treasury. Not only has Mr. Mellon made several statements which have proved to be grievously erroneous, but he has issued them under circumstances which leave no doubt that they were released as propaganda. A vast number of service men resent the propagandizing of Mr. Mellon which, all in all, has made much more effect than any other.

Harold W. Ross

*Ross went on to edit* Judge, *a venerable humor periodical, but he was increasingly determined to develop a magazine of his own. By late summer of 1924 he had worked up a prospectus and prototype for* The New Yorker *and was circulating them widely in search of backers.*

TO CHARLES SHAW

*THE NEW YORKER*
*NOVEMBER 15, 1924*

Dear Mr. Shaw:

You will recall me as having been with *Judge,* I think.

I am taking the liberty of sending the inclosed [*sic*] which attempts to outline the plan of a new magazine I am involved in starting. I wish you would read this over and keep us in mind. I should like very much to see you and wish you would drop in some time when you are in this neighborhood.

Very sincerely yours,

Harold W. Ross

## TO J. B. MILGRAM

*DECEMBER 8, 1924*

Dear Mr. Milgram:

I am very much interested to know you had a plan for a magazine of the kind we propose. Since we announced ourselves, I have learned that several people considered such a field as an opportunity.

I should be interested, too, in the details of your plan, if you should care to let me see them.

H. W. Ross

# II

# "NEVER GO INTO ANYTHING LIKE THIS . . ."

## 1925–1929

Launched in February of 1925, *The New Yorker* nearly died before it had a chance to live. As Ross was the first to admit, those early issues were so confused and unpromising that within months circulation had plummeted to almost nothing. In May, Ross and Fleischmann actually decided to kill their creation but didn't have the heart to go through with it. Instead they regrouped for the crucial fall season with better content and a more confident tone, and the magazine gradually began to attract the kind of discerning readers its editor had always imagined for it. Soon *The New Yorker*'s prospects were secure enough that Ross could lecture Fleischmann and the business side about staying out of editorial affairs. His newfound confidence also stemmed from the talent he was recruiting: such astute editors as Katharine S. Angell (later White), Ralph Ingersoll, and Rogers E. M. Whitaker, and some unknown but marvelously fresh young writers, most notably E. B. White, James Thurber, and Wolcott Gibbs. But if *The New Yorker* was improving, it was primarily because Ross was willing it to happen. Nothing, not even his marriage to Jane, came before his commitment to the magazine.

---

*After the usual setbacks that attend a magazine's launch, Ross finally picked mid-February for* The New Yorker's *debut. But with the dead-*

*line imminent he was presented with another distraction: the deteriorating health of his father back in Utah. The illness turned out to be stomach cancer, and George Ross died several months later.*

## TO GEORGE ROSS

*THE NEW YORKER*
*FEBRUARY 6, 1925*

Dear Father:

I told my doctor that you were having trouble with your stomach, and he became quite concerned as to the kind of medical advice you are getting. He is an expert and on to the fact that most doctors are no good. He told me to have you see Dr. Sam Pinkerton at once.

You go and see Dr. Pinkerton as soon as you can and tell him that you were recommended to him by Dr. Erdman of New York. Dr. Erdman is about the foremost surgeon in the world and as I understand it a classmate of Dr. Pinkerton. Do this for me at once and let me know what they say.

Harold

## TO CONTRIBUTORS OF *THE NEW YORKER*

*THE NEW YORKER*
*FEBRUARY 21, 1925*

To contributors:

The first issue virtually sold out in New York City in the first thirty-six hours and we were as surprised as the next one. We printed thirty thousand of which eighteen thousand were distributed in town. Reports from outside New York are encouraging. Amount of mere curiosity, non-repeat sale is unknown. The print order on the second issue is forty thousand.

We had not intended to look so much like a humorous magazine and regret that the appearance, together with the contents, tend to give a wrong impression. We are changing our make-up somewhat and are trying to be a little more serious and purposeful.

It is hoped that the early issues will give a better idea of what we want. We are going to try to be exceedingly topical. We will go to press on Wednesday and be on sale the following Tuesday morning, which will help. Short stuff may be taken even on a Thursday. Longer material will have to be got in a week or two earlier than this.

Most of the departmental stuff will be done by staff writers although contributions are wanted for the Talk of the Town department, anecdotes about people more or less well known, new stories, etc.

If these are roughly set down as notes it will be acceptable. Items for In Our Midst also are sought.

The paragraph department (In Our Midst) has been weak and offerings are earnestly sought. We want to *say something* in this department and at the same time keep it more or less entertaining and bright.

We hope to give a prompt reading in the future (admitting and apologizing for some dereliction in the past due to getting the early issues to press).

We also want humorous drawings and cartoons, and ideas for same.

*Educated at Bryn Mawr and possessing confident, discerning taste, Katharine Sergeant Angell had many qualities that the unsophisticated Ross lacked. She joined* The New Yorker *soon after it started and quickly became Ross's most trusted lieutenant. In 1929 she would marry E. B. White.*

TO KATHARINE S. ANGELL

*[1925]*

Angell:

This is a materialization of something I foresaw a year ago and, unless I am away off in my thinking, hopeless as is, i.e., we do not want such a Wall Street column. We could have a Talk dept. of Wall St., yes. But if so we could have a Talk dept. on Theaters, the Art World, the night clubs, the butter and egg market and every other specialized field in town. Our Talk dept. is a reflection of the high spots in all fields, or is intended as such—though I realize that it could be ten times as long, or one hundred times. It could fill the whole book, and maintain its present, or an improved, standard.

I invite your thought on this subject, and opinion. Am I away off?

If not, the anecdote about the man wanting a wholesale price on a Cadillac is a Talk anecdote and some of the other stuff in here is Talk stuff. And the one of the industrial magnate sounds like very interesting stuff for a Profile. Likewise the Vanderlip stuff. (The mere fact of his return as a banker at large would make In Our Midst stuff.)

You see, your suggestion attacks a fundamental decision long since made.

At any rate two other questions come up: Do we want, and can we keep interested, specialists in various fields to give us such incidental stuff as this for Talk? Wall St. especially is important.

Do we want to invite a man like this to do Profiles or ask him to collaborate, to the extent of supplying the facts, at least, upon Profiles of financial people? We have never been able successfully to get ahold of them yet.

R.


*Spaulding was* The New Yorker's *first general manager.*

MEMO TO EUGENE SPAULDING

*JULY 8, 1925*

Ben Hecht ran a paper in Chicago for three years up against something of the problem we are up against. He says that his circulation was beneficially effected by this method:

> Take a good show which is nearing the end of its run so that it has space in the theatre and make a deal with it to advertise the show in exchange for theatre tickets, then take the theatre tickets and judiciously hand them out to newsstand dealers, thereby getting their goodwill and better display.

Have you done anything towards experimenting on the idea to write letters to hotel guests telling them that they should read *The*

*New Yorker,* which can be had at the newsstand in the lobby. This might make a good tie-up with the newsstand man downstairs, it would boom his business.

H. W. Ross

*Wiley was a friend from the war.*

TO HUGH WILEY

*THE NEW YORKER*
*SEPTEMBER 9, 1925*

Dear Lieutenant:

Get a fur coat and come on to New York for the winter. Would undoubtedly be good for your future....

I have been working like a dog. Terrible! We have just started on some forty page issues with a lot of advertising and the book is beginning to look prosperous. It is taking a lot out of me although I am not doing so badly at that.

I am away behind in my work including, I think, some letters from you and your story, which I thought was a little rough in spots and which I put aside for future reading, which I have been unable to do.

Your first advice, to stick to a covering of New York, has been adopted, incidentally. So you have already earned your wage. I became convinced of that myself some time ago and we stopped fiddling around on extraneous things.

Just as soon as I see Fleischmann, the business end of this enterprise, I will find out about stock. I don't know what the situation is. I will let you know at a very early date, however. Maybe he does want to sell some.

Sincerely yours,
Ross

## TO HUGH WILEY

THE NEW YORKER
OCTOBER 15, 1925

Dear Lieutenant:

Everybody talks of *The New Yorker*'s art, that is its illustrations, and it has just been described as the best magazine in the world for a person who can not read. Our text is not as good as it ought to be, but I guess we will get it better. . . .

Sincerely,
Ross


## MEMO TO RAOUL FLEISCHMANN

JANUARY 11, 1926

I suggest that we register with the copyright bureau all titles in *The New Yorker*. Think this very important. Specifically suggest registering the following:

Talk of the Town
Heroes of the Week
A Reporter at Large
Of All Things
Profiles
Critique
Tables for Two
On and Off the Avenue
Goings On and Goings On About Town

I am inclined to think that "This and That" ought also to be registered. I assume that the title "The New Yorker" has been registered, but come to think of it, am not certain. I believe it would be advisable to do this.

A lawyer would know what assurance such registration gives us. I am not quite clear on it—possibly Spaulding knows.

H. W. Ross

*For all its progress,* The New Yorker *was still so pinched for cash that Ross was not above hoodwinking even close friends, such as sometime contributor Alexander Woollcott. Ingersoll was the infant magazine's managing editor.*

## TO RALPH INGERSOLL

*[1926]*

Ingersoll:

On the rate. Try this—pay him for one of the pieces, the longer one. If he complains tell him bookkeeping error, other not paid for yet. He will get over the fifteen cent [per word] idea soon. I will get him over it if necessary. You have got to take the brunt on Wooll. Alibi vaguely, or what you think of. He will write more....

*Through the magazine's turbulent first year Mankiewicz helped Ross in countless ways, from writing funny promotional copy to contributing theater criticism to consoling the editor when his Round Table friends failed him ("The half-time help of wits is no better than the full-time help of half-wits," Mank famously remarked). So when Mankiewicz was lured by the money of Hollywood and stayed longer than expected, he was outraged when Ross fired him—by telegram.*

## TO HERMAN MANKIEWICZ

*THE NEW YORKER*
*FEBRUARY 16, 1926*

Dear Mank:

Your letter, dated, received and, since you recognize my right to edit *The New Yorker* as I see fit, I don't think you make sense when you say I am guilty of a low, dirty piece of behavior.

I will not discuss the merit of your dramatic criticism which, of course, was a factor. Aside from this, I was forced to the conclusion three months ago that it would be impossible indefinitely to continue our relations. Your disposition and your attitude seemed to make it impossible. My accumulation of grievances was too preposterously great. About that time you braced up to a certain extent and we decided to let matters stand for the time being. But I will tell you now, Mank, that I had no confidence that they would stand on more than a temporary basis and doubted if they would last out the present season. When you decided to go west, I told you that your going would not affect your status. You assumed that I "assured you flatly and positively that my job would be waiting" upon your return. I didn't, because I know what was in my mind, and I wanted to be careful not to mislead you. I thought this over and, two or three days later, decided that I had better tell you before your departure that we were making new arrangements. This, so that there would not be any misunderstanding, and it was not, then, the result of a chance meeting a day or two before you left.

I haven't a short memory and I am still grateful personally for the help in the early days, but I sincerely feel that your subsequent omissions and actions removed that obligation a hundred times over. I would point out too that I am responsible for other persons' property, other persons' money, and have no right to let my personal feelings influence me beyond the point of what practically is the best thing to do. Damn it, we are not playing magazine, and we are not children.

A few specific things: You drew one hundred dollars a week from *The New Yorker* for a good many weeks with the understanding that you would do the criticism and considerable other work. You did very little of the other work. In fact, while you were neglecting this you were actually writing pieces for other magazines. Unpardonable breach of faith.

While at this salary, which was to have included your good will, you denounced me to contributors we were trying to line up. A dirty game.

You went squalling to a third person over a request of mine and thus broke a confidence which was painfully embarrassing.

You were negligent in your covering of shows, being inexcusably late with important reviews. We have the statistics on this.

Your personality is such that you cannot be fitted into an organization. You are too disturbing—announcing to the assembled staff that you were resigning and coming into my office to paste me one in the mouth, haggling boyishly about things such as the Fields Profile, etc., etc. My God, Mank, you resigned publicly at least six times. Probably the whole office would testify to this.

The first few of the things set down above wipe out, many times over, the obligation of the early days; on the whole, they made continuation of relations impossible. . . .

As ever,

Ross

*By the magazine's first anniversary,* The New Yorker *not only had survived but was experiencing growing pains.*

MEMO TO *THE NEW YORKER* STAFF

*FEBRUARY 20, 1926*

To the Editorial Staff:

The contractor says he will finish the quarters on the ninth floor by March 1st. Judgment of the undersigned is that he will be a few days late.

We have taken such a large amount of space because it was as cheap to take over a floor as to get a smaller amount under other arrangements.

The elaborateness of the partitioning does not indicate lavish expenditure as it is to be amortized over a period of years. . . .

Our plan is to move in at the earliest possible moment to relieve the present situation. Certain suggested additions to partitions etc. are not being made now. Necessary changes and additions will be made later.

H. W. Ross

*The independence of the magazine's editorial staff from the business side was a bedrock principle for Ross. He would pound his benefactor, Fleischmann, on that subject for the next twenty-five years.*

## TO RAOUL FLEISCHMANN

*THE NEW YORKER*
*APRIL 17, 1926*

To Mr. Fleischmann:

I think it essential that all members of the advertising staff be tactfully but firmly taught that they are in no wise to have direct contact with the members of the editorial staff or with me—that they are to deal with the editorial department only through the head of their department.

In my opinion this is most important. Unless stern measures are taken my present efforts to keep the editorial department independent, uninfluenced, honest and—more important than all—slightly aloof, will be more or less defeated. I do not want any member of the staff to be conscious of the advertising or business problems of *The New Yorker.* If so they will lose their spontaneity and verve and we will be just like all other magazines. In my opinion it is this burdening of practical problems on editorial departments that makes them timid, self-conscious and afraid, and produces a flat book. In this kind of publication the flavor is practically the whole thing.

There is no doubt of the soundness of this policy. If there is I am a one-legged blind man. Witness the advertising already in the book. Witness the contracts coming in; witness, specifically, the Rolls-Royce account which, I humbly believe, came in because they wanted to be in this magazine. . . .

This morning Mr. Price asked to see me. He came into the office and explained that he wanted to meet Mr. Shane, the movie critic, and get contacts to help him get movie advertising. This would have been very bad. I called him off, at the outset, but he had the more or less conventional idea that the Editorial Dept. would help him. Of course we could help him, if the writers are good humored enough and weak enough to do it, but it would affect immediately the work of these people. They would be made conscious. The fact in Shane's case is that when I gave him the movie job I told him I didn't want him to have any personal relations with the movie people. I pointed out that most of the critics are useless by the very fact that they get their personal relations mixed up with criticism. It is true of most critics in New York except the bigger theatrical and book reviewers. . . .

Ross

TO RAOUL FLEISCHMANN

*The New Yorker*
*May 1 [1926]*

Raoul:

There was no boy on duty in the outside hall this (Saturday) afternoon despite my memo of a recent date which was returned with the notations that arrangements had been made to keep someone there Saturday afternoons until five o'clock.

There was no telephone service. The girl simply went home. Moreover it was impossible to get into the telephone room to get at the board ourself.

That such things can happen is beyond my belief. I have never been up against such an exasperating situation in my life.

While we are in the middle of a mess occasioned by this, Mr. Rose, who does "As to Men" column in the Fifth Avenue department, came in to resign as the culmination of happenings which followed the receipt of a memorandum from Mr. Baldwin of which I attach a copy. That Baldwin should have written thus direct to Rose is incredible. He was in the office this afternoon and I asked him about it. What is more incredible, HE SAYS THIS WENT THROUGH [advertising director Raymond] BOWEN. HE SAYS HE HAS NEVER BEEN ADVISED NOT TO DEAL DIRECT WITH EDITORIAL PERSONNEL. This despite our recent decision on the subject. Moreover Bowen has paid no attention whatever to my request that he keep away from Miss Long and not attempt to influence her stuff. He is still at it. This situation is very delicate and this must be held absolutely confidential since I get it from neither of them.

The fact is that Bowen has NEVER PAID ANY ATTENTION

TO THE ONE MILLION THINGS I HAVE SAID ON THIS SUB-JECT and that your decision to notify the staff that they were not to deal with editorial personnel has never been conveyed to the advertising salesmen.

I am bewildered, frustrated, defeated, powerless. I am absolutely flat this afternoon and unfitted to do the exacting work of getting out fifteen pages of copy. I am too nerve worn to do anything under such circumstances.

Ross

*A young Yale graduate, Ingersoll was bright, efficient, socially well connected—and about as incompatible with Ross as two people can be. He would endure several years of sometimes withering criticism before going to work for Henry Luce. At Time Inc. Ingersoll edited* Fortune *and helped develop* Life *magazine. Later he founded the legendary New York newspaper* PM. *Here Ross had been away several weeks after oral surgery.*

TO RALPH INGERSOLL

*[1926]*

Ingersoll:

If I have been cranky I am sorry and I haven't intended to be. Please don't think I am because I am not although I may indicate impatience, even exasperation at times and on the whole this is good for the business if nobody minds it because we are not making Ford automobiles. I admit that frequently I make unwarranted criticisms etc. but it is the way I am and please don't mind.

I have been impatient lately probably because, having been away three or four weeks, I returned with the idea that I would never get close to the picture again and by God I won't! At all costs. My head was full of little reforms and tucking up of loose ends, and I have been exceedingly anxious to get them done before the big book starts and you go off on vacation etc. because I don't want to take on anything new that we can't do well. I am exceedingly desirous of taking them on but won't be swooped into it until I know that we have a reasonable chance of getting away with them. Witness the weekly cartoon which can't be done in our present state. Certainly until that organization settles down a little I won't have the freedom of mind necessary to create cartoon ideas. I want to spend a lot of time thinking, coping and getting around and I want to be carefree. Now, I can't be carefree as long as you are either tired or too busy to talk to me. In fact it makes me downright uneasy....

While we have gone miles toward an organization, there is still a lot to be done to put the house in order. This is going to take calmness. Incidentally I don't want to think about the organization, personnel etc. as much as I have in the past and I think you and I can settle most of the details pertaining to it in about fifteen minutes a day if we are both receptive. If I am fretful don't bother me. Kid me.

Ross

And please be advised that I think you did wonderful work while I was away. I am bad at compliments but I think this.

R.


MEMO TO RALPH INGERSOLL

*JULY 2, 1926*

Mr. Ingersoll:

I doubt if, under the circumstances, Miss Shanley and Miss Pearce are entitled to a week off each, especially since it means hiring extra people. This runs the expenses up perhaps unwarrantedly. I think it would be fine to either give these young ladies time off at the beginning and end of the week, so that they would have a very long weekend or, possibly, after other people are taken care of, a full week. Giving Miss Shanley eight or nine consecutive days is too much, to my mind.

R.

*Rockefeller was a Salt Lake City banker tending to the finances of Ross's mother, who was living in California with one of Ross's cousins. Her assets included twenty undeveloped acres on the city's western outskirts.*

## TO W. V. ROCKEFELLER

*THE NEW YORKER*
*NOVEMBER 9, 1926*

Dear Mr. Rockefeller:

I have your letter of November 4th and my viewpoint is that if you get any reasonable offer for the ranch you had better sell it—and, if time is an element, not waiting to write me about it. As you know I was home little during the latter half of my thirty-four years and had been led to believe that the land might be quite valuable some day. This, it is obvious, was romance. My father had a lot of it in him, as all that worthless mining and other stock will testify. Sell the place and deposit the money, I say.

I am glad to know that my mother's account is in reasonably good shape. In a pinch, of course, I could relieve any situation that might arise but I haven't been so hard up in years as I am at present. Such money as I could spare I have felt obliged to send down to my cousin.

I shall see that you continue getting the magazine and I hope that it means something to you in Salt Lake. It is rather local, though. It is succeeding but it is a much bigger undertaking in every way than we thought when we started.

With renewed thanks, I am,

Sincerely yours,

H.W. Ross

## HANDWRITTEN NOTE TO RALPH INGERSOLL

*[1926]*

Ingersoll:

The typewriter and stand are gone again from the end room, God damn it!!!

Ross

TO DOROTHY PARKER

THE NEW YORKER
FEBRUARY 26, 1927

Dorothy:

The verses came and God Bless Me! if I never do anything else I can say I ran a magazine that printed some of your stuff. Tearful thanks. Check, proof etc. to follow. We want to use one of the verses under [this] title. . . . Think this a good idea. Is it satisfactory? If not please say so and we will jump in the lake. It is better, though, to spread your stuff out because it reminds people of you oftener and will help sell your book. I'm nothing if not practical, and one of the leading men in New York although still in my early thirties.

Ross

TO E. MCNERNEY

THE NEW YORKER
AUGUST 25, 1927

Dear McNerney:

Of the last batch of drawings you sent in we found one usable. I regret very much that we did not like the others. The one we are taking is the sketch showing the colored gentlemen in Harlem (the colored lady passing in an automobile, etc.) and we have tinkered the caption to read as follows: "She passin', boy?" "Yassuh. And in passin' is how yo' got to note her." I presume this will be satisfactory with you. This picture we liked very much. The others are going back under separate cover.

Very glad to have had these offerings from you.

Sincerely,

Ross

*Wilson was an army buddy who worked for the Warner Bros. studio in Hollywood.*

## TO A. C. WILSON

Dear Wilson:

You could have knocked me over with a feather when, upon getting back to town today, I got a letter from you and then, in the same batch, one from my mother saying that she had gone to stay with you for a few days. I wired you a few minutes ago and I wish to God I had been in town two or three days earlier to have got the letters when first they got in. To plunge into it—

I don't know what to do about my mother. My father died a little less than two years ago. I went out to Salt Lake then and, on the spur of the moment, decided to send my mother to Los Angeles because I have a cousin living there. He isn't there now, being away on a construction project, but he usually is there. I didn't want to bring her to New York because this town is hell for anyone who can't hop-skip across the street through traffic. She couldn't have left the house alone. Moreover the climate is terrible here for a person in her position. New York is a place only for people who *have* to live *here* to make a living. It is hotter than you-know in summer and colder than Salt Lake in winter. And my mother is very sensitive to climate. Well, she didn't make out very well with my cousin. For one thing, the generations don't mix, and my mother is an unusually difficult person. I say this in all kindness, but in recognition of the fact. She left my cousin (Jimmie [Dodds] is his name, and I have been trying to get him to go around and see you—you would like him) to live with another cousin and that didn't work out either. The trouble is that she is a very unworldly person, out of touch with what is going on, and hell on giving advice and asking intimate questions. Also, she has got a streak of the miser in her or, rather, she is frightened to death about money. When my father died I fixed it so that she could have enough to live on. I put the whole thing in trust. They were to pay her about two hundred dollars a month and I could have pieced that out. She juggled around, however, until she doesn't get nearly that much out of the trust company and, of what she does get, she saves some. I am morally certain of this. It is all nonsense. I wanted her to spend the whole thing but she won't do that.

At that time I was hard up as hell myself. This magazine had just started, I had put all my capital into it, it was losing money so fast it would make your head swim, and I couldn't take much out. It has now got thoroughly on its feet, however, and I am, or am on the verge of being, wealthy beyond my fondest dreams. This isn't much, of course, to an old 18th Engineers boy but at that I've got enough to support my mother in any style she wants. The trouble is that if I did send her any money she would salt it away somewhere in some savings bank. You can't get that idea out of her head. When she was living with my cousin I used to send him some money and in that way a little was spent on her. I have been trying to get out west for the last three or four months but the duties of this job at this time are so numerous and strenuous that it is all but impossible for me to get away. I could, in a great emergency, duck away for a couple of weeks, but if I went to the coast that would allow me only a few days there and a fleeting visit would be no use. I don't know what to do. I have half made up my mind to have her brought on here, or to go out there and get her, and, traffic, weather and all, establish her in New York. I was going to wait before making up my mind to hear from Dr. Devol, a very close friend of mine, who is now in California. He promised to go around and look her up and advise me. From the last letter I got I gather that he hasn't turned up yet. I suspect that he tried but that he missed her because she moved. Now, what do you think? How is her health, for one thing? Let me know all about this and I will be undyingly grateful.

Well, as to my welfare the last couple of years: I started this magazine a little longer ago than that after some preliminary work. I got tired of working for other publishers, newspapers, etc., and thought I would like to run something of my own. I blocked this out, got a gent with a lot of money to back it and here we are. It was just as tough a proposition as was expected but now it has come through and, as I said, is rather firmly established. This fall we will begin making money and, what with my interest in it, salary, etc., I will be doing well. I won't really cash in for two or three years at the earliest but neverthe-less am quite a substantial citizen considering that I am nothing but an old buck private. But never go into anything like this. It is killing until you get up momentum. I don't know whether I will ever recover or not.

I will have your young lady looked up. I don't know what we can do about her in *The New Yorker* but I will try to do something somehow. Glad to do it. I don't see how you can be of service to *The New Yorker* out there; you have already been of enough. Give my regards to White, Williams, Muldoon and the rest and tell them I am coming out to get them someday with Corporal Clark. Love to Mrs. W. and the children.

Ross

P.S. If you ever see Laurence Stallings or Herman Mankiewicz, tell them to go to hell. Also Wally Young. Needless to say, don't show this letter to my mother.

R.


MEMO TO RAOUL FLEISCHMANN

*SEPTEMBER 9, 1927*

Mr. Fleischmann:

I have permanently taken over for private offices the two rooms in the front corner. An outer office and an inner office. The inner office being the only place in the entire *New Yorker* organization in which it is possible to hold a private, uninterrupted conversation. It is, there-fore, very valuable. I suggest, therefore, that when you have anything private to talk to me about you have your young lady tip me off on the telephone that you are coming up and we can talk it over there.

I find that talking to people in an office where an interruption is likely or possible at any moment, or talking before a third person, is too much for my nervous system and that is all there is to it.

R.

*Long wrote the magazine's popular On and Off the Avenue and Tables for Two columns.*

TO LOIS LONG

*NOVEMBER 28, 1927*

Miss Long:

Will you please talk to me about Russek's? Mrs. Angell says it is not a very high class store—or was not the last time she visited it two or three years ago. Spaulding tells me that they have made great efforts to bring it up the last two or three years and he rates it as superior to Macy's from our standpoint. He says that they have very good imported merchandise.

Am I asking too much when I suggest that you tell the girl at the operating desk when you are coming back? I looked for you all over the place—to find that you had gone out.

Ross

*Ochs owned* The New York Times.

TO ADOLPH S. OCHS

*THE NEW YORKER*
*JANUARY 18, 1928*

Dear Mr. Ochs:

I take the liberty of addressing you thus because I have something on my conscience. You will recall that you entertained Mr. Fleischmann and me at luncheon in the *Times* offices a few weeks since.

In the next issue of *The New Yorker* is a humorous drawing laid in the office of the *New York Times.* I do not want you to think that I left the luncheon with the idea for the drawing which we are using. The fact is, it had already been done at that date and it was the idea of the artist—not of either Mr. Fleischmann or myself. Not that there is any harm whatever in the picture. It is merely slightly irreverent and I hope you will pardon this irreverence and will find it amusing. In fact, I feel quite sure that you will.

I also wish to take this opportunity to thank you for having had me to luncheon. I enjoyed it much and I deeply appreciate the honor as the *Times* is one of the institutions in the world which I admire much.

Very sincerely yours,

H. W. Ross

*"I'm married to this magazine," Ross once told James Thurber. "It's all I think about." Indeed, by 1928, the accumulated stress of launching and sustaining* The New Yorker *was undermining Ross's marriage to Jane, who had considerable emotional and financial capital tied up in the magazine herself. Early that year Jane traveled to Florida to revive her health and give them both time to think. Ross stayed behind in the rambling apartment on West Forty-seventh Street that for four rowdy years he and Jane had shared with Woollcott—another strain on their relationship. When Jane returned to New York sooner than planned, Ross, caught off guard, sent her this letter. They would divorce in 1929.*

TO JANE GRANT

[*MARCH 1928*]

Dear Jane:

Your note received just a few minutes ago. I had not expected you back so soon. I have, of course, done a lot of thinking about our affairs and have, in fact, made up my mind as to what we ought to do. I have some rush work to do this morning before the art meeting this afternoon and I won't attempt to outline and argue the thing here in full. Tuesday and Wednesday are such brutal days with me that it is hard for me to get my mind on anything for a long stretch at a time. Briefly, however:

We have different tastes, different interests, different instincts, different ideas. We are distinctly two entities, two personalities. We differ in almost everything. We are both terribly sot. Living with you on the basis that I have in the past is, I have concluded, impossible. You are a disturbing and upsetting person. From your standpoint I undoubtedly have most objectionable characteristics. I truly realize that I must be almost impossible. In the past I have yielded much to you, much, much more than I now am willing to yield. My brief period of freedom from you, while it has frequently left me at a loss, has convinced me that I am quite capable of arranging my own life on a much more satisfactory basis than it has been on in the past seven years, or than it could possibly be on, by continuing to live with you as we have been living in the past. I find that, with a place unrestrictedly my own, I can quite easily handle the social end of things and that, planning my own time, I can get more work done and have more relaxation and time for reflection. Literally, the only real moments of placidity that I have had in several years have come during the last few weeks.

In view of this I definitely urge that we maintain a status of separation for some time to come. I would propose now a permanent and final separation but for the fact that, some months from now, when we both calm down and when things at my office are more settled, and when it would be possible to reorganize our physical arrangement, we might do something in the way of the two apartment idea. Frankly I haven't much faith in this for when you analyze it it means two separate households and that reduces the ties to so little that they are scarcely perceptible. I do not present this as a final judgment, however. We neither of us know now what our state of mind and our moods will be six months from now and it is remotely possible that we might find such an arrangement suitable to both. As for myself I feel at the moment rancor and resentment, or something like these, and I would fear to engage in any dual household plan now. Moreover, the physical readjustment would entail so much thought, work and planning that in my present jaded condition I simply couldn't face it.

I propose that you let me go on living in the house indefinitely. As I feel at present I simply could not live with you here as it is now constituted. It would be intolerable. For years, over my protest, we went on building this thing in the wrong direction and we have made it such that it is impossible for two people who have different interests. It is bigger, God knows, than either of us needs. The reason I nominate myself for residence here is a very practical one. I have and will have during the next six months a crush of work to do (people at the office are planning vacations, a big reorganization is contemplated, etc.), I simply must have a place *which I control* for the fulfillment of certain social obligations (which, largely due to your attitude and the state of fuss you kept me in, have been neglected in the past), and I must have a place to work. I have found that, training Arthur not to interrupt me and with no danger of interruption from others, with, in fact, a consciousness of complete privacy, I can really relax and concentrate. Moreover, I want to experiment and see whether or not I cannot handle the domestic and social ends of a household alone. I already am certain that I can. I want an opportunity to make a practical test.

That is why I propose that I continue to live here. I think it is more important that I be efficient for the next six months than it is that you be, and moreover your work is not comparable to mine in volume and complexity. Should I leave now I would have to organize another household. I found that the hotel was impossible because of inconvenience and expense. I would have to get an apartment. This would be such an ambitious step that it would lead almost necessarily to a permanent and irrevocable separation. Moreover it would inconvenience you terribly because I should certainly take Arthur along. Arthur I regard as my attachment and he is one of the few things I would not consider compromise on. Finally, we haven't enough income to support both this house and such a household as would be necessary for me. Nor have we an immediate prospect of realizing on the *New Yorker* stock or other assets. You are planning to go to Europe in the summer. That is not a long way off. It certainly will be impossible for me to go and I will have to live in New York continuously all summer. My moving out of here temporarily and then returning would be absurd. Couldn't you take things rather easy so far as your work at your office is concerned, a trip or two on the pretense of health, until you want to go abroad? It is now March and I presume that you would go in April or May.

I am setting this all down hastily. As I said, your note was unexpected and I was not ready to formulate my ideas on paper finally. The fact is that I feel hopeless about the whole thing. What I have proposed above is temporizing. If you feel that a definite separation now is preferable to what amounts to an experimental (and clumsy) separation for a limited period I am, by all means, for it. My opinion is that such a step would be best. We are so far apart in most respects that compatibility is probably impossible. As for myself, I am a monstrous person incapable of intimate association.

Ross

More, after pacing the floor a few minutes:

I think indecision is the killing part of a thing like this and I suggest that probably it would be wisest to separate now and have it over with. That will at least make us human beings and we will know where we stand. I will leave this at your office and you should get it during the afternoon. I will return from the office as early as possible this afternoon, probably about five-thirty, and will be in more or less all evening. I shall take dinner here. If you could send me a note here outlining your viewpoint I would appreciate it. I feel that it might be better if we didn't see each other because that would be almost certain to bring in the emotional element, which is the last thing that ought to be brought in, but if you wish to talk to me on the telephone you will be able to get me on the private phone, Pen 6623.

Ross

*The work of Elwyn Brooks White first appeared in* The New Yorker *in late 1925, and Ross knew almost at once that here was the voice he had been listening for—unforced and elegant all at once. Soon White had made the opening Notes and Comment section his own, and Ross came to regard him as the magazine's one indispensable writer. So when White suddenly slipped away from New York, as he sometimes did when the office began to seem claustrophobic, Ross tracked him down.*

TELEGRAM TO E. B. WHITE

*MARCH 23, 1928*

This thing is a movement and you can't resign from movement. It has just started.

H. W. Ross

*A picture of Ross accompanied a story on* The Stars and Stripes.

## TELEGRAM TO IDA ROSS

*MARCH 23, 1928*

See how well I am looking? *Saturday Evening Post* page one fifty-eight.

Harold

*Stout was an associate editor of* The Saturday Evening Post.

## TO WESLEY STOUT

*THE NEW YORKER*
*MARCH 27, 1928*

Dear Mr. Stout:

I was born in Aspen, Colorado. I first came to New York on my own (I had been here before that as a minor) in 1912. I stayed here a year or two, if that is relevant, then I went out to California where I remained for three years. That brings us up to the war. After the war I came here and stayed. I have lived in San Francisco, in New Orleans, Atlanta, New York, Paris, Panama, Denver, Salt Lake City, and numerous other cities in periods of various lengths.

I knew this subject would come up sometime.

Sincerely yours,

H. W. Ross

## TO RALPH BARTON

*THE NEW YORKER*
*JUNE 27, 1928*

Dear Ralph:

I was on the brink of writing you when your letter came—this morning—telling me about your latest predicament. I knew, of course, that you had reached some such conclusion as this. You are a creative soul and therefore a restless soul; therefore, a damn fool. I would leave this to any fair-minded banker. I wish I were a banker. I also wish I were Henry Ford or anybody who can accept the church, the government, conventions, and all those things.

I also had house trouble. I am thinking of burning the damn thing down. The insurance would net a tidy bit of cash and would enable me to get a room somewhere and fit up what I really ought to have. I am not competent to manage more space than this. I would be if I were a fairy. Fairies are the happiest people there are. All editors ought to be fairies. I fuss around with commas, semi-colons, dictionaries, and wordings, and it drives me crazy. I am too virile. I ought to be building subways. I was thinking of going to the South Pole with the Byrd expedition but that would take a year or two and I can spare, at most, only two months. It probably would be a bore anyhow. All life is a bore if you think at all. . . .

As ever,
Ross


*Byfield was a Chicago hotelier.*

TO ERNEST BYFIELD

*THE NEW YORKER*
*JULY 4, 1928*

Dear Byfield:
We have to maintain tone in *The New Yorker* and have a rule against mentioning bartenders, sheep-herders, bootleggers, portrait painters, Long Island millionaires and Chicagoans. Especially those that have insulted my mother. Everyone must draw the line somewhere.

Well, I spent the weekend with [Charles] MacArthur. We were two of a small party invited to Madge Kennedy's camp which was on the shore of a lake in Connecticut. We arrived at daybreak Sunday morning and I started everything off by pushing Miss Kennedy's mother into the lake. When she was finally rescued it turned out that a cat which she held in her arms was missing. The cat, it was subsequently learned, God be praised, had swum ashore. Within half an hour we had made so much noise and general whoopie that the occupants of all the twelve residences on the lake were up and raising hell. One thing happened after another until MacArthur and I finally set fire to the place. We departed Monday afternoon leaving the burning embers containing several bodies. Otherwise everything is going well with both Charlie and me.

I want to know about Mrs. Lillie because my conscience got to troubling me. One weakness of mine is making promises of aid and assistance and I told her that I would be at her service when she got to New York. I am a systematic person and had a reminder down.

Sincerely yours,

Ross

P.S. I hear you have been calling me a fairy. I don't like this.

## TO JANE GRANT

*[1928]*

Dear Jane:

Here is a check for eight hundred with a small deduction for books bought for you. I make this because I am keeping close books on all expenses now to see how we stand and this is chargeable to your account only (under my primitive system). I am going away Sunday. I think it will be Sunday for three weeks. I would like to talk to you about the house but if you would rather not I will try to arrange to shut it down temporarily. Will this last you for three weeks, the period of my probable absence?

Ross

*Samuels was an early* New Yorker *editor.*

## MEMO TO ARTHUR SAMUELS

*AUGUST 13, 1928*

Mr. Samuels:

Jed Harris remarked to me—and he was supported by his publicity agent—that he has found that we do not follow type specifications in setting our theatre ads. He has had quite a bit of trouble about this, he says.

Incidentally, he thinks our page of theatre advertising is the most unsightly advertising page in New York City. I agree, I think.

H.W. Ross

*Ross's mother was vacationing in Florida.*

TELEGRAM TO IDA ROSS

*JANUARY 11, 1929*

I am doing business as usual and haven't got the flu or anything. You and Aunt Sally get fixed up there now and have a good time. You had better buy some gay clothes.

Love,

Harold

*Adler was a New York City printer.*

TO ELMER ADLER

*THE NEW YORKER*
*MARCH 11, 1929*

Dear Mr. Adler:

I shudder at the idea of my suggested presence at a tea. I am shy and incompetent socially. Moreover, I would not undertake to nominate who, among the vague body of people called the staff of *The New Yorker,* ought to know about your business. They are all crazy to begin with.

Let me drop around from time to time and bring someone.

Sincerely yours,

H. W. Ross

TO GROUCHO MARX

*The New Yorker*
*April 4, 1929*

Dear Groucho:

We cut this as I said we would. Read it over, and if you have any objection, let me know soon as we are going to use it right away.

About your writing more, you are a fairly well known figure, and as I told you when I first suggested that you write for us, other magazines are bound to offer you more if they like your stuff at all. They buy names, and pay for them. We don't. We would not pay you any more than an unknown writer.

It is literally true that I was after Will Rogers to write before he ever broke forth. I was [editor of] *Judge* at the time, and I could have had him writing for that magazine, I think. After I nibbled at him, then dropped him, *Life* took up his stuff. They couldn't hold him long because the big boys went after him. Now he is as recognized a writer as he is an actor. I don't know whether you could attain that or not, but you have a gift which, perchance, can be reflected successfully on paper. I would certainly keep on writing something if I were you, and give it a whirl, whether you write for us or not.

I am honestly unselfish most of the time, and not just an impractical dreamer—I am being eighty five percent unselfish in this.

Sincerely yours,

Ross

TO F. SCOTT FITZGERALD

*April 26, 1929*

Dear Fitzgerald:

We got a piece of yours through your agent, Mr. Reynolds, a very good piece for us. This makes us happy.

I wish to God you would write other things for us. You wouldn't get rich doing it, but it ought to give you satisfaction.

Sincerely yours,

H. W. Ross

## TO GLUYAS WILLIAMS

*THE NEW YORKER*
*MAY 1, 1929*

Dear Williams:

Your Industrial Crises [cartoon] on Tudor City kicked up a big fuss. A lot of people spoke to me about it including Douglas Fairbanks who, it turns out, is an admirer of yours.

I just thought I would tell you.

Sincerely,

Ross

## TO FATHER FRANCIS P. DUFFY

*THE NEW YORKER*
*JUNE 3, 1929*

Dear Father Duffy:

Will you do me a favor? I need some expert advice. We are running some reminiscences by Balieff in which he mentions our friend, Morris Gest, a couple of times—once in connection with an episode involving a Catholic archbishop. What we want to know is whether or not this instance would be insulting, or in any way offend our Catholic readers. We don't know whether to kill it or not. It is fairly amusing but I don't want to put it in print if it will needlessly hurt people's feelings. As I am a Presbyterian, I wouldn't know about this. I am not even certain in my mind as to what the holy sacraments are.

I am enclosing a proof of this piece, and I am wondering if you will read it (on the third galley marked "Here") and then let me call you about it over the telephone in a day or two. I will be grateful.

With best wishes.

Sincerely yours,

Ross

## TO ROGERS E. M. WHITAKER, HOBART WEEKES, REED JOHNSTON, AND FRED PACKARD

*JUNE 14, 1929*

Mr. Whitaker, Mr. Weekes, Mr. Johnston, Mr. Packard:

Page 104, May 25 issue, paragraph one, story "Subway Recreation," in the penultimate line, the word "in" is italicized without any justification that I can see.

In the June 15 issue, on page 26, column 2 (see attached) is a bit of sloppy writing which ought to have been caught. The clause which terminates the sentence might (obviously) better have become the first clause of the succeeding sentence.

There have been quite a number of such minor oversights in the book lately. I wish that all you gentlemen would watch not only for typographical errors—not so much for typographical errors in fact—as for such things as oversights in writing and editing, wordings which will sound untimely when appearing in print (such as mentions of overcoats, straw hats, and other seasonable things as well as events), uniformity in style, and all such things. We are running misprints and clumsy wordings from other publications, and otherwise being God-like, so WE MUST BE DAMN NEAR PURE OURSELF.

Please query everything, taking up all questions with Mr. Whitaker (or in his absence, or at his delegation, Mr. Weekes), who will settle all questions.

Ross

*Knapp, Ross's friend and a contributor, had been mayor of Saratoga Springs, New York.*

## TO CLARENCE KNAPP

*THE NEW YORKER*
*DECEMBER 14, 1929*

Dear Mayor:

Whatever became of that song you once offered to Beatrice Lillie? I know that you gave her a copy of it. She undoubtedly lost this. I saw her last night, and she said that she had signed a contract with the Lido, to appear there next month, and that it was specified that she had to introduce one new song a week.

If you have that song around, or anything that you think might be good for her, and can lay your hands on it easily, let me have it, or them. Don't bother unless you have something handy as she will probably lose anything given to her anyhow.

I sent back your last Sob Ballad. I get an absolute cold fit about running humorous stuff about the stock market because of the Riordan suicide and others. Suicides are fairly numerous these days. I had, however, some constructive suggestions which I trust Mrs. Angell conveyed, and which I trust you will act upon.

Sincerely yours,

Ross

III

# "AN ANGEL DESCENDED

## FROM HEAVEN . . ."

### 1930–1934

The magazine weathered the Depression considerably better than most New Yorkers did. It would be criticized, not unfairly, for maintaining its carefree pose as millions suffered, a mistake Ross later acknowledged and vowed never to repeat. Nonetheless, *The New Yorker* thrived as its weaker competitors faded in large part because it was giving readers a welcome respite from their troubles. Ross always maintained it was a high calling to make people laugh, and he had assembled the staff to do it. Besides his stable of comic artists, Ross was happily publishing the likes of Thurber, White, Robert Benchley, Dorothy Parker, Arthur Kober, Frank Sullivan, S. J. Perelman, and Ogden Nash, making this a kind of golden age for humor. For his part, Ross, divorced from Jane and with a firmer grasp on the magazine, was also enjoying himself, as his letters from this period demonstrate. He was dating attractive young actresses and socializing with the Broadway and Hollywood elite, from the Lunts and Noel Coward to the Marx brothers.

———

*Busch, later an accomplished novelist and screenwriter* (In Old Chicago, Duel in the Sun), *was an early* New Yorker *writer. In dispute was a Talk item on Primo Carnera.*

TO NIVEN BUSCH

*FEBRUARY 4, 1930*

Dear Busch:

Stopping that check is not absolutely unfair. You were wrong in your principal facts, and would have made us ridiculous if we had printed them. Good God, it was impossible to have confidence in anything else in the piece after your glaring errors in the lead. We may be able to fix it up, but frankly, I get terrorized when dealing with one so careless of fact as you are. You know my feeling in this matter.

H. W. Ross

TO JOHN O'HARA

*THE NEW YORKER*
*FEBRUARY 28, 1930*

Dear O'Hara:

I don't know of any job and I'm not likely to hear of one, but if I do, I will let you know. Maybe the only thing for you to do is to keep on writing and become a writer.

Sincerely yours,

H. W. Ross

*Marquis was a popular New York newspaper columnist.*

TO DON MARQUIS

*THE NEW YORKER*
*MARCH 5, 1930*

Dear Don:

We cannot use these, I regret to state. I would have told you this long ago, but your letter has been on my desk for ten days. I intended to write a personal answer at length. But you know how things are. I get swamped. I get swamped most of the time and all my good intentions go by the board. Not only do I get swamped but I get bewildered. Never start a magazine or you will find yourself bound up by the most terrific executive responsibilities and exhausting details—how much ought we to pay for this poem? who left that comma out? do we raise Miss Snell five dollars a week? and so on. You have no idea. It keeps you crazy all the time.

As to our departments: As a boy, I never dreamed I would have to deal with any publication running critical pieces about women's underwear. Here I am, though. My viewpoint on these departments is that they are necessary evils. I wanted to make certain that *The New Yorker* would succeed commercially, and I therefore realized it had to be of some use; that you just cannot start an entirely idle magazine such as *Punch* in this country in this century. I regard these departments as more or less of a nuisance, and as a matter of fact have paid little attention to them the last year or two, trying to build up the other part of the magazine, which, as a matter of fact, is the only thing that interests me.

I know about our Profiles. I know a lot of other things that are wrong too, but we have to get out fifty-two issues of this damned thing, and that is a terrible order. Love.

Sincerely yours,

Ross

## MEMO TO EUGENE SPAULDING

*MARCH 12, 1930*

Mr. Spaulding:

Well, I am as bitter as ever about some of the advertising we have been carrying, and since the situation has recently led to embarrassing complications, I think we ought to do something definite about it. I propose as follows: That we establish a rule that we will not use any endorsement advertising containing a palpable lie, or a statement we are morally certain is a lie.

The Fleischmann Yeast advertising is certainly hocus-pocus. I haven't read it much lately, but I assume that the statements made therein are more or less true—certainly they are such as cannot be, without pretty thorough investigation, branded as untrue. I don't like the tone of these advertisements, but would say (speaking offhandedly) that we should continue to use them. Such advertisements as those run by the Lux people are, however, palpable lies. So are the Simmons Beds. The recent endorsement of coffee by the Messrs. [John] Held and Woollcott, both contributors to this magazine, are also lies.

We were very much embarrassed by the appearance of the Held and Woollcott endorsement. We have been rather severe with the newer and less widely known contributors, being strict with them even in the matter of the use of their drawings in advertisements appearing in the magazine. This is possible with the newer people because they are inclined to trust us and accept our advice, and have grown up with us in an atmosphere which has inculcated in them some sense of truth, honesty, dignity and integrity. Our viewpoint has not been so readily impressed upon certain money-grabbing writers and artists who were established before *The New Yorker* was started. A few recent examples, such as the Lux stuff and the Held-Woollcott endorsement, have seriously embarrassed our policy.

Obviously, the thing for us to do is to attack the matter at its roots, by making it a rule not to print advertising which we know of our own knowledge to be untrue, or which we are morally certain is untrue. That would be a simple, clear-cut rule. I urge that we adopt it. If it is not adopted we will, editorially, have to deal in our own way with contributors who offend, but we haven't much face left if our own management isn't with us.

I urge this policy not as an idealistic measure in any way. I may be idealistic in it, but I would point out also that it is not good business to print palpable lies. It is not bright to do so. Our readers, or the readers we hope to hold and to get for *The New Yorker*, are intelligent enough to know that this stuff is the bunk. We are being short-sighted in running it. We have an opportunity to live honestly. We have also the great privilege now of being in a position to lead the advertising industry. For Christ's sake let us no longer pussyfoot. Let us be really honest, and not just slick. I think that in our present prosperous condition we could afford to suffer even a temporary small loss in revenue to keep our own conscience clear. Moreover, it is never too late to reform. We have offended often in the past, but that is no reason why we shouldn't institute a reform now. We can at least stop being cheap.

H. W. Ross

P.S. I am not certain about this, but I am of the opinion that the *New York Times*—a great monument to simple integrity—will not run this stuff.

MEMO TO KATHARINE S. WHITE, RALPH INGERSOLL, RAYMOND HOLDEN, WOLCOTT GIBBS, JOHN MOSHER, SCUDDER MIDDLETON, WILLIAM LEVICK, AND GEOFFREY HELLMAN

*APRIL 10, 1930*

With the view to making the book department more intelligent and timely, we will try out this system: When a list of new books is received it will be passed to the above named. You will glance over it and promptly return to the information desk, with a notation about any book listed thereon which you know or suspect is especially timely, important, or worth special treatment.

No one person can possibly be well enough informed to take the responsibility of going over the vast number of titles now coming in each week. It is thought that this fractional check by several people will help.

Will you please return the book lists promptly as they come to you. They will be issued twice a week.

H. W. Ross

TO HARPO MARX

*THE NEW YORKER*
*APRIL 18, 1930*

Dear Marx—

While I think of it, if you are going to buy an automobile don't move until you see me. I think I want to sell mine.

Sincerely,

Ross

*Wilcox apparently was acting as an agent for Benito Mussolini, who wanted to submit an essay entitled "Women Are Not Fit for Politics." Nothing came of it.*

TO U. V. WILCOX

*THE NEW YORKER*
*APRIL 25, 1930*

Dear Mr. Wilcox:

Well, it gets down to this: I would not want to take a chance on running the piece without a signed statement by Mussolini that would protect us absolutely. The only signature that would do is his.

I suggest that if you want to take a chance on it you mail it to him and ask him to sign his name to it. You can tell him if you wish that *The New Yorker* is interested in it and would use it if he proclaimed his authorship. I really think it is worth trying because most statesmen pride themselves on answering all correspondence; also, most statesmen like to see writings by themselves in print.

Sincerely yours,

H. W. Ross

*Mrs. White, Mosher, and Gibbs were responsible for reading the fiction submitted to the magazine.*

MEMO TO KATHARINE S. WHITE, JOHN MOSHER, AND WOLCOTT GIBBS

*APRIL 28, 1930*

The piece sent in by Donald Moffatt on the Yankee Clipper brings forth these observations: Let's all get clear on the fact that all departmental stuff in the book is FACTUAL, all the non-departmental stuff FICTIONAL, and that the two kinds of stuff have no other place than in their regular one. This holds true always, with the minor exception of certain factual stuff which is considered novelty or freak and is used in the back of the book. It is easy always to draw the line. Moffatt's piece is a review of the Yankee Clipper. Therefore, it cannot be considered for non-departmental use.

In this instance, I think it would have been well to have offered this piece for departmental use. Trimmed down (with the author's consent, should it be forthcoming) it would make a good item for the Out of Town department, the department into which this item happens to fall....

At any rate, please be conscious of our departments and remember that the incoming manuscript should provide occasional items for them, and undoubtedly a lot of ideas. We review or report on almost everything from a baby's nursing bottle to a new steamship. Please remember. Ideas will be appreciated.

H. W. Ross

TO ALFRED A. KNOPF

*THE NEW YORKER*
*MAY 19, 1930*

Dear Knopf:

I knew those names would interest anyone at Sacramento. They will also interest the state politicians in California. Most of the laws of that state were decided upon in one of those three places; or the old Western Hotel, which was respectable at all times except when the California Legislature was in session. At those times it was wild, with beautiful girls all around and everything.

I am sorry to learn that Fanny is dead. I didn't know it until I read your letter. She must have been ninety. She was reputed to be the mistress of that fellow who was the coroner for several terms, and Carmen Gray was supposed to be friendly with the chief of police. It was a great city in those days.

Sincerely yours,

H. W. Ross

*At the time of this note Nash was working for the publisher Doubleday, Doran. Ross had already discovered his ingenious comic verse, but for some inexplicable reason he decided Nash was executive material and soon recruited him as the magazine's managing editor, a grueling position that had been a veritable turnstile. Nash lasted less than three months but remained a contributor for years.*

## TO OGDEN NASH

THE NEW YORKER
AUGUST 6, 1930

Dear Nash:

A suggestion: Bring out a book of [Otto] Soglow drawings as one of your first much-heralded dollar books. Here is an artist who, so far as I know (although I am not certain), is not otherwise committed and whose stuff, it would seem to me, would be very good for wide circulation. You ought to have a book of humorous drawings in your dollar books anyhow.

A further suggestion: Write a lot more of those verses for us. They are about the most original stuff we have had lately.

Sincerely yours,

H. W. Ross

## TELEGRAM TO JOE COOK

AUGUST 8, 1930

Picture swell, much funnier and better than you led me to believe. You're a big success in the movies and so is Dave Chasen. Thanks for the seats.

Ross

## TO WILLIAM ROSE BENÉT

THE NEW YORKER
AUGUST 27, 1930

Dear Bill:

We like your stuff, God knows, but this verse, damn it, is obscure. I read it three or four times and wasn't quite certain what you are getting at. We have been getting kidded for using obscure verse, and I don't think we should. I showed it to two or three other people and they were slightly baffled too. There are too many lines to throw you off.

Please don't mind.

Love,

Ross

MEMO TO E. B. WHITE

*[UNDATED]*

Mr. White:

If you get that story done, I'll take steps to get you a new cushion for your chair.

H. W. Ross

TO ETHEL BARRYMORE

*THE NEW YORKER*
*SEPTEMBER 8, 1930*

Dear Ethel Barrymore:

That girl was not authorized to do a piece about you. I checked up the office today. I didn't think she was, but I wanted to make sure. Often people go around and write these things and then submit them, for better or worse, and we have no control over such people. There is nothing we can do about it, even when we do learn about their activities.

Will see you soon.

Sincerely yours,

H.W. Ross

TO RING LARDNER

*THE NEW YORKER*
*SEPTEMBER 15, 1930*

Dear Ring:

The fact that we used your piece obscurely in the last issue doesn't mean that we didn't value it more highly. We were all jammed up, and the book was trimmed four pages at the last minute because of a fall-off in advertising. Instead of giving you a full page opening we used it with a two-column head on it.

Anyhow, it is my experience that if a piece is good they read it in *The New Yorker* no matter where it is. Moreover it isn't every publication that can play down anything by Lardner.

Hope you will send in pieces right along.

Love and respects,

Ross

*Whedon was an early* New Yorker *writer and editor.*

## TO JOHN OGDEN WHEDON

*[UNDATED]*

Whedon:

An angel descended from heaven last night bearing word direct from God that this piece is to be used with the blurb as is, in full, leading Mr. Irving's casual. Said God felt that, having got into the mess, we ought to accept it wholly. Two-col. opening, BoB [back of the book], big issue. This will satisfy God. Gibbs is of exactly the same mind.

Ross

*The occasion was a* Stars and Stripes *reunion.*

## TO ALEXANDER WOOLLCOTT

THE NEW YORKER
OCT. 9, 1930

Alec:

Baldridge, Ochs, and I went up in the compartment. We discovered Waldo on the train half way up and he came in and visited. Ochs was very disappointed at not seeing you, so I would get ahold of him in town here. He will be here a few days. He also got cock-eyed on the train and by the time we got to the hotel was putting in calls for you all over the country. He called Swope's and says he got a hell of a bawling out. It was all right, he says, until he mentioned my name. Bliss was tight and passed out stolidly early in the dinner, which was served at a French restaurant outside Boston in the old army style, red wine and all, and very charming. Wally passed out. Britt is the same, quite shocked at your not coming. He says he can fix anyone up on income tax difficulties. Waldo was swell, all full of Coolidge and the Pershing reminiscences he has been trying to buy. The General lost all his money in the market, owes debts, and has got to have $$ at once. Kenyon was a good host. Very little drunkedness outside the cases noted. Oh yes, Starett, Ochs's old assistant, was there, Dick Jones, Ryden, Wint. and Chauffeur Howells, who used to tell the dirty stories (under my encouragement) while Baldridge blushed in the back seat. He is New England representative for a paint company, looks very respectable and prosperous. Wint. sent a limerick to Hawley. It didn't rhyme.

Alec, I wish you would get the [Shouts and Murmurs] page going again soon, as I think it important to both of us.

Ross

P.S. John Clark returned on train with me. He is unchanged.

*For a time Ross dated Kennedy, a leading stage actress of the day.*

TELEGRAM TO MADGE KENNEDY

DECEMBER 23RD, 1930

Have a happy and Merry Christmas, Madgie, and I got the book, which is just what I wanted. I guess you have intuition. Also, I have a small token for you which I will deliver to your house here. It's not an opium smoking set.

Love,

Ross

TO ARTHUR KOBER

*THE NEW YORKER*
*DECEMBER 31ST, 1930*

Dear Kober:

I don't think we could run a Hollywood Letter. I don't think there is enough interest in it. We might run Hollywood Notes or something like that, but even so, you would be writing about *New Yorker* contributors who are adequately handled by Walter Winchell and the other columnists.

My life in this office is a constant fight to keep people from writing about our contributors. Hollywood Notes ignoring the writing colony would be a good occasional feature, perhaps.

Yours sincerely,

Ross

TELEGRAM TO NOEL COWARD

*JANUARY 26TH, 1931*

I realized in the middle of the night I didn't pay that sixteen dollars but I got to sleep almost at once and have now succeeded in completely dismissing the matter from my mind. Don't give it a second thought.

H. W. Ross

*A fellow Round Tabler, Dietz was at MGM. Ross's mother had moved to New York.*

TO HOWARD DIETZ

*THE NEW YORKER*
*JANUARY 26TH, 1931*

Dear Howard:

Say, is there any way I could get a season ticket or a pass, or something, for my mother, Mrs. Ida M. Ross, age seventy-six, of the Poe Cottage, the Bronx, to your Paradise Theatre up there?

I am not asking that you give me this. I am willing to pay for it. I would be willing to pay for it through the nose. I can't get her out of the house much, but she would get out once in a while and get to the movies if she felt she had to live up to some kind of a free weekly admittance. I know her. Among other things she is a miser. Let me know about this. Do something if you can.

Yours sincerely,
Ross

*Pulitzer, publisher of the* New York World, *was one of Ross's card-playing colleagues.*

## TO RALPH PULITZER

Dear Ralph Pulitzer:

About that cover of the butterflies: the art man reports that the artist, Mr. Alajalov, did not sell it to the man who first inquired about it, the latter being unwilling to pay seventy-five dollars for it. It is therefore available at that price if you want it.

It was someone's suggestion that since it was you who were inquiring about it, the price ought to be put up to one hundred dollars, but I opposed that. It also occurred to me that I ought to send it to Peggy as a wedding present, but my limit on wedding presents is twenty-five dollars. Or thirty dollars. And I am two or three years behind on them.

Yours sincerely,
Ross

## TO DOLLIE ROSS

*THE NEW YORKER*
*FEBRUARY 16TH, 1931*

Dear Aunt Dollie:

I was very pleased to hear from you. I have been neglecting you people out there, I guess, but I am a long way from San Jose and my mind is in the east here. Moreover, I have been pretty busy of recent years.

I haven't been in California since the last time I dropped by to see you when my father and mother were out there. After all these years I intend to try and get out this summer. I don't know whether I shall make it or not but I am going to make a definite effort to spend two or three weeks out there. I would rather do it than anything I can think of and if I do get to the coast I will, of course, call on you.

On the whole, my mother is as well as she ever has been. She has been rather ill the last two weeks and has been in bed most of the time, but it turns out to be nothing more serious than an attack of the flu followed by complications which apparently always follow the flu. She has her own little apartment here and I have a lady to live with her who takes very good care of her, and, on the whole, she seems happier than at any time since my father died. She seems contented most of the time but, naturally, has her blue spells.

I am glad you are all getting along so well out there. Will you give my regards to Ethel and Verne and Hazel and William and also to Harold and Henry when next you see him. Tell them all I will see them if and when I get out to California.

Sincerely,
Harold

*Nothing came of Ross's amorous intentions toward the young actress, but they remained lifelong friends.*

TELEGRAM TO GINGER ROGERS

*APRIL 18, 1931*

Oh dear, oh dear, but you are forgiven if you really would rather be with me and I will call you Sunday and say so personally. I tried to call you this morning for solid hour but your phone was busy. Princeton boys, I guess, and if they go too far they will find the city isn't big enough to hold both them and me.

Very bestest,
Non Princeton Boy

## TO NEWMAN LEVY

*MAY 8TH, 1931*

Dear Levy:

Yes, we would be interested in a series on operas but we would rather consider a bunch of them than just one, and buy them that way. Damn it, nobody ever finishes a series if we put through just part of it, and we're always left on a limb. As to this one on Faust, damn it again, there are two or three things about it I don't like—"Gland Opera," "family way," and another phrase or two. Aren't these a little brash, or something? I know you're writing it in the vernacular, of course, but still these make me gasp, mildly. I suggest that you hold this and let it come along with the others when you get them done and then let us size them up all together—say four or five of them.

As to price, I don't want to be discouraging, but—.

It's no time for increases. The business office is hopping on me all the time now about expenditures, business not being what it was and expenses having gone up in anticipation of doing better than we are. Might be better in the fall and if so we'll pay more. You probably won't get these done much before then, and we wouldn't want to use them until the music season starts, so let's wait awhile on the price question.

Regards,

Ross

## TELEGRAM TO BEATRICE LILLIE

*JUNE 1ST, 1931*

I know you wouldn't be much help but will you marry me?

H. W. Ross

*Stark, who edited a Detroit newsletter, had written Ross about the genesis of one of the magazine's most famous cartoons.*

TO GEORGE W. STARK

THE NEW YORKER
JUNE 5TH, 1931

Dear Mr. Stark:

The dope on the "spinach" caption is this. Sometimes, not very often but occasionally, we get a caption in the office here for a picture, rather than use the artist's caption. This is because we insist on the artist putting the idea into the picture rather than into the wording. I say this in preface.

Now, Carl Rose sent that drawing in and E. B. White saw it and wrote the caption we used in the picture: "It's broccoli, dear." "I say it's spinach, and I say the hell with it." I didn't think it was anything special and put it aside for two or three weeks, largely because of the word "hell" in it. We get so much profanity in our captions that I usually hesitate over a "hell" or a "damn." Anyhow, I didn't think it was anything very hot. I went away to Florida and Mrs. Katharine Angell, who subsequently became Mrs. E. B. White, and who always insisted it was hilariously funny or something, printed it. It very shortly became a by-word much to my surprise.

Yours sincerely,

H. W. Ross

*When they divorced, Jane didn't seek alimony from Ross but did want compensation for all the work she put into the early* New Yorker. *Ross agreed to pay her ten thousand dollars a year, ostensibly from his* New Yorker *stock dividends. With the deepening of the Depression, however, those dividends would shrivel, and the "Jane Grant agreement" would become a bitter burden for him.*

TO JANE GRANT

*THE NEW YORKER*
*JUNE 8TH, 1931*

Dear Jane:

Herewith two checks, the situation being this:

| | | |
|---|---|---|
| Regular quarterly payment | | $2500 |
| Minus advance | $1000 | |
|    Dividend | 765 | |
| Balance | | $ 735 |

Also a second check, for $625, under the second agreement.

I am making these out separately for clarity and because, as I understand it, the agreements may as well be kept separate. I will be out west when you get this. Hence am mailing it now. The checks are pre-dated, July 1st. I will make a deposit to cover them by that date.

I hope to God your health is better. Don't forget that you have to turn a stock certificate over to the Guarantee Trust. I am writing Henderson a note now asking him to follow you up on this. My present intention is to be gone about four weeks but I may not stick it out that long. Decision very sudden. If I don't go now I won't get away until fall.

Sincerely,

Ross

TO LEWIS MUMFORD

*NOVEMBER 24, 1931*

Dear Mr. Mumford:

In checking over a card index system upon which are noted a collection of ideas for pieces which have accumulated through the years, we came across one which I want to put up to you. It might hit you. It is this: to run two or three articles, or whatever number is necessary, on the statuary of New York, the public statuary. There are, I think, about a hundred statues on display in public places in the city. We once had a book around the office which enumerated them all, the poets on the mall in Central Park, Joan of Arc, Sunset Cox (whose upraised arm is said to be longer than either of his legs, and who was erected by the mailmen of the city because he got them a raise in pay) and all the rest. Our idea is for a critical but waggish series which would recognize and place (in the reader's mind) the good ones and have a little fun with the other. There is some kind of a wooden statue of a soldier in the Harlem River, for instance.

As I said, perhaps the idea will hit you. If it should, we can give you help in the research work entailed. Also we can get a copy of the book. I hope that you will like it. And will you let me know? No hurry about it.

Sincerely,

H. W. Ross

TO ALVA JOHNSTON

*NOVEMBER 30, 1931*

Johnston:

For some years I have been told from time to time that the H-T [*New York Herald Tribune*] has kept a private account of Mayor Walker's attendance at his office, the hours he came and went, and the days and weeks missed. One night at the Players Club, when good fellowship prevailed, your Mr. Draper and I fell to conversation and he said it was true, that the H-T did have such a record. He said, moreover, that he wasn't going to use it himself, or that the H-T wasn't going to use it, and that he would be willing to turn it over to us.

I now wonder, what the hell? I wonder if we couldn't get this and do something with it, and, if so, if you wouldn't be the man to do something with it. Please give this matter thought and let me know your conclusions. I certainly would have nerve enough to run it, I think.

Your old admirer,

Ross

TO RUSSEL CROUSE

*THE NEW YORKER*
*JANUARY 27TH, 1932*

Dear Crouse:

Here is some additional dope on Scarr, got by one of our earnest workers, and which I think will make the piece stand up. You see if you don't think this stuff will add somewhat to it.

I think further that, as I said before, it would be a good idea to explain how storms come east and any other interesting dope you can get on how weather gets here. As I told you, I read something somewhere on all the storms coming from the west and that there was some point south of New York at which they either turned and headed for here or else passed out to sea. The point was that after they passed this point it was easy enough to tell which direction they were going but sometimes Scarr couldn't wait for this but had to make his prediction by schedule and was occasionally defeated by the storm turning at this point. The story I read said if he could wait until the storm passed this turning point he would never make a mistake. I told you the source on that.

Will you please return these facts with your piece as I want the young man to get credit for them.

Yours sincerely,

Ross

*Thurber's celebrated drawing—"All right, have it your way—you heard a seal bark!"—marked the start of his second* New Yorker *career, that of a cartoonist.*

TO JAMES THURBER

THE NEW YORKER
FEBRUARY 10TH, 1932

Dear Thurber:
I was over to Benchley's and he talked at great length about your seal drawing. He wants to know if you will part with the original and if so, for what.
Love,
Ross


*Bergman was the magazine's managing editor.*

MEMO TO B. A. BERGMAN

APRIL 8TH, 1932

Mr. Bergman:
I asked the telephone girl if Alva Johnston was in. She said "Yes." I went to find Johnston and couldn't find him—one of those office hunts.
I stepped back to the booth and asked the boy if Johnston was in. He asked her and she said, "How should I know?" I then asked her again and she said she was quite certain he was in as she hadn't seen him go out. He was out. She should know, not be "quite certain."
H. W. Ross

MEMO TO RAOUL FLEISCHMANN

APRIL 11TH, 1932

Mr. Fleischmann:
May I respectfully call your attention to the fact that in asking Mr. Mosher to get you an extra ticket for the opening of the movie *Grand Hotel* you violated a very important rule of the office, or two or three. We have a rule, definitely ironclad, that we do not ask managements

for free tickets except for critics or other writers or artists actually on assignment. Everybody in the editorial office has been advised of this, repeatedly if necessary. We frequently ask managements direct for extra tickets, but always insist upon paying for them. I have never taken a free ticket, at a considerable cost to myself. . . .

Moreover, I have made a strenuous fight to keep the critics and other writers aloof from the press-agent, bally-hoo, special-favor gang. I have been especially anxious in this respect about the movies department, as it happens, for a systematic and powerful effort is made to bring the movie critics into line. I have repeatedly warned Mosher against falling into the rut.

Mr. Hague in this office is responsible for getting tickets for staff members, artists, etc. and does a considerable volume of business in this respect. He arranges admissions for editors, artists, writers, etc. on assignment, by pass if they are on specific assignment, by payment otherwise, always. Usually he can get good seats at box office prices. I consider this legitimate, the whole racket being what it is. He offers a service which you are, God knows, welcome to take advantage of and which would be useful, I think. Won't you please help me out, however, by not requesting such favors of writers, as it runs directly counter to my efforts?

H. W. Ross

TO JANE GRANT

*THE NEW YORKER*
*[UNDATED]*

Dear Jane:

Here is this. Consider it an advance, or loan. I'm very sorry I snapped at you on the phone and I apologize. This subject, as you know, drives me crazy—the financial one, I mean.

Ross

*Norris was Columbia University's general manager. Schindler was a well-known private investigator and one of Ross's best friends. Sadly for Ross, the paint gun proved to be ahead of its time.*

TO HENRY NORRIS

*THE NEW YORKER*
*JUNE 15TH, 1932*

Dear Mr. Norris:

You will recall me as the charming gentleman you have met around [Ray] Schindler's a couple of times, or with Schindler. I have a story to tell:

Several months ago I invested in an invention at the behest of my attorney, B. W. Henderson, who is a patent lawyer. It is a new kind of paint machine and it looks to be very good. The sales manager for the machine told Henderson he would be helped a great deal if he had a letter from some authoritative source stating that the gun was not harmful to health. I mentioned this to someone recently who told me that Columbia University has a bureau which tests out commercial products and what we should do is to have it tested before this Columbia bureau. I told Henderson about this and someone from his office called you up, asking you if you wished to see a demonstration of this gun from a standpoint of buying it. You might want to. In fact, I think you would find it a quite wonderful thing. I wanted to make this explanation, however, and ask you if there is such a bureau at Columbia and if you would be kind enough to let me know who is at the head of it and how we could go about approaching it.

I wonder if you would have the time to do this. It would be a favor.

I hope to see you soon.

Yours sincerely,

H. W. Ross

*Flanner, who had been recruited by her friend Jane Grant in* The New Yorker's *desperate first summer, wrote the Paris Letter. Ross gave her the pen name Genêt and this instruction: "I don't want to know what you think about what goes on in Paris. I want to know what the French think."*

TO JANET FLANNER

*JULY 6TH, 1932*

Dear Janet:

Mrs. White has gone on her vacation, so I am writing you. I've been intending to write you for about a year. I have always had it more or less in mind, but Mrs. White does most of the work around here, especially the letter writing, and I always passed the task along. Moreover, I don't like to inject my personality into things when they're going well. And I haven't the disposition to do so. I devote my life, it seems, to the things that are going wrong and it wears me down. Mrs. W's last week prior to departure was cluttered by the fact that her husband, E.B.W., was going to specialists to see about his stomach. Gallstones were feared but the diagnosis was fallen stomach which isn't so serious; it doesn't mean an operation apparently, anyhow. She was to have written you about a multitude of things, of which I will endeavor to take up a few, to wit:

The depression has finally hit us and the issues are away down in size. We had one of forty pages a couple of weeks ago, the smallest since the first year. We expected some cutting, but not that much. Not nearly that much, God knows. This situation has necessitated a revision of our departmental schedule downward. For the next six or seven weeks we are going to have practically no space at all and it's a question whether it wouldn't be better to get out a few well selected words on a paper napkin. The new schedule calls for omitting at least one of your departments in August, and if you should want to go away or otherwise engage yourself during that period we would be content if both August Letters were omitted. . . .

As to the general outlook, we anticipate an increase in business in the fall and hence more space. A certain increase is inevitable, but nobody knows when it will be like the old days when we never had to think about getting pieces in with a shoe-horn. Your stuff is among our very best departmental stuff and, believe me, we hate to drop even one department.

I'm to tell you that we sent a reporter to a newspaper morgue to get things about the Dolly Sisters but that he got little that would be of value. Mostly fluff stuff, no facts. He is seeking elsewhere for a source and we will send you what we dig up as soon as possible.

I was to say that your arrangement for the other magazine writing was satisfactory so far as we are concerned. I read your letter to Mrs. White about it but I haven't it at hand now. It's O.K. though; I know we agreed to that.

I had a vague notion a month ago that I might possibly get abroad this summer, but I'm not going to. I'll be right here, and it's hot. Rather aggravating, for with the issues as small as they are there isn't a full week's work for me. I take long weekends. The Connellys are over there somewhere and maybe you have seen them. You will have if you've been around the Guaranty Trust. Give my regards to Rousseau and anybody else that I know, and accept sincere and hearty same for yourself.

Ross


TO ALICE HARVEY RAMSEY

THE NEW YORKER
JULY 27TH, 1932

Dear Alice Ramsey:

As promised, I am writing you further about that drawing, although in the absence of Mrs. White, all the secretaries in the office and, apparently everybody but me, I cannot give as full and complete a report as I thought I could. What I think happened is that you were given the idea a long time ago and that between the time you got it and the time you drew it up the idea came in from some other source, to wit: Helen Hokinson. She had one with almost the identical idea. The caption was different but the situation so similar that everyone would think it the same idea if we ran both drawings. I'll tell you what you do: Send the drawing back here and see if we cannot get another caption for it here. Let us have it for a little while. The business office will positively not issue a voucher on anything but a finished and accepted product. When such things come up they clamp down, and I think they're right as we would be tying up tens of thousands of dollars in unusable stuff otherwise. At any rate, I see their point.

Your letter brings up something which, to my mind, is a thousand times as important as a single drawing, however, and it is this. I'll begin at the beginning:

For years and years, before *The New Yorker* came into existence, the humorous magazines of this country weren't very funny, or meritorious in any way. The reason was this: the editors bought jokes, or gags, or whatever you want to call them, for five dollars or ten dollars, mailed these out to artists, the artists drew them up, mailed them back and were paid. The result was completely wooden art. The artists' attitude toward a joke was exactly that of a short story illustrator's toward a short story. They illustrated the joke and got their money for the drawing. Now, this practice led to all humorous drawings being "illustrations." It also resulted in their being wooden, run-of-the-mill products. The artists never thought for themselves and never learned to think. They weren't humorous artists; they were dull-witted illustrators. A humorous artist is a creative person, an illustrator isn't. At least they're not creative so far as the idea is concerned, and in humor the idea is the thing.

I judge from your letter that you apparently don't realize that you are one of the three or four pathfinders in what is called the new school of American humor. Your stuff in *Life* before *The New Yorker* started might well be considered the first notes of this new humor. I remember seeing it and being encouraged by it when I was thinking of starting *The New Yorker*. It had a lot to do with convincing me that there was new talent around for a magazine like this. And now you speak of "illustrating jokes"! The very words in your letter to me. I always see red when an artist talks of "illustrating" a joke because I know that such a practice means the end of *The New Yorker*, the new school of humor, and all. Unless an artist takes ahold of an idea and does more than "illustrate" it, he's (she's) not going to make a humorous drawing. I haven't any quarrel with your work to date in this respect. You still draw Alice Harvey drawings and God knows give something to them, but I've simply got to run on this way when I hear or see the word "illustrate" in connection with a joke.

What I started out to say was this. Your letter and one or two similar complaints have decided me to try out something that I want to put in effect while Mrs. White is away. I have long felt that if I participated in the selection of an idea and then turned around and had to judge the drawing when it comes in, I am a disqualified judge. I can't be both collaborator and judge too. Therefore, I am going to let [Wolcott] Gibbs go over the ideas hereafter and show them to the artists without me ever seeing them. In effect, he will be turned over by *The New Yorker* to the artists to help them, if he can, by picking out ideas that come in and showing the artist an idea that may or may not hit them, the artist to draw them up only if they hit her—or him, and *The New Yorker* (meaning me as editor and final decider) to take no responsibility whatever for the merits of the idea, any more than we (I) take it for an artist's very own idea. This puts the buck directly on the artist which, according to my way of looking at things, is where it ought to be. I'd like to try out this scheme, at any rate, and see if it doesn't work to the better satisfaction of all.

Pardon me for having written at such length. I got started and off I went, it seems. I'd like to talk to you about this, but how can you talk to anyone who retires to Connecticut and is never seen around, which is what most of our contributors have done. Send that drawing back in. Incidentally, it occurs to me that you probably have other drawings around that we or somebody might think of lines for. In the fall, when the staff gets back, we might try.

Sincerely,

Ross


MEMO TO RAOUL FLEISCHMANN

*OCTOBER 27TH, 1932*

Mr. Fleischmann:

Could I have a copy of my contract with *The New Yorker*? I have mine but it is in a safety deposit box and would be hard to get, and anyhow I would rather use just a mere copy for what I want it for, which is to show to the lawyer in re my income tax complexities. They are trying to get thousands out of me.

H. W. Ross

TO HARPO MARX

*THE NEW YORKER*
*NOVEMBER 19TH, 1932*

Dear Harpo:

Never mention the first issue of *The New Yorker* to me. Never mention any of the early issues to me. There are none around. I will think up some other appropriate thing to give you for Christmas.

As for my Christmas, all I ask is that you allow Chico to stay in town for a while. He is a big help to me financially and if I can get enough of his time I think he will do something toward making up the debt the Marx family has owed me for the last year or two. He helped out considerably night before last.

Yours,

Ross

HANDWRITTEN NOTE TO E. B. WHITE

*[UNDATED]*

White:

Will you pls. look in on me when you wake up? I never disturb a sleeping man.

Ross

*Markey was the magazine's first real journalist and in 1925 originated
the Reporter at Large department.*

TO MORRIS MARKEY

THE NEW YORKER
DECEMBER 28TH, 1932

Dear Markey:

O.K. except that this week the business office broke the news that
the long postponed cut in prices is very seriously contemplated for the
near future. That may affect you ten percent on the price of your articles. I talked it over with Bergman, who says Fleischmann will probably feel that you would be affected, although the thing is still vague
and I am not certain whether you would or not. Fleischmann and
Bergman are handling it as I have resigned from finances. I am the
writer's friend, trying to get as much money for them as I can.

If you consider any reduction in the figure mentioned a breach of
faith, let me know frankly and I will tell them so, and try to get it
through for you. As I understand it, the proposed bonus would not be
affected. Don't hesitate to say so if you think the cut will be unfair. . . .

Happy New Year.

Sincerely,

Ross

TO CAROLINE DUER

THE NEW YORKER
JANUARY 20TH, 1933

Dear Caroline Duer:

I wouldn't be interested. I have nothing in the world to show for my
life except a few pieces of crumpled wastepaper.

I am, however, passing the word along to the Messrs. Arno and
Thurber in your behalf. You may hear from them, but my experience
with them leads me to believe you won't. They are rarely heard from
by anyone.

Yours sincerely,

H. W. Ross

TO S. J. PERELMAN

*THE NEW YORKER*
*FEBRUARY 14TH, 1933*

Dear Perelman:

I have been a little baffled and disappointed in the three or four (oh, I know it is four exactly) pieces you have sent in lately. Two of them I didn't like at all and I think Mrs. White sent them back. I told her I would like to handle this one as it might possibly give me a chance to make a constructive observation.

For one thing, I think you ought to decide when you start to write a piece whether it is going to be a parody, or a satire, or nonsense. These are not very successfully mixed in short stuff; that has been my experience. You have some funny lines in this, but on the whole, it is just bewildering. It goes into dizziness and then goes into a parody of H. G. Wells, and then gets dizzy again, and then into clubmen stories in general, Sherlock Holmes, etc. You have got too much of a mouthful for one piece and the germ of five or six pieces, it seems to me.

That's the way I look at this piece and the others you have sent in recently. I write in sorrow and hope, not in anger, of course. And I write as an old admirer of your stuff. Damn it, it is annoying.

Yours sincerely,

Ross

*The playwright and screenwriter Charles MacArthur was married to Helen Hayes.*

TO CHARLES MACARTHUR

*THE NEW YORKER*
*FEBRUARY 18, 1933*

Dear Charles:

Two things:

1) Kindly ask Mankiewicz to forward the $1,460 which he owes me.

2) Woollcott told me that you ought to do a Profile of Helen Hayes. If you will write one, we will run it. And perhaps it is not a bad idea as

from the little I have seen of your work I think you are a very promising young writer.

Oh well a third thing: I have seen your show [*The Twentieth Century*] twice; paying for it once and going through the kindness of Mr. Maney a second time. It is a very good show. I am going to go again and maybe more than once again. You ought to see it sometime.

Sincerely yours,

Ross

P.S. I love Helen.

*Tony's was a New York speakeasy.*

TO MRS. EDWIN KNOPF

THE NEW YORKER
FEBRUARY 28TH, 1933

Dear Mrs. Knopf:

I regret to say that we did not like this piece well enough to use it. We feel it is too much on the depressing side of things for us at the moment. We have just run two or three stories on unemployment and feel we have done our bit. Moreover, the theme of this is rather old from our standpoint, or we thought it was.

I can't give your love to Tony at the moment because he got raided the other night. I saw him afterward and he said it was a very unusual raid. Apparently they sent strange Prohibition men up from Washington to get him. They are now in the process of moving all his furniture out. That has been seized. He is going to reopen, I understand, as soon as they get the old furniture out and he can get in with some new.

Yours sincerely,

Ross

*A New York broker sold some of Ross's F-R [Fleischmann-Ross] Corpora-*
*tion stock without telling him—and without passing along the proceeds.*
*Ross sued but to little avail. Mintz was Ross's attorney.*

## TO IRVING MINTZ

*THE NEW YORKER*
*FEBRUARY 28TH, 1933*

Dear Mr. Mintz:

I have read your letter and the Parker letter. I frankly don't think he
has anything and therefore don't think there is any chance of getting
anything out of him. I recommend merely waiting. It was a crooked
deal and probably a criminal one but you can't very well put a man
like this in jail for a couple of thousand dollars. I told Mr. Ernst about
this and he agreed with me—(I mean I told him a long time ago about
the whole matter)—and he thought criminal proceedings would be
fruitless and just leave a blot on our consciences. I will defer to your
judgment, of course, if you have any other suggestion than one of
waiting.

I appreciate the thorough and expeditious way you have handled
this and the other matters.

Yours sincerely,

H. W. Ross

*Contributor Bonner lived in England.*

## TO PAUL HYDE BONNER

*THE NEW YORKER*
*MARCH 14TH, 1933*

Dear Bonner:

. . . You missed our little bank holiday which was quite amusing.
Nobody I know in New York was bothered much, but I think everywhere except in New York City people did suffer. Roosevelt allowed
all the sound banks around here to open yesterday. He apparently
worked the whole thing out beautifully: shut them all and now is going
to let the sound ones reopen, which is much better psychologically

than ignominiously shutting down the insolvent banks here and there. The dope is that two hundred banks in New York state are insolvent to a greater or lesser degree and three hundred solvent, and New York state is better off than most states.

Sincerely,
Ross

TO NOEL COWARD

*The New Yorker*
*April 3rd, 1933*

Dear Noel:
I have seats for the circus next Sunday night, the 9th. Do not forget. I am taking you all to dinner and will advise later as to the time and place.

Sincerely,
Ross
cc: Miss Lynn Fontanne
    Mr. Alfred Lunt

*Crowninshield was the editor of* Vanity Fair.

TO FRANK CROWNINSHIELD

*The New Yorker*
*April 20, 1933*

Dear Frank:
The use of daring words is one of our most serious problems, or at any rate, one of my most serious concerns. I, too, suspect frequently that I am a generation behind. Much of my activity the last couple of years has been fighting the use of words which I think are shocking in print. I am completely disqualified as a judge of what is shocking. That is my difficulty in the present situation. I am an old-fashioned double-standard boy who is shocked at nothing, absolutely nothing, in a stag gathering, but who is embarrassed poignantly at any word or reference which used to be called off-color in mixed company. I remember I went to see the opening of a show written by Ben Hecht and suffered

terribly because of the obscenity. None of the others of the first night audience seemed to be suffering. The ladies for whom I was embarrassed seemed to enjoy it all. I was glad to note, however, that the show closed a week after it opened, although it had considerable merit.

A magazine is certainly something for circulation in mixed company and I always keep in mind *The New Yorker* will be left around the house where it is available to women and children. That is a practical consideration and, it seems to me, a very important one. The hell of it is that in these days of frankness and disillusionment, when fathers insist that they want their daughters to have "experience before marriage" and when Vassar graduates turn up with a vocabulary which you haven't heard since the old days in Fanny Brown's hook shop in California, I don't know how to gauge the standards of mixed company. I frankly suspect, however, that the present vocabulary is superficial socially, temporary and fadistic, and that the conservatives are in the majority. Every once in a while I get out into non-writing and non-modern circles which I find conservatively "decent." They are dull but homelike.

On the other hand, I am theoretically in favor of a certain amount of frankness, sex freedom, and all the other things talked about today. This is intellectual and not instinctive. I cannot dismiss my puritanical inheritance and training.

Especially do we hedge on "Christ" used as an expletive. Usually, we use "Jeez." Sometimes in fiction stories and where the writer is entitled to considerable privilege, we let "Christ" go through; "bitch" probably yes; "bastard" I would shrink at. I have argued three or four "bastards" out of print in the last three or four months....

I could discuss this subject further but I won't. We are both in the same situation, although I have been beaten down further than you have, I think.

Yours sincerely,

Ross

*For a time Ross was experimenting with London Letters.*

TO PAUL HYDE BONNER

*THE NEW YORKER*
*MAY 8TH, 1933*

Dear Paul:

I feel sheepish writing this, but I'll plunge in, asking pardon for the tardiness. I sent you a cable, however, at the earliest moment we could make a decision on the Letter and was entitled to procrastinate a few days on this explanation. Anyone is entitled to a few days in a disagreeable matter. What happened was this. Your first Letter came in in time, cable on the Grand National and all, but we didn't think it quite came off. Partially this was due to the fact that you had just completed one letter covering the same period for *Vogue* and partially to a lack of assurance, uncertainty, etc., inevitable in a first offering of this kind. The Letter could have been fixed up and used readily, I think, but I didn't want to come out about the same time *Vogue* did with the same stuff by the same author. . . . That fact, and a bad and chronic space problem, led us to omit the first Letter. I didn't want to cable you or write you to that effect, having found by experience that it is best to let writers remain in blissful ignorance of such things when they are making their second attempts, so as not to distress or disturb them. . . .

The second Letter was better, from our standpoint, but in the meantime I had found out more about the space situation, which was that it was terrible and would continue to be. We simply had to can the London Letter for the summer and make the best of it. For your information (and possible sympathy) I have been urging Fleischmann to spend a couple of hundred dollars more a week and let us have more space for the departments, as it is impossible for me to do anything but break my great heart under the present circumstances. He can't see his way clear to spending the money, however.

The Letters weren't exactly what we wanted but I think that by experience and coaching we could have got together. No early departments by any writer are ever what we want. No matter who the writer is he has to get accustomed to what he's doing. . . . Maybe the opportunity will come up again sometime, and we can go ahead, but there isn't a chance of any relief of the space situation before next fall. It's a hell of a note. . . .

With regrets and regards,
Sincerely,
Ross

## TELEGRAM TO GEORGE S. KAUFMAN

*AUGUST 3RD, 1933*

George, old fellow:

Joe Cook, too shy himself, asks me to ask you if any possible chance your giving two-three days to his show helping direct and advising in cutting book, or could you at least give Corey Ford day or fraction thereof to read book and advise cuts which are necessary, Ford being eager for advice. Otherwise everything OK here.

H. W. Ross

*Althea was married to Hawley Truax, Ross's confidant and* The New Yorker's *longtime liaison between the editorial and business sides. Ross's mother had broken her leg in a fall.*

## TO ALTHEA TRUAX

*THE NEW YORKER*
*AUGUST 29, 1933*

Dear Althea:

If I left my book on the migration of fishes at your place, will you please preserve it for me as there are certain facts I must brush up on if I am to talk with thoroughness on the subject in addition to interest. Have Hawley bring it back to town with him and that will be an excuse for him to come and have dinner with me.

And if you get over Hillsdale way please call on my mother who is reported today as resting easy, but who will be laid up for several weeks at best. To find her place you take Route 22 North (or toward Albany) from Hillsdale. This road goes down one side of a valley for about three and a half or four miles. On the left you will see a store— a grocery store—which is run by Robert Dawes, the name being upon the building. This is about two and a half or three miles out of Hills-dale. You can stop here and get directions on how to get to William Dodds' farm, which is where my mother is. It is highly necessary to do this, however. This Route 22—at aforesaid three and a half or four miles—goes straight across the valley and up and across a hill, the road running diagonally up the hill from right to left. About two-thirds of the way across the valley a farm house will be seen one-quarter of a mile across the road on the left. This is down a dirt road and is the Dodds farm in which my mother is laid out in a second-story room.

With thanks for everything.

Ross

## TO DOROTHY PARKER

*THE NEW YORKER*
*[OCTOBER 19, 1933]*

Dottie, my Heart:

Under separate cover I am having sent you a copy of Alice Long-worth's new book. (If it isn't obtainable yet, you will receive it when it is.) I am also having sent Dolly Gann's book, issued some weeks ago. These are being sent in the hope that you will do a piece on the pair, or brace. I am also having forwarded a copy of Pitkin's book. There might be meat in this also. He is said to advise that you sleep alone in a big wide bed. Not you personally, of course, but you generally. Also, you must keep your desk clean.

You are further advised that we have an idea for a department to run occasionally, when warranted, and when we can get copy for the God-damned thing, called "Onward and Upward With the Arts." We had a piece by Sigmund Spaeth on popular lyrics which we ran under this title, thinking to start it off. The ideal writer, as we visualize this dept., or react toward it, is you, personally. We would like you to write articles on books, movies, plays, authors, the radio, or certain radio programs, George Bernard Shaw lectures, and a variety of other things. Maybe on mixing drinks, or drinking itself. You will see that this department has unlimited possibilities, offering a rare field for your unique talents. From time to time we will forward books and sug-gestions to you, and damn it, please do something about them.

Ross

Dottie: Quite a few ghouls have written in asking for Ring Lardner's radio "job," most of them remarking that it would be hard to follow Lardner but—. I don't think we ought to start a radio dept. yet, and I don't think we ever want a regular radio review column. Nuts to the radio. But I think that later, some time hence, we would do well to run occasional pieces on the radio and I want you to consider doing them. Now, please.

R.

## TO BERNARD BARUCH

*THE NEW YORKER*
*NOVEMBER 2ND, 1933*

Dear Mr. Baruch:

Not in ten years have I asked a personal political favor of anyone but pressure has been put on me lately by the lawyer who has handled my modest legal matters for some time to use my influence to gain him a brief moment with you, looking toward your giving him a letter which would assist him to gain appointment as an assistant attorney general in Washington. He is favorably considered, he advises me, by Attorney General Cummings himself, but needs some word from an influential person to swing it.

He was for some time associated with Judge Bayer who was, I think, a friend of yours. I finally promised, reluctantly, I would write and ask if you would see him. He is a worthy gentleman, honest, and able, who has had more financial misfortunes than the average in recent years, and was an attorney general in the Wilson administration. So he has had qualifying experience.

I'll make this as simple as I can: Will you please leave word with your secretary, and then I'll call up and find out what it is, one way or another and, in any event, the matter will be off my conscience.

Warmest personal greetings,

H. W. Ross

P.S. His name is Barclay W. Henderson.

*Mrs. Smith, Ross's cousin, lived in California.*

TO HAZEL ROSS SMITH

THE NEW YORKER
NOVEMBER 27TH, 1933

Dear Hazel:

I am terribly sorry to hear about your mother. It is just one of those things about which I never know what to say. My mother, you know, broke her leg this summer and has been laid up ever since August. She is just beginning to walk around a little now and, on the whole, came out of it pretty well. Or perhaps you didn't know. I didn't write it around very much.

Please give your mother my love and all the rest of the people too.
Sincerely,
Harold

TO JANE GRANT

THE NEW YORKER
MARCH 5TH, 1934

Dear Jane:

Here is a check for one thousand dollars, which I got from *The New Yorker* in your behalf. It is labeled a temporary loan. As I told you, I didn't want to put it through my books which the government keeps under constant suspicious surveillance. Ernst told me this morning he has a trust agreement tentatively drawn up but that it must wait for the return of Truax, who has gone to Florida, just to make my life more complicated. Ernst wants to get Truax's approval and assent from you, I think, before putting it into effect.
Sincerely,
Ross

Anyhow, here is the money, and have a good time in China, which I probably will never see.
R

*This is a draft of a letter Ross wrote to protest being evicted from his Park
Avenue apartment. It's unclear whether he ever sent the letter.*

## TO THE IRVING TRUST COMPANY

*Camp 277 Park Avenue*
*[March 1934]*

Gentlemen:

I hereby wish formally to call your attention to the matter of my
being served with a notice to vacate my apartment at the above address over the signature of Colonel Copp, U.S.A. Retired, who, as I understand it, has been put in command here by the Irving Trust
Company, acting as bankruptcy administrator for the premises, to see,
among other things, into the moral conduct of the tenants. I am advised by the colonel that under the seventh clause of my lease I am
being evicted for having ladies (or as the colonel more tactfully puts
it, "persons of the opposite sex") in my apartment overnight.

I know you gentlemen are busy but I wish to call your attention to
some facts. I am more than forty years old and while I have knocked
about the world a lot, I am naturally home-loving, and when I signed
the lease for this apartment I did it under the assumption that I was
renting an apartment for a home. It is an apartment of seven rooms,
and I would call your attention to the fact that three of the rooms are
bedrooms, three of them, and that I rented an apartment with three
bedrooms for the specific purpose of entertaining overnight anyone I
considered fit to entertain in my home. For some years, before the
Irving Trust Company took over the moral welfare of the community
in addition to its bankruptcies, I had lived in other apartments in this
building and, I would call attention to the fact that I had never been
questioned in the matter of entertaining guests. I assumed that the
management considered that I was renting the bedrooms for the purpose of entertaining guests in them, not to raise goldfish in them, or
to sit in alone and crochet, or to myself sleep in each one successively
for two or three hours each night, or for any other mysterious purpose you and Colonel Copp think a tenant engages extra bedrooms
for. . . .

*A long article in* Fortune *magazine, written anonymously by Ralph In-gersoll, pulled back the curtain on how* The New Yorker *was produced. Many at* The New Yorker *found the piece upsetting, especially Inger-soll's educated guesses as to how much money everyone made. And some of the artists, including Williams, were angry at the assertion that they didn't generate their own ideas—which at the time was largely true.*

## TO GLUYAS WILLIAMS

*THE NEW YORKER*
*AUGUST 7TH, 1934*

Dear Williams:

I have a note from Mrs. White today telling of your visiting her and expressing a determination not to accept ideas from others hereafter which distresses and alarms me. That damned, as I call it, *Fortune* piece has kicked up all sorts of unhappiness in subtle ways. It's got all the payroll figures wrong, or practically all, it says Steig's drawings are printed over Irvin's protest, that you don't have your own ideas, etc. I haven't read the thing, being afraid to, but I am hearing about it end-lessly.

Now, to argue the ethics and advisability of an artist doing draw-ings which are not his idea I would cite the case of the Waring's Penn-sylvanians idea. It was mine. I thought of it out of the clear air. I can't draw it. I'm employed by *The New Yorker* (although not at the forty-thousand-dollar figure) largely as an idea man. That's what I regard myself as, at any rate, and what I think my chief value to the magazine is. That's White's value partially, Mrs. White's and Thurber's. This magazine is run on ideas, God knows, and we naturally hire the peo-ple that have them and hire them for that purpose.

My God, a very large percentage of the contents of *The New Yorker,* drawings and text, are based on the ideas originating with the staff and suggested to writers. Now please reconsider your resolution. We don't ever try to cram an idea down an artist's throat. We always send it as a suggestion made on a take it or leave it basis. I'm flatly against our buying ideas as the old humorous magazines used to do and then sending them out to an artist to do at so much per picture. That is ruinous to humorous art, I think, or to anything creative. Our attitude, honestly observed, I think, in practice, is that we submit an idea to an artist and that if he sees fit to use it as a suggestion for a picture into which he is going to put something of his own he will proceed to draw it; otherwise not. It's the same with our text pieces. We've suggested a lot in our time, of course, and one significant thing is that I never remember a writer announcing that he was through taking ideas from someone else, although every artist seems to do it every once in awhile. Or every really sensitive artist. All good artists, either with pencil, pen or typewriter, are hypersensitive, thin-skinned, and apt to be influenced by crude observations. I think Winchell's observations are all crude, I suppose most of *Fortune*'s were. I don't know whether *Fortune* said so or not, but the one thing that has made *The New Yorker* successful is that it is a collaborative effort, switching ideas back and forth to find the man best adapted to doing them, and I hope to high heaven that you aren't going to be discouraged into not being willing to work collaboratively. I'm a steadfast believer in collaboration and *The New Yorker* is a monument, or something to it. Please stick with us, and please remember this: So help me, there's no sin, no harm, and nothing unethical in drawing up an idea suggested by a man who can't possibly draw it himself. You're just robbing the public of something entertaining. I hope you'll think it over and reconsider and do that Pennsylvanians idea to begin with.

We're desperately short of page drawings and have been more or less depending on this and other things from you. As a matter of fact this comes just after we had resolved to put pressure on you somehow for more work.

Don't bother to answer this. I'm going out west at the end of the week to get away from it all and wouldn't get it until I got back anyhow.

Sincerely and hopefully,

Ross

P.S. I just happened to think. I was talking to E. V. Lucas of *Punch* a month or so ago and he told me that ninety percent of the *Punch* ideas are suggested to artists. (Our average is, of course, nowhere near so high.) This proves that the honorable and ancient institution of *Punch* sees no sin in offering ideas to artists.

H.W.R.

*When a cash-strapped Ross needed to sell some of his stock in the magazine, he asked Wall Street friend Philip Boyer to locate a purchaser. Boyer in turn had gone to Ingersoll, who arranged for Time Inc. to buy the shares.*

TO RALPH INGERSOLL

*THE NEW YORKER*
*SEPTEMBER 4TH, 1934*

Dear Ingersoll:

I just got back and am hastening to write this to correct an unfortunate blunder I made in my letter to you about Boyer. I didn't mean to accuse him of "chiselling." The letter you received was copied from a previous draft elaborately amended with pencilled corrections in a laudable effort to make myself clear. What I meant to say was "wisely," but there is some excuse for the stenographic error as it has been pointed out to me that I spelled it with two l's. My only explanation for all this is that it happened the afternoon I left on a vacation and I was doing many millions of things at once. I didn't, of course, carefully read the final draft of the letter.

Therefore, please be advised that I meant to say: "... for all I know he was doing it wisely." Not "... doing it chiselly," a strange word which, so help me God, I had never thought before this hour could possibly be committed to paper by anyone.

I have never had the slightest doubts of Boyer's integrity, cleanness, openness, general above-boardness, and first classness and naturally deeply regret the slip-up.

Sincerely,

Ross

*On May 16, 1934, Ross quietly married a young Frenchwoman, Marie Françoise Elie, whom everyone called Frances. Ross had known her but a short time, and even many of his friends were surprised when F.P.A. belatedly broke the news in his "Conning Tower." McIntyre was a newspaper columnist.*

## TO O. O. MCINTYRE

THE NEW YORKER
OCTOBER 17TH, 1934

Dear O.O.:

Yes, it is true, and thank you for the good wishes. We kept it secret because there was reason for it first and then it was difficult to announce. I let [Franklin Pierce] Adams do it as I was afraid the Winchells would do it and make dirty remarks.

Sincerely,
Ross

## TO JANE GRANT

THE NEW YORKER
[OCTOBER 22, 1934]

Dear Jane:

I guess I am hard to reach by phone but I don't know what to do about it. I've got to do a lot of concentrated work and the only possible way I can do it is get into a hole away from a telephone and lock the door. That does take me out of the office a lot, and out of communication. Of course, ninety-nine percent of the calls, letters, etc. I get [are] all unnecessary and time wasters. Anyhow, thanks for your good wishes. Sooner or later I will have some kind of a proposal to make about our agreement but it won't be for some time and I'll take it up with Hawley first, anyhow, as he is the trustee. The tax business is killing and I want somehow to slip out of giving all my money to the government, or all the velvet. That's a future, however.

Your caricaturist hasn't called. Now there isn't much use in my talking to him personally, but if he does call, I'll do so if I can. It would be best for him to see Gibbs, who is handling the caricatures now, or Mrs. White. Anyhow, tell him to come around if you see him again.

Love,

Ross

*Before he became the magazine's book editor, Fadiman worked at Simon and Schuster. He sent Ross a dollar bill to "option" his autobiography—should Ross ever write it.*

TO CLIFTON FADIMAN

THE NEW YORKER
OCTOBER 29TH, 1934

Dear Fadiman:

Come, come, come. I can't have you throwing Simon and Schuster's money away on such remote speculations. I will undoubtedly never write anything in this generation of Simons and Schusters anyhow, and for all I know, the little Simons and Schusters may all be black sheep who would squander the money foolishly.

Moreover, Dorothy Parker has been a great lesson to me. She signed up with at least five different publishers for her first novel and is practically deadlocked now in writing one because it could not possibly be published for years because of the litigation which would ensue. I cannot even make a modest start toward such entanglements.

Yours sincerely,

Ross

*Random House proprietors Cerf and Klopfer invited Ross to a reception for Gertrude Stein and Alice Toklas.*

TELEGRAM TO BENNETT CERF AND DONALD KLOPFER

OCTOBER 31ST, 1934

Nuts to Gertrude Stein. If you want to play backgammon tonight telephone me.

H. W. Ross

## TO CORNELIA BRUCE

*THE NEW YORKER*
*NOVEMBER 23RD, 1934*

Dear Mrs. Bruce:

I have been intending to answer your letter of last August for a long time but I took it home, and like a great many things I want to do there it got sidetracked. By a strange coincidence, your letter arrived during my absence from New York and during a trip which included Aspen—my first visit to that town since I left at the age of seven or eight. I regret I didn't get it before I left as I should have looked up your mother. The fact is I didn't know anyone there and although the man who ran the hotel remembered my father he didn't remember very much about him. I was there only a couple of hours and left intending to go back but I never did. The distances of the mountains out there proved too great. I got a thrill out of visiting the place though and found the house I was born in which is still standing. It looked much smaller than I thought it would.

My mother died about eight months ago. She survived my father by seven or eight years. He passed away in Salt Lake City and then after a year or two my mother came here to live. She was seventy-nine at the time of her death. I have often heard her speak of your mother although I was so young when I left Aspen I scarcely remember anybody definitely. You are wrong in one thing. There weren't any "Ross boys." I was the only son. The only brother I had died when I was three and he was one. I don't think he could have raised much of a rumpus. I think it was Benny Smith of the house next door who joined me in throwing rocks at your mother's windows. I remember him all right although I have never known what became of him.

I was very glad to hear from you, I assure you, and as I said, regret I didn't hear earlier. If I ever get to Aspen again I shall look your mother up and I think I will get there again as that region is wonderful, all I had expected it would be.

Sincerely yours,

Harold

MEMO TO RAOUL FLEISCHMANN

Mr. Fleischmann:

That was, of course, Woollcott's one hundredth resignation. He always resigns under such circumstances. My opinion was merely that I certainly wouldn't run his stale and off-color anecdotes if I owned the magazine, which is really all I can say under such circumstances, for perhaps I am, as is often charged, a nice-Nellie, or an old moss-back, etc. Whatever I am, *The New Yorker* has got to decide what kind of a magazine it is and that can be up to nobody but you. You said you were in favor of running the last piece, under the circumstances. I was flatly against it under any circumstances, with some very slight misgivings because of a suspicion that I am too conservative. I'm open to conviction on the latter, but I've got to be convinced. It's not just vacillation. I've heard a vast and an alarming lot of complaint about Woollcott's off-color anecdote:—people cutting them out of the magazine so the children wouldn't see them and so on—and actually there is damned little doubt in my mind. I don't want to be connected with smut, moss-back or not.

Possibly this matter could have been handled better with Woollcott. I think we should have had it out with him as a general subject before we had to pick up a specific issue in copy at deadline time. But Woollcott is difficult in such matters at best and things are complicated now by his radio success, which is wine to him, and by his secretary, Mr. Brown, who has become an intermediary.

In any event I don't think we ought to be bullied into running dirty stories if we don't want to run them, no matter who it is. And I would point out that Woollcott can't get "five times as much for this stuff elsewhere" because, pure as we are, we're the most liberal magazine he can write for and he can't print dirty stories anywhere else. He doesn't try it on the radio, either. Moreover, some class connection is very important to Woollcott, no matter how mighty he is nationally, and divorce certainly has common disadvantages.

Ross

*Denver attorney and businessman Quaintance was married to Ross's cousin. "Alma" was an unproductive gold and silver mine they had invested in.*

## TO ARTHUR D. QUAINTANCE

*THE NEW YORKER*
*DECEMBER 24, 1934*

Dear Arthur:

I have the note with the assay report. Very good, and tell Eddie Snell best wishes and to keep warm up there. I'd like to have a week of Alma this winter but not more than that. It's been cold enough here, but we have steam heat and so on. Tell Mary and Uncle John and everybody Merry Christmas from Frances and me, please.

I'm going to Florida at the end of this week, Frances having set her mind on it and the doctor supporting her. She is still somewhat underweight, and although her general health is good, he thinks that some sunshine will be good for her and that she will get some exercise, which she doesn't get in a large city this time of year. I am going to try to get her sister to go with her and stay with her a week or two. I can only take a few days off and if it works I will leave her there and come back.

You know, my mother had a broken leg or a broken thigh. These things seem to be common to old people. They did not put her in a plaster cast at all, because it seems that the inaction might have produced some kind of pneumonia. Instead of a cast, they put her leg between two boards, which acted as splints although she merely lay there with her leg between them and wasn't tied up at all. She came through that all right, or at any rate recovered the use of her leg partially, although a thing like that is a shock, of course.

Your candy came and thank you. I got almost sick on it yesterday. Frances is to acknowledge this formally, but I will here announce its receipt. I didn't send anybody any Christmas presents this year, as usual. I am on strike as to Christmas, because it always comes at the very worst moment in the year for me.

Merry Christmas, as I said, to all.

Sincerely yours,

Harold

# IV

# "THE NEW YORKER IS

## AS SOUND AS EVER . . ."

### 1935–1939

This period of Ross's life starts happily enough: he has a charming new wife and a baby daughter, and builds himself a large country house in Connecticut. It also sees him stumbling into what would be the best investment of his life. Purely as a favor to an old friend down on his luck, Ross gave Dave Chasen the money to open a small restaurant—then watched in astonishment as it quickly became a Hollywood institution. But Ross's tranquility wouldn't last. The effects of the lingering Depression and impending war in Europe finally hit home, discouraging *The New Yorker*'s humorists and putting a big dent in its advertising. Ross's already strained relationship with his publisher suffered a near-permanent rupture over Fleischmann's financing of another magazine. Ross's second marriage was faring no better than his first. And perhaps worst of all, his twin pillars at the magazine, the Whites, had moved to Maine full-time, with Andy quitting *The New Yorker* to write a column for *Harper's*.

———

## TO FREDRIC MARCH

*THE NEW YORKER*
*APRIL 16, 1935*

Dear March:

The belief that "none" is a singular pronoun is an old American legend which grew out of an error made in a common-school grammar many years ago. I quote from Fowler's *Modern English Usage,* the last word on such subjects: "It is a mistake to suppose that this pronoun is singular only and must at all costs be followed by singular verbs, etc. The Oxford English Dictionary explicitly states that plural construction is commoner."

The last complainant about this was Mr. Alexander Woollcott, who is nearly always wrong in his issues on the fine points of grammar, being an old Kansas City public school boy.

My regards to Mrs. M. My regards to everybody in Hollywood.

Sincerely yours,

Ross

## TO E. B. WHITE

*MAY 7, 1935*

Mr. White:

Reference yours of May 3rd, regarding mention of toilet paper. I appreciated your sincerity and the legitimateness of your intent and am, I think, among the first always to distinguish between a *Ballyhoo* joke about toilet paper and a "would be serious, or reasonable comment on an abstract idea." Nevertheless, the word toilet paper in print inevitably presents a picture to me that is distasteful and, frequently, sickening. It would, for instance, ruin my meal if I read it while eating. It might easily cause vomiting. The fact that we allow toilet paper to be advertised, under the name "Satin Tissue," has nothing to do with this matter. I have never been nauseated by a Satin Tissue ad, possibly because I have never read it. . . . While I have a sensitive and easily-upset stomach, and may on account of that shrink from things that would be unobjectionable to most persons, I am totally depraved in most other matters of taste, nothing whatever shocking me. I merely am embarrassed that others may be shocked. Hence, for years, I have tried to defer in matters of taste to others, principally to a lady you know well, a fellow stockholder....

H. W. Ross

*Ross's quest to motivate contributors to write more often, but with greater brevity, led to ever-changing pay systems that were sometimes breathtaking in their abstruseness. This sheepish "explanation" to his good friend and regular contributor Sullivan appears to date from the mid-thirties. It suggests the convolution of a new Ross system as well as the sorry track record of its many forerunners.*

TO FRANK SULLIVAN

THE NEW YORKER
THURSDAY
[UNDATED]

Frank:

I must write you in connection with this check, which you probably will see instantly is not as big as you have been getting, although the story is of a very unusual degree of excellence. It's one of the best by anyone in a long while, in fact. We have a new and revolutionary scheme for payments, an explanation of which is now being mimeographed.... Briefly, the plan is to pay somewhat more per word (in your case twenty cents) than we have been paying for all pieces under one thousand two hundred words in length and for the first one thousand two hundred words of pieces that run longer than that. Then, after one thousand two hundred, pay half the word rate. This, we hope, will accomplish several things, one of which is to make it profitable for writers to do quite short pieces—a few hundred words—or to encourage them to do it anyway. The flat word rate didn't encourage them. The flat price per piece didn't. The fact is that both *dis*couraged them....

Although, perhaps unfortunately, your first check under the new system is a little smaller than your flat price check would have been (this piece being a short one—just over one thousand two hundred words), an average (of the past) sized piece would have been as much, or greater. We have gone over all our writers, and especially you, I will say, and found that there would have been no suffering of loss except in a few cases of long-winded persons that ought to be choked off anyhow, probably. You won't lose, on the basis of past performance, and if you write some short pieces, God damn it, you'll profit to a considerable extent and can buy more Pennsylvania R.R. stock. For instance, you'd get eighty dollars for four hundred words, the length of some of the best things you used to do in your good old newspaper days, and haven't done since. One hundred dollars for five hundred words. Think of it!

    Your old admirer,

    Ross

*Ross's only child was born on March 17, 1935–St. Patrick's Day—and was named Patricia.*

TO MOSS HART

*THE NEW YORKER*
*JUNE 17TH, 1935*

Dear Moss:

So help me God, I didn't know you were back until I was told so yesterday and I regard your not notifying me as a social slight. Perhaps I am not good enough for the famous traveler and petted darling of world capitals. I called you up today about a business matter—not a social one, for God knows I have my pride and would not be the first to make advances. It is this:

My old friend, Joe Cook, said yesterday that he had heard something about the show you and Porter are doing or have done, whatever the case is, and from what he had heard the lead seemed to be one he would like to do. Joe, for some time, has had a strong secret ambition to play a straight role, no gags, no clowning, no broad comedy makeup, etc. He has been told there is such a part in your play. I therefore advise you of this. His desire to play such a part is deep-seated and sincere. He was broken-hearted, for instance, that he didn't get to play that leading part in *Three Men on a Horse*. He thinks he'd have been perfect for that and I think so too. Nobody would think of him for such a role, of course, but he would be fitted for one, nevertheless.

In your absence I have become the father of a beautiful daughter, now aged three months and weighing fourteen pounds. I may call you up in her behalf, at that.

Sincerely,
Ross

## HANDWRITTEN NOTE TO E.B. WHITE

*THE NEW YORKER*
*[AUGUST 1935]*

White:
Was very sorry to hear about your father, and send my sympathy, which is about all I have to say, except that after you get to be thirty people you know keep dropping off all the time and it's a hell of a note.

Ross

## MEMO TO JAMES THURBER

*SEPTEMBER 23RD, 1935*

Mr. Thurber:
While bathing this morning, it came into my mind that what that dog is doing on your New Year's cover is winking, dog winking. I'm not exactly clear on how a dog winks but it's probably as you've drawn it. It's important that it be clear in the final picture, of course. I will not take a bath again for some time.

H. W. Ross

*Department store magnates Bernard and Adam Gimbel were Ross friends.*

## TO ADAM GIMBEL

*THE NEW YORKER*
*OCTOBER 17TH, 1935*

Dear Adam Gimbel:

I take great pleasure in announcing that after you left the other evening Mr. Seeman suffered reverses and lost forty-eight games, which at one dollar a game is forty-eight dollars for you. Subsequently, after we had played Red Dog I played three more games with Seeman and lost sixteen points, so you owe me thirty-two dollars. I will not hesitate to call this to your attention when I see you again. Keep it until then.

Yours sincerely,

Ross

*Whitaker arrived at* The New Yorker *in 1926 and was a pivotal editor there for half a century. But as a writer he contributed in many guises, producing nightclub coverage (as "Popsie"), Talk pieces (as "Old Curmudgeon"), railroad tales (as "E. M. Frimbo"), and, beginning in 1934, the football department (as "J.W.L.").*

## TO ROGERS E. M. WHITAKER

*[UNDATED]*

Mr. Whitaker:

Would say that your football stuff has interested me this year. From where I sit, which is almost never in the stands, you seem like a good football writer, with a proper technique for a weekly magazine with a deadline like ours. This is important as an example to the rest of the sports depts., too.

Ross

TO ERNST LUBITSCH

*THE NEW YORKER*
*DECEMBER 19TH, 1935*

Dear Lubitsch:

I am doing something I rarely do, but anyhow I am doing it: writing to put in a word for my old friend, Dave Chasen, who is out around Hollywood trying to get started in pictures, mostly at your studio [Paramount]. I went to see a picture he is in, running at the Paramount this week, and he is damn funny. Dave is a very able and funny actor and comedian, and if he is given a chance I know will be a big success in the movies and an asset to someone. He is exceedingly anxious to get into the W.C. Fields picture which your company is going to put on. He says he has a lot of good ideas for Fields which he is willing to turn over without any strings. This is undoubtedly true. I know when Dave was working with Joe Cook he was a great help all around. Moreover, he understands working with a star comedian as well as anyone can.

If you give him a break I guarantee you will not regret it.

Sincerely yours,

H. W. Ross

TO JAMES THURBER

*THE NEW YORKER*
*MAY 14TH, 1936*

Dear Thurber:

Now in connection with the Talk of the Town rewrite situation, I mentioned the matter to [Russell] Maloney and he said you had more than that one piece you talked about (Alexander Dumas, lawyer). Checking our records, find you are credited with having three others, listed as follows: "C.W.R. Knight, lecturer who lives by falconry and lecturing on it;" "Harry Krakaur," the rabbit man; and "The Macfadden for President Headquarters." I think you should have a lot more than this, of course, and for Christ Sake! I thought you did, because Maloney has repeatedly assured me that you had "plenty," etc. Did you ever get these stories and if so, weren't any of them any good?

The Macfadden thing sounds good. I didn't read this, or any of them. I'm trying to put pressure in and get some rewrite for you, for we need Talk sorely. I am, sir,

Yours sincerely,

Ross

*The tempestuous Woollcott was not only one of Ross's closest friends but one of the nation's favorite writers in the twenties and thirties. For six years his Shouts and Murmurs page was a popular feature of* The New Yorker, *but he quit in late 1934. Now Ross was trying to get him back.*

## TO ALEXANDER WOOLLCOTT

*THE NEW YORKER*
*JUNE 2, 1936*

Dear Alec:

I may have been somewhat dilatory about this but I understand there is no cause for hurry, because of the dilatoriness of the surrogate's court. It's about Shouts and Murmurs, and resumption of same, upon which I was appointed to write you. All concerned are naturally very pleased and happy, of course. The price you suggested to Mrs. White is unquestionably high by our precedent and present standards, but turns out, after due discussion and consideration, to be feasible if you are willing to assume certain responsibilities and to submit to certain indirection. In the first place (our viewpoint) there is no question that the value of having you continuously, or more or less so, is the important thing. A page of yours now and then is a doubtful asset and probably no asset at all. (Interruptions and suspensions are a damned annoyance, certainly, with letters from subscribers and replies to be written and all; a serious factor.) Therefore the conclusion, rather obviously, that you are worth more if continuous than occasional, and, carrying this further, and to get to the point, I am authorized to make, and herewith do make, the following offer to you: *The New Yorker* will pay three hundred fifty dollars per page for Shouts and Murmurs plus a bonus of fifty dollars for each page printed providing you do a minimum of forty pages in one year.

Or something like that. For your information, these bonus arrangements are in general use around this office, their purpose being to stimulate, or coerce, writers into doing more work. One of them sent Frank Sullivan back to his psychoanalyst within two weeks and another brought an attack of agoraphobia on Gibbs in a few months. Nevertheless they have been frequently effective and I think in many cases where we make increases of pay, they are helpful, fair, and advisable. . . .

If you don't get your place in Nyack, don't worry, because Connecticut is a wonderful place. You can get both banks of a river up there and have full control. They have one footing in for my bridge. It looks like the portico of Grant's Tomb. That's on the larger place, where house construction will begin upon completion of the bridge. I call it Ross's Tri-Borough Bridge. Or Ross's Try-It-Once bridge. I expect to break ground on the house in two or three weeks and may invite you up for the cornerstone laying. You can break wind. My smaller place, a mile down the river, is about done. Lederer called me up and asked me to Hecht's weekend before last and I said I was committed to Connecticut and probably would never see him again. If you get the Nyack place, I may never see you again. It's sad, but I'm always swept on by currents I can't control.

My family all fine. Regards to all.

Sincerely yours,

Ross


TO RAOUL FLEISCHMANN

*THE NEW YORKER*
*JUNE 13TH, 1936*

Dear Raoul:

I herewith set down a few words to make clear my position around here. I want, at the earliest possible moment, to go frankly and fully and by general announcement on a status of advisory editor, or consulting editor, or whatever you want to call it. Maybe call it Founder. At any rate I want to be relieved of a great part of what I have repeatedly called the financial and personnel end of my job. I'm so Goddamned tired of dealing with personalities I'm dizzy. Whatever little patience I once had is all gone. I've got no talent for it and want to turn that phase of the job over, as fully as possible, to someone who has a talent for it. I don't mean that I won't associate with the members of the staff, etc. The fact is, I think, that I would associate with them a damned sight more than I do now and would be several times as useful as I am now in that phase of the work, because it would work a great psychological difference in my relations with them. I'd be one of them, a fellow working here, and they'd talk to me frankly and not with suspicion as they do now. That's the way I want to be and that's the way I'd be most valuable to the magazine. You and I have a different definition of "editor" and I want to resign the editorship as you define it. I started the damned magazine anyhow only to get out of what you call editing, thinking that much of the executive work, or all of it, would be turned over to someone else and, as I've often said, the magazine is a flop, so far as I am concerned, until I do. . . .

In this connection, I would state that my present salary is not inviolate and that, in fact, because of the tax situation, and my having moved my residence to Connecticut (I trust) where they have no state income tax, I will be around with a proposal for an adjustment myself in a few weeks, as soon as I can talk some more with my tax man and get the situation better in my head. I'm ready at any time to take less money for less work, my old standing proposition.

[Philip] Hoyt shows great promise of developing into the long-sought executive. He says he wants to go ahead with it, try to work into it. (He doesn't mind dealing with people as much as I do, apparently.) I think it is now up to you to have a talk with him about going ahead as the money-bags and the Legree of the place . . . offering to him rewards, present and future, as warranted. . . . We've become a big-money magazine with a great deal of subtle and not-so-subtle competition, a staff of prima donnas that require constant watching, dealing with, and keeping track of. It's a big job, a hell of an important one. The guts of the whole business. This place isn't what it was seven years ago when I could slap [Otto] Soglow down and take a drawing away from him at thirty dollars. It requires efficient and scientific management. . . .

As to my stand, there is little new in the foregoing, but I do want to commit it to paper to clarify things. . . . It might work out, of course, that sooner or later it would be better from your viewpoint for me to go on a part-time basis. That would suit me fine. Or it might be that I would work out of the organization entirely. And that would suit me fine. I would be perfectly content to walk out, confident that I was leaving an organization that would support you, and Jane Grant, and Ruth Fleischmann, and John Hanrahan, and me in the style to which we have become accustomed.

Ross

TO ERNEST BYFIELD

*THE NEW YORKER*
*JULY 17TH, 1936*

Dear Ernie:
I write this in the middle of a big rush. It looks as if I am not going to get out west at all this year. It has been one damn thing after another, mostly the house I am struggling with in Connecticut. I have been so busy and had so many problems the past few weeks that I haven't been able to think about anything personal. It is barely possible I will change my plans and duck out west next month. If I do I will communicate in ample time. I meant to write you before this but have been putting it off.
Sincerely,
Ross

*William Shawn, a shy young man from Chicago, had scant editorial experience when he joined the magazine's staff in 1932. But Ross, still on the lookout for his perfect executive officer, detected Shawn's potential. The younger man's responsibilities were gradually increased until he became managing editor for factual material. Upon Ross's death Shawn would replace his mentor as editor of* The New Yorker.

TO E. B. WHITE

*[SUMMER 1936]*

White:
... Now, briefly, for it's late P.M. and three people are waiting to see me to settle pre-vacation problems (the shutdown begins tomorrow evening). [Geoffrey] Hellman is going on his vacation for the next two

weeks so Shawn will be handling your stuff (and most everything else) for the present. After that I suppose Hellman again, although he has just turned writer, having delivered a casual and a two-part Profile and I suspect is about concluded for desk work. Why don't you just turn your stuff in marked for what it is and not worry about who handles it. For instance, a packet marked Comment Rejections would find its way to the right place, I think. How helpful has Shawn been in the past on the occasions when he's handled Comment? Would appreciate knowing; and how well does he do your Newsbreaks? He's bright, by all indications....

Love to all. Tell K. I have a letter of hers but it's at my country home, where I have stayed practically every night, and a couple of the days, this week. I left it in a pile of unfinished business. I'll write her later. I'm not going away until the end of next week at the earliest as there are a lot of loose ends, as you might call them. One loose end is a steamshovel now digging out a swimming hole in my beautiful Connecticut plot. I've got to see that through. I've got to get a train and get right up there and see what it's done today. It's not a steamshovel. It's a gasoline shovel. Strange thing.

Ross

*Through the years Ross had an increasingly unpleasant relationship with Fleischmann, whom he viewed as having profited to an outsize and unfair extent from* The New Yorker's *success. But a major breach occurred when the publisher quietly used* New Yorker *capital to underwrite a glossy, entertainment-oriented magazine called* Stage, *published by Fleischmann's own business consultant, John Hanrahan. Ross despised Hanrahan and considered* Stage, *a fairly transparent* New Y rker *knockoff, to be a direct competitor.*

MEMO TO RAOUL FLEISCHMANN

THE NEW YORKER
NOVEMBER 2ND, 1936

Mr. Fleischmann:

Forwarding the attached from Mrs. White on which I would remark as follows:

As to *Stage* I am frequently amazed to a point of speechlessness. For instance, several times lately I have been asked if *Stage* magazine is "cutting into us much." I then have to make the rather embarrassing explanation that *Stage* has been backed by *The New Yorker*. This always greatly astonishes my listeners. Of all the magazines extant now, *Stage*, I think, offers the most direct commercial competition and is the most successfully imitative. This is generally recognized in the publishing business, which is offered the unusual, and to my knowledge unique, picture of one magazine supporting its leading imitator and competitor.

I think *The New Yorker* has enough strength to hold its own with all competitors and imitators, probably, if it is given a fair run, but there are elements in the present situation that are certainly alarming. You and the other gentlemen who pass on the payments and personnel problems, which are the biggest factor in the handling and control of our staff and contributors, of course, are also vitally interested in the well-being of *Stage*.... It seems obvious to me that you have brought about a situation which inevitably creates a peculiar and a dangerous case of divided allegiance. How with one hand you can pass on, for example, [A. J.] Liebling's salary and performance, and with the other help lift *Stage* up I don't know. Liebling, according to my understanding, was supposed to be working full time here and being paid on that basis. Yet he writes for *Stage* and that is countenanced by the business meeting. Where in God's world do we stand on Liebling? . . . Pretty much our whole salaried staff is affected; if they haven't written for *Stage* it isn't because they haven't been asked repeatedly to do so. And, of course, our contributors are besought constantly by *Stage*, frequently to do the same thing they should be doing here. It is a constant and hard struggle to get enough good contents to fill up *The New Yorker* and the editorial department efforts have certainly been seriously complicated by *Stage*, which, from the editorial standpoint has certainly come to have the highest nuisance value of all competing magazines. I have no solution; am just mildly dismayed.

H. W. Ross

*Mining engineer and bon vivant, Baragwanath was married to the glamorous illustrator and Round Tabler Neysa McMein. He had dedicated a new book,* Pay Streak, *to Ross, who because of his upbringing had a lifelong fascination with the mining industry.*

## TO JACK BARAGWANATH

*THE NEW YORKER*
*NOVEMBER 11, 1936*

Dear Jack:

It's obviously up to me to say something, so I'll say I read the God-damned book clear through last night and during certain hours of restlessness early this morning without having seen the dedication at all. This is my tribute. Then I accidentally stumbled on the dedication and, after recovering from the double shock of being mentioned at all and of being called son of a bitch and bastard in print, a very unusual thing (in print), I was duly appreciative and grateful. Any mention at all is gravy, is my viewpoint.

My ambition (I must now tell you about myself) is to write that kind of a book on Aspen and Silverton, Colo., and the other mining towns of the west that so impressed me in my youth. There's the damnedest mess of stories out there you ever heard of; you get it from the mouths of old-timers. I've been back there twice in the last three or four years and am constantly in a dither. Met an old fellow who had been with my father when he died, the "geologist" who advised the Browns in the discovery of the Molly Gibson mine. They went down with a diamond drill, which didn't make much progress after three or four days. It had bored into a nugget of solid silver (on view in the state capital, Denver now) which weighed a ton after they'd dug down to it and got it to the surface, "and then we had to cut one hump off it to get it up the shaft." [The] Browns were going to quit when this happened. The Molly Gibson shipped, by the old ledgers which they got out and showed me, two hundred fifty thousand dollars in gold the tenth month after being opened and kept that up, or better, for years. In Silverton we had dinner in the restaurant of the old Palace Hotel which, so help me God, after all these years, still has something of the atmosphere of the first-class, snorting western restaurant of those days. When we finished I got talking to the city marshal who was standing in front with his badge on. I wanted him to settle a question that came up in an earlier talk with another old-timer: What year was it that it snowed three inches on the Fourth of July and they had to call off the ballgame in the fifth inning? He was my man, had played on the team, which was financed by Jack Slattery, owner of the Hub, the leading (of forty) gambling places and saloons. It was 1902. At the end of the third the snow started and by the first of the fifth it was all off, despite the bonfire near the pitcher's box. I inquired about a certain block of granite they used to use for rock-drilling contests. The marshal said he remembered it, and, as a matter of fact, it was right over on Blair Street then.

The mention of Blair Street stirred up poignant recollections. There were three streets in Silverton, the residential, which included the school and the church; the business, which included the forty saloons and gambling rooms; and Blair Street, which was the red light district. (We lived on the residential street; my mother was easily the most righteous woman in town.) I said to the marshal, "When I was here Blair Street was the red light district—full of wild women." "Still is!" he said. "And still the same women. They're all right over there now—never had money enough to get out of town." Next morning I took a walk down Blair Street to the granite block, which I easily discovered. It was ten o'clock and, by God, there were the women: fifty-five- and sixty-year-old hookers, still doing business in their little wooden houses, which hadn't been painted or repaired in all the time since I'd left. Or still there for business: they didn't seem to be doing any. At that time only one mine was working in Silverton. The old girls were sitting out on the porch shelling peas or sewing, hanging up washing, and doing other household chores. There was considerable interest in me, although somewhat half-hearted. I was obviously the best prospect that had come down Blair Street in a long time but the gals seemed so despondent, discouraged, and downright old you could hardly call their solicitation better than listless.

I saw the marshal later that day and asked him about prices now on Blair Street. Fifty cents he said, if you were a slick bargainer. Fifty cents, by Jesus, is calamity. Used to be five dollars, when the North Star and the other mines were going. Grover Cleveland did it, and he had a hell of a lot to explain when he got to heaven.

When I see you I'll tell you about Charlie Nelson, three card monte dealer at the Hub and his marrying Gussie right out of Blair Street and moving next door to us. My mother raised hell.

Please do something about my seeing you and again, accept my thanks, for the unusual honor.

Sincerely yours,

Ross

*In 1936 The New Yorker published one of its most famous pieces, a Profile of the founder of Time Inc., Henry Luce, done in a wicked parody of Timestyle ("Backward ran sentences until reeled the mind"). The Profile was written by Wolcott Gibbs. In exchange for Luce's cooperation in the reporting of the story, Ross agreed to let Luce see it in advance; upon reading the piece Luce was acrimonious. In a long and boozy evening at Ross's apartment, he recited his many grievances. Ross promised to discuss each objection with his editors and report back to Luce. The adjectives and phrases in the letter's close were all descriptions of Ross that had appeared previously in Time and Fortune.*

TO HENRY LUCE

*THE NEW YORKER*
*NOVEMBER 23, 1936*

Dear Luce:

I assume it is up to me to make certain explanations; at any rate I do so, to clear my conscience, with which I always struggle to keep current. I enclose a copy of the final proof of the parody. I have just been over this, reading the piece for what I pray to God is the last time and making notes of a few points I want to explain. . . .

The staff here wanted to be fair and McKelway and I put all of the important "matters of opinion" (as [Time Inc. general manager Ralph] Ingersoll called a great many of the points raised in the *Fortune* piece on *The New Yorker*) which you raised to a sort of committee, consisting of Mr. and Mrs. White (founders of a dynasty, *Fortune,* August, 1934), Gibbs, McKelway and myself. We considered these matters with a full sense of our responsibility, rather solemnly. Our office differs from yours in that our contents are signed and the writer of an article has the final say on changes, if it comes right down to it. In this instance, however, Gibbs abided by the group decision in every instance. To the special points:

You complained that there wasn't a single favorable word in the piece about you. It was generally felt that the total effect of the article and its being in existence at all were enormously favorable, and that our listing of your remarkable growth, the figures themselves, were complimentary in the highest degree, presenting you, in fact, as practically heroic. It was decided, however, to go further and we generously gave you each a favorable word, or phrase: you are, as you will note, "revered by colleagues," Ingersoll is "able." As Gibbs pointed out subsequently in a memo written to me: "Having chosen this (parody) form (and I think it's the only way we could possibly write about another magazine) the piece was bound to sound like *Time,* and you will go through a hell of a lot of copies of *Time* without finding anybody described in a way that would please his mother." I was astonished to realize the other night that you are apparently unconscious of the notorious reputation *Time* and *Fortune* have for crassness in description, for cruelty and scandal-monging and insult. I say frankly but really in a not unfriendly spirit, that you are in a hell of a position to ask anything. And, as was pointed out, the kindly adjectives inserted may throw the piece slightly out of key, so rare is a pleasant adjective printed by *Time....*

We decided that our estimates as to some of the [Time Inc. operating] figures were as good for our purposes as yours would have been, since the article was a parody and some errors would only contribute to the general effect; *The New Yorker* figures in the *Fortune* piece were amusingly wide of the fact in certain instances. (Your passion for accuracy is in no wise doubted; your ability to attain it in many instances is questioned, naturally, by practical journalists.) We felt that the figure on average pay could not possibly be taken as anything other than a parody figure, since it went to five decimal points. (The figures are just as Gibbs happened to hit the typewriter keys.)

I was confronted with an ample mass of evidence to substantiate the statements that the writers put "jokers," or "slithering insults," in their copy. Remember that there has been a considerable duplication of writing talent by *Fortune* and *The New Yorker* and that writers talk much. Quite a number of anecdotes about this.

The paragraph on *Fortune*'s methods of getting facts was allowed to stand as being justified, beyond doubt. Not only did we have *The New Yorker* piece as evidence on this point, but ample reports on several others. For instance, we were informed that your original piece on the Astor estate contained one hundred and thirty-eight misstatements, or errors, which had to be painstakingly worked out.

Your unavailability for lunch for three weeks was based on a statement made by one of your own men to one of ours in the course of preparing our article.

I didn't get anywhere on your argument about the inaccuracy of "indiscriminate admiration for business success." This [was] held to be amply justified on superficial evidence of [Time] publications [themselves], and on strength of various reports. ". . . Indiscriminate" used loosely, perhaps, but justifiably.

The passages about the first Mrs. Luce were changed, as also were the ones about Mrs. Clare Luce. The quote from Richard Watts [in which the critic tweaked the playwright for an unprovoked curtain call at the opening of *Abide with Me*] was taken out of the text and run as a footnote. This was given solemn consideration, I assure you. It was unanimously felt that it should be retained in the parody, as being exactly the kind of item *Time* would pick up and use itself. . . .

Ingersoll's hypochondria was adjudged to be still existent. Not only did we have the advice of one of the greatest psychiatrists in the city on this (he told us, once a hypochondriac always a hypochondriac; on occasion it may be latent or nearly so but such periods are only temporary and that the patient should be watched carefully during them) but from direct testimony. One of our investigators reported that the second drawer on the left-hand side of Ingersoll's desk contains twenty-eight bottles, phials, boxes, etc., of remedies, an impressive assortment. I would transmit the list of them if space and time permitted. Moreover, there was testimony that Ingersoll is still dosing, still exhibiting a morbid interest in medicines. Seems a bottle of mange cure, which a fellow worker had got for use on his hair, was accidentally broken recently; Ingersoll came up, plunged a finger into the liquid, and was about to put his finger to his tongue when someone shouted at him and restrained him.

The now-famous [Luce] apartment was left at fifteen rooms, and I trust to God that it has fifteen rooms. Our earnest reporter-checker on this fact swears it is, itemized the rooms, and supplied us with a real estate announcement calling it a fifteen-room apartment. He is a faithful lad and feels the whole thing deeply. He ... points out that you are offering the place for rent as a fifteen-room apartment, a pretty state of affairs if it isn't true. I hope you will realize that Gibbs's point at getting this was one of expediency: he wanted to use his coinage "Newyorkereporter." You were adjudged to be by tradition a Tory, and no doubt whatever. Ministers of the gospel are the very spearheads of toryism; then Hotchkiss and Yale, both conventional, Tory.

Retention of the paragraph on presidential ambitions was also a unanimous decision. It was regarded as exactly the kind of thing *Time* is doing constantly: denying the weird and, as we called it, "grotesque" rumor after stating it, thereby getting the full news value of it. Moreover Time enterprises are always speculating on people's ambitions. This seemed the perfect item for parody purposes.

That finishes my itemization of special points in the story. . . .

After our talk the other night I asked at least ten people about *Time* and, to my amazement, found them bitter, in varying degrees, in their attitude. You are generally regarded as being mean as hell and frequently scurrilous. Two Jewish gentlemen were at dinner with me last night and, upon mention of *Time,* one of them charged that you are anti-Semitic, and asked the other if he didn't think so too. The other fellow said he'd read *Time* a lot and he didn't think you were anti-Semitic especially; you were just anti-everything, he said—anti-Semitic, anti-Italian, anti-Scandinavian, anti-black-widow spider. "It is just their pose," he said.

There was telephoning about these proofs last week but we didn't send them over to Ingersoll because I wanted to send some explanation with them when they went, and the whole thing seemed to get to a childish stage. Perhaps it still is in one, for I feel rather childish writing all this. It's all over now, anyhow.

Sincerely yours,
Harold Wallace Ross
Small man . . . furious . . . mad . . . without taste

*In the twenties Ross became good friends with vaudeville comedians Joe Cook and Dave Chasen. When Cook retired and his partner got nowhere in Hollywood, Ross gave Chasen, an accomplished amateur chef, the money he needed to open a small barbecue and chili shop in Beverly Hills. To Ross's everlasting astonishment, bankrolling what metamorphosed into the celebrated Chasen's restaurant turned out to be the best investment he ever made. McNamara, a former New Jersey police officer, was another vaudeville veteran—"The Singing Cop"—and he sometimes roomed with Ross between the editor's first and second marriages. As the restaurant was getting established Ross was nearly as attentive to it as he was to* The New Yorker, *and he relied on McNamara to keep an eye on things for him.*

TO EDWARD MCNAMARA

*The New Yorker*
*December 23rd, 1936*

Dear Mac:

I just sent a wire addressed to Dave telling him to go ahead with the addition. That will be O.K. Apparently, he's got more kitchen and barbecue facilities than seating capacity. This is admittedly a sad situation, providing he's got the people to seat, as seems to be the case. There's no point in feeding thirty people, for God's sake.

If he's got class carriage trade like Capra and Cagney he ought to have a back room for them and run it as a club; no riff raff admitted whatever. That's the only way to do it. It's how "21" made its success in New York. If you can afford to be snobbish that's the thing to do. Have a doorman and nobody who doesn't belong is admitted. Think this over and, if sound in your opinion, get President Chasen's ear and read these remarks to him. And tell him about my coming west. The facts are as follows:

Unless something serious prevents (such as sickness of baby, broken leg, or something like that) I'll leave Sunday, December 27th. I don't know yet where I'm going. The original plan was (and the trip really came about that way) to go to the new skiing and winter resort the Union Pacific has built in Idaho. Adam Gimbel and his wife are going along with us, or I'm going along with them. Today Mr. Gimbel learned to his astonishment that there is no snow (for the first time in sixty-one years) in the St. Moritz of America and is trying to change the routing to go to California first and come back by the St. Moritz of America. This is probably what will be done and we will be in Los Angeles on the 30th. I suppose, knowing how things are, that we'll spend New Year's Eve in Los Angeles. The point, however, is to get to some quiet place where there isn't any traffic. Palm Springs seems to be the most likely place, from here. Anyhow, I want to get out into the quiet as soon as possible. No parties first. I can consult with Dave about the party after I get there. It will require some planning, as you will realize after your long social training in Paterson, because we don't want any faux pas. (Just read *that* word to Chasen.) Now the question is, will Dave need any money before I get out there, or will the five hundred dollars now en route hold him until I arrive? If it doesn't please wire me at the house, 22 East 36th Street, immediately upon receipt of this and I will forward check.

I can't quite figure out what your role in this venture is, unless you're Dave's corresponding secretary. Maybe you're a candidate for doorman to the clubroom. If so, Mac, I'll put in a good word for you the minute I can buttonhole Chasen. Don't let him give too much food away—unwisely, I mean. It's all right to treat millionaires well, but don't let him start doing things for the poor.

Merry Christmas to all,

Ross

P.S. On second thought, I'm enclosing the second five hundred dollars now. Dave will need it anyhow, and I might just as well not squeeze it a few days more. So here it is, and if I go by Idaho and don't get to California for a week after that, it won't worry me.

H.W.R.

*Ross was surprised to receive a letter from Wallis Simpson, the American*
*for whom Edward VIII had just abdicated his throne. Mrs. Simpson was*
*thanking the magazine for its relatively sympathetic treatment at a time*
*when she was being vilified elsewhere, and Ross was trying to figure out*
*what to do with her letter. It never ran in the magazine.*

TO JANET FLANNER

*THE NEW YORKER*
*JANUARY 29TH, 1937*

Dear Janet:

. . . You will hear from Mrs. White later, undoubtedly, in answer to
the long letter from you which she has just given me. I read only the
part in which you referred to Mrs. Simpson (but will read the rest
later with deep interest). The letter came in from Mrs. Simpson, cre-
ating a mild sensation in the office and also a quandary. We didn't
know whether to print it or not and still don't. It came in like any other
letter to the editor with no request that it be kept confidential. One
school of thought here was that she wants it printed as a slap at *Time*
and some other American publications. We finally, a little while ago,
cabled her asking if we might use it. That will settle it. It would be
good journalism to use it and bad manners to use it if she didn't want
it so used. I enclose a copy of the letter for your interest. It is undoubtedly the result of your handling of the situation. I don't think it
will do any harm if the letter is printed, as it is, after all . . . evidence
that she is human.

Sincerely yours,
Ross

MEMO TO RAOUL FLEISCHMANN, EUGENE
SPAULDING, PHILIP HOYT, AND IK SHUMAN

*FEBRUARY 15TH, 1937*

Mr. Fleischmann, Mr. Spaulding, Mr. Hoyt, Mr. Shuman:

I think it's short-sighted and unfair to pay only six cents a word to
Ruth McKenney for her piece "The Prince," which is first-rate humor,
something rare and valuable. This girl should be encouraged, and she

should be paid what she's worth, and I think she's worth, say, ten cents a word.

H. W. Ross

## TO ZEPPO MARX

*THE NEW YORKER*
*MARCH 1ST, 1937*

Dear Zeppo, Inc.:

There is a girl in Hollywood named Janet McLeay, an actress of experience, who wants to get a job in the movies. She's the sister of Sophie Gimbel, of Saks-Fifth Avenue, the lady you met with me New Year's Eve at the Trocadero, the good old Troc. She complains that she's tried to see you and that you won't even talk to her on the telephone. Will you please see her and take appropriate action? If you don't, I'll write no more letters to President Roosevelt for Harpo about your indigent cousins in Germany.

Did you do anything about Hugh Wiley? Might be gold there.

Love to all,

Ross

## TO DAVE CHASEN

*THE NEW YORKER*
*MARCH 15TH, 1937*

Dear Dave:

I was down for the weekend at a hunting lodge in New Jersey and am able to tip you off on one of the world's finest delicacies, which would fit right into your business. It's smoked turkey. They had one, and it's among the best things I ever ate. I investigated how they did it, and here is how: They take a fresh turkey and soak it in brine for three days. I think they told me they used four pounds of salt to five gallons of water. At any rate they put in salt until a fresh egg floats on top so that the little end is sticking out only to the size of a quarter. They also put two pounds of brown sugar in. At the end of three days, they take the turkey out and begin smoking it. They smoke it for four days, using hickory wood and a little sassafras. The sassafras presumably helps to give it the flavor.... The turkey is absolutely black when it is done, but tasty beyond belief, and a beautiful sight. (If you put a whole one on display you'd knock 'em dead.) ... You can prepare them to keep forever if you soak them in brine long enough. This is a gilt-edged idea and don't forget it. A smoked turkey sandwich would be a great feature, also all sorts of smoked fish. Or for appetizers. Or sold to the family trade. I'll bet you could do a whale of a business, for home consumption and mail order, in whole turkeys if you ever got this thing started. They can be shipped all over the country.

Your old pal,
Ross

## TO ERNEST BYFIELD

*THE NEW YORKER*
*MARCH 17TH, 1937*

Dear Ernie:

Have a problem, as follows, which please take up with the proper person in your organization and let me know about:

I'm one of the backers of Dave Chasen in the barbecue-restaurant business in Hollywood. (You probably know Dave, Joe Cook's old partner.) Dave started off with spare ribs, chili, etc., a couple of months ago and was so successful he filled his place up. He's enlarging and now wants to serve steaks, chops, etc., and he's having trouble getting good steaks. It seems there aren't any good steaks on the Pacific Coast, except a few imported by the first-class places from a man named Davis in New York, who ships them out from here by train. Through my old friend, William Seeman, I got in touch with Davis and learned, to my amazement, that he feels committed to his old customers in Hollywood (two of them gambling joints) and is doubtful whether or not he'll sell Dave any meats. He's written out asking them if they are going to have any objection. The answer is going to be, undoubtedly, that they have objection and that will choke Dave off from getting these Davis steaks. This may be a good thing, for he'll have to get his steaks from somewhere else and you can't tell me he won't do better, in price at least, by getting them nearer where they grow than

New York. For Christ's sake, Byfield, it is uneconomic to ship steaks from the Middle West to the east and then back again (probably right through Chicago) after the aging. What I want you to do is have the aforesaid proper man in your organization tell me where and how Dave can get good steaks shipped to him regularly from Chicago, or Omaha, or wherever good steaks grow and are properly aged, etc. Please let me have this information at once and oblige

One who loves your wife,

Ross

P.S. Come to think of it, send a copy of your letter to me to Dave direct: Dave Chasen, Chasen's Southern Pit, Beverly and Doheney drives, Hollywood, Calif.

H.W.R.


TO DAVE CHASEN

*THE NEW YORKER*
*MAY 13, 1937*

Dear Dave:

I may have told you about this before but I came across a piece of paper with a recipe on it and send it on for what it's worth. In the old days in San Francisco there was a famous drink called Pisco Punch, made from Pisco, a Peruvian brandy. It was distilled from some berry that grew ten thousand feet up in the Andes. I used to see it coming into San Francisco on coastwise boats in crude little clay jugs made by the natives there. . . . It's a unique liquor and one of its distinctions is that it makes that drink which (as served in S.F.) used to taste like lemonade but had a kick like vodka, or worse. A great drink, though. All San Francisco bars used to serve them and one or two served nothing else; one of the latter being old Duncan Nichols, who ran the oldest bar in the city and the only bar at which women were allowed to drink in the whole town. You might, with profit, introduce this drink in Los Angeles. It used to be a great favorite with the ladies, account of its mildness, kick. It also was reputed to be an aphrodisiac, which it may be and which would probably be velvet to your customers.

The recipe, which I've just discovered, is this:

1 part sour ...................................................lime
2 parts sweet............................................grenadine syrup or sugar
 (I think syrup the best probably)
3 parts Pisco
4 parts water and ice. My recipe says mix in a cocktail shaker....

As ever,
Ross

## TO ROBERT BENCHLEY

*WEDNESDAY (JULY 7, 1937)*

Dear Bob:
 ... I am writing this on the desk you loaned me, which I have moved
to my townhouse, 22 East 36th Street, for the summer. I think the desk
will be a success in its tryout but to date I have been handicapped by
having only a chair with high arms against which I bang my elbows at
practically every word, a portable typewriter that is loose in every
joint and, today, by the fact that I brought the wrong glasses to town
and can't see very well at less than four feet. This, plus the example of
your usual neat, pansy typing has put me under a considerable strain,
so I will draw this to a close, with the news that it's very hot here.
 Ross

*This was about the time E. B. White decided to quit writing Notes and
Comment, weary after having produced the column for a decade. The
Whites had summered in Maine for years; its pull was strong for both of
them, but especially for Andy. In early 1938 they would move there permanently.*

## TO KATHARINE S. WHITE

*TUESDAY (AUG. 24, 1937)*

Katharine:
We were talking yesterday and came to the conclusion that there's
no reason you couldn't stay up in Maine, or anywhere else you want,
for two or three weeks more if you think it would make you feel bet-

ter in the end. This was apropos of the statement in your letter that White found he felt better when he didn't work and that you did too. With me, that's completely understandable. I feel better when I don't have to spend a day in town. If you wanted to stay in Maine we could send up stuff to keep you fairly busy there and make the continuation of absence logical from a standpoint of good business. Think this over. I am writing this hurriedly as have to go to lunch with Fadiman in ten minutes. I was going to answer your letter fully this morning (at home) and also several postcards White has tauntingly sent but I got tangled up with the telephone, domestic matters, etc. and this is all I'll write today. Tell White I thought he was still stuck behind a reef because of rough weather and handling no mail. Tell him I'm sending a letter of recommendation, the customary one when an employee leaves. I shall give him a first-class rating in the publishing world. It will be a letter he could show Simon and Schuster without fear.

Gibbs hasn't had a drink in months, is clean-eyed and in command of everything since he came back from the sanitarium, and there is no theatre to speak of this month. He could carry on all right. The latest tragedy is the Shanghai war, which has caused the suspension of Emily Hahn's stuff. The strangest things happen, as usual.

Ross

TO E. B. WHITE

*THE NEW YORKER*
*TUESDAY*
*[SEPTEMBER 1937]*

Dear White:

You're a common stockholder and entitled to know what's going on, so will say that we're starting the new movie guide thing in the next issue and that you'll be startled to see it isn't what you thought it was going to be. We finally—and when I say finally I mean after the damnedest river of palaver and debate around here in years—decided that the best thing to do was just list thirty or forty neighborhood houses and have done with it. Otherwise we'd have been letting the magazine in for three pages which would break the world's record for dullness, both as to text and typographically, and our readers would have been going to bank nights, getting lice, and winning chinaware. We are going to cover the city as well as warranted, and I hope the feature will prove useful to you upon your return to town.

There has been only one other departmental change of consequence. The "How's that again department?" has been changed to the "How's that again? department." You were scarcely cold on the Maine shore when you were ganged on this. Maloney is doing Newsbreaks in almost a sufficient quantity and Orr has turned in several that I thought pretty good. Your departmental heads are saving the situation, or I think they will. . . . Worst break of the season: we had an Emily Hahn series on Shanghai boarded up and the damn Japs ruin Shanghai and our series and we're as bad off as usual this time of year, if not worse.

A gentleman from Montreal wrote in suggesting that your last piece be set to music. I suppose you got that letter. There was some talk that I ought to write you a letter upon completion of ten years service and I started a couple of times on it, my idea being to have *that* set to music and sing it to you. Deems Taylor, a composer, lives nearby and, owing to the fact that his cook left him, has to eat here and is under heavy obligations. My first letter began, "Dear Old White colon," fine for the bass notes. But I hardly knew who the letter would be to. I tried using Ingersoll as a sort of dummy and pretending that you wanted to get a job on *Life* as "Life Goes to a Party" editor. That didn't seem to go very well. I then thought of Colonel Blethen, but gave him up in the end. I then gave the whole thing up in the end, but if you ever should want a letter, by God you'll have one if I have to call Woollcott in to help me.

Do you and Mrs. W. want to stop off at my Connecticut establishment on your way down? If you do, advise. Or don't advise. Just stop. The only thing is that we may not be here and there may be no food. We're always here on weekends, though, and you wouldn't have to do more than telephone, if that.

I hope your God-damned stomach is better since you've quit writing. I was cheered when Katharine said you felt better when you didn't work, but have heard nothing since. She said she was better, too, when she didn't work. I've long known that about work but never mentioned it. I am doing as little work myself as possible now, but they keep nagging me. Let me know if you want to visit me. You could stay several days if you wanted: suppose it gets too cold up there; you could finish your vacation out here. We could fill our pipes, light the fire in the grate, and have a good long talk about the old days.

Ross

P.S. This written in Conn.


TO DAVE CHASEN

*THE NEW YORKER*
*SEPTEMBER 20TH, 1937*

Dear Dave:

Dan says he has a late statement from you, or, I guess, Mr. Aye, which is very encouraging, both as to the volume of business you're doing, the profit, and, what is probably more important, the matter of finding out where you stand. . . .

I now wish earnestly to recall my earlier suggestions that you drop all the nonsense of having a French, or half-French restaurant and French, or half-French menu. I think your present situation is grotesque. You start out to open a barbecue, then serve steaks, chops, etc., and go into a more or less all-around American restaurant, then you get in the hands of a gang that wants you to imitate "21" and a French chef and get delusions of grandeur. I think you veered wrong when you went in for the Continental stuff, which isn't in your line. My advice is be yourself: stick to your barbecue stuff, your steaks, chops, corned beef (which I don't see on the menu despite all the dust-up about it in New York when you were here) and the Dinty Moore line of stuff. Get out a homely American menu, serving top-notch stuff and let it go at that.

To begin with, your present menu looks like something the railroad eating house in Ogden, Utah, used to hand out to travellers on day trains in 1902. It is one of the most uninviting typographical messes I've ever seen in my life. The sloozy varnished finish is highly distasteful, suggesting that you wash the gravy and fly-specks off for reuse. Your French spelling is fantastic. You have at least fifteen or twenty errors in your French, which ought in itself to be evidence that you'd do better to drop the French language and leave it lie. You, or your printer, or your chef, or whoever got out this menu can make enough mistakes in English without tackling the rich field of French. These errors are apparent to me, and I'm no French scholar; for all I know you haven't got a single God-damned French word right. You've dropped "con Carne" from your "Chili" in favor of a mess of pottage. . . .

I could go on at considerable length about your menu, specifying the misspellings, but that probably isn't necessary for one doing business in your cultural center of Hollywood, but I want to know whether you're in sympathy with what I say before I waste any more typewriter ribbon. If you are, I'll express myself further, giving some really excellent advice. . . .

Regards,
Ross

*Raoul and Ruth Fleischmann had divorced. Peter Vischer was editor and publisher of* Country Life.

TO E. B. WHITE

*THE NEW YORKER*
*[AUTUMN 1937]*

Dear White:

Just a line to let you know that all is well. I am well, too, but working rather hard as Ruth Fleischmann just married Peter Vischer and we have another little mouth to feed.

Sincerely yours,
Ross

*The legendary McKelway was one of the early* New Yorker's *great writers, but for several years in the late thirties he was the magazine's managing editor for fact. Here Ross is reacting to a trial piece from Ann Honeycutt for a prospective department on dogs. Honeycutt, incidentally, had been briefly married to McKelway (he wed six times in all), and was the lifelong flame of James Thurber.*

## TO ST. CLAIR MCKELWAY

*[Autumn 1937]*

McKelway:

Promising, I should say. I finished it with a definite feeling that it was scant and bare, which it is, partially because of its shortness. I say let her take the project seriously and figure to start up sooner or later. I doubt starting off a dept on which we are all so uncertain over a weekend, and think my ideas of testing out a department writer with a department which is not on a show, or an event, is a very good one. It would be good moral example, too; deptal [departmental] writer otto be able to get up a good dept. with no event to talk over. . . .

I was disappointed in this piece because it didn't tell more about the small dogs; we spoke, for instance, of the smallest dog in the show for Talk. Who was he? Novelty stuff like that would be mighty interesting, generally, and could certainly be got, along with lore, of which there is encouragingly some here.

Ross

The point is, damn it, I think this department could be worked out by Miss H if we had enough well-directed power here to help her enough, both in feeding ideas, helping her develop ones she has, and in editing, for this is ragged copy, rather.

R.

## MEMO TO WILLIAM SHAWN

*December 22, 1937*

Mr. Shawn:

In re handling of ideas, while I think of it. When you get one, for anything, I say sit down and write it out then and there and put it through, i.e., if you have no doubts about it. If you have doubts, save up for news meeting, or if more timely than that, to talk to me about. I'd save for news meeting only ones that are debatable, or require discussion of some sort. It's quicker for me to read an idea than it is to listen to it in news meeting and the practice I propose would considerably cut down the palaver there and save time all around. I'd like to have all Talk, Reporter, and Profile ideas routed through me for the time being. I'll mark whether preferred or not (or confirm your marking) make any comments or advice I have (as to whom to assign to, etc.) and pass along for copying, filing, etc. You can send the ideas to me in rough note form, if you want—any way: your own typing, dictated off, on back of an envelope, or anything.

I say also send to me any very important notions you want to pass along for other departments of the magazine. The lesser ones, the big stream, pass direct to the editor or writer concerned and check in post mortem only. All art ideas to [William] Maxwell for the present; with Gibbs transferring from his desk. Mrs. White should not be burdened with these.

Ross

TO ST. CLAIR MCKELWAY

*MARCH 11TH, 1938*

Mr. McKelway:

I finally got to this piece and read it faithfully. There is unquestionably a story here and unquestionably a way to organize it as suggested by Shawn. I agree with all his observations (although I didn't read his long list of numbered points). It's not right as is certainly and it suffers badly from the old trouble of [Charles] Cooke's, tightening up when he writes original stuff. Also, he's got quite a number of trite phrases in it, a few old gags ("including the Scandinavian") and he's attributed human emotions to animals (eyes twinkled, etc.) which gave me the creeps and will never be recorded in this magazine if I'm here and alert. I regret to say that I doubt Cooke's ability to re-do this thing. I think he's got stuck on it. He's asked me about it twice (see notes attached) and will you please handle with him, presenting my apologies for being so long but at the same time making the point that the piece had had the benefit of extremely competent criticism already.

Ross

TO RAOUL FLEISCHMANN

*THE NEW YORKER*
*APRIL 1ST, 1938*

Dear Raoul:

Publication of the annual report for 1937 has had an extremely de-moralizing effect and it is up to me to make some explanation to the staff and, if possible, to give some reassurance. The situation has got to the grave point where I feel I can no longer take the responsibility for this department if any further contribution is made to *Stage,* or to the Hanrahan Publishing Company, and if announcement is not made to the effect that we are to invest no more money in it. The general assumption here has been that the investment was much smaller than it is now revealed to be. This has been based largely on the word of several directors who, after a meeting last June, said that the amount was six or seven hundred thousand dollars and that no more money was to be sunk. Several months ago you yourself told me that the investment was only seven hundred thousand dollars. Or so I recall it, and if my recollection is correct, the F-R Corp. has been pouring more money into *Stage* at a dizzying rate since then. May I ask, therefore, for a statement telling exactly what your intentions are as to *Stage,* or what the F-R Corp.'s intentions are? I should like to know also the nature of the security for the Hanrahan account spoken of in the statement of the auditors. It is given as fifty-three per cent of the account minus the reserve (as I dope it out) and that would mean something over three hundred thousand dollars. I understand, by hearsay, that either part or all of this consists of notes from the Hanrahan Company to this corporation secured by *New Yorker* stock. Would it be possible for you to let me see copies of these notes? Considering the fact that for thirteen years I have given all that is in me to *The New Yorker,* I know you will understand that these requests are made with the best interests of the institution at heart.

Sincerely,

H. W. Ross

*Days later Ross resorted to an ultimatum.*

TO RAOUL FLEISCHMANN

*APRIL 5, 1938*

Dear Raoul:

I have your note of yesterday regarding the investment in *Stage* magazine and allied ventures, and will show it to the persons you suggest. As for myself, I have decided upon a course of action as follows: Unless, before five P.M. Friday of this week, I have your written promise that you will stop the financial contributions to *Stage* (or to any company or enterprise headed by John Hanrahan) at the earliest moment it is legally possible to do so, and that in the meantime you will hold these contributions to the minimum amount legally possible, I shall terminate my services with the F-R Publishing Corporation with the closing of the present issue of *The New Yorker*. You are requested to consider this communication as notice to that effect.

This decision has been made after deep consideration. As I have said many times, I think *Stage* is a preposterous enterprise for the F-R Corporation, my reasons being that it is frankly imitative of *The New Yorker* and is a serious nuisance as competition to the editorial department; that it is directly competitive to us in circulation and advertising; that it is an unsound publishing idea which, if it did succeed would do so in only a piddling manner and the return would not even be sufficient to make up for the nuisance of its competition; finally, as I understand the set-up between the F-R Corporation and the Hanrahan Company, whatever might happen, we would own only a minority interest in the latter corporation and I think such a minority interest would be worthless.

To put it more briefly, if *Stage* did succeed it would be directly competitive to *The New Yorker*, and it wouldn't be worth anything to *The New Yorker*. I could understand your spending money to put it out of business; I cannot understand your spending one cent to support it....

Sincerely,

H. W. Ross

*Fleischmann acceded and withdrew* The New Yorker *from* Stage, *which eventually went out of business.*

*The "Jane Grant agreement" obligated Ross to pay his former wife ten thousand dollars a year. He set aside a block of* New Yorker *stock for that purpose, but when the dividends fell short—and for years they did— Ross had to make up the difference out of his own pocket.*

TO RAOUL FLEISCHMANN

MAY 24TH, 1938

Raoul:

I have your three recent memos. I will try to refrain here from going into any detailed argument on the various points involved, for I think nothing would be gained by doing so and time would be lost. To me time is extremely pressing now because we are in the middle of an involved and intricate editorial reorganization, as you know. My purpose in asking for the access to the figures, which you grant in your note of May 20th, is, of course, to substantiate certain points I want to press upon you, but that must necessarily be future work. I want to be constructive and specific in what I say, and I want to have the facts when I speak, and I merely ask now that you keep an open mind and give my remarks due consideration. I want merely to take up one detail in your note of the 20th here. You say "I don't think you know our [business-side] men *nearly* well enough." I would point out that I know all the old-timers rather intimately, or did. I used to have much contact with them, including weekly lunches, etc. I have no confidence in them as managers. I think they are men raised far above their stations, men who should not be giving direction but taking it. I know them well and know much about them and this is not just an "impression."

As to your memo about my remuneration: I regard your proposition as inadequate. I will try to explain my situation and my viewpoint. My association with *The New Yorker* for some years has been in two capacities, as a stockholder and as an employee. As a stockholder, I had hoped that my F-R holdings would be sufficient to satisfy my financial ambitions for life and enable me to meet my rather extensive personal obligations, not the least of which is the Jane Grant agreement. When this was signed, it seemed a reasonable document. *The New Yorker*'s earnings warranted it. You immediately adopted a policy, however, of putting a large share of the earnings into reserve instead of paying them out in dividends and this resulted in my having to meet heavy annual payments out of my pocket. This was not serious until the earning power of my own stockholdings were threatened by what I considered an extremely extravagant business management and a hopelessly ill-advised investment in *Stage* magazine. My misgivings grew until they amounted practically to terror and I sold most of my holdings at a heart-breaking figure, my confidence gone. I point out that, of $1,600,000 carried on the last balance sheet as gross assets, about one million dollars has been dissipated, and this on top of other amounts I consider needless expenditure, notably certain salaries in the business office (and a few in the editorial department), extensive and unnecessary promotional efforts, a vast amount of free advertising space given the Hanrahan publications, the extensive intelligence service supplied Hanrahan in his various efforts (giving him duplicates of the reports of our salesmen), etc. The fact that my forebodings proved entirely justified is no satisfaction whatever. It does not mitigate my present situation, which is that my capital has been reduced by fully fifty percent; I have suffered a loss of a couple of hundred thousand dollars and find myself in what I must candidly call my late forties with my finances depleted to a point where I have no confidence in keeping up with my obligations. Hence, something must be done.

In my other role, as an employee of the magazine, I have for years been probably the lowest paid editor in the big league magazine business. As you know, I tolerated this only because of assurances that my job would be allowed to work into a part-time one (two-thirds, or three-fourths, or some such) but it never has worked out that way and no effort ever was made to work it out that way.

I am certain there have been several years when Bowen's remuneration from the magazine exceeded mine. Several other people, not nearly comparable to me in value, have received remuneration close to mine. There were years when Hanrahan's remuneration was twice mine, and more, and that not for full-time, seven-day-a-week slavery, but for luxurious part-time advisory service. My earnest conviction is that compared to equivalent jobs on other magazines and compared to other employees of this one, I have for long been underpaid. I believe that you, and the board of directors, have a false idea of my value....

I don't know what the "circulation difficulties" are but I know you have none not of your own making. I pleaded until I was hoarse for a not-too-greedy rate-setting policy, for a cushion of ten thousand circulation above our guarantees, against the inevitable setback. We should have had that. As it was, you went ahead for ten or eleven years gaining, and that was too much to expect really. *The New Yorker* is as sound editorially as ever, if not sounder; it continues to monopolize its field. It could be an extremely profitable property still, but it cannot carry the staggering, ruinous overload that has been asked of it.

H. W. Ross

TO ROBERT BENCHLEY

*September 1st, 1938*

Dear Bob:
... I am just back from Europe with four suits of clothes bought in England which turn out to have no hip pockets and this has almost completely demoralized me. On top of that I have lost my eyesight and my senses of hearing and smell, leaving me only the sensation of feeling, or touch. I will try to get along on this basis for the few remaining years. Let me hear from you at once, please, and if you should happen to see Dave Chasen please tell him to communicate, too, God damn it. Have had no word from anybody in months.

Yours briskly,
Ross

## TO FRANK SULLIVAN

*THE NEW YORKER*
*FRIDAY*
*[SEPTEMBER 1938]*

Frank:

I had just started to answer your letter Wednesday when the God-damndest flood known to the Rippowam valley in my day, and the day of my contemporaries, was noticed outside the window, rapidly approaching. I didn't get any more things done beyond pumping out the cellar for more than twenty-four hours. It's a damned good thing you didn't visit me, although you would have been useful. You could have helped man the pump. Thursday I managed to fight back to the city, leaving the baby marooned, but with a raft for use in case of emergency. No great harm done, except a mildly flooded cellar and my road out for 100 feet. This is now being filled in and I shall return tonight, boldly.

When the flood started, I was on the verge of saying that By Jesus, you are a problem, what with the pieces for the Connecticut nutmeg and the Dutch Treat Club book and having a lot of fun doing them. There's something wrong with the magazine business, or the humorous business, and I don't know what it is. If I did I'd live happy ever after, though. It's that when a man starts to write professionally it becomes work. Why this should be so, I don't know, but it is. Ask your doctor about it. A scientific man ought to be able to explain this. The solution may be to stop paying for writings hereafter, putting the whole thing on a strictly amateur basis and allowing people to write things only after an inspection for the commercial taint.

The only trouble with you on the conversation pieces is that, as you yourself say tersely, you got stymied. You probably were in a state of some kind. Don't try to tell me not; writers have feelings like other people.

I mind your doing the piece for the *Atlantic Monthly* but won't say anything, because what the hell is there to say? I mind anybody doing any piece that we might use here. Broadly that's how I feel. I realize I may be narrow. Please come and stay with me. Don't answer this formally. I'll be living in the country for weeks yet and it's very pleasant. After I leave you can stay there if you want, letting me in weekends. I'll take you up when you come to town. My regards to your sister.

Ross

P.S. Your new piece is in. I haven't read it.

*To Ross's dismay, White had agreed to become a columnist for* Harper's *magazine. To White's dismay,* Harper's *placed an advertisement in* The New Yorker *to trumpet that fact.*

TO E. B. WHITE

*STAMFORD, MONDAY*
*[SEPTEMBER 1938]*

Dear White:

I (replying to your recent letter, which would have been answered sooner but for the flood) wouldn't have got you down off the barn roof for the *Harper's* advt. but Shuman thought we ought to advise you as a personal matter. They sprung it at us on press day, as is usual with advertisers, but I had enough time to read it and conclude that it was truthful, honorable, and justified with one possible quibble about the wording. The photograph was removed and the caricature put in. Which is better I don't know. The caricature is certainly vaguer and if vagueness is what you're looking for you have it.

Oh, I see why you're writing two thousand five hundred [words] a month for *Harper's,* and it doesn't matter whether the hell I do or not anyhow. It is my instinct to make such remarks, and it is probably my duty to do so, too. I am not God, however. The realization of this came slowly and hard some years ago, but I have swallowed it by now. I am merely an angel in the Lord's vineyard.

If you will do a very little bit of timely Comment it will help out. We don't need more than that the way things are working now. Gibbs hasn't had any jitters lately that I've seen or heard about. I thought they were going to be recurrent and maybe they are, but if they are the interval is apparently longer. I should think you'd have afterthoughts on Christmas and things like that after you've got the *Harper's* piece done: say thirty-two days after your *Harper's* deadline you want to say something on the same subject, or even refute what you've said, you still have time in the quick-acting *New Yorker*. . . .

With best wishes for Christmas,

Ross

P.S. Your first *Harper's* piece is on my desk as I write this. I haven't read it yet but will get to it presently, no doubt. I plan to read it the minute I finish Charles Cooke's book, which I also have. According to an accompanying note from Cooke, it contains 144,000 words which he wrote over a period of 1170 days, an average of one hundred twenty-three words a day. Jack London used to write one thousand words a day every day of his life.

R.

## TO E. B. WHITE

*Monday*
*[October 1938]*

White:

Katharine says she'd have cut Benchley out of your Comment on the lost generation but not Parker. Well, would say that there's been some talk of her writing for us some more, via Alan Campbell and others, and that I think she will sooner or later, and perhaps sooner, and that if she'd have been mentioned she probably would have shied off, vociferously, for years. Moreover, I don't think we ought ever, probably, to print anything slighting about her, or anything she might construe as slighting, because of the mountain of indebtedness the NYer is under to her. There's no question that the NYer is. Her Constant Reader, in the early days, did more than anything to put the magazine on its feet, or its ear, or wherever it is today. . . .

I was in Biarritz for a week and it was the God-damndest experience I ever had; first time I really saw the inside of the International set. More sophisticated than the New Yorker [set], I give you my word.

I could go on about it for an hour, but mention of Parker reminds me of one thing. An old International nymphomaniac with dyed red hair who was giving me a buzz about going to Spain and writing the right stuff (and even went to the American minister under the misapprehension that I might do so) said, "Mrs. Parker was down here. She went to Spain, you know. She is a very strange woman. We got her papers to go to Spain, and we couldn't have been nicer to anybody, and after she got back she talked terribly about all of us."

R.

*Almost from the beginning Benchley's droll essays, theater reviews, and press criticism had graced, even helped define,* The New Yorker. *But increasingly Benchley was torn between his growing success as a movie performer and his writing allegiance to Ross. Wolcott Gibbs was Benchley's understudy as drama critic, and in 1940 he officially assumed the job.*

TELEGRAM TO ROBERT BENCHLEY

*OCT. 28TH, 1938*

Dear Bob:

Certainly we want you back but I dry my tears to say that if it is great sacrifice on your part you needn't let your conscience get you down. Gibbs now in sanitarium after recent strenuous period but no theatre this week anyhow and doubtless he can carry on when he gets out as rest of season promises little. I am partially reconciled to saying this after talking to nameless man from coast who said you would be a fool to drop what you're doing now for this chore and that you felt that way about it. If this true I say do as you think best for you. Reviewing our relations through the years I should say the obligation is mostly on our part and if your decision is to stay this will be understood by your friend and admirer Ross who realizes that people frequently outgrow his enterprise.

[No signature]

TO PAUL HYDE BONNER

*THE NEW YORKER*
*MARCH 2ND, 1939*

Dear Paul:

... I went to my rectal specialist yesterday and he was just back from Florida. He told me he caught a tarpon down there and that reminded me that one thing I really want to do is go tarpon fishing on the West Coast and if you and Archie [Crabbe] will go tarpon fishing after your Bimini trip, I'll go with you. Even if you don't go, God damn it, I'll likely take Archie up on his six days to spare and make him go; but it probably would be better if we all went. The more the merrier, up to a certain point. Think this over and let me know. If you have any great yen for tarpon fishing you might rearrange things and go tarpon fishing first. This probably would suit me.

I trust it's Jean that John is bringing. She'd be easier to handle in this country than her older sister; quite a good looking girl, and quite companionable and pleasant. It must be Jean, as Ida is married and as I recall it, was to become a mother late last year. She'd hardly leave such a young baby, if everything came off as it should have.

Sincerely,

Ross

TO E. B. WHITE

[*SPRING 1939*]

Dear White:

... When you are in town Bennett Cerf of Random House and the Modern Library wants to see you. I spent much of last evening with Cerf and he has a plan for putting you in the Modern Library, which, it seems, needs light stuff. It has no light stuff and apparently has no hopes of any unless they take you or *Huckleberry Finn,* when the copyright expires next year, or both. Cerf doesn't think your last book would make a Modern Library volume. He speaks of some kind of omnibus volume. I told him to write you about it, but no, he wants to see you and me to tell you so. Publishers always seem peculiar to me in their approaches. So I tell you so. I think it's a good idea all around, a damned good idea. The Modern Library has a big sale all over and inclusion of you in it would be important recognition of some sort. I don't know whether they pay a royalty, lump sum, or what, but think it's catch-as-catch-can in arrangements. Mostly their authors are dead and the copyright expired so the question doesn't come up much. I will undertake to get you together with Cerf when you come, if you want. Of all the publishers I know, I think I'd rather talk to him. A quite nice and sane fellow.

Ross

*After the Whites moved to Maine, Katharine continued editing manuscripts and performing assorted tasks for Ross, such as critiquing just-published issues of the magazine. The long-distance relationship was hard on them both.*

TO KATHARINE S. WHITE

*[1939]*

Mrs. White:
As to your sharp-shooting of the issues, and your recent memo about this, I say do it your way. I deplore your way, but since you can't do it another way, I'll settle on it. One of the earliest and most distressing discoveries I have made in administering an office (after my fashion) is that a piece of paper won't go two ways. Your report has to go twenty-four ways, including back to you in instances where you ask outright questions. I make one exception to swallowing your method. I won't be responsible for answering personal questions asked by you in the body of a report. These are so preposterously unfair that I'll stand on that. If you want to know who P.W.W., the author of the Court Games Dept., is, it's up to you to put the question on a separate piece of paper and send it in here *not personally addressed to me.* It is unfair to bother me with such things. . . . (P.W.W. is [Philip W.] Wrenn, but that's the last time I tell you.) . . .

Ross

TO KATHARINE S. WHITE

*THE NEW YORKER*
*FRIDAY*
*[SUMMER 1939]*

Dear Katharine:
Briefly and chronologically: I'm going to Colorado, or somewhere near there; I don't quite know yet. I won't fly. Not by a damned sight.

Gibbs and everything else will undoubtedly be O.K. while I'm gone. It will be mostly the mass vacation period and we've got the issues for that well in hand and they'll both be made up by the time I go, or will be all set. . . .

Maxwell isn't leaving the first of the year; not until next spring. I rather think that both he and McKelway will be available longer for part-time work if it becomes necessary to put the pressure on them when the time comes. . . . We decided against Max Schorr [as an editor] because he would have needed too-heavy guarantees. He's been teaching nine years and is not in a frame of mind to take a chance in the hurly burly of non-academic life; wanted to know what becomes of magazine editors in their old age. Well, what does?

Love to Andy,

R

V

# "WAR IS SIMPLE,
# IT'S PEACE THAT IS COMPLEX . . ."
## 1940–1942

With the outbreak of war in Europe, Ross found himself in an un-comfortable position: He was increasingly pressured to commit *The New Yorker* to the Allied cause and even lobby for American intervention, but his own strong preference was to remain neutral. This struggle with conscience is most evident in letters to and from the Whites, a correspondence that flourished at this time, ironically, because these two key resources were still exiled in Maine. Ross was relentless in his efforts to get Andy to contribute to Notes and Comment, and he needed Katharine's editing help more than ever. After Pearl Harbor, of course, Ross threw *The New Yorker* into the war effort wholeheartedly. And even as they lost a large percentage of their mostly male staff to the armed forces, Ross and Shawn still managed to orchestrate some of the most literate and compelling journalism of the war.

———

*In September 1939, with France anticipating war and Janet Flanner's mother ill in California, the Paris correspondent returned to the States. In her place the magazine sent the intrepid Liebling. Despite her intentions, Flanner would not get back to Paris until late 1944.*

TO A. J. LIEBLING

*THE NEW YORKER*
*JANUARY 19TH, 1940*

Dear Liebling:

Your letter of January 5th received, and also two addressed to Shawn, which I have just read. If we knew what was going to happen over there, we'd be able to answer your questions. Damned if I know how long you ought to stay over, and there is no way of telling unless we can get to Hitler and some of the others and find out what their plans are. For the time being, I say mark time, and be prepared for excitement if it starts. As for your passport, you've got six months. I should think that, if you stay longer, we would be able to fix things up over here for an extension. It stands to reason that we can and my experience in such matters has been that the obviously best course is possible, with pressure and effort, even with governments that like paperwork.

Aside from future events there are two other factors in the situation, the principal one of which is what you want to do. If you have any strong desires about staying over there or coming back please express them in due course. The second one is what Flanner wants to do. She is in California now. When she left she spoke of wanting to go back to France in the spring but that was very vague. If there is an active war in France or vicinity, or the prospect of it, I should think that she will not want to go back, and I should think also that you would be a better correspondent for us. She sounds timid and you sound brave, if slightly bored. I say let's see what happens.

Meantime, anything you have to say personally should be said. We are looking anxiously for your Reporter piece on the front and the Profile on Gamelin and hope to God that the censor doesn't ruin them, or ruin the latter. I suppose they will let a front visit piece stand. . . .

As to your Letter, it is a great success. The only trouble with it is that Paris is quiet and much the same from week to week. That is not your fault. If you could vary it more with non-Paris pieces you would remove a certain threat of mild monotony. But don't strain on this. After all, there is a real interest in Paris and your Letters are avidly read over here and any sameness in your report is the fault of what you are reporting and not your own resourcefulness. If the generals don't do something, you can go only so far.

Your copy will be labeled "By Wireless" when it comes by wireless. It was stupid of us not to do so sooner, in line with our policy of honesty and frankness.

Meantime, business is about as usual at the water cooler. [Richard O.] Boyer, who was set upon by highwaymen and beaten up (I think before your departure), has taken several weeks off to go to Florida to recuperate. He's still weak but will be O.K. with rest, they say. A hell of a note. You may be safer in France.

With regards from most everybody,

Ross

TO JOHN O'HARA

*THE NEW YORKER*
*MARCH 5TH, 1940*

Dear John:

I have given full attention to the matters brought up in your letter, although so help me God, I begrudge any time given to Chasen and his affairs, having enough on my mind and conscience here. I am only a remote investor and silent partner in that venture and I intend to remain remote and silent, although I hear on all sides that he is a big success and gather that I made a brilliant investment. I deplore the feeling between you and Dave, both of whom I regard as old friends, and on Dave's behalf I will say that any crimes committed by him are not of the heart. I've known him too long. I think he got swamped out there, starting a barbecue and suddenly developing into a big-scale restaurant, and was on the ropes part of the time, groggy. If any gypping goes on, it must be the waiters, but for Christ's sake, don't you sign checks in his joint? I can't believe he just sends out a bill without having a signed dinner check for the amount. I don't see how he can sue you for thirteen dollars unless he has your signature. It seems to me to be as simple as that: either you signed a check for thirteen dollars or you didn't. If you didn't the lawyer will be left whistling, I should say. As to your overpaying a bill by several dollars and the balance not being sent you, I should say that this is either a bull in bookkeeping, or a pilfering. It can't be anything else. I think you should have written Dave about it, or told him. I know by long experience that he wouldn't personally take a dime from anyone, and nobody can tell me that he would. Christ, he lived with me off and on for years and I know him. I'll tactfully bring this overpayment to his attention and see if he can trace it in his books. But don't come to me with any more restaurant problems, for the love of God. It violates my contract with *The New Yorker,* which buys all my time. . . .

Maxwell has written you about your last piece, which we thought not quite clear. I won't go into details here. Maxwell has left, damn it, and that means another shift in the office. We will carry on, though, despite these, I guess.

With regards to Mrs. O'Hara and my best to you,

Sincerely,

Ross

## TO ST. CLAIR MCKELWAY

*THE NEW YORKER*
*APRIL 10TH, 1940*

Dear Mac:

. . . The three hundred dollars is O.K. Financing you has become an undertaking of such magnitude that it's out of my sphere of responsibility, but Shuman says Fleischmann says O.K. to the advance. Let me know what you want done with the dough: put to your credit, sent to your wife, or what. Since you bring the subject up, I will make an observation that I've made before, I think: As an old payer-through-the-nose of alimony, I'm against giving a woman a God-damned cent more than is necessary and your seventy-five dollars a week sounds too much to me, too heroic under the circumstances. It's your own God-damned business but I wanted to get on record.

I had a letter from Dr. Richardson saying your prospects are fine and wanting to know if I had any suggestions about you. I had none, or none that I wanted to express to him. There's a chance that I'll be in the country on Monday, the day of your return; if not, fine for lunch. Let us know about the money.

Ross

*The A issue was the impending issue, the B issue two weeks away, etc.*

TO PETER ARNO

*APRIL 18TH, 1940*

Peter:

Come, come. In the last five issues we've used five of your drawings, two of them [full] pages. You've had pages in two of the three April issues out to date. You are in the A issue, and you were in the B tentatively, with the drawing of the Indian young man and his mother, but I postponed that because spring is exactly the wrong time for us to use a drawing of the Indian country. There are only four Arno pages on the bank. I haven't looked at them, but by experience I know that some or all are held up for timeliness, conflict with other contents, etc. We need more than four drawings on the bank to do any decent scheduling, for God's sake, and please get some drawings done at once.

Ross

TO CHADBOURNE, WALLACE, PARKE & WHITESIDE

*THE NEW YORKER*
*MAY 2ND, 1940*

Gentlemen:

I am enclosing a check for five hundred dollars, which I hope will hold Miss Grant for a little while. I have never been so pressed for money as I have lately. I would like, somehow, to advise you of my intentions, as you request, and of my abilities along with it. It's a long story, however, and I won't attempt to go into it at this moment. I shall do so, however, as soon as I can gather the facts and marshal my wits.

Sincerely yours,

H. W. Ross

TO E. B. WHITE

*THE NEW YORKER*
*MAY 31ST, 1940*

Dear White:

I got your letter about the Comment and do not hesitate to say that it was disappointing. Gibbs has been working long and steadily and I had hoped to get him some relief—out of sheer decency, if nothing else—this summer, as well as to have you back in the magazine, if only by the thimble-full. Your practically complete cessation of writing for us has long been a disappointment to me, both as editor and human being. As editor, my philosophy is that I do my reasonable and conscientious best and let it go at that, and as a human being I enjoy reading your stuff, as we call it here in the office, and feel a sharp lack when there is no stuff. In neither role will I nag you, however, or I won't nag much, having a deep understanding of a writer who doesn't want to work, especially at this season. . . .

By the way, did you know Gibbs had come into money? I suppose so, as Katharine's news service probably is still working out of here. If not, or if the details aren't known, the details are these. His uncle died and he went to a reading of the will, four other heirs being present. One of them was Gibbs' sister. The lawyer read the will in a very rapid tone of voice; there were a number of bequests to the Presbyterian church, etc., and then a statement that the residuary estate was to be divided among the five heirs, equally upon the death of the deponent's sister (aged eighty-four), except that in the case of Gibbs, at least; don't know about the others—they were to get the income but not the principal. All the heirs were quiet after the reading, the silence being broken by Miss Gibbs, who asked how much the residuary estate would be. The lawyer said comfortably over a million dollars. So Gibbs gets the income for life on a fifth of comfortably over a million dollars. How it will affect his work, his life, etc. I don't know. The income won't be as big as it was in the old gentleman's day, I'll tell you. Maybe it won't be anything, under decree by Hitler.

Great pressure is being put on me to have *The New Yorker* swing over strong to preparedness and the hop-right-over-and-aid-the-Allies viewpoint. Wish you were here.

Sincerely yours,
Ross

*The magazine was on the verge of publishing McKelway's withering six-part Profile of gossip columnist Walter Winchell.*

MEMO TO ST. CLAIR MCKELWAY

*JUNE 4TH, 1940*

Mr. McKelway:
I asked Alice Duer Miller, whom I saw lately, if she had ever asked Winchell to dinner and she said positively not; that she never had. I told her I was almost positive that I'd seen him there at a buffet thing, supper or dinner, and she said that was likely, that Woollcott might have brought him. I think that is the case. She'd remember if she'd asked him and would, as a matter of fact, say so. I think, in fairness, [the story] ought to be changed to Winchell was taken to a buffet dinner at her place. It's a hell of a thing to say about anyone, that they asked Winchell to dinner.

H. W. Ross

TO JULIAN STREET

*THE NEW YORKER*
*JUNE 21ST, 1940*

Dear Mr. Street:
The war had me down and I didn't get around to answering your letter until now. God knows what the future holds for a topical magazine. It's hard to get one's mind on reminiscent stuff of old New York and so on at the moment, but in my calm moments, I realize that the magazine will probably go on largely as it has and that such pieces will

be usable. We will continue to have fifty-two issues a year and that takes a lot of text....

You needn't have told me who you are. I am well aware and, while some of the detail is interesting, I surmised it. As a youth I was a steady reader of *Collier's*, and during the war I used to hang out at a place on Montmartre directly opposite one that bore an endorsement from you across its front. That one was, at the time, too expensive for me.

Sincerely yours,

Ross

## TO PAUL HYDE BONNER

*THE NEW YORKER*
*JULY 2, 1940*

Dear Paul:

Your various communications received. I regret to report that the enclosed piece drew a negative decision. It seemed to us too damned mild for these days.

Of the other communications I was most interested in the news of the cable from Yvette. If Archie [Crabbe] was not in Narvik I figured he might have been in the second expeditionary force to France. From the dispatches speaking of Norwegian veterans there and crack regiments, etc., and since England could have very few outfits that answered this description I thought possibly Archie had made a second foray. There's no telling. The poor bastard is in for it sooner or later anyhow, although I have a rather strong hunch that casualties in this war are not going to be great. It's deadlocks over a long time that kill people in vast numbers.

Your fishing enterprise is interesting to me only academically. I am positively committed to going to Colorado if it is in any way possible this summer. I think it will be although with the war and the presidential campaign on it's hard to get away.

As a journalist I am concerned about the story about the eyes that arrived from Germany, and I regret to state that I don't believe a damn word of it. I went through one and a half years with the intelligence service of the A.E.F. and we were never able to track down a single such atrocity story, and God knows they were numerous. I am still conscientious professionally, however, and I should like to investigate this, looking toward getting some evidence, preferably the eyes or responsible witnesses who saw them. If you could give us names, or names that would be leads, I would be very grateful.

Sincerely yours,

Ross

## TO WOLCOTT GIBBS

*THE NEW YORKER*
*JULY 10TH, 1940*

Dear Gibbs:

A second (to the *World-Telegram-Herald-Tribune* memo) interruption of your vacation. I went over all the Comment killed in recent weeks, following what you told me the other evening. Attached are proofs of all Comment killed, five pieces. Weekes tells me that you were the man who dictated the kills in all instances, especially in the case of two which it was my opinion should not have been killed. One by one—

1. I guess this Comment should have been killed in view of the rapid collapse of the Allies; would have sounded heartless, I think, and it probably was unsound on the basis that the U.S., after all, is endangered definitely in some ways.

2. I suppose this might be classed as "unavoidable." On the other hand some system of checking might be put into effect if such duplication happens often. Weekes says this is the only instance he recalls over the years.

3. It rends my heart to realize that this Comment was killed. Weekes says that you said to use it only if necessary and that it wasn't necessary, or that it got crowded out. I should think it could have been salvaged by de-timing the lead somehow.

4. I don't know whether the use of an item by Danton Walker or some other columnist ought to kill such a thing as this for us. I doubt it. What the hell? The duplication of readers can't be extensive and, if it is, people can smile at a thing twice. I doubt if this should have been

killed and I say in future think twice before killing something under such circumstances.

5. This shouldn't have been killed to my mind. Weekes says it was squeezed out of two issues by war Comments and that you said the hell with it. I think it's a shame it was wasted.

Of the five, then, there are only two that to my mind palpably should have been killed. Now if Weekes is giving me a run-around on these, if he argued you into killing some of these items against your judgment and wishes, I'd like to know about it. If he did tell me. Or if anyone did. You don't have to interrupt your vacation to do it, but do it sometime.

Yours conscientiously,
Ross


TO FRANK SULLIVAN

*WEDNESDAY*
*[UNDATED]*

Frank:

So far as the time element went, that piece would have been as good a week later, or almost as good, but when Lobrano left he had scheduled three issues ahead, and it was easier to break into last week's issue than this week's. We had simply to remove a light Perelman piece to make room for a light Sullivan piece. So we decided to do that.

Let me know about the ending—whether it was fucked up or not, and while I'm at it, I wish you and O'Hara and a few other hardy boys would stop writing *fuck, shit,* etc. in letters to this office, because they have to be handled by pure young girls and I don't want to embarrass them, whatever the new attitude is toward such things. . . .

As ever,
R

*The Stork Club was Winchell's base, and he generally had his way there.*

MEMO TO *THE NEW YORKER* STAFF

In the interests of avoiding possible embarrassment, I would report that I was kicked out of the Stork Club last night, or asked not to come in again (suavely), because the sight of me causes distress to Mr. [Sherman] Billingsley, the proprietor—something I'm doing my best to take in my stride. It's because of the Winchell pieces. I don't know to what extent Mr. Billingsley's aversion extends into this organization, but it certainly includes McKelway.

H. W. Ross

*Introduced in 1936, Ross and Mencken became fast friends and faithful correspondents. Mencken's reminiscences and pieces on language were* New Yorker *staples.*

TO H. L. MENCKEN

*THE NEW YORKER*
*SEPTEMBER 6TH, 1940*

Dear Mencken:

O.K. on the proofs, and as I said before, I hope the delay here will not be taken as indifference, and won't delay you in doing further ones. Also, thanks for the quotation from the *National Intelligencer* on Horace Greeley's old *New Yorker.* I'll think about it. It's interesting to me, even if it doesn't turn out to be grist.

But what I want to say especially at the moment is this: Your name came up the other day at a session here in which the political campaign was being considered. It came up when somebody said, "I wish we could think of a story for Mencken to do." It is unquestionably true that for a certain kind of political story, you would be the best reporter there is. We didn't have any specific idea for a story, though, and the matter died right where it was. It now occurs to me that you might have an idea for a piece, or pieces. If you have, I wish you would let us know. We could use Reporter at Large pieces (of which you've never done one), for instance, although we're local and would want it on something with a New York tie-up, probably—a meeting, conference, gathering, headquarters, or something like that. Or there might be an Onwards and Upwards department piece. There probably damned well is an Onwards and Upwards piece but nobody had an idea for one. If you should happen to have any ideas and the time and disposition to execute them, please be advised that we would be receptive.

Sincerely yours,

Ross

TO E. B. WHITE

*SEPT. 16TH [1940]*

Dear White:

I read the piece in *Harper's* [on the meaning of freedom] and I think it is a beautiful and elegant thing, probably the most moving item I've read in years and worthy of Lincoln and some of the other fellows that really went to town. I recognize myself as several of the skeptical bastards you enumerate, but am perfectly willing to be kicked around in such a cause. You'll do some good with an argument like that, but all your eloquence can't convince me that there won't be wars in the world for the next two thousand years, and maybe twenty thousand, and honeys, too. The human race isn't ready for peace yet. Christ, my cousin Sallie thinks it's wonderful that her son has joined the air corps and my cousin Art Quaintance in Denver is hollering that the manhood of the country is soft, and hop to it at once. So are you, I guess, but you're using more than wind and you're not blind about it. Anyhow, knock me down anytime you want.

Ross

TO HOWARD DIETZ

*THE NEW YORKER*
*SEPT. 17TH, 1940*

Dear Dietz:

I would respectfully submit a constructive suggestion for an improvement in the Loew theatre service. I wanted to see *The Great*

*McGinty* the other evening and, going to the Ziegfeld Theatre, found that it didn't go on for an hour and a half, the screen being occupied at the time by a second picture called *South of Pago Pago*, which is pronounced Pango Pango. (I knew this beforehand.) I thereupon went to Loew's Lexington, where I found ditto. I figured the management of the theatres wouldn't play the same two pictures at the same time in all the places, but they were doing it; or so the girl at the ticket office said. She said this is the custom. The picture of the surf beating on the edenic shores of a south sea island all over the city at exactly the same moment, and, for all I know, all over this broad land, smacks of Hitler regimentation in the Loew theatres. It doesn't take care of the case of a man who doesn't want to have to sit through some such wonder picture as *South of Pago Pago* to get to see something he wants to see. I would suggest what I believe is called the stagger system: I'd have *Pago Pago* showing at one theatre while *McGinty* is showing at another, and vice versa.

No charge for this suggestion.

Sincerely yours,

Ross

## TO NUNNALLY JOHNSON

*THE NEW YORKER*
*SEPTEMBER 19TH, 1940*

Dear Nunnally:

... [Joseph] Mitchell, to put it bluntly (and I'm a forthright fellow of the old school) isn't interested in this. I don't know why, figuring that it was hardly worthwhile asking him. I'm one who has had a lot of experience with writers. Will you please explain this to the padre and will you also, damn it, stop teasing me with contributions which, at first glance, seem to be by you. Damn it, you write for other people every once in a while and you ought to write for us, as a sort of penance, or for the sake of art.

I appreciate the plan to give a series of parties in my absence and approve of it. I've had some experience with this absenteeism. Charlie MacArthur gave a party for me one time, throwing his home open in a grand old Southern manner and then spent the evening flying in an airplane over Boston with Laurette Taylor. This is no reflection on the name of a good woman. I don't know what it is. The situation was the more peculiar because I went into MacArthur's room when the party started, locked the door, and went to sleep. From all accounts it was one of the most successful parties ever given in the pre-Elsa Maxwell days. Charlie had to quit after she came along.

Anyhow, I've been kicked out of the Stork Club and told not to come back, and Christ knows what will become of me socially if my friends don't rally and do something. Winchell said it was him or me.

With love from Louella Parsons, who, so help me God, threw kisses at me night before last. There's one friend I've got.

And with deep admiration,

Ross

## MEMO TO RUSSELL MALONEY

*OCTOBER 16TH, 1940*

Mr. Maloney:

Some [Talk] anecdotes hastily set down in the emergency, ones I've had notes on, thinking to do something about them, and haven't.

The five-year-old daughter of a Greenwich couple came home from school and sat down to her lunch and complained about some item of food. I don't want any of the God-damned stuff (you can use your imagination here, as elsewhere throughout these anecdotes) and her mother said that if she was going to talk that way she'd have to leave the house; she could go right up and pack up and go. The little girl did so, packing her doll and a couple of other things and went down and roamed around the grounds for awhile and then sat down on the stoop of the kitchen door. Grocer came up and said, making conversation, did your mother order so and so today. "God damned if I know," said the girl, "I don't live here any more."

xxxx

One of the DuPonts of Delaware, most likely Harry DuPont, who has a valuable collection of Ming china, was showing a lady guest at his house a valuable vase, a very valuable vase. She dropped it to the floor and it broke spectacularly. The lady reeled and lamented appropriately. "There, there," said Mr. DuPont, "it was an accident, etc.", and fainted. ...

xxxx

W. C. Fields was married years ago, living in New York, and once he wrote a letter to the manager of a theatre here: "My wife and I are attending your theatre tomorrow evening. Our seats are J2 and J3. I am advising you of this because my wife will lose a pair of long gray suede gloves. ..."

xxxx

Maybe you can make something out of the foregoing. As stated, the imagination may be used freely, and may have to be.

H. W. Ross


*Arno was staying at the Garden of Allah in Hollywood.*

TELEGRAM TO PETER ARNO

*OCTOBER 29, 1940*

Dear Peter:

No drawings from you in weeks and we haven't an available one in the house and few for any other season. Please draw up some of the pending ideas. We are desperate and people beginning to talk.

Love,

Ross

*In the summer of 1939 few were surprised when Ross and Frances divorced, considering that about all they had in common was daughter Patty. But in 1940 Ross again managed to catch even close friends off guard when, for the third time, he slipped out of town to get married. The bride was Ariane Allen, a vivacious actress and model originally from Texas. She was twenty-five; Ross was forty-eight.*

TO PAUL HYDE BONNER

*THE NEW YORKER*
*JAN. 6TH [1941]*

Dear Paul:

This is in acknowledgement of your note of Nov. 14th, regarding my marriage, which (the letter) has what I quaintly describe as come to light. My personal correspondence got all sidetracked in clumps, what with being away awhile and then running headlong into Christmas and its inflow. I loathe Christmas because it brings most of my relatives from all parts of the country in on me with letters which sooner or later have to be answered. I loathe it for other reasons, too. However, thanks, many thanks, and I trust I will see you sooner or later. Are you going to Florida this year? If you are, let me know. I am going to try seriously to get down about the middle of Feb. It won't be the same as in recent years, but I guess the sun will be there, and the ocean. . . . I had a letter from Archie [Crabbe] but it was cut to hell by the censor and I didn't send you a copy of it. I gave it to [Ernest] Hemingway when I ran into him one evening and he said he was going to write Archie, whom he referred to as a "very wicked man."

Regards to all,

Ross

*The cover illustration Ross mentions was of a valet strapping kneepads onto an affluent weekend gardener.*

TO PERRY BARLOW

*THE NEW YORKER*
*MAY 1ST, 1941*

Dear Barlow:

I was laying for you this week, but Geraghty tells me that you didn't come in today and probably won't be in tomorrow, and, in fact, that you haven't been in for several weeks. I was just going to praise you on the cover on the April 26th issue, which is generally regarded as superb and which, from all I have heard, won wide acclaim. Everybody reports having heard much comment. It's a fine and a funny thing, I think, and not seeing you I will get on record to that effect in writing.

I think all your recent work has been wonderful, my only complaint being my chronic one: volume. I wish you'd do two or three times as much as you do. By God, there are only two first-class character artists in the United States—Hokinson and you—and you, for one, ought to do more. You are a fine and an important artist, and I think you would hear more about yourself if you weren't so generally taken for granted, which, I guess, is the fate of one who maintains a standard through the years.

Anyhow, I appreciate you and I will try to tell you so once in a while.

Sincerely yours,

Ross

P.S. I think that series drawing of the old lady sewing the chevrons on the pajamas is excellent. My favorite of the last two or three years is the boy eating the candy bar but pausing to read the label, telling about all the ingredients. I'll never forget that one.

H.W.R.

TO E. B. WHITE

*SUNDAY*
*[MAY 1941]*

White:

Here I go on some kind of an answer to your letter, although it is hard for me to spend any time or thought on such matters as this for my mind is preoccupied by medication. I take eleven doses of one thing or another a day, counting a rinse of my mouth with peroxide before going to bed following my annual gouging of the gums for pyorrhea but not counting fifteen minutes of exercises daily for sacroiliac. Honest to Christ, I'm more dilapidated at the moment than Yugoslavia. Since you bring up the subject of what will happen in this country at next presidential election time, I will say that I have heard nothing whatever spoken on this subject except for an occasional offhand remark that Lindbergh may be the Hitler of the country and that I have thought nothing about it. Now that you have mentioned it, I regard this situation as extremely odd. The reason for it is that the war itself, as a day-to-day proposition, is about all anyone can think about and all thought and all talk goes onto that subject. I'll be damned if I know what will happen to the country. I haven't any idea. As you are probably aware, I have long felt that the American machinery of government, or system of government, is too cumbersome, too lawyer-ridden, too bureaucratic, and too theoretical for the accomplishment of the business of government in ordinary times (if there be such), let alone in great emergencies like the present. As to the present emergency, though, I think that the government will probably function efficiently and with a single purpose once the time comes. War, after all, is simple. It's black and white. It's peace that is complex.

Internationally, there is no question that there is a way of dodging the fight (your phrase) indefinitely. In theory this country can go on the basis that Japan was on until Dewey changed all that. We can cut ourselves off from the rest of the world, reorganize our economy to exist on domestic activities alone, and live happy ever after. We produce within our boundaries ninety-seven percent of what we consume and we can get substitutes for the other three percent. This includes rubber. We can sit tight for a generation or a century, until things blow over. We can't be invaded, or bombed, or harmed. That is my conclusion after much thought. A German victory with us in the war would put us in just about that position of isolation, I should say, unless we want to carry on a world-wide sniping naval warfare for a period of considerable duration. Somebody is going to run the world, police the world, and along with it, exploit the world, and it's, of course, going to be Germany if England loses. If England wins with our aid it will be England. Alone. My judgment is that if England and we won the war we'd go back into our shell immediately after the war, restore England to her former position, more or less, and turn the world over to her. America has been too long steeped in isolationism, hands-off, self-determination of all peoples, etc., to take a role of boss in the world. We fought for Cuba's freedom and for the freedom of the Philippines. We are not an aggressor nation by nature. We don't even want to hang on to the Philippines; we didn't want Cuba. We want them to be young republics in our prototype and that's all. I'm merely saying in this that I think that the United States now has the clear opportunity to go out and make a bid for boss of the world but that we won't do anything about this opportunity (if it is that) because it is contrary to our nature. . . .

Ross

*After several years at* The New Yorker, *Gill had encountered Ross in person on only two brief but intimidating occasions. Feeling underappreciated, the young writer sent Ross a prank gift of a wooden skunk.*

TO BRENDAN GILL

*THE NEW YORKER*
*MAY 16TH, 1941*

Dear Brendan Gill:
I got your letter all right and carried it around showing it to various people until it got sidetracked under something. Receipt of the skunk didn't bother me much but it puzzled me and I mentioned the matter around. I used to be bothered by such happenings, but I don't even

blink anymore, for I've become reconciled to from six to twelve people being mad at me at any given time. I've come to accept that as normal and routine. Every week there is a certain amount of pique over drawings and stories turned down, something printed about somebody in the magazine, etc. I now go on the principle that a journalist isn't entitled to friends, or an editor, either. Further, I have abandoned any attempt to try to keep personally in touch with all the contributors of the magazine. I used to try to, but I was just going to rattle myself to pieces and I gave up. Since then I have rather avoided meeting new contributors, depending on other members of the staff to ... keep in touch with them. This is the most difficult magazine in the world to get out, and it involves, I think, more people and contact with them than any other. It's appalling. When you count up the people in the office, artists, humorists, fiction writers, idea men, agents, fact writers, departmental writers, etc., you have a total of two or three hundred. Obviously hopeless for me, especially as I must do pretty much a full week's work at a desk to begin with. Moreover, the turnover is heavy. A lot of promising young people around here are gone after a fairly short while, writing for the movies, or other magazines, or somewhere.

You do me only one injustice: I don't try to scare anyone, although occasionally I don't give a damn if I do probably. Anyone I can scare must scare easily, so easily you can't help scaring them. There are, I suspect, some such. I didn't try to scare you. The profanity was natural. My manner is not orthodox, but I've given up trying to curb it, for often as not it serves (astonishingly) to put people at their ease. I think it relaxes more people than it excites. I hope so, anyhow.

Sincerely yours,

H. W. Ross

P.S. As I look back on it, I did intend to get better acquainted with you because I was interested in your work and counted on it. I did keep in touch with you religiously though, if not first hand, and still do.

H.W.R.

*Ross was trying to keep the magazine editorially noncommittal on the war,*
*but he was under mounting pressure to throw in with the Allies.*

TO E. B. WHITE

*JUNE 24 [1941]*

Dear White:

. . . I have been strongly suspicious that you disapproved of what we
have been doing in the Comment page and elsewhere in relation to
the international situation. I am not positive of this, of course, but I
gather you would have gone a lot further. My decision is that we have
been doing it right and that we ought to go on as we have been going,
call it slacking, call it escapist, call it what you will. I'll be God damned
if I've got the slightest bit of confidence in the opinions and emotions
of all the people who have advised me, denounced me, ridiculed me,
tried to lead me, etc. Nor have I any in myself. I have been an earnest
clutcher for a straw but I haven't got ahold of a straw yet. I doubt if
there is any mind on earth that [can] work out a solution to the present situation or tell me what I ought to do, in positive action. I am,
therefore, for drifting. After a great deal of thought, I think the thing
for American publications to do is follow the President, for better or
for worse. That's all I see to do. He knows more than anyone else here
and presumably is in a position to make the wisest decisions. I haven't
the confidence in him that a great many of you people have (although
he may be just the man for a big philosophical situation such as this),
but I don't see anything to do but do as he says from now on.

In this connection, I have sought the best counsel I could get and I
had Bob Sherwood up here for a part of a weekend, concluded yesterday. He and his wife and Dottie Parker (who has just written a piece for
us, in the old manner), came up and stayed Saturday night and then
tore down to Harlem to address five thousand colored Sunday P.M.,
Dottie with no lunch and four martinis and Sherwood with a speech
somewhat disqualified by the attack by Germany on Russia that morning. Anyhow, Bob is supposed to be the closest man to Roosevelt now
on propaganda and public relations matters. . . . Much to my astonishment, he thought the editorial policy of the NYer was O.K. No criticism whatever; didn't expect anything more, etc. All right, the fact is

this: R himself is marking time. He no longer fears (I am indirectly quoting S. from now on) that the country isn't solidly behind him; he is not considering Lindbergh or Sen. Wheeler at all any more. He will go to war when the time comes or take any military or naval action he thinks advisable short of war without any misgivings as to the situation at home. If he was worried about domestic unrest, he isn't any more....

Ross

TO FRANK SULLIVAN

*JULY 12TH*
*[CIRCA 1941]*

Dear Frank, old fellow:

... I don't know who that drunk was that showed up at your place, but there is no doubt that he is an old pal of mine. All bothersome, noisy drunks that show up anywhere—in elevators, in restaurants, in men's rooms, at Mrs. Harrison Williams's—are always old pals of mine, without exception. It has been that way all my life. It is my fate. It is something I did when I was young.

I may roll up to your place in the next few weeks, as my daughter is again at Cooperstown and will take me into those parts, but I will be erect, firm, dignified, and in complete control of myself, and my breath will be that of a Jersey cow's, a zephyr from the gardens where green vegetables grow, with a slight flavor of Amphojel blended with Creamalin. I called you at the Cornell Club one evening a couple of weeks ago. You had gone.

I cannot refrain from urging you to write a piece. If you don't do one, you are a little bastard. GOD DAMN IT!

Ross

*Liebling had returned to New York after covering the fall of France. Ross and Shawn sent him back to England, where the reporter initially was uncertain as to what he should report.*

TO A. J. LIEBLING

THE NEW YORKER
SEPTEMBER 11, 1941

Dear Liebling:

Here is another letter right away—following one of a couple of days ago, which I trust got through. In talking to Shawn today about you and your last letter we found that we were both astonished at your suggestion that you are getting bored over there and thinking of coming home. Shawn's idea was that your stay in England was a minimum of six months and, while mine wasn't as to any definite period, I thought you'd be there more than a few weeks, or several weeks. In this connection, I hasten to say this: I think you are inclined to underestimate the value of the "minor piece," as you seem to consider such a thing as your Reporter on the trip across on the bomber. You seemed sheepish about sending it in, evidently, because it wasn't of much substance. Well, damn it, it was a fine piece and of general interest to most everybody. That it may have been obvious, that there wasn't much to tell, etc., isn't against it. It's news that there isn't much to tell. I've asked several people about this piece and they all found it interesting. Lobrano, for instance, says it was exactly what he wanted to know about the bomber business. I certainly felt the same way. We're typical of a vast public, one hundred sixty thousand, at least. I haven't read your second Reporter piece yet but, slight (in your eyes) or not, it probably will be interesting. I think things that seem commonplace to you over there are of hot interest here. You don't have to do four-part [Roy] Howard or Winston Churchill series to be writing interesting and valuable stuff. So much for that. Don't underestimate the seemingly unimportant. Next point—

Shawn and I got the notion that you might visit my pal Major Archie Crabbe (formerly Capt.) who is in charge of an air field (Hendon, The Hyde, N.W.9) and spend some time around there and do a piece on it. For months Mrs. [Mollie Panter-] Downes has had a project to visit some air field and tell about planes coming, or going, or something. There must be a good chance, or several chances, there. She hasn't been able to get permission to do the piece or even get to the air field, I guess. You ought to be able to crash one, and maybe Crabbe would be useful. He'd do what he could, I can assure you, going the limit even if you lean a little on army regulations if insured of protection. It seems to me that a piece about bombers taking off, or bombers coming back after a raid, or a night in the mess, or combat planes getting the alert, or anything like that would be gilt-edged. I'm for such a piece, and for any others that look good which you might think too light or unimportant. Color is the thing, etc., or one big thing.

Shawn and I are not inclined to argue in the matter of a scarcity of Profile subjects. Churchill is the only man who stands out over here, of course, or rather, he stands out overwhelmingly, and we wouldn't want to encourage you to write on the lesser fellows if you aren't enthusiastic. But think of the Reporter possibilities, etc.

With best regards,

Ross

P.S. I think I forgot to tell you that Roy Howard has developed a bad, or tired heart, and his doctor has ordered him to spend six months away from it all, on his yacht. This affliction overtook him before your pieces came out, and you have no responsibility. This in case you get a garbled or incomplete version.

R.

*Dewey was New York's district attorney. Winney for years had access to Ross's personal accounts; he killed himself when he realized the editor was about to discover the forgeries. No one was ever prosecuted in the case, and Ross recovered almost none of the money.*

TO THOMAS E. DEWEY

THE NEW YORKER
SEPTEMBER 12, 1941

Sir:

My secretary Harold D. Winney, who had been in the employ of *The New Yorker* for nearly eleven years, committed suicide on Thursday, August 14. Soon thereafter my accountant found a shortage in the accounts he kept for me. This shortage is approximately seventy thousand dollars and was effected by forgery. It seems to me that facts now in possession of my attorneys, Greenbaum, Wolff & Ernst, indicate that Winney might have acted in concert with others and warrant investigation by your office. Messrs. Greenbaum, Wolff & Ernst, through Harold H. Stern, will give you any information you may require.

Sincerely yours,

H. W. Ross

*Kober had been married to Lillian Hellman.*

## TO ARTHUR KOBER

*THE NEW YORKER*
*OCTOBER 17, 1941*

Dear Arthur:

A personal matter, as follows: Margaret Harriman has written a piece on Lillian Hellman and you seem to come into it, as per type circled on the attached galley, which is a fragment of the piece. I always deplore the mention of *New Yorker* writers in the magazine and go to extreme lengths to lobby mentions out, but in this case it's inevitable. Everybody connected with the joint has accumulated engrossing personal history as he (and, I guess, or she) went along, evidently. Anyhow, please read this over and see if there is anything in it that will cause embarrassment. I hasten to say that I am not thinking about embarrassment to you personally but rather to the present Mrs. Kober, and the possible rebound from same. The first reference to you, as a wealthy Hollywood writer, I questioned in a routine manner myself, although it may be good build-up for the magazine at that, and encouragement for younger writers. The piece has a certain amount of banter all the way through, and I guess that could come under the head of banter. As for the rest of it, it seems all right to me, and unobjectionable, and don't you be captious or hypersensitive about it. In other words, unless you think it's terrible, O.K. it as is. In case you, being personally involved, can't get a sufficiently detached viewpoint to have confidence in your opinion, I will say, for what it is worth, that I think the passage is all right, with the possible reservation that maybe Mrs. Kober won't. I write as a man who has been married three times.

Let me know about this at once in the enclosed envelope, please, and I trust to God I will see your name in the magazine soon as a contributor rather than as one of a cast of characters.

Best regards,

Ross

*Private citizen Ross wrote this hysterical, regrettable letter to the governor of Connecticut as part of a neighborhood effort to stop a state park. When it was leaked to the press months later Ross found himself in the most uncomfortable spot of his career. The park was never built.*

TO ROBERT A. HURLEY

*THE NEW YORKER*
*NOVEMBER 5, 1941*

My dear Governor Hurley:

I address you in a state of considerable panic and alarm over the proposal of the State Highway Commission of Connecticut to make a public park of the state-owned plot of land at the junction of the Merritt Parkway and High Ridge Road in the town of Stamford. The whole neighborhood has been thrown into a state of excitement over the proposal, including me.

I own eleven acres adjoining the state land and have my home there, acquired after half a lifetime of effort, and I feel absolutely certain that the peace and privacy of myself and family are threatened and the value of my property endangered. I reach this conclusion on actual observations and experience. When the Merritt Parkway was first opened there was a brief period when the state land was open to the public, and immediately an appalling situation developed. Dozens of automobilists on the parkway stopped off, parked, changed into and out of bathing suits in their cars, explored and overran the neighborhood, littered everything up with cans and paper, shouted and sang, swam in the little river there in their underwear or less, and committed the worst kind of nuisances in the stream, obnoxiously and dangerously polluting it from there on down. The river reaches my property a few hundred feet after leaving the state land and I have a swimming pool on it. I had to give up swimming during the period of invasion, the water was so foul, and for the rest of that summer my family, including my little daughter, couldn't go swimming in the water, for fear of infantile paralysis, or worse. This wasn't a conjured up fear; I was warned by a doctor that the danger was real.

If the park were intended for residents of Stamford, town or city, there might be some point to the idea . . . but I understand it is just to be a stopping-off place for travelers on the parkway. Well, sir, what your highway commission would be doing is just inviting Harlem and the Bronx, New York City, up to Stamford to spend the day. I do not mean to be undemocratic, but by God, you couldn't choose a more alarming bunch of people anywhere in the world. The parkway has put Stamford within thirty or forty minutes of the northern sections of New York City, and Stamford is sitting on a keg of dynamite as it is. If some of your officials would spend a summer Sunday or two along the country roads in that vicinity, they would realize this. Stamford is on the verge of becoming the playground of the Borough of the Bronx and the dark, mysterious, malodorous stretches of Harlem, without doing anything further, and why the state of Connecticut should gleefully go out of its way to complicate the situation, I don't know. I don't see why Connecticut should be host to Harlem and the Bronx.

And I think there are dangers beyond the noise, litter, and disease, and destruction of privacy, too. I think you'd encourage a wave of petty thieving, and thieving not so petty, if you opened up the park and, inevitably, the rest of the countryside. The studio of the late Gutzon Borglum is down the river a short distance from my place and that building is broken into on the average of once a month, winter and summer, as it is—not by big-scale burglars, of course, but by roving tourists of the quality such a park . . . would be encouraging in vast numbers.

I'm addressing this letter to you and am sending copies to other officials of the state I am advised are of influence in this matter, and I most earnestly pray that you will think twice, and two or three times more, before such alarming open-handedness. I write in sheer terror.

Sincerely yours,

H. W. Ross

*The bombing of Pearl Harbor occurred on a Sunday, the day* New Yorker *staffers typically were closing that week's issue.*

## TO E. B. WHITE

*[DECEMBER 15, 1941]*

White:

We got the picture ideas, oceans of Newsbreaks, and the interview with Neal Vanderbilt. The last named will enable me to carry on in my efforts to get aboard the war, which takes considerable effort. The pix ideas are appreciated and one of them, the sinking Japanese ship, ought to be through this week. I didn't know what a "grease monkey" is but everyone else did. I think that will materialize. We are appreciative. Further reports later.

Ross

P.S. By God, the boys generally responded on pictures and ideas. If the war had started a day or two earlier than Sunday we'd have had good coverage, or reflection, in last week's issue. Sunday was a bad day.

R.

## TO H. L. MENCKEN

*THE NEW YORKER*
*FEBRUARY 5, 1942*

Dear Mencken:

Lobrano passed me your last letter, mentioning that you hadn't heard about me. This is my fault. I *intended* to write, but the habits of the hospital, where I spent two weeks, hung on. The doctor wanted to get me relaxed, and evidently did. I put everything off indefinitely and am continuing on this path, more or less. It may work out fine. I wasn't operated on, having, as they say, responded medically. I still spare myself a great deal of the time, rushing home from the office and getting an hour's rest before dinner, etc. I neither drink nor smoke. If I keep it up I will have no further gastric troubles and will go to heaven when I die, maybe. Let me know when you're coming up and I'll try to go on the loose for an hour or two and have a glass of milk. But not two. I don't want to overload my stomach.

One of your pieces is going to press immediately and I guess the series will be run now regularly—or irregularly but frequently—but God knows what the war is going to do to us next. Advertising is off twenty-five percent they tell me. Lobrano had some problem in one of the proofs which I think he took up with you—a policy matter involving mention of constitutional government. He mentioned it to me and I told him to take no chances with the patriots from now on. The U.S. Navy is already after us for disrespect for the opinions of Gene Tunney.

With best wishes,
Sincerely yours,
Ross

## TO DOROTHY GARFINKLE

*The New Yorker*
*February 9, 1942*

Dear Dorothy:

I've got to ask you to do something for me, a little chore, but I'm more interested in Jerry than that, so I'll take him up first. Ariane and I got a letter from him from San Francisco last week, saying you were there, too, but telling little more than that. Since then I've seen pictures of his late ship, the *Arizona,* and wondered more than ever what happened to him. I have it figured that he must have been on leave or, anyhow, wasn't on the ship when it was hit, for I doubt if there were any survivors. What did he tell you about all this? I'd like very much to know. Also, what address have you for him? He didn't give us one. I'll write him, which is the least I can do, I guess, and the most.

What I want you to do for me is ask your husband or some competent person what [Salt Lake City] land is worth on the edge of the desert, about Tenth North and Fourteenth West. I've got a plot of land there from the days of my father and I know it isn't worth much, but at the same time I don't want to get euchred on it. I have a letter from one Keith Holbrook of the Cook Realty Co., 11 East First South, offering twenty-five dollars an acre for the place. I think it is about twenty acres, which would be five hundred dollars. This seems small, but I guess west side land in Salt Lake City isn't worth much. It has been obvious to me that it never would amount to anything unless someone wanted to build steel mills, or some such, there, or air fields. If there's any talk of that, do you know—or do you know anyone you could ask? I'd appreciate anything you could dig up for me but don't want you to bother, of course, beyond casual inquiry. . . .

As ever,
Harold

TO A. J. LIEBLING

*MARCH 9, 1942*

Liebling:

I have just read the pieces on the convoy trip in proof and they are certainly fine, epical, and epochal, too, I guess; worth all the time and trouble. However you look at it, you got a whale of a story here, and you wouldn't have got one on an airplane, probably, or a passenger boat. In my notes I remarked that I thought you ought to write in a little more on two subjects, i.e., the restricted deck space on the tanker and the limitations placed on getting about, and the picture it presented. At the start of the first part you say water goes over the low decks, but after you get to sea you never tell about this, never give the picture. As an old sea saddist [*sic*] I'd like a little on this. Also, something on your meals with the silent captain, which are certainly noteworthy.

Anyhow, your reputation ought to grow with the appearance of these pieces.

Ross

## TO GEOFFREY HELLMAN

Hellman:

All I know is what I read in the papers, and from these I learn that George White is your wife's former husband's lawyer. He was my first wife's lawyer, and a man I bitterly resent. I am ready to gang him at any time you say.

Ross

## MEMO TO KATHARINE S. WHITE

Mrs. White:

What I would like to feel is that there is a responsible, close watch of the whole magazine field and that I will be advised if there is anything I ought to know about. It's as simple as that. I don't think I ought to know about every single possible idea or drawing that we may have missed in *Collier's* or the SEP [*Saturday Evening Post*]. I would like to feel, however, that if some phenomenal artist comes along in one of the other magazines I would know about it in reasonable time; or if their quarry improves or deteriorates I would be told about it eventually. It's something that cannot definitely be done by routine or it would take twelve people churning around, all needlessly, more or less.

I talked to Shuman about this today and told him that every once in a while you could take one dollar and go to the newsstands and buy the new magazines that are around, look into them, and report to me anything that I ought to know. I am interested, for instance, in the fact that Norman Anthony is issuing a new magazine designed for sale in doctors' offices. But I am not interested much beyond that mere fact and possibly a report that it contains a lot of *New Yorker* rejections and that it is as terrible as should be expected. Shuman says that you say that magazines don't get to Maine. I suppose some of them don't, but on the other hand a lot of them do, and we could depend on them to a certain extent, at least. If it gets down to a question here of having somebody buy the magazines and send them up to you there's a chance of incompetent judgment in the selection of the magazines. It takes an old-timer around here to do it and a person of comparatively great judgment. My only idea of euchring you into doing this job is that you qualify in both respects. . . .

Ross

*Ross and Woollcott's friendship, while deep, was never easy. The two nearly broke, however, over a* New Yorker *Profile of Woollcott, written by Gibbs. Woollcott maintained he was most hurt by its embarrassing disclosures about an old* Stars and Stripes *colleague, Seth Bailey, who was called Sergeant Quirt in the story.*

## TO ALEXANDER WOOLLCOTT

TUESDAY
*[APRIL 1942]*

Dear Alec:

I am late in writing this because I have been in Washington for three days where I not only had no typewriter or other writing facilities but barely more than half a room. They are now putting two in a room down there, to speed up the war, and I saved myself from a roommate only by registering "and wife," although my wife is in California. In the event that your alert mind instantly turns this into a blackmail opportunity, I will report that I have already advised the lady, and while I may not be believed entirely, further notification would be anticlimactic. I went down to see my daughter but also saw a number of people I craved to see, including Winterich and Giegengach, who I would report are unchanged as far as I can see and are great men. . . .

As I said in a telegram which I assume you have received, I'd rather have got that letter from you than anything else I can think of, except possibly full restitution by the Guaranty Trust Company, which recently allowed me to be forged out of all my worldly cash and securities. I have Lloyd Stryker on that case but will probably get nowhere. I don't give a damn, really, and, as a matter of fact, am able to get a big laugh out of the new tax proposals of Roosevelt, which will cut everybody in the world down to about my size. I chuckle when I think of

Fleischmann, Jane Grant, etc. As to the Bailey business, to change the subject in the middle of a paragraph, I want to say just a few words and then never any more. I was brought into consultation when he got that job in Chicago, by an old employer of mine who knew much about Bailey through having been involved in the efforts to spring him from San Quentin. Gibbs and I thought that Bailey had been completely protected in his piece (which turned out to be the case) but as a precaution I called my old employer and asked him what would happen if Bailey should be suspected as the hero of Gibbs's piece. The o.e. was amazed that I'd called him. "Nothing would happen," he said. "What is one more ex-convict on the *Chicago American*?" In just those words. I'm always getting blamed for things I certainly didn't write and didn't have much to do with. Gibbs is almost as jealous of his pieces as you are, and either of you would tear an editor to pieces and not think about it twice. That Bailey story got to be a classic and I'd heard it dozens of times from the raconteurs: it was in the public domain if anything ever was.

I should like to visit you if you want me to. I am having dinner tonight with [Daniel] Silberberg, who says he has a letter from you inviting him up. I could go up with him sometime, or otherwise. My ulcers raised hell but are quiescent at the moment. I made Washington and back without complications, and probably could travel more. I haven't had a drink in sixteen months, although I smoke, which is worse, theoretically. If you're in a position to be called on, let me know—and in a mood. One anecdote and I will close. I always told Aunt Fon an anecdote in conclusion. *Time,* the magazine, called up the other day to ask about the *Stars and Stripes,* and I (who probably should never cast a stone) said that a piece they'd had on the S&S the week before had mistakes in it. The lady researcher (who was doing the telephoning) jumped me for details. I said [Franklin P.] Adams and [Grantland] Rice weren't privates, etc., and where did *Time* get the dope that Harpo Marx was on the staff? She said Harpo had told *Time* he was on the staff and that *Who's Who* said so. By God, Harpo has got it in there, evidently. I meant to look it up but forgot. If so, his gag is ruined so far as *Time* is concerned. There is much talk of a new S&S. I am going to dinner to mark the appearance of the new one, or of "Yank" I think they are going to call it. They are going to print in New

York and distribute it all over the world. This would take two Waldoes, and I don't think God ever made more than one.

Much good will and many good wishes,
Ross

## TO KATHARINE S. WHITE

[CIRCA 1942]

Dear Mrs. W:

The tooth dope is this, briefly: I had two out, upper left, two or three weeks ago and was told to chew on my right side, where I developed soreness. I thought it was my gum, under a bridge I had there, for five or six days. Then a tooth there—the one the bridge was attached to—kicked up unmistakeable and I pegged it as that. Soon afterward, I got so drowsy at the office that I thought I would come home and sleep a couple of hours and then get my work done, that evening. I was drowsier than ever when my wife woke me up and she put a thermometer in my mouth and discovered I had considerable fever. I couldn't get the dentist, my doctor was out of town getting married, etc. I finally got another doctor and he said to take sulfa-something, which I did. The fever was soon gone. The doctor came around and shot some penicillin into me the next morning. I never had any more fever, but I still had the tooth, and I couldn't get it out there because the dentist—the tooth-pulling dentist—was going to be away over the weekend and didn't want to leave me with a wound during that period. I went up to the country, took sulfa and penicillin all weekend, with occasional codeine, and then on Monday had the tooth out. I have just this minute returned from the dentist's, to have the dressing changed. Everything all over, except that my chewing capacity is limited. Reconstruction in my mouth starts next week, and will be extensive because two of the extracted teeth were anchor teeth. My mouth now undoubtedly presents an interesting, and an expensive, problem. I kept on working, but was somewhat slowed down....

Comment is by far the most glaringly weak thing now, and if White should write some it would save the day. Gibbs spoke of writing some a week or so ago, but he hasn't turned in any yet. I rather think he will, because he is getting into shape now.

As ever,

R

P.S. Thurber did a piece, very good, except for paragraphing.

*The* Stage *debacle had weakened* The New Yorker's *financial position just as war broke out in Europe and eroded its advertising. When in early 1942 the company's nervous directors chose to pass on a dividend, key shareholders—including Fleischmann's former wife—decided they'd had enough of the publisher.*

TO RAOUL FLEISCHMANN

*APRIL 16, 1942*

Raoul:

For purposes of secrecy I will write this out and ask Shuman to hand it to you personally.

I have been aware of the stockholders business for a few days. For one thing, two of the minor ones, the very minor ones, called me on the telephone and wanted to know about it. This alarmed me and I called up one of the leaders and told them for Christ's sake to let the small stockholders alone or they'd have scandal in the columns and general, probably ruinous, embarrassment. I understand that this has been headed off and that there is to be no general canvass now. For one thing I was approached to go along with my stock. This I have not done, pointing out two things: First, that I have practically no stock and can't be considered a stockholder really. Second, that I am an employee of the company and consider it my duty not to take my eye off the ball with side issues. This has ever been my policy, and to my cost apparently. I said that I would answer any questions asked by a director, which I take it to be the role and duty of an employee. I pointed out, though, that asking me questions would be pretty much a waste of time for the reason that, by hook and by crook, the facts of life have very largely been kept from me here.

Since this subject has come up, however, I will take this opportunity to advise you that I, personally and as head of my department, have problems which you must consider sooner or later, and rather sooner than later, which are probably equally important from your standpoint. I long ago sold the bulk of my stock, foreseeing the hole which the organization seems inevitably to have gone into, and my interests are therefore not those of a stockholder. I am an important employee of the organization, however. I have made a career out of this magazine, and I am nearing fifty. I have reached the conclusion, or the resolve, that between now and my fiftieth birthday, which will be in November, that all the various misgivings I have had about this organization must be cleared up or that it will be inadvisable for me to go on here. At fifty a man must take stock of his situation coldly and take some path, for better or worse, for the remainder of his life. As you know, there are several points of difference between me and the management of this organization and one of them will undoubtedly have to come to a head in the matter of wartime retrenchment. That is one of the things that will have to be settled. There are two others. First, an employee of my position—and in the position of the other employees in responsible positions who are more or less making this magazine their life's work—are entitled these days to know what provision is made for the future in the event of the demise of the owner, or controlling stockholder. I think that since the present taxes have got so extensive, it is customary in corporations to advise the employees where they stand in the event of a change of management. I think that some provision should be made for the future here and that the so-called key employees ought to be told what it is. Second, there have been general rumors around for a considerable time that you are in a jam with the government on taxes and that, for all anyone knows, the government may at any moment take over your stock and appear as owner. You may not know it, but that rumor is wide in certain circles. I gather that little has been done to keep the matter quiet, as far as that goes.

These latter matters are extremely important to me, I know, and I know that they are extremely important to the organization as a whole. I had intended to bring them up with you soon anyhow, and I take the opportunity of this stockholders business to do so now. The picture of some management man from the trust department appearing at the office some morning, or some government tax collector, and saying, "Whee, I'm the new boss and I want so and so done" is one that can't be relished.

H. W. Ross


TO KATHARINE S. WHITE

*[APRIL 1942]*

Dear Katharine:

Some of the stockholders are preparing to investigate things and raise hell, I guess, but I am surprised to learn that Vischer wrote you, for I was told there was to be no canvass of the small stockholders (nothing personal) for the present. At any rate, I was told something of the proposed activity and immediately thereafter soon got the echo of it right back in my ear, via Rollin Kirby and Woollcott (second hand, although Woollcott has since, in anticipation of death, I take it, written me a strong letter of reconciliation after all this time). I called up Lloyd Stryker, the lawyer who has been engaged, and told him for Christ's sake to choke people off on going after the small stockholders, of whom there are scores. It seems that Miss Grant told Kirby, whom she met, and wrote to Woollcott. I was told there was to be no more of this, and I assumed that went for you, too. Widespread rumors of the business would be serious, I think, possibly fatal, so please keep it quiet. I have told no one around the office, or anywhere else, except Shuman, who is a director of the company and knows all about it.

I didn't start the activity. I think I know how it started but I won't go into that here. I may have been partially responsible, by expressing opinions, declarations of intentions, etc. There was a meeting of stockholders which, I think, included Ruth Vischer, Jane Grant, Hawley Truax and, I think, Alice [Duer] Miller, or Henry Miller as her proxy. I am not sure about the last named, but I am sure that the Millers are with the bunch, for I talked to both of them when Alice was in the hospital recently and gathered they were curious and indignant. Alice, I recall, once went to a stockholders meeting and was treated like a leper, etc. (Come to think of it, what really started it, of course, is that no dividend was paid at the last directors' meeting. That was bound to touch things off.)

I didn't go to the stockholders meeting, taking the stand that I was such a small stockholder I didn't rate as such and that I was an employee of the magazine and that our interests weren't exactly parallel, in any event. Also, I said I didn't want to confuse my situation. I had another reason I didn't voice: I haven't time for all those goings-on. I have to make my own stand with Flmann anyhow and I guess I'm the man that in the long run will bear the burden. Vischer is in it legitimately to this extent. He's Ruth's director on the board, Ruth is the second largest stockholder, and she owns a considerable amount of stock. Also, and very important, it will be up to her to bear the legal expenses, or nearly all of them.

So far as I know what's up, I am in full sympathy, although not participating. They certainly are entitled to inquire into some circumstances here, beyond any doubt. There have, God knows, been many rumors about, and I think Flmann and his gang ought to come clean. I've always thought I was entitled to know some things, even though of recent years a minute stockholder, but I never wanted to bust things up completely by getting into a death grapple. It would have been better if I had, I guess. I got onto the *Stage* thing enough to know that it was a near-disaster and sold most of my stock then, thank God, or my ruin would have been complete.

As for me, I have sent Flmann a note explaining my situation (in answer to a query from him) and going further, have told him that I have some points of my own that must be settled reasonably soon. These are, briefly, a declaration of intent as to business policy (this involving his weakening of our stand on advertising accepted, which may get damned serious); a policy as to retrenchments; what to do in war contingencies, etc.; what provision he is making for the continuity of the magazine in the event of his death, which I think the old-time employees here are entitled to know, as they would be in any business these days; and what happens in case the government seizes his stock in the pending income tax case, in which event it would seem that Flmann would be sold out and some stranger would show up some morning as new majority owner and, presumably, publisher. I'm to have a session with Flmann next

Monday, which may be momentous. I was going to have a showdown in any event. The stockholders thing was completely independent of this but it had the result of making me state my attitude to Flmann.

The main thing to keep in mind now is that publicity would be ruinous, and to say nothing to anyone.

Ross

P.S. I have been asked to answer certain questions by Stryker, and shall tell what I know, assuming he is legally authorized, which I understand he already is. I told Flmann I understood it to be an employee's duty to answer any question asked by a director, and that seems to be the law. Whether it is or not, I'm going to do it in this case. I've always [thought] that *Stage* business, for one thing, is a matter Flmann and Ives ought to have been run out of town for, especially Ives, whom I regard as the principal villain.

R.

P.S. Maybe you better tear this up.

R.

P.P.S. (Handwritten) No time to read this. Much work to do.


TO H. L. MENCKEN

*THE NEW YORKER*
*APRIL 22, 1942*

Dear Mencken:

I am not clear at the moment exactly how many Days of Innocence pieces are on hand. I think it's four, two of them not being in the series for some reason or one of them not being, anyhow. This is probably tentative. It is again near the end of the day and I won't look into it now. Three of the pieces aren't set, I think, because we thought we'd put them aside until more started coming and reshuffle then. The need is not acute but we think you ought to start up again fairly soon. We run into peculiar scheduling problems all the time, this office being haunted, and like to have as much bank as possible. Get to the things when you can, in any event.

I will take steps to investigate the Edgar Lee Masters sketches, and thank you very much.

I am quite comfortable but not quite reasonably secure in my mind. My man has a mild desire to operate. He's a surgeon and that would be his solution, I assume, in any event, but he makes out a plausible case. Says I'll have to be on a semi-invalid (his word) basis indefinitely and an operation would solve everything in two weeks. That sounds like a way out. I'm smoking some again and have loosened up the least little bit to see what happens.

Sincerely yours,

Ross

P.S. By God I had a letter from Edmund Wilson today suggesting that I get him started in a literary magazine. He mistakes me for a publisher. He remarks that the *Mercury* presumably made money in your day. I have written him that I think it did, but that you quit there because the advertising manager was getting more money than you were, which I have found a fascinating fact. (I didn't tell him you'd told me this, to save possible embarrassment.) Damned if I know. I told him I'd help him any way I could. I guess if anyone, next to you, could run such a magazine it would be Wilson.

Ross

TO REA IRVIN

*MAY 13, 1942*

Irvin:

I put through the Halloween cover with Hitler, although it violates my solemn stand about no more specific people on covers. Also, there's a business question involved: who takes the risk of Hitler bumping off or resigning before we go to press? I am putting payment through in full but if anything happens to Hitler I guess it's partly your responsibility. I pass the buck to you in this matter, you being a director of the corporation.

Ross

TO RAOUL FLEISCHMANN

*THE NEW YORKER*
*MAY 15, 1942*

Dear Raoul:

I had a session with some of the other early and original minority stockholders on Monday and decided to join with them in the investigation, or movement, or suit, or whatever it is or is going to be, and want to clear the record by advising you of this. My decision was governed, and my viewpoint in general crystallized, by the bringing out there of certain things I hadn't known about before—facts or alleged facts which I deeply feel should certainly be inquired into.

I give you my word, I am not interested in a post mortem for the sake of a post mortem (nor were the others) but am motivated by trying to do what's right for the welfare of the business.

I am sending this to your house for secrecy,

Yours,

H.W. Ross

TO ALEXANDER WOOLLCOTT

*THE NEW YORKER*
*MAY 19, 1942*

Dear Alec:

I have your letter and will take steps to come up [to Woollcott's Lake Bomoseem retreat] as soon as I can get in the clear. I am up to my nipples in hot water, what with half of the staff going off to war, a limitation of fifty-seven gallons of gasoline for six weeks, the Holy Name [Society] demanding that we stop printing "son of a bitch," and so on. This war is much harder on me than the last one. I don't know how to get to Vermont, or to the lake after I get there, but will take this matter up later. I am very anxious to see you.

Sincerely,

Ross

*E. B. White wrote a wartime Comment about how the government's various information agencies should be consolidated, and commentator Elmer Davis put in charge. In short order Davis was named director of the new Office of War Information.*

TO ELMER DAVIS

*THE NEW YORKER*
*JUNE 16, 1942*

Dear Davis:

Your amazing appointment is our first editorial accomplishment since getting the information booth at the Pennsylvania Station moved into the middle of the floor fifteen years ago, and is unexpected and overwhelming. E. B. White wrote that paragraph on what I have assumed was an off-hand, irresponsible impulse, after listening to you on the air. It seems you shot off about censorship, which we here had been shooting off about considerably, but not, fortunately, before a microphone. I read the item in my normal mood of hopelessness and frustration. Subsequently, when a considerable lobby got behind you and the situation looked serious, I was abashed and since then have listened to the goings-on with probably as much trepidation as you have, my concern being about what I will call the executive or administrative aspects of the job, which will unquestionably be a bitch. I was pleased to note in the paper this morning that you are going to put in a good executive and devote yourself to policy and dreaming. That is just simply elegant if you get the good executive. I have been trying to get associated with a good executive for my entire adult life, rather desperately, and I've never found one. My entire career has been spent in close association with horse's rosettes.

You will find us lenient political bosses. We have a few changes we want made in the government, which you will God damned well hear about if your instinct doesn't tell you what they are, or hasn't already. No heavy patronage demands, though—just jobs for a few relatives and so on. And the Lord knows we fervently wish you good luck under the circumstances.

Sincerely,

Ross

*With the war in full swing Ross was desperate to get the Whites back
from Maine—Katharine for her editing and Andy to help produce Comment.*

TO E. B. WHITE

*JUNE 19, 1942*

Dear White:

The Davis Comment came in and saved our life. I don't think we
could have risen to it otherwise, and you rose with mastery and, I guess,
triumph. . . . I have great faith in your wisdom and in emergencies—
and otherwise, too. The collaborating and conferring power in this office [for producing Notes and Comment] is limited now, and is going
to get limiter [*sic*] as things go on, I guess. The able-bodied men who
haven't gone to war are so busy with their arrangements to do so, or to
find out something, that they are greatly preoccupied. Anyhow, the
deplorable fact is that we haven't you writing Comment and there is
no use in me (or your wife) trying to think us out of the fact. There is,
it is increasingly borne in on me, only one White.

In connection with this, and the Davis situation, the Davis accomplishment, I am impelled to again urge you to do Comment, and to
make you, in fact, a tangible, concrete proposition. It is that you take
over the subject of the war in the department for the time being.
There is, I regret to say, a wide-open field there, and a clear-cut one,
free of duplications and complications. . . . [N]o one is writing on the
war for us (except McKelway occasionally, and he is going off to war
shortly). I think it buffaloes everbody; either they have no convictions
or they haven't confidence enough to put them out if they have. Gibbs
writes stuff up to standard but he touches on the war only as the war
touches him and he gets at the edges only.

Here, in one little paragraph, you got Davis appointed (and from all
I have heard this week, which is considerable, he is the best appointment that anybody could think of; there is great unanimity about it).
Damn it, there are other things you could do in the department, all the
time. . . . I think that if opportunity ever cried for a man it is crying for
you. . . .

Please give weight to what I say. If you'd do one piece a week it would make all the difference in the world. I write on behalf of the public as much as mine.

Sincerely,

Ross

*Half a year after Ross had written and forgotten it, the inflammatory letter objecting to a state park near his property was leaked to the New York papers. Walter Winchell, by now Ross's sworn enemy, took a shot at the editor on his national radio program. Lyons, Bronx borough president, had castigated him, too.*

TO JAMES J. LYONS

*The New Yorker*
*June 23, 1942*

Sir:

I finally received last evening your letter addressed to me on June 20th and widely heralded in the press and ballyhooed, I understand, over the air by Commander Walter Winchell, U.S.N. I will answer it, even thus belatedly, to get a few facts on record and to try to defend myself against you two screaming, self-appointed superpatriots.

You say, "I was amazed to read your comments in Saturday's *Herald-Tribune*..." and, emitting a prize, prime, and juicy jet of cheap demagogic spouting, you continue, "While our brave boys are fighting on land, at sea, and in the air to preserve the cherished freedoms, it is revolting to find a so-called editor trying to create caste and rank in America."

Nonsense, Mr. Lyons. Those statements are foully unfair, and you knew it when you wrote them. While my comments, as you call them, were printed last Saturday, they were written a long time before last Saturday, and a considerable time before the United States entered the war. I haven't taken any action at all "while our brave boys are fighting on land, at sea, and in the air" as you, evidently, have been using the boys to grab a headline now and then, even if you have had to scratch out some citizen's eye to do it. That letter happened to have been dragged out after the better part of a year and you seized upon a few printed fragments of it, misrepresented it, and, romping out the war as a background, used your official position to get in a few blows below the belt, which is a cheap and brutal trick.

What I did, briefly, was to write a letter last fall to Governor Hurley of Connecticut arguing against turning a few acres of state land adjoining the Merritt Parkway and also my home into a public park. I was one of many residents of my neighborhood to do this. I think sentiment in the matter was unanimous. If I was a "creature ... in an ivory tower," there were many like me—self-respecting, inoffensive people, most of them commuters to the city, most of them simple seekers after peace and quiet. We sought merely to preserve the privacy of our neighborhood and of our homes, seriously threatened by the opening of the new Merritt Parkway, which put this area thirty-five or forty minutes by automobile from the northern part of New York City, which happens to be the Bronx and Harlem. This has inevitably created a serious problem, one which I believe even such a superficial person as you seem to be might grasp if he should pause long enough to digest an idea fully. In haste and in the vehemence of argument I used a phrase or two which I now sorely realize might be twisted into misrepresentation, but my letter contains not one word which can honestly be construed as calculated to "create class or rank," as you assert. The simple fact of the matter is that my neighbors and I want quiet and privacy and a decent respect for common-law property rights, and I doubt if we'd welcome an extensive invasion of our driveways, yards, and lawns, even if the invaders were all from Newport, Rhode Island, and every one of them listed in the Social Register, and I assume that even such a self-starting democrat as yourself would be perplexed by a dozen or so strangers moving into the foyer of your home for their weekend diversion. As I recall it, I did not argue against the establishment of any parks whatever by the state of Connecticut but endorsed an alternate and more comprehensive plan to open larger tracts of state land farther from the solidly settled communities. But you didn't know about that because you didn't bother to find out what my letter, a communication of considerable length, contained before you shot off in arrant unfairness.

Since you bring up the subject of my profession, I will say that for seventeen years I have been editor of *The New Yorker,* which, if you'll pardon my saying so, has an outstanding record for supporting democracy, decency, and tolerance, and even of tolerating such obstreperous phenomena of the age as flag-waving politicians.

Yours,

H.W. Ross


TO FRANK SULLIVAN

*FRIDAY*

*[JUNE 26, 1942]*

Dear Frank:

I'll write you, but I really shouldn't be wasting my time on a private citizen, the demands by governors, borough presidents, and the heads of big organizations being heavy. I'm touched by Kate's support, however, and I'll take the time and that's all there is to it. My last letter was to the head of the Blue Network of the National Broadcasting Company asking that Winchell be made to make a retraction, or that NBC damned well do it itself. Winchell went too far in that spouting and I think I've got him. If they don't retract I'm going to write next to the Federal Radio Commission asking them to revoke NBC's license. What the hell. Then I'll write Congress. I smoked a transcript of the commander's remarks out of NBC, after considerable monkeying around, and it is pretty bad. He lost his head. That letter was written last fall long before the superpatriots had the war to rant about and was dragged out on me and I was ganged. Your *PM* started it, in retaliation for the [Ralph] Ingersoll Profile (which I didn't think was so bad, and which, by Jesus, could have been a lot worse). They misrepresented the thing, pretending that the letter had been written the day before, or recently anyhow. Also, they didn't say that I was just one of the many members of the Stamford Hills Association that wrote the governor. I was certainly indiscreet in my remarks, however (and I'll never send another letter off without reading it carefully—to a governor), and if the boys had taken the other tack they'd have had me. If they'd said that anybody might object to a picnic grounds next door, but that nobody had a right to insult the colored race and Harlem and the Bronx and, by inference, the Jewish race, they'd have had me cold. But they lost their heads and said I was a heel for not letting the proletariat in next door with their loud-speakers and not turning over my lawn for fornication by all races. So I came out all right, I guess, or what the hell anyhow? I'm going to keep pressing the matter, I think, and see what happens to the commander and his channels of distribution, oral and printed. So help me God, I didn't think of the Jews when I wrote the letter and, since I have come to think of it, I have no complaints against the Jews as trespassers and nuisances in my vicinity. It's members of some other races. Jews seem very orderly, neat, and stay at home. I wrote the letter the day after I had a run-in with four carloads of flashy and slick coons, the bad boys, in sports clothes and yellow roadsters with convertible tops. But that was long before the war and the gasoline shortage, etc., and the matter would have been dead if it hadn't been for my pals on *PM*.

I'll be in trouble all my life, regardless of what you say. I'm fated that way. I'll write it all down someday in my biography, which is to be called "My Life on a Limb."

I will now write as a private citizen and an editor. By all means go ahead with the John Morrissey piece. It's a damned good thing for you to do, I think. Take your time about it; there is no hurry whatever. Meantime, interrupt it to do the piece on vichyssoise and various other subjects. We get practically no humor these days, and if some of you older men, as I call you, would just start in and do something, we might scrape through. By "we" I mean this magazine and the people of the United States. We both need humor and encouragement, and it is up to a few of you fellows to give it to us. Say, in connection with vichyssoise, you might go into the names they call it by now, cleverly, in various restaurants: Ex-vichyssoise, V-ssoise (V for victory), and so on. I'm an observant fellow, and always try to be helpful.

Love to you and Kate, in a most democratic spirit.

Ross

P.S. Woollcott is offering reconciliation and I may go up to see him—if I can get the gas. If so, will certainly see you, and Kate.

R.

## MEMO TO E. B. WHITE

*[JUNE 1942]*

White:

I put through the Fascinating Story of the Week proofs as you had it originally and you can regard this series as now under way.

Say, have you heard anything further about your draft status? I would appreciate knowing, for among the things we've got to worry about are the Newsbreaks, let alone whatever else we might hope you'd do, including Comment. If you go in the army I might get you assigned to the army newspaper. I've got two or three assigned there now, but doubt if I've done them any particular favor. The exodus from this office is getting strongly under way: McKelway, Cooke, Hellman, Whitaker, Weekes, Shaw, Cheever, Newhouse, and God knows who else. I don't know what will become of us.

Ross

## TO GUS LOBRANO

*THE NEW YORKER*
*JULY 9, 1942*

Dear Mr. Lobrano:

This letter is to commit to paper our oral understanding in the matter of your activities in connection with possible military service by yourself. *The New Yorker* recognizes that many men in your position, facing the possibility of eventually being drafted and thereafter facing the prospect of supporting their families largely on their service pay, are seeking commissions in the armed services for purposes of insuring a larger income. In view of your not doing so, but awaiting the decision of your draft board as to your service, *The New Yorker* agrees that, if you eventually are drafted into the army it will, for a period of two years from the date of your induction, pay you the difference between whatever pay you actually receive from the army and the base pay of a captain in the army, these payments to be made monthly to you, or to your wife if you so direct, or to anyone else you nominate.

Sincerely yours,

H. W. Ross

TO H. L. MENCKEN

*NEW ENGLAND BAPTIST HOSPITAL*
*BOSTON, MASSACHUSETTS*
*AUGUST 3, 1942*

Dear Mencken:

I am in the custody of the Lahey Clinic, old ulcer people, and primarily surgeons. My doctor, however, one Dr. [Sara] Jordan, a lady, is wild-eyed against surgery unless there is no way out, and says that an operation for ulcer is not to be taken lightly, but is a major matter. It would seem to be as they do it here, for when they open up the abdomen and go for the ulcer they always take out from three-fourths to four-fifths of the stomach with it. This is on the theory that the abbreviated stomach won't put out much hydrochloric acid and therefore won't cause further ulcers, perhaps in the small intestine, which is looked upon as a very bad place for ulcers. God knows, maybe. At any rate, I have taken a vast quantity of warm milk and cream mixed at one-hour intervals, with various acid killers on the half hour. I must have taken more medicine in the last three weeks than anyone ever did previously. I have taken it every few minutes, through all of the well-known orifices of the body except the ears, and including a good many pores.

I will tell you all about it sooner or later if we both survive. Did I quote Don Marquis's old line about a man of fifty when I saw you last: a fellow who thinks he's going to feel as good as he ever did in about two weeks....

I am supposed to do no work now, but will violate the restriction to say that I hope you are after some of those pieces for us. I don't know what will come of the magazine with everybody being either an invalid or an armed wonder, and I don't care much.

With regards,

Ross

## TO KATHARINE S. WHITE

*SEPT. 14TH [1942]*

Mrs. White:

Tucking up on the personnel and manuscript situation, would report that Gibbs is going back to desk work, which changes everything, of course. This has been vaguely in the air for some time, or vaguely in my mind for some time, at least, for Gibbs has found it harder and harder to do Comment—found it hard to reconcile himself to the war, or his writing to the war, at any rate, didn't have enough opinions on things, etc. He has been doing less and less, and damned if I know *what* the page would have been if White hadn't come through this summer. From my standpoint, that was God's doing. We get to the end of the rope here, and then God does something.

If White can keep a little Comment coming and Gibbs works out on a desk, that will be God's doing, too, I guess, for Comment will be better and the desk work also. Gibbs says he'll do anything at all except talk to [artists] Leonard Dove and Alan Dunn, and if he works as of old it will be a great relief for Lobrano, Shawn, and me. . . .

I'm in the country, trying to do fifty-five things that have accumulated and was doing fine until my new Underwood typewriter collapsed on me. After trying for thirty minutes to get it restarted, I am writing this on my wife's portable, which in the long run would give me ulcers right back. I'm going to take the Underwood to town and try to get it fixed, and my wife will try to get sugar tickets at the same time. That will put us two days behind in our gas supply.

Ross

## TO ALEXANDER WOOLLCOTT

*THE NEW YORKER*
*SEPTEMBER 22, 1942*

Dear Alec:

. . . I have been going to write you for some time, and as a matter of fact damned near called on you [at Lake Bomoseen] or at any rate was on the verge of a call up there. I was in the hospital for three weeks with my duodenum and afterward had to take a couple of weeks off, to rest, and made a sweep over the countryside, calling on my daughter who was in camp, visiting my mother's grave, seeing various relatives in the vicinity of Albany, and eventually getting as far off as Saratoga, where I put up at Sweeney's Hotel, for the benefit of my diet, which was very rigid. I was out of gas, the time was short, and I got tired of the strenuous life, so I came back home without trying for Bomoseen. I had seen a couple of people who said you were coming down this fall and I figured it might be best all around if I waited for that. I think you had a gang at the island anyhow.

Since then I have seen Harpo and interviewed him on your condition; he is alarmed because you won't stay put and take it as easy as your doctor wants you to. I wish to God you would do this, as does everyone else. As for me, I seem just wonderful and unless circumstances bother the ulcer again, I think I'll be all right. I've certainly laid it low for the present, though. I had a woman doctor, quite a person.

I am looking forward to seeing you this fall, at which time I will be at your disposal to any extent you want—presuming my dope on your coming down is correct. I trust you are coming down, for by God you shouldn't stay up there when it's cold and when there's ice around.

I have taken Henry Miller to dinner a couple of times and talked about Alice. We had a fine time, and he perked up.

As ever,
Ross

*Connelly had sent Ross a twelve-dollar check for a two-year subscription, which cost only nine dollars.*

TO MARC CONNELLY

THE NEW YORKER
SEPTEMBER 22, 1942

Dear Old Subscriber:

Your loyalty and confidence is much appreciated. I enclose a check for three dollars, and your subscription is entered for two years. Such transactions always embarrass me, for they remind me that, after all, this is a commercial venture, which I try to forget from time to time.

Frankly, my ominous rumblings were due not only to ulcers (which are gone now, for the moment, at least) but to a chronic feeling that this thing is going to blow apart, or be blown, at any moment. In the long run I am right. If we could present a story by Marc Connelly occasionally, it would please all the old subscribers, who would be glad to send in nine dollars.

Thanks, old man.

Sincerely,

Ross

P.S. Marc, why don't you do a Christmas story for us, God damn it, for old times and the good of your soul, etc.? Why don't you? Or some kind of story. You ought to keep your hand in, old man.

Dorothy Parker called me up the other day. She wants a job. I haven't been able to get her since. Alan [Campbell, her husband] has gone into the army, as I suppose you know. Dottie is living at the Ritz Towers. She says it isn't expensive. I'm going to try to put her in charge of make-up.

H.W.R.

*Private Shaw was stationed at Fort Monmouth, New Jersey.*

TO IRWIN SHAW

*THE NEW YORKER*
*OCTOBER 1, 1942*

Dear Shaw:

You don't sound buoyant, and I don't blame you. I may be hypersensitive to the army life, however, because of age and ailments. I privately get a great deal of solace out of the fact that they couldn't possibly hope to do anything with me, and at the same time, with two years heroic service behind me, my conscience is clear.

I am positive there was nothing personal in *Yank*'s decision in your case. The fact is that at last count they had seventy-two writers, editors, etc., and I guess that's enough. They turned down a couple of other nominees of mine, too, and there could have been no suspicious history in their cases. They simply got over-manned, and also they faced a new order (exactly the same order that was issued at about this point in the last war) that hereafter such outfits could not request men by name. If *Yank* wants a writer now all they can do is request a writer (I suppose giving qualifications needed) and take what is sent them. That won't work out in practice any more than it did in the last war. Meantime, I think the thing for you to do by all means is put in for Officers' Training Camp. Of one thing I am positive: it's better to be an officer than an enlisted man, unless you're an enlisted man with a very special nook. The very special nooks all get filled early; it's a law of civilized warfare.

I don't know what is going to happen to us. We'll carry on until cornered, I guess. The prospect is dismaying, though. Keep in touch with us whatever happens. Once you're through your preliminary training we might be instrumental in helping you get where you want to go, and anyhow it's another law of warfare that writers bob up like corks. You'll be discovered fairly soon and be in the journalistic or intelligence end of things. This is inevitable, even if you fight it. Keep in touch, and we'll keep you in mind. Sooner or later, I believe you will write; inevitable. I hope to God that you and certain others do, for we'll probably go for a loop if you don't.

With warm regards,

Ross

MEMO TO LOUIS FORSTER, FRED PACKARD, AND A
MR. ANDERSON

*OCTOBER 1, 1942*

Mr. Forster, Mr. Packard, Mr. Anderson:

As several people have pointed out, we had the island of Guadalcanal eighty miles wide and twenty miles long. I started this bull off by misreading the copy when I passed it: mistook "eighty" for "eight." I'm liable to do this, being human, and sloppy on top of it. This should have been caught somewhere along the line, though, it seems to me. If the fact that *I* made the change was a factor in not changing back, I will say that I don't hold myself responsible for such matters any more than the preliminary editor or the rewrite man and, anyhow, don't do a thing wrong because I say so.

H. W. Ross

## MEMO TO KATHARINE S. WHITE

*OCTOBER 19, 1942*

Mrs. White:

I have your memorandum about the follow-up of contributors and it is just as discouraging to me. I agree with all you say about the list sent you. What discourages me more, though, is that I don't think that effective follow-up can be done from Maine, or not on this basis and not with the system we have in this office, or the lack of same.

I will go over this memorandum with Lobrano and Shuman and try to arrive at some decision as to procedure and report to you later. This communication is a preliminary one.

I am convinced that our follow-up is proceeding very well. It may have holes, but not many. As you say in your note, follow-up is a constant, everyday routine business. This is the way it is being done. The formal semiannual checkup as it was made—at a grand session—has gone by the boards here because I concluded it was needless. Lobrano is practically heroic in his follow-up work. I know this by vigilant watching. I am somewhat in your position on this business; that is, on the outside. But there is the difference that I am on the spot and when I get wondering about writers (as you do in this memorandum) I can check up and find out. I am, God knows, a natural worrier about such matters, but my findings over a long period have given me considerable confidence, as much confidence, probably, as my system will absorb. I am always thinking of names (as you are in your memo) and then (being in the office) investigate. In every recent instance I have found the writer has been followed. I thought of Bessie Breur, who heads your list, some time ago, and asked Lobrano. He had been in touch with her three or four times. I've asked Lobrano several times lately about five or six other people on your list—McKenney, Benet, Moffat, Thielen, etc.—

and found that he was up to date. On the other hand, putting a writer like Schulberg on your list was bad, it seems to me, and is disquieting.

More later. Meantime, the follow-up is pretty good, at least, and no cause for you to worry. What is worrying me now, as I wrote you the other day, is that our system for nominating new writers has collapsed almost completely. A total of only two nominees in several months (these from you), which is preposterous. . . .

Ross

TO ELMER DAVIS

*THE NEW YORKER*
*NOVEMBER 5, 1942*

Dear Davis:

I write you to clear my conscience. There's an artist recently come to this country who might very well be highly useful to your department in its foreign propaganda work, it seems to me. His name is [Saul] Steinberg. He is a Roumanian by birth. He went to Italy as a young man (which he still is, comparatively) and, as nearly as I can make out, became one of the leading humorous and satirical artists of the country, if not the leading one, and a terrific satirist. He got jugged after the war started for drawing anti-Nazi things, or, I guess, for having drawn them before. He escaped and got to this country after much tribulation. He has drawn a lot of things for us lately. He is the ablest humorous and satirical artist to appear in this country in the last ten years, and maybe in the last fifty years. I should think he would be perfect in drawing things to stir up unrest in Italy, where he is famous. He knows the country, the people, the language, and is eloquent on paper. He also would be useful in all of the Balkan countries, too, and all of Europe, I should think, as he speaks six languages and knows the lay thoroughly. At the moment he is working on a per diem basis with the OWI [Office of War Information] in New York. I think you ought to know how he is about. . . .

You don't have to answer this. As I said, I'm clearing my conscience.

With best wishes,
Sincerely yours,
Ross

## TO KATHARINE S. WHITE

*FRIDAY*
*[LATE 1942]*

Dear Mrs. W:

I have read your letter of Tuesday and will now tear it up. Those boys on the Writers War Board are just full of ideas and, as nearly as I can make out—and I've had a lot of opportunity to make out, because I play poker with Crouse, F.P.A., Marc Connelly, and several others and they are full of talk of projects of great scope and mystery—are on the whole wild-eyed and amateurish, and all of the ideas that have been put up to me by them have ranged from silly to not so hot. We got one story from them, or through them, which was all right, but that's the net effect so far as *The New Yorker* is concerned and I've been receptive through it all. That one story was one Mrs. [Margaret] Harriman did on the wives of aviators. They got in touch with her, suggesting it, and she then queried us. As I said, it was all right; it was no better than the average run-of-the-mill idea around here, of which we have dozens, of course. I feel deeply that the established channels of expressing thought are adequate, and ought to be used. I feel that White is one hundred times as important when he says something in the NYer as he would be in some propaganda sheet. I've seen propaganda sheets all my life and I've never seen any of them readable, or read. The government is using up a trainload of paper a day to not much purpose. I've told several of the boys that we're at their service, but they haven't made any constructive suggestion of any kind yet. . . .

Ross

*Best was editor in chief of Viking Press.*

TO MARSHALL BEST

Dear Mr. Best:

It turns out that I have a couple of other matters to take up with you Vikings, both relating to the eerie practices of the book publishing boys mentioned in my last letter to you, regarding the [Ludwig] Bemelmans stories.

In due course I acquired the new Hemingway book *Men at War,* and the first thing I did, as is the habit of one in my profession, was go over the table of contents.

I quickly realized that five or six stories in the volume had first been printed in magazines of which I had been editor, which I considered a most creditable between-the-wars record. Pride welled in my bosom. This welling subsided almost instantly, however, when I realized that in only one instance—apparently as a result of some slip-up in the book publishing business—was the magazine that originally published the stories given credit. The others were printed kindness of the book boys who had reprinted the stories. Two of the latter were by Alexander Woollcott, which appeared through the generosity of Viking Press.

Confronted with this situation, this office wrote to Crown Publishers, who issued Hemingway's book, and we have received a letter reading in part: "We obtained permission for them (Woollcott pieces) from Viking Press. We shall be pleased to give *The New Yorker* credit if requested to do so by Viking Press." Very well. A simple question: will Viking Press be kind enough to request Crown Publishers to give *The New Yorker* credit for original publication of these stories in subsequent editions of *Men at War,* thus pleasing both Crown Publishers and *The New Yorker* magazine?

The next matter concerns stories by Dorothy Parker which were originally published by *The New Yorker* and subsequently appeared last year in *The New Yorker* volume of short stories, published by Simon and Schuster. I was going through this book the other day and, so help me, Mr. Best, I discovered something I hadn't seen before. I'll be damned if there isn't a credit note in front of that volume which, among other things, says that these stories are published by courtesy of the Viking Press (or some such wording). Thus *The New Yorker* is placed on record as being indebted to Viking Press for republishing its own stories in its own anthology—this when it expressly reserves the right for such republication. Why Simon and Schuster let Viking horn in I don't know. I guess it was just you book boys playing ball with each other, as you occasionally do so prettily, with daggers sheathed.

One thing leads to another. I now find that *The New Yorker* received a bland letter from Viking Press requesting that checks for Dorothy Parker's share of the royalties from the short story anthology be sent to Viking Press and not to Mrs. Parker, and I find that we blandly did this. This would seem to leave *The New Yorker* out on a limb in a matter involving a considerable amount. Therefore, another simple question: will Viking Press please return the amount of these payments to *The New Yorker* or else provide *The New Yorker* with evidence which will convince our finance office that Viking Press was legally authorized to receive the checks?

I will ask a third simple question, which you may regard as rhetorical: where does Viking Press, or any other publisher, get off to horn in on a percentage of an author's royalties in such a case as this?

If the tone of the foregoing seems to you to be one of exasperation, be advised that it is written in that mood. Among the things I am exasperated about is the simple-mindedness of my office and of myself. At the same time I am grateful to you for making me aware of our naivete. I am not going to be so trusting as in the past, and I herewith swear a small oath to make a junior crusade of doing what I can to protect our rights and those of our authors, who in my mature opinion have in quite a number of instances been subject to unholy gypping and exploitation by you book publishers. I trust you will hear more of this.

Meantime, I would appreciate an answer to the first two questions above.

Sincerely yours,

H. W. Ross

TO BEN SMITH

*THE NEW YORKER*
*NOVEMBER 20, 1942*

Dear Ben:

I have just learned that your race track in Mexico City has hired an old and faithful employee of this magazine as a steward. He is G.F.T. Ryall, who has written our racing column for many years. He is a sterling, high-type character and I am positive has never doped a horse in his life. I know he is honest because the few grudging tips he has given me at race tracks on my occasional visits have cost me plenty, in my modest way. Only a man completely above reproach could have been as thorough. I thought you should know about this. I trust I will see you soon.

Sincerely,

Ross

TO MARSHALL BEST

*THE NEW YORKER*
*DECEMBER 2, 1942*

Dear Mr. Best:

I have finally got around to answering your two letters, neither of which I considered too unkind. I say let's be frank, and if you should have any further correspondence, please don't feel obliged to hold any punches. I earnestly want to get this self-centered viewpoint of you fellows in the book trade and I'm willing to learn the rough and rugged way. If God gives me strength I'm going further with this magazine-author-book publisher relationship business and the more I know about it the better.

I will take up several points you raise in your letter, one by one.

You ask if it occurred to me that you published Bemelmans long before we "caught on" to him. The answer is no. I didn't give that matter a thought. It has no pertinence. Regardless of who got Bemelmans first, the fact is that, having got Bemelmans, whenever we have bought a story from him we have reserved magazine rights, as we do with every item we purchase.

Your next remark, "Why a magazine should feel proprietary about an author's rights, other than the right to publish a given work in a given issue of the magazine, I can't quite see." All right, I'll say I can't quite see why a book publisher should feel proprietary about an author's rights, other than the rights to publish a given work in a given book. I say that only rhetorically, however, knowing damned well why a publisher feels proprietary about a writer's work after its appearance in a book. The reason is that he has blandly cut himself into all subsequent auxiliary profits from that book (fifty percent, it seems to be in your case and in some other notable ones) and he feels proprietary because, by God, he *is* a proprietor. We don't make money that way, and the fact of the matter is that we don't feel proprietary about an author's rights. What you mistake for this is a proprietary feeling about our own rights plus a feeling of friendliness toward an author.

When we buy a story or a drawing in this office we buy all magazine rights. Why we do so is a long, dull story which I won't bother with here. I will say only that we have found this necessary to protect our own rights and the rights of our authors and artists, and that specifically, one of our purposes is to avoid awkward situations that are likely to arise these days because of the large number of reprint magazines here and abroad, and that another is to protect ourselves against you book publishing birds who, after reprinting stories from *The New Yorker,* have the weird and disconcerting habit of hogging all the credit upon subsequent publication. I will pause to give an example. In this month's *Reader's Digest* is a piece by James Thurber originally printed in *The New Yorker* and subsequently published by Harper's. Does it appear with credit to *The New Yorker?* No. It appears with credit to Harper's. This is an instance of one kind of high-handedness on the part of book publishers that we are resisting. By reserving magazine rights we are in a position to insist upon proper credit to *The New Yorker.* We do not, however—mark you—insist upon sole mention, or even first mention. We are reasonable. We are willing to let the book publishers ride along with us, or to ride along with them. We merely want to be there. I know that this insistence of what we consider a magazine's rights vexes and distresses you boys. My viewpoint on that is that it's just too damned bad.

As to authors, I regard it as no more than friendly to warn them against practices in the book publishing business which I vehemently believe lead often to their being rooked out of an unholy share of the financial fruits of their work. I think that frequently they'd do better to go along with some amiable highway robber. I have seen a lot in my editorial life. For instance, I have seen writers innocently sign up with book publishers thinking they were signing up merely to get a book published only to find that they have signed away an unholy fraction of their dramatic, radio, motion picture, and republication rights, along with other things, possibly including their suspenders and the refrigerator in the kitchen, and I have seen book publishers drag in tens of thousands of dollars on these deals and buy twelve-room houses in the country. My hair has curled, and uncurled.

Where do you book publishers get off to collect fifty percent of the secondary publication rights to a story? That's another thing I can't quite see. Take, as an example, the case of Bemelmans, since you have brought up his name. Ordinarily, when a magazine wants to republish a story from *The New Yorker,* the magazine gets ahold of either *The New Yorker* or the author. In either event, we give the author a release on his story (or, more likely, handle the office work for him) and he gets the proceeds, in full. It's as simple as that, and as profitable for the author.

In seventeen years we've never taken a cent from an author under such circumstances. But it is not that simple in the case of Bemelmans. He is signed up with you, presumably on one of those fifty-fifty deals, and you naturally feel proprietary about the $37.50.

You speak of "the general nuisance of handling permissions" and of other things, and say that book publishers "are equipped to act as agents for their authors in a way that magazines don't pretend to be." I regard this, insofar as *The New Yorker* is concerned, as, to a considerable extent, hogwash. It is true that we have no facilities for plugging and ballyhoo-ing our authors, if that's what you mean, but we do do a vast amount of ordinary agent work for our contributors as a matter of course, and as far as that end of it goes, we are, I will dare say, better equipped than any publishing office. And, oh, boy, if we were getting fifty percent of the proceeds, couldn't we give them the works! We could put in full valet service and pedicures in the little room off the reception hall....

You say, "Your good friend Woollcott turned over to us all his book rights to his pieces. . . ." I know Woollcott's old, expansive self-headedness, and I will say that it's good work if you can get it.

You say, "The impertinence, arrogance, and general obscurantism of a magazine claiming book rights . . . would interest a lot of book publishers. . . . It would force them to be on guard against magazine malpractice. . . ." O.K. You warn the book publishers and I'll warn the writers and we ought to make a hell of a stir, and it might damned well be the most profitable thing for the writers since sound came to the motion picture. Whee! Let's have oceans of obscurantism.

Sincerely yours,

H. W. Ross

## TO ERNEST HEMINGWAY

*THE NEW YORKER*
*DECEMBER 6, 1942*

Dear Ernest:

I enclose a copy of an exhaustive letter I have sent Marshall Best, a book publisher. Please read the God-damned thing. I can't come to Cuba now but Archie and I both may be there, for good, after the war.

I am embattled on all sides, and rushed, but I will take time to say that you are a horse's fetlock to give any publisher fifty percent of the reprint proceeds of your story—you of all people. Suppose Kipling had signed away half of the reprint rights of "If." Christ Almighty! I'm going on the road about this thing. . . .

If you do some short stories for us, they would be God-damned welcome, I'll tell you.

Sincerely yours,

Ross

P.S. I forgot to say what was most on my mind. I wrote to Crown Publishers and asked them to credit *The New Yorker* for the Woollcott stories. They replied that they'd be happy to do this if requested by Viking Press, Woollcott's publishers. Viking Press said nuts. Will you write Crown Publishers and tell them to give *The New Yorker* credit? And while I'm at it, you might also tell them to give the *American Le-*

*gion Weekly* credit for the Marquis James stories. I was always proud of these latter, and I was mighty glad to see that you had picked them up.
H.W.R.

MEMO TO WILLIAM SHAWN

*DECEMBER 10, 1942*

Mr. Shawn:
An Irwin Shaw short story as long as your left leg is going through for early use and will have to go as a Profile substitute. I see no other way out.
Ross

*Mumford, who wrote the magazine's Sky Line department and also contributed art criticism, was at Stanford University.*

TO LEWIS MUMFORD

*THE NEW YORKER*
*DECEMBER 22, 1942*

Dear Mumford:
Two months ago I was appointed to write you and tell you to keep us in mind out there and write anything for us that might come into your head—fact, fancy, rhyme, or reason, and I herewith do. I forgot it for awhile but was reminded by the piece in *Commonweal,* which I read duly, after a lapse of a couple of weeks. I am always way behind these days, like war production. Every once in a while I read or hear something that makes me proud to have been associated with you. Gibbs and Thurber and I had lunch the other day and Thurber brought up your observation that there is hardly a bed in the United States suitable for sexual intercourse. This set us all to speculating. Thurber said you hadn't been constructive. The interest, however, was largely academic and wistful, something like men talking over their adventures in the last war.
There is positively no building in New York now. I trust you will be back some day, however, to pen those parkway and bridge designers who build walls beside their works so that patrons of their handiwork can't see the river and landscapes.

Keep us in mind, as we do you, and while I'm at it I will wish you a Merry Christmas.
Sincerely yours,
Ross

*Westbrook Pegler was an influential newspaper columnist who lived near Ross in Stamford.*

MEMO TO E. B. WHITE

*[UNDATED]*

White:

... I went to dinner at a neighbor's and Westbrook Pegler was there and bursting with an inspiration that all citizens should turn in their car bumpers for scrap metal. He took three or four drinks and then got a wrench and was going out to take two fenders right off my car. I reasoned him out of such impulsive action, feeling that I would be naked and powerless without fenders, not being an overconfident driver as is. I think I'll have to give up my fenders, though, for I have an idea feeling is going to run high, and it's probably a good idea, too. I'm going to get planking put on, though, as a precaution and comfort. I have just found a two-ton scrap boiler in the old Gutzon Borglum studio for Pegler. Mrs. B. has been trying to turn it in for two months, but nobody takes any interest. She also has about one ton of pipe. I'm going to telephone Pegler, come to think of it. Your Comment last week on the scrap situation in the country [is] exactly true around here. Plenty of scrap.
Ross

P.S. Your Comment enormously appreciated last week, as usual, damn it.
R.

# VI

# "I HAVE BEEN LIKE
# CHRIST IN MY PATIENCE . . ."
## 1943–1945

Everyone who knew Ross understood that he was an organic complainer. But during World War II his plaints were fully justified. "Things are dismal here," he writes to Katharine White in the spring of 1943, just before she and Andy are finally persuaded to come back to New York. "Many writers have gone and more are certainly going. . . . You say there weren't any funny pictures in a certain issue. You've got to be prepared for worse issues. I can see that coming plainly." Plagued by paper rationing and a sheer dearth of material, Ross on more than one occasion lobbied for skipping some summer issues, which the *The New Yorker* never did. The loss of so many editors was particularly hard on Ross and Shawn, who worked virtually every day until war's end directing their own army of sorts, the energetic young reporters who were following Allied forces to the remotest parts of the globe.

—

MEMO TO KATHARINE S. WHITE

*JANUARY 18, 1943*

Mrs. White:
   . . . The main thing that's worrying me now is some ideas for covers to fence over the end of the war with. I feel that we should have these

on hand pretty soon to run quickly when the time comes. If you or White should think of any "war's end" ideas please send them in. It's not only the end of the war, but any overwhelming good news, such as the cracking-up or defeat of Germany or something that would cause rejoicing. What we will have to do when the time comes is scrap the war covers we have in plate form and run in buffer covers carrying some kind of note that the war is over.

H. W. Ross

TO H. L. MENCKEN

*The New Yorker*
*January 21, 1943*

Dear Mencken:

The book [*Heathen Days*] has arrived. It is on my desk here and I haven't opened it yet. I won't until I get it home, whereupon I will read it and undoubtedly enjoy it. I usually have a fine time with books containing reprints from the magazine, being able to read them with a sense of irresponsibility that was impossible at the time of original reading because of my deadening professional apprehension. Mine is no job for a man with hydrochloric acid. Regarding that, I went to Boston the other day for a check-up and the stomach pump showed the acid still running freely. My lady doctor expressed alarm over this and said that there was no hope if I didn't quit smoking. I probably will do this—tomorrow. The duodenum is in fine shape, however. The half-hour dosings of milk, aluminum, bella-donna, and so on lay the ulcer.

I was advised by my wife that you were in town the other night and [I] intended to get around and see if you were at "21" but got tied up on heavyweight matters and didn't make it. I'm sorry. I intended to.

Thanks for the book and best regards,

Sincerely,

Ross

*Adams was writing a biography of Woollcott, who died in January 1943.*

TO SAMUEL HOPKINS ADAMS

*THE NEW YORKER*
*FEBRUARY 4, 1943*

Dear Sam:

... Now as to [Woollcott's] quarrel with *The New Yorker*, so called. All the time Alec wrote for us he was a trial—something of a nuisance and an embarrassment. That was just at the time he was getting drunk with power. He did the page for us, radio broadcasts, pages for other magazines, personal appearances, and Christ knows what. There was usually a jangle every week because he'd want to put in some off-color thing, a dirty word, or a for-men-only story. At that period he was for utter frankness of expression between the sexes and everybody else, free living, no marriages, recognition of the nobility of bastards, and so on. We had to fight to keep him printable, and he was harder to deal with than a Gila monster, which he sometimes resembled. One week he wrote the same story for us that he wrote for the *Pictorial Review* and then, when we at the office were dismayed by the simultaneous appearance of the pieces, said he was doing it to determine the extent of duplication in readership—a scientific experiment. At that period, too, as I recall it, he was doing that un-Christly Town Crier phony business on the air and his picture was blazoned all over the country on billboards smoking a pipeful of Ranger tobacco, one good whiff of which would have bumped him off permanently. He endorsed the new Chrysler automobile (saying he wrote his stuff in it while going sixty miles an hour on a dirt road), endorsed tennis balls and Christ knows what. It was at this period I got embarrassed. I made up my mind that if he quit the page for us it was O.K. with me. I figured he was too big for us; was becoming a big national personality and the magazine couldn't hold him. At about that time he announced that he wanted to quit the page temporarily. I said O.K. without argument. That was the deal, anyhow, from the beginning, that he could do the page whenever he wanted. I think he suspended the page because he was taking a part in a play. Or it may have been that he was going to China—I forget.

There never was any definite final row, at all. It was merely left that he was to resume the page later. The question never came up directly, however, because we ran that piece in our Profile department on him and from then on he was my enemy. There was no question of his doing the page after that. My policy of recent years is that when a person gets mad at me I let them stay mad, and I did this in Alec's case. He was a friend who demanded much and would pull you apart if you didn't watch out. Being close to him was like being in the army with an exacting and imaginative corporal: you had to turn out instantly every few minutes and hold yourself on the alert at all times. I was too damned busy to have time for this. What he was mad at about the piece we had I don't know. I've tried to figure out for years what it was, but he was too complex for me on this point. I am certain it wasn't what he said it was. I let him lay, with one attempt at friendliness when I ran into him personally, and then last summer I got a letter of reconciliation from him. . . . The fact was he withdrew his offer of reconciliation because he had written it in anticipation of death and then didn't die. That was about it. . . .

Sincerely yours,

Ross

*The writer Gellhorn and her husband, Ernest Hemingway, were living in Cuba.*

TO MARTHA GELLHORN

*THE NEW YORKER*
*FEBRUARY 15, 1943*

Dear Martha:

The circulation department went belly up, due to the draft, illness, breakdown of machinery, a greatly increased volume of subscriptions, and God knows what. I've been pounded on all sides but the business office doesn't seem to be able to meet the situation and my reputation there is so bad I haven't brought the point up personally. I have never in my life worked on a publication that could deliver itself, and it seems the simplest thing in the world, too. I don't know—all magazines are cursed with circulation departments that collapse. Ernest

himself hasn't the words to meet such a situation. I will have someone
look into your case and see if I can get the thing started up. Last I
heard they were about caught up. We ran a notice in a couple of issues
of the magazine but that didn't do any good because the people who
didn't get the magazine didn't see them and they were the ones concerned. Paper is rationed now, the newsstand distribution has been cut
away down, and the subscriptions are coming in like sheep.

It's hell about Alec, but I had long since written him off. There was
no chance for him unless he went to bed and stayed there for two or
three years, and he wouldn't do that. He got more rambunctious than
ever. It was one of those semi-suicide things, of which I've seen several in recent years. I saw him about a week before he died, and he'd
fallen off a lot in weight and his clothes were loose; his face was
peaked and white and he acted like a man who had an unbearable burden on his mind. Anyhow, he didn't die in bed, which was something.
*Time* is terrifying, and ought to be put out of business but it gets more
powerful daily. If Clare [Boothe Luce] isn't president Henry will be,
and I'll probably get run out of the country.

I'll try to get the magazine fixed up and regards to Ernest and tell
him that if he ever writes a short story that he thinks *The New Yorker*
ought to have, for God's sake to send it in to us. In the early days I never
went after him because we didn't pay anything. We don't pay much
now, but we pay more than *Esquire* (although not using fishing stuff).

Best regards to you both,
Ross

MEMO TO IK SHUMAN

*MARCH 4, 1943*

Mr. Shuman:
I think the business office ought to consider the proposition of
skipping four issues in the summer, two in June and two in August.
Aside from the paper saving this would effect, there is the question of
a decrease inflow in contents, especially fiction at the moment (we are
scraping bottom now) and pictures. We would save considerable space
by omitting the four issues. It may damned well become necessary to

do so, if the inflow of stories and pictures continues as low as now. The principal difficulty I foresee is the damned stencils in the circulation department. Probably circulation department would collapse.

H. W. Ross

*Ross made several runs at this during the war but the magazine never did skip any issues.*

*When* Harper's *magazine published a profile of Ross, he took quite a ribbing from friends. Mencken wrote him that the piece "makes me groan. There was material enough to scare half the children of America to death, but all the authors managed to do is to touch the edges of it. I am almost tempted to spit on my hands and do one myself. If I ever get to I'll print it in either the* Christian Herald *or the* Police Gazette."

TO H. L. MENCKEN

*THE NEW YORKER*
*APRIL 1, 1943*

Dear Mencken:

I didn't read the damned thing. The author was quoted to me as saying that it was going to be thrilling, and that was final with me. E. B. White read the piece, as a courtesy to *Harper's,* for which he does a column, and told them it was dull and no good. I found long ago that if you don't read these things they don't bother you. . . .

Let me know ahead of time when you come up and I will try to rally. As a matter of fact, I've been feeling just dandy and such of my complaining as isn't habit—and due to having to live the life of a well-behaved Methodist minister—is defense mechanism. My ulcer has come to be my pal; it's the best alibi I've ever had and has simplified my social life beyond belief.

God bless you,

Ross

P.S. If you write a piece about me I'll read it, but I can't be bothered by any bush leaguers any more.

R.

TO SAMUEL HOPKINS ADAMS

*THE NEW YORKER*
*APRIL 5TH [1943]*

Dear Sam:

... I didn't read the *Harper's* piece. The hell with it. E. B. White said it was the dullest document of the year and I don't want to get bored by myself.

R

TO H. L. MENCKEN

*THE NEW YORKER*
*APRIL 8, 1943*

Dear Mencken:

Yes, it will be all right if you give us another story for the one that got caught in the tangle, or some such. You wrote in a letter a long time ago that this story was a surplusage of *Happy Days* and "would probably never go in any book," but it is half our fault, too, because Blanche Knopf sent us a list of the contents of the last book and we didn't catch the title of this story on the list. We will bear at least half the burden and probably more. I will make a stand with the business office and will prevail. I don't give a damn about the money, anyhow; it's the loss of potential contents that breaks my heart. The inflow is very limited now, with so many writers in service, and the loss of even one story is serious and painful. Lobrano had this one scheduled and was about ready to go to press when we found out that it was in the book.

When you feel the urge to write some stories again, know that there's an eager maw here.

I am going up to Boston to see my lady doctor for a check-up next Monday. She will pump my stomach out and find the usual amount of acid. I have done everything right but work too hard, and smoke, otherwise I have been like Christ in my simplicity and patience. She will find acid and that will be that.

Sincerely,
Ross

## TO NUNNALLY JOHNSON

Dear Nunnally:

. . . I got what, with me, passes for a chuckle a few days ago when one of your potentates shot off with the sweeping challenge to the American mind, "Think what Goering would do if he had Hollywood at his disposal." That's an easy one, and it offers a mental picture of considerable interest, Goering being a roomy man. I still think we'll win the war.

Yours till Mankiewicz freezes over,
Ross

*A draft-depleted staff, paper rationing, and other wartime exigencies often got Ross down. That discouragement was plain in his letters to the Whites—whom, not coincidentally, he had finally lured back to New York.*

## TO KATHARINE S. WHITE

Dear Mrs. White:

. . . I've got drops in my nose, etc., having had La Grippe accompanied by a fever. Dr. Devol appeared with a thermometer over the weekend and advocated my going to a hospital and I went for a couple of days, largely because of household deficiencies. My wife is still away—being unable to get train space for her return—and no cook, and with the ulcer diet and all I turned in to the Roosevelt hospital, where I rapidly recovered. . . .

Things are dismal here, and the outlook generally not bright, although the desk staff is still intact to a greater degree than anticipated. But many writers have gone and more are certainly going, and things are going to get tougher, and no question about it. You say there weren't any funny pictures in a certain issue. You've got to be prepared for worse issues. I can see that coming plainly. Most of the artists are still around, but they are getting an overwhelming amount of advertising work, other publications are after them, and so on. The main thing, though, is that our two best idea men are gone (although somewhat productive)—[Richard] McCallister and [James Reid] Parker. I doubt if [Helen] Hokinson has had an idea of her own in years; they're all Parker's. As far as that goes, none of the artists have had an idea of their own in years, I guess. When the issues get really lousy, I will revive the every-other-week scheme....

R

TO E. B. WHITE

APR. 22ND [1943]

Dear Mr. W:

Very good. I am greatly cheered by your statement of intention, and will look toward the future with a bit more confidence. On the whole the future is dismal, as I told your wife in a recent note, and it has been getting dismaller. There is no way of telling now what the situation is from day to day. This day [Sanderson] Vanderbilt is finishing up and going to the army, along with a lad named Howard who has been useful on proofs and copy. Christ knows what July will bring. As for writings, we need casuals as much as we need Comment, and maybe more. It is hard to tell from where I sit. We need verse, too, but it's been so long since we had any light verse that I have practically forgotten about it. In other words, the magazine is still going.

In the matter of rates, I think you are entitled to a bonus, anyhow. By your own statement you are not taking on another regular writing chore, you *intend* to write for us, etc. That would seem to me to warrant the additional pay that was proposed, or at the rate that was proposed, and we will pay it, and settle up quarterly. I am making a note to this effect and the bonus will be paid, unless the note gets lost. There is about an even chance of that. There is a further practical reason for paying the bonus: the magazine is having a slight boom now and I'd rather have contributors getting it than Flmann, who would just lose it at the races. It would come to the same thing if we just raised the rate and had done with it, but there are several reasons against that, at least two of them devious.

If I had any confidence in the righteousness of the cause, I'd argue for your coming to New York this winter. It would be simply ducky, as a social as well as a business matter. I told Katharine you people can have my house in Connecticut next winter if you want and you might damn well consider that. It's remote and at the same time handy to the train, roads, schools, etc. I mean it has the feeling of being remote. I'd rather have you living in it than [it is] now, and you could pay the oil and telephone.

Meantime, welcome to the little group.

Ross

P.S. That extra gas allowance is certainly legitimate, and you ought to insist on your rights. Perhaps you ought to have gas for two trips. All sorts of extra allowances are being made for artists to send in drawings, writers to get their copy to the station, and so on. Connecticut is criss-crossed with the trains of artists and writers darting about.

R.

TO KATHARINE S. WHITE

*SUNDAY*
*[SPRING 1943]*

Mrs. White:

I am writing this in the country, in the evening, and it's so damned cold I don't think I'll be able to hit many of the right keys. . . .

It was inevitable that White would get those [endorsement] offers and I suppose they can be taken as evidence of arrival—at something. He could easily go Woollcott and clean up all around, and get his picture all over. I was thinking that the other day. I got a telephone call from the Mission Bell Wine Co. (or some such) asking me to head up a program on the air to sell wine. The gent was very confident about it. When I declined, and made my decision positive by saying that I always had an uncontrollable impulse to say dirty words over the microphone every time I got near one, he wanted to know if White and some of the other lads whom he mentioned would be interested. He's looking for another Fadiman, of course. I didn't bother to transmit the offer to White, or anyone else, but I think it still stands. . . .

I'm going to try to get a big bonus for the writers and artists unless paper rationing knocks the profits in the head. I don't know whether I'll get away with it or not, but when the directors start to pass a dividend to the stockholders (or maybe before) I'm going to propose one for the contribs. (The payroll people are pegged, and hopeless, without intricate conniving.) . . .

Ross

*Ross was thrilled and relieved when White rejected DeWitt Wallace's lucrative offer to write a column for the* Reader's Digest, *a publication Ross deplored.*

TO E. B. WHITE

*MAY 7TH [1943]*

White:

After a brief spell of breathlessness, I had several loud chuckles over your defiance of Wallace, and I continue to have them. I am carrying your note around with me and referring to it whenever life seems grim. My admiration for your boldness is unbounded. You have defied the biggest giant in the business and, by God, it's the first time I ever heard of anyone turning down his big dough. Whatever Wallace may think of your merits and your wordage, he cannot exceed me in the former, and as for the latter, I have never seen you use an unnecessary word. I am willing to take an oath to this effect. Take your Comments this week, exactly right as to length. You are a man who should not be digested; hydrochloric acid should never be applied. . . .

Ross

TO SAMUEL HOPKINS ADAMS

*[1943]*

Sam:

There is one wonderful anecdote about Woollcott that you might possibly be able to work in, although I doubt it. You may or may not know that he sort of took charge of President R's library, or anyhow, his shelf of mystery books (and then writing pieces about what the

President was reading). Well, Alec, the Prest. and a number of other people were sitting around some room in the White House one evening a few months ago and Alec shouted across the room to the President, "Did you get those mystery books I sent you?" "No, I didn't," said the President, then in an aside to a few people near him, "I got them all right, but I wouldn't give him the satisfaction of knowing I did." One of those close to the Prest. at the moment was my informant. True enough, but doubtful [for use in the book], maybe....

Ross


TO ERNEST BYFIELD

*THE NEW YORKER*
*JUNE 2, 1943*

Dear Ernie:

On April 28th, at 3:05 P.M., I sent a telegram to you at the Sherman Hotel, saying that Mrs. Ross was arriving in Chicago on the Chief that evening and might not make connections, and asking you to see that she had a room for the night if she had to stay over. Mrs. Ross got off the Chief about nine o'clock that night and had a hell of a time. She couldn't get anyone by telephone at either the Ambassador or Sherman, and finally went personally to the Ambassador, where they said they had no room for her. Subsequently, being bedless, she took a plane out at midnight, and eventually got here. She told me that one of your clerks at the Ambassador obliged her by cashing a small check for her to help pay the airplane fare.

What I want to know is whether you ever got that wire at all. The matter comes up in a bill from the Western Union, and I will be God damned if I am going to pay them if it didn't get there. I have had a lot of trouble with the Western Union lately, having been thrown for several loops. I want to have it out with them. Maybe the telegram came at night and you didn't get it until the next day. Maybe you were in Honolulu at the time. I know nothing.

I am still carrying on here, but I don't know why.

Sincerely,

Ross

MEMO TO RUSSELL MALONEY

*June 23, 1943*

Mr. Maloney:

I have your second memo (6/13/43) on the matter of new offices and regard it as a mass of constructive and helpful criticism and observation. As I think I told you, there has been some revision in the management of this enterprise and as a result of this I am hopeful of getting action in such situations as this, whereas I have been hopeless in the past. If I don't get action on such things I will damned well fly the coop. The story of how we landed in this hell-hole is a long and fantastic one, hard for a sane man to believe. I am more irked by the present office set-up than anybody else in the place, I believe, with the exception of you. It is straight hogwash and that is all there is to it.

H. W. Ross

*Block was the editor of* Current Biography.

TO MAXINE BLOCK

*The New Yorker*
*June 23, 1943*

Dear Madam:

This is in reply to your letter of May 18th, inviting me to point out errors in the piece about me in *Current Biography* for May, 1943. The delay in answering is due to one thing and another, including a spell in the hospital. The *Fortune* and *Harper's* pieces (neither of which I had previously read) contain some misstatements and I will point them out below in detail, since you are going to put me between covers. The fact is I'd very much like to get an accurate biographical piece printed somewhere and be able to refer writers to it in the future, if I am ever written about again. So:

In your second paragraph you might well say a little more about Aspen, which was second only to Leadville as a silver mining camp, a very spectacular place. It was on the other side of the range from Leadville. It went flat with the collapse of silver in 1896 and everybody in town was broke, including my father. You might do better by the old gentleman, too. He was a well-known mining man in the west for forty years. In Salt Lake City he was mostly a contractor—the wrecking you mention was a side issue—but he was pretty much a mining man all his life, his other interests being dilettante-ish, really. The trouble was, mining went out from under him, except for the big-scale, low-grade copper mining, etc.

I was *never* an office boy on the *Salt Lake City Tribune*, and I don't want it said that I was. It isn't pride on my part, for I was an office boy, or an errand boy, once, but I want to do justice to a gentleman named Frank I. Sefrit, who at the time I began newspaper work was general manager of the *Salt Lake City Tribune*. He is one of the few constructive journalists I have encountered in thirty-five years of journalism. I was one of his proteges, and he is entitled to the credit, if any. He started off a number of boys in their early teens as auxiliary and apprentice reporters, as an educational undertaking. I was one of these. I was something of a reporter at twelve or thirteen, really. After I started in high school I did the High School Notes, along with other reporting chores outside of school hours, and did them with a considerable amount of professional ability, if I do say it myself. After two years of high school, I drifted off into full-time newspaper work. That is one way of putting it, anyhow. I found high school too dull and newspapers glamorous (what with riding on the fire engines, the police patrol, and all), and I still find journalism glamorous. I really left Salt Lake City at sixteen, going to visit an uncle at Denver, Colorado, and then lighting out for California on my own with an older lad. That was in 1908. The older lad ditched me with our joint capital in Albuquerque, New Mexico, and I hoboed my way to Needles, California. I wasn't a very good hobo, and the Santa Fe didn't have many trains in those days, and I walked most of the distance. At Needles I got a job as a timekeeper on a construction gang (being competent because I had done the same work for my father). I went back to Salt Lake City (as a first class passenger) but I didn't stay long, deciding to see the world. I was off schools and colleges by that time. As to the *Marysville Appeal*, I worked there as the sole reporter, doing a competent job. The editor died and the owner was in India on a trip around the world. I got out the paper until he could get back, which was a considerable spell. It was unquestionably that experience, at eighteen, that gave me an idea I was an editor, God forbid. Anyhow, in those two or three months I got out a daily paper almost single-handed and after that was a pretty confident newspaperman, if not a very experienced or able one. It wasn't the present King of Siam (as of *Fortune*'s date of issue) that I chaperoned at the World's Fair in San Francisco. He didn't last long— died. He was a Harvard graduate, or maybe it was Yale.

Your next paragraph: You are wrong in saying it was necessary to be an officer to get on the *Stars and Stripes*. The *Stars and Stripes* was edited by enlisted men. The fact was that I couldn't have got on the *Stars and Stripes* if I had been an officer. I tried to resign from the [officer] training camp and remain a private. I finally succeeded, after much turmoil. I didn't get demoted because I was never promoted. I was just a candidate (for second-lieutenant). I was no "junior member" of the staff. We didn't have senior or junior members on the editorial staff. We were all enlisted men and we kept the rank we had arrived with. To lay the apocrypha, here is how I came to be the so-called editor of the *Stars and Stripes*. Our commanding officer had a nervous breakdown and the editorial department was left without authoritative direction. Six of us, Sergeant Alexander Woollcott, Private John T. Winterich (now colonel in the army censorship section at Washington), Private Hudson Hawley, Private (Marine Corps) Albian A. Wallgren (comic cartoonist) and C. LeRoy Baldridge (serious cartoonist) held a meeting to decide what to do. My idea, which prevailed, was that we should elect an editor and that that editor would have full authority to give instructions to the others and to run the paper but could be removed at any time by a meeting of the six of us. My candidate for editor was Winterich but he backed out. Winterich was more the editor than anyone else, from start to finish, but he shied away from the personal contacts that went with the job, many of which were disagreeable. I took on the job. I was never fired by the staff and we finished the war that way. Winterich really did most of the editing, though. Woollcott used to say that after my election I sent the staff out on so many assignments and such distant ones that it never got to meet again. That was a joke.

Next paragraph: I was never offered a job on *Redbook,* that I ever heard of.

Next paragraph: I'm afraid you can't say "and still is" about the Thanatopsis Club. Broun and Woollcott are dead and a lot of the boys have strayed. I didn't play poker myself for about ten years, although a little now. . . .

Later in your article you say ". . . Ross, who was able to make a big business of frivolity." Two things wrong here. We have never been a big business; we're a peanut business compared to the other magazines. And I don't think we're so frivolous, either. My personal opinion of our promotion is that it was terrible and probably gave unobservant people the notion that we were frivolous. My own impression is that my salary is thirty thousand dollars a year, but don't say I said so. I don't own any ten percent of the stock and haven't for many years. I own less than one percent at the moment. I sold my stock partly as a psychological matter; I wanted the workers' viewpoint, not the magnates', or the investors'.

I don't think (same paragraph) we're "aware" of our readers. It's the other way around with me. All I know about getting out a magazine is to print what you think is good (or as near to your standard as you can get) and let nature take its course: if enough readers think as you do, you're a success, if not you're a failure. I don't think it's possible to edit a magazine by "doping out" your audience, and would never try to do that.

Third paragraph, page 73. You say after the war Jane Grant became a reporter on the *Times.* The fact is, she was on the *Times* long before the war. As to my present wife, she was never a cinema actress (being to date thwarted in that respect) and she wasn't a stage actress either, except for four days, in a failure. She took dramatic courses at schools, though. She went to Barnard and is a graduate of the University of Texas.

In the next paragraph you have me "working best in a rage," which is arrant nonsense. Nobody can do editorial work in a rage. I suspect that was written by [Ralph] Ingersoll, who worked on *The New Yorker,* and who would drive any co-worker into a rage, or a leap out of the window. I am not full of phobias. That must be a couple of other guys.

I have just a couple. I am normally bold in crossing streets, for instance. I'm afraid of boats, but not of crossing streets. Also, I claim I understand all the jokes that we've printed—and everything else that we print, too. Our motto in the office is, "Don't print anything you don't understand."

Next paragraph. For what it's worth, it's "Use the rapier, not the bludgeon."

Next paragraph, toward the end. Well, I never told anyone to tell an office boy not to say "Good morning" to me. It is true, though, that I haven't time for the idle amenities and frequently don't shout salutations to people in the hallways and so on, and stop to chat with them. There is usually something on my mind, and there is usually something on the minds of the other members of the staff, too, if they are functioning.

Last paragraph. I haven't got an "estate," for God's sake. That is tabloid journalism use of the word. What you ought to call it is just a home.

All right, there are my quibbles. I could go on further, but I won't burden you. And I'll appreciate it if your piece is fixed up according to your new enlightenment. I would welcome some source thing about me that is reliable.

Sincerely yours,

H. W. Ross

*The flamboyant Beebe was a columnist for the* New York Herald Tribune *and Ross's friend. He had written a note in his column about how the editor's prominent "missing front tooth" was becoming a New York landmark.*

TO LUCIUS BEEBE

*The New Yorker*
*July 7, 1943*

Dear Lucius:

Come, come, you are making an eccentric out of me. I am not missing a front tooth. I have all my teeth (if you are willing to accept a few artificial replacements in the rear of my mouth). The space in front is a natural one, although it is true that a committee of the U.S. Army Medical Corps had to take a painstaking tooth census once to be convinced of the true situation. It is also true that my dentist, who is a creative and imaginative gentleman, has suggested that he could insert an artificial tooth into the gap and improve my appearance, and has several times urged this procedure with wistful artistic sighs. I have stood firm: God made that gap and I'll stand by it.

Sincerely,
Ross

*Ross was trying to explain why he shouldn't be the arbiter of taste for the Notes and Comment department.*

TO KATHARINE S. WHITE

*MONDAY*
*[UNDATED]*

Mrs. White:

... The trouble is an old one: I am a straight old-fashioned double-standard boy and nothing whatever shocks me. I grew up that way. I have two entirely different vocabularies, one for men, the other for mixed company and women, children, and ministers. Any standard I set up is artificial. All such standards must, by their nature, be artificial, of course, but I am completely disqualified. I'm the boy who worried himself into ulcers about "bum," used by Woollcott, son of a bitch, bastard, etc., used by everybody, even "hell" used weekly by Gibbs, "behind" used by White, and so on. I was trained in the newspaper school that played safe in all of these and simply never took a chance. I'm shocked by seeing these words in print, because women and children and members of the Holy Name Society are going to read them. It's contrary to my training (although not to my taste). ...

Ross

*From* The New Yorker's *inception, Ross resented any money the business side spent to publicize the magazine, insisting that the best promotion was editorial excellence. The previous year's shareholder revolt had resulted in the formation of this three-man executive committee, designed to weaken Fleischmann's grip on the company.*

## MEMO TO RAOUL FLEISCHMANN, LLOYD PAUL STRYKER, AND HAWLEY TRUAX

*THE NEW YORKER*
*AUGUST 23, 1943*

I quote below a memorandum given me by Mr. Cook:

"Please note the free and unsolicited promotion (which is more valuable than anything we can concoct or buy) that *The New Yorker* has received this week— ·

Orson Welles read our Comment, 'The Meaning of Democracy,' over CBS network, with full credit to *The New Yorker*, Saturday night, August 14.

During the Invitation to Learning radio program, CBS, Sunday, August 15, Lionel Trilling, professor of English literature at Columbia, compared Oliver Wendell Holmes to E. B. White, and Lt. Lawrence Thompson said, 'If Holmes had lived today he certainly would have published his things in *The New Yorker* with pleasure.'

*Time*, August 16, quotes two hundred words with credit from our Comment on the definition of the word 'fascist.'

*Life*, August 23, used three pages of pictures of McSorley's saloon, and refers to [Joseph] Mitchell's book of *New Yorker* pieces. But *Life* does not mention *The New Yorker*—refers to Mitchell as a New York newspaper reporter.

[Ed] Sullivan, in *PM*, August 19, starts off a piece under a four column head by calling attention to Geoffrey Hellman's Profile of Harry Hopkins in *The New Yorker*.

*Newsweek*, August 23, reprints the Richard Decker drawing of the bloodhounds hunting for the escaped welder, with full credit to *The New Yorker*.

*The New Yorker* of course got its weekly plug when the *Post* picked up some of Mark Murphy's piece and mentioned Thurber's short story.

During the week we received thirteen requests to reprint or purchase cartoons and two requests to reprint poetry from *The New Yorker*."

This is a very interesting showing, although of course it is but a fraction of the publicity we got through the press and radio in one week, for there is always a sprinkling of reprints and comment the country over. It is unquestionably true that we get more such publicity than any other publication in this country, and get it free, and to my mind it is unquestionably true that this fact ought to be borne strongly in mind in all our promotional or publicity planning. The boys can wrinkle their brains for two weeks and spend ten thousand dollars on a newspaper ad and not get the value out of it that we got out of Orson Welles's reading of White's Comment on the air.

I have preached for years that the contents of this magazine itself afford us our best promotional opportunities and that, generally speaking, the best way to spend money on promotion is in contents. White's Comment, in itself, frequently is promotion. . . . I have got headaches from people asking me over and over who wrote certain of White's recent Comments. A good [Alva] Johnston series is promotion. An exceptional picture is promotion. It gets into print, it gets on the air, and, what is more important even than that, it gets mouth-to-ear publicity all over. God only knows how many people exclaimed over and discussed that White piece defining democracy. It has already become sort of a classic.

Pardon me for intruding upon you gentlemen with another memo, but I think a big matter of policy is involved here: the magazine is its own general publicity getter. Any other promotion we do ought to be aimed directly at specific people, whoever they are—certain advertisers, or certain potential readers, or whatever. Cook has shown me a vast collection of advertising that other magazines are doing, in the newspapers, in other magazines, etc. It all looks crazy to me, although those publications, none of them, get anything like the break we get in free publicity, and do have to pay for theirs. I think we were crazy when we went in for that sort of thing, and I think we'll be crazy if we do it again. When we have done so we are just playing the other fellow's game; we're just playing at being *Saturday Evening Post*, and we're not, fortunately.

H. W. Ross

TO MOSS HART

*THE NEW YORKER*
*AUGUST 26, 1943*

Dear Moss:

Herewith a proof of the piece on you. Margaret Harriman said she was going to send you a proof but we worked it out that it would be more efficient for me to mail this and let her keep a proof she has in her possession. We save motions where possible, as a part of the war effort. Report any errors and complaints in this to Miss Harriman direct, please, and quickly, for having this in type we want to rush it to print, you having suddenly become the man of the hour, apparently, in journalistic circles.

Don't take anything said too seriously. Some changes are to be made anyhow, without your bringing them up, but you bring anything up you want to.

It is an unusual procedure for us to send a proof of a personality piece to the man written about but in this case I see no harm for you seem to be such a generally worthy bastard.

Sincerely,

Ross

TO JAMES CAGNEY

*THE NEW YORKER*
*SEPTEMBER 16, 1943*

Dear Jim:

I have checked up on the tractor and I find that I paid $873.50 for it, $105.00 for the dump wagon, and twenty dollars for tractor chains. That comes to $998.50. I am advised that a fair price is one-half of that cost, which would be $499.25. If you agree with this viewpoint, then done and done. I am told that I bought a flywheel too, at additional expense. I don't know whether you got the flywheel or not. If so, you can have it for seventy-five cents, this price being a special one for the public spirited citizens of Martha's Vineyard. That brings the total neatly to five hundred dollars. If you want to argue, do so, and if you don't want to buy the tractor at all, that will be all right. You can send it back. I don't give a damn one way or another. I got a certain amount of pride out of owning a tractor, even if I didn't use it much, and that is worth something, and I can use it anyhow after the war.

I don't know where the hell you are. I got overwhelmed with work and forgot this tractor business until a day or two ago, when I read that you had gone on the road with a cavalcade of talent. Best wishes in your travels. I will send this letter to the Vineyard. Maybe you are going back there and will get it there. If not, I assume it will be forwarded. I am enclosing another version of this letter to show Mac [Edward McNamara]. For Christ's sake, give him this with a dead pan and stick to the story. Make him write me a letter about it. There is nothing in the world I enjoy so much as a letter from Mac, and the picture of him writing it.

Mac has been very firm about this tractor business. He was very expansive until the tractor was delivered, but afterward said darkly, "You're not going to get what you think you are", etc.

With best wishes,
Ross


*After Ross fell behind in payments to Jane Grant, he skirmished with her attorneys in a vigorous, and at times sardonic, correspondence.*

## TO CHADBOURNE, WALLACE, PARKE & WHITESIDE

*THE NEW YORKER*
*SEPTEMBER 17, 1943*

Gentlemen:

Good news! Please read the attached, pertaining to the matter you inquired about in your favor of recent date. I'll be remitting some cash if this check comes through, although I won't get the full amount of the check (due to other legal and bureaucratic complications that I won't burden you with here), and there are others in line also, among them an attorney or two. There is always an attorney or two in my line. I was going to try to have you all in for cocktails, but I don't think there will be enough left over....

Long life to the legal profession! In just about ten years you boys will have this country so thoroughly tied up that it can't turn a wheel, and then everybody will just go gracefully out of business.

Very truly yours,

Ross, Ross, Ross, Ross & Ross

sgd/H. W. Ross

By H. W. Ross

*Ross was no fan of the FBI director—he called him a "flatfoot," even to his face—and Hoover certainly didn't appreciate* New Yorker *humor. This exchange was prompted by a brief* Talk *anecdote wherein an FBI agent was said to be conducting a background check. Said the agent to his interviewee, "I notice, in reading over back copies of your college daily, that your friend was sometimes referred to as Lefty. Was this because he was interested in communistic activities?" Hoover had written Ross to ascertain who the agent was.*

## TO J. EDGAR HOOVER

*THE NEW YORKER*
*OCTOBER 12, 1943*

Dear Mr. Hoover:

I have your letter of October 8th, and simultaneously a letter from the source of one of our little items that you brought up in your earlier correspondence. The source of this item asks that his name not be divulged to you and this makes it unanimous, for I had previously had a letter from the source of the first item making a like request. So I guess the only thing I can do is stand on my constitutional journalistic rights and not reveal the sources. I am disappointed that they both preferred to remain in the background. I wrote them fair and square, telling them your problem.

It is too bad I was not better trained as an observer, or I would unquestionably have been more useful in describing the man who asked about Sherwood, et al. Perhaps we ought to keep the names of callers at this office, or at least government representatives, but we don't. Mr. Shawn, as I think I told you, estimates that he has been interviewed about twenty-five times by F.B.I. men and, allowing for even a fifty percent error on his part, it would seem odd that your New York office can get track of no man that interviewed him. I'll ask Mr. Shawn to make a note of the F.B.I. men that interview him hereafter, although I doubt if his government callers will be so numerous from now on, for most of our staff is already gone—and investigated.

Sincerely yours,

H. W. Ross

## TO GILBERT GROSVENOR

*THE NEW YORKER*
*OCTOBER 13, 1943*

Dear Mr. Grosvenor:

Thank you very much for your thoughtfulness in writing, and if it is true that *The New Yorker* has helped you in lightening the geographic descriptions, that is no more than right, for I feel that I have owed something to the *National Geographic* for many years and that it is no more than right that I should make a contribution to it, although obliquely. The *National Geographic* was my father's favorite magazine. He stayed put geographically from a point shortly after I was born but he went all over the world vicariously with your writers. When he died one of the problems I faced was what to do with his store of *National Geographic*s, to the number of two or three hundred. I finally presented them to another old friend of his, another *Geographic* admirer. If he were alive, I'd show him your letter and impress him as I never was able to impress him during his lifetime.

Sincerely yours,

H. W. Ross

TO EDMUND WILSON

*THE NEW YORKER*
*OCTOBER 14, 1943*

Dear Wilson:

Pending the end of the war and the starting of that magazine, why don't you review books for *The New Yorker*? Fadiman is giving up this job and you seem to be conspicuously the man for it if you should be disposed to take it on. In fact, from our standpoint, you seem to be the only man, standing alone among the possibilities like a large, isolated mountain.

I should like to know right away if there is a chance of your being interested, at least to the point of giving it a whirl. I know that you have never done weekly reviewing and my recollection is that I was told that you once shuddered at the thought of it, but I may have been misinformed, and anyhow, this is not a hard job as reviewing goes. Fadiman has been picking out two or three books a week and writing about them, leaving the other books for brief mention by others. That procedure could be continued, or it could probably be changed to suit your ideas.

Fadiman at first said he wanted to leave about the first of the year but now says he would like to leave sooner than that if we can get a successor, so the job would be open at any time you chose between now and January. The financial arrangement would be adequate, I believe. (The magazine is prosperous now and will continue to be so until paper rationing really hits us, but regardless of our present success, it was a damned good thing that you didn't try to float a new magazine during this period. It has been just worry, worry, worry.)

As I said, I'd like to know soon and I'd appreciate it if you'd telephone me (collect) when you get this letter. I'll be at the office all day tomorrow, Friday, if you should get this in time, and at Stamford, Connecticut, 3-1290, Saturday and Sunday. I hope to God that your answer will be yes, for the Wilson sentiment in this office is practically unanimous and everyone ... will be disappointed if you don't give this job a try. If you are disposed to talk about the proposition we would gladly pay your expenses down here for the conversations.

Sincerely yours,
H. W. Ross

*Hahn was bound for South Africa.*

## TELEGRAM TO EMILY HAHN

If you have red-hot fact stories please transmit by telegraph. With anything else air mail.

H. W. Ross

## TO ARTHUR D. QUAINTANCE

*THE NEW YORKER*
NOVEMBER 1, 1943

Dear Arthur:

The bearer of this note is Mr. E. B. White, who is in Denver with his wife spending some time with a relative in the Colorado branch of the army. I have asked Mr. and Mrs. White to look you up. They both have been closely associated with me on *The New Yorker* for so long I can't remember, and are very close personal and professional friends. I want them to meet you, Mary, and the rest of the family, especially Uncle John, and anything you can do for them in Denver will be appreciated deeply. Show them where I kept the eagle that Uncle John made me turn loose.

Sincerely yours,
Harold

## TO FRANK SULLIVAN

*[NOVEMBER 1943]*

Dear Frank:

I won't tell Flanner that. What the hell do you think I am? Don't answer.

Ariane was driven into a terrific state of excitement by the [El] Morocco piece. It was a sensation. You just don't understand women; that's all. I met Jerry Geisler the other night, that attorney [who] defended Chaplin, Errol Flynn and others, and he told me that on the first ballot the women on the Flynn jury all voted for acquittal, all the men for conviction. That's the way women are. I don't know what that's got to do with the argument, but it's a point about women.

Call me up and I'll buy dinner at any time. Write a piece.

Ross

*Steinberg was filing illustrated dispatches from China. James Geraghty was the magazine's art director.*

TO SAUL STEINBERG

*THE NEW YORKER*
*NOVEMBER 19, 1943*

Dear Steinberg:

We have got your various letters here and the forty-some drawings you sent have largely come through at this writing, although not all of them have arrived yet. Those that have been received came in good shape and caused great rejoicing throughout the office. I will leave it to Geraghty to report in detail on the drawings. We certainly will be able to make good use of all of the Chinese drawings and of several of the others. The Chinese drawings are wonderful. We have enough now for a double-page layout, or thereabouts, but we haven't laid them out finally yet. We thought we would wait and see what more came in and then make our plans with everything in hand. If the other drawings are delayed, though, we will use what we have now and await the others.

As I said, we rejoiced upon the arrival of these drawings, and we will rejoice upon the arrival of any more that come in. Please keep them coming. Your going to war so suddenly was a sore loss to us, and I have felt sad about it ever since you went, but if you can give us service and foreign drawings—either sketches like the Chinese ones or idea drawings—we will be reconciled to your going in the service and, as a matter of fact, it might work out to the ultimate advantage of both of us. We haven't many artists in the service and our coverage of the war in drawings is largely by ear and therefore not as good as we would like to have it. You may save the day for us, in a big way. The hell with *Life* and the other magazines. I think we can use a great deal of the stuff you send, and be glowingly happy to get it. If you can keep up at your present rate, you ought to have a reputation when you come back that will warrant a parade. I speak as one American to another. . . .

[Albert] Hubbell is gone and Geraghty is carrying on. Hubbell expected to be drafted but he hasn't been drafted yet, after several nervous months. The magazine is in better shape now than I thought it would be. I thought for a time, as a matter of fact, that we were going to blow up, but we have had some luck lately, and not the least of it is your productivity. Please send on everything you draw. We will handle it with despatch, turning over to Mr. Civita promptly anything we can't use.

The office is somewhat the same as it was when you left it, and New York is much the same, I guess. The blackout has been lifted to a considerable extent. That is the biggest change in the city. Hurry up and kill those Japs and get back here.

I would write this letter with greater enthusiasm if I were sure you would get it. China seems far enough away in peace times, but in days like these I have a feeling when I write to such distant points that I might as well tear the letter up and throw it out of the window. But I earnestly hope that you will get this, and God bless you.

Sincerely yours,
Ross

*Sayre was in Europe attached to the Special Service Division of the War Department.*

TO JOEL SAYRE

*THE NEW YORKER*
*NOVEMBER 22, 1943*

Dear Sayre:

We didn't see our way clear to using this piece by Sergeant Hine, I regret to report. We are getting quite an inflow of pieces on the war now, largely from old timers around the place who of course know pretty well what we want, and on top of that space is getting scarce, and going to get scarcer. We don't need so many secondary pieces.

Primary pieces, now, are a different matter, and why in God's name don't you write some, may I ask? We hoped that when you got over there you might send back some good stories, or anyhow I personally hoped that. I've been hoping for many, many months now that you'd write, and I take this opportunity of urging you again to do so, damn it.

I hate to send this piece back so far, but I don't know what else to do with it. It is, thoughtfully, on flimsy [paper] and won't burden the mails so much. I am returning one copy only, though, and if you or Sergeant Hine has any instructions as to where to send the other with a view to possible publication, we will send it, having a nice clean copy made if necessary. Let me know if we can do anything about it.

You have been put on the complimentary list to receive the magazine, and I hope to God you get it, but magazines don't seem to get through the mail to you fellows abroad much. All we can do is send the copies off, properly addressed, which we are doing faithfully.

Good luck, and God bless you, and please write something. I hope some copies do get through to remind and encourage you.

As ever,

Ross

TO FRANK SULLIVAN

*[UNDATED]*

Dear old toff:

I inquired about a job for your young lady secretary and regret to report nothing doing. All I've been doing the last two weeks is to inquire about jobs for people, unsuccessfully in every instance. I even wrote Mrs. Vincent Astor, in re Red Lewis, of old Company C, 18th Engineers, my old squad mate, who was under the blissful impression that if he could get to Mrs. Astor he'd get a job as deck steward on one of the Astor steamships. I don't think I ever told you, Frank, but Mrs. Astor was one of the canteen lassies at Bordeaux, France, when I was stationed there and I have social contacts far more important than Alma Clayburg (who has just started seasonal operations on a broad front, incidentally; you otto come down). Red said Mrs. Astor had once said if you're ever in need of anything in civilian life, come to me. On Red's behalf I wrote Mrs. Astor. No answer. As a matter of fact, my association with the wealthy has never profited me a cent; just cost me money. I'm going back with the Irish. . . .

Yours sincerely,

Ross

## MEMO TO JOSEPH MITCHELL

*[DECEMBER 1943]*

Mr. Mitchell:

I have read the piece on Mr. Flood and am a great admirer of it. I may be prejudiced because my father was Scotch-Irish and would have been like this old fellow if he'd lived long enough. My Uncle John, the famous founder of the Pillar of Fire, was more like Mr. Wall in that he got in his rut and stayed there despite everything, by God. He lived with his daughter, though, which this fellow didn't. I suggested a couple of little additions on points I was honestly interested in, but you know what to do about those if you don't agree.

Ross

## MEMO TO RAOUL FLEISCHMANN

*JANUARY 3, 1944*

Mr. Fleischmann:

Peter Arno asks that he be put on the complimentary circulation list. He has always had to buy the magazine. I say yes unless there is some government regulation against it. His address is 417 Park Avenue.

H. W. Ross

MEMO TO JANET FLANNER

*THE NEW YORKER*
*JANUARY 31, 1944*

Miss Flanner:

To me the Pétain pieces were engrossing and thrilling and I think they will undoubtedly be considered likewise by a large number of readers. There was a mental hazard between them and me before I started reading them because of the mountainous responsibility I had assumed in lightly suggesting them—or in suggesting a "piece" on Pétain. It would be desecration, God knows, to call this work a piece, so I shall hereafter, through the years, refer to it as a "study."

I don't think I've ever seen so thorough, so interesting, and so engrossing a study in a magazine, and printing this will probably be a milestone in American journalism. I don't know what our debutant subscribers and the younger married set will think about this, but our savant clientele will be profoundly impressed and a great many other adults, for the series has a surge to it that makes it almost a romantic adventure piece.

I now think your time was well spent and that probably you'll be offered a chair of French History in some Middle Western University.

H. W. Ross

TO CHADBOURNE, WALLACE, PARKE & WHITESIDE

*THE NEW YORKER*
*FEBRUARY 10, 1944*

Gentlemen:

I have your letter of February 9th. It seems to be written in ignorance of my letters to you of September 1st, 1943, September 17th, 1943, and December 30th, 1943 (enclosing a check for seven hundred fifty dollars). I refer you back to these letters for a partial explanation of my situation. As soon as I get some dough I'll send it along. At the moment, I'm not very flush, and also I'm bewildered. I call attention to the fact that I have pulled the Jane Grant account down from $10,775 to $6,177.50, one way or another, which seems heroic to me, and that

I'm working like a little major here seven days a week trying to keep this publication going in the midst of an incredible manpower shortage, and thereby keep Miss Grant going, which also seems heroic to me. What I ought to get is a vote of appreciation and confidence, but then life isn't that way, I guess.

Sincerely yours,

H. W. Ross

TO JOHN O'HARA

*THE NEW YORKER*
*MARCH 8, 1944*

Dear John:

I regret to report that there is nothing doing as to the proposed $3,200 advance. I formally put it up to the big-scale fiscal man and the result was a laugh, in which, in the end, I joined. I couldn't put up any story as to how the company would get its money back out of bonuses, or anything else, since you've had just one story in here since the last chunk of dough went to you (to the best of my recollection), and when we asked you to fix that up slightly you refused to do it. I fervently hope that some day you will be fair with the world and with yourself and rework your stories when warranted. All other writers that I know of do it, and they all can't be wrong.

Sincerely yours,

Ross

*Streger was a literary agent.*

TO PAUL STREGER

*THE NEW YORKER*
*MARCH 30, 1944*

Dear Paul:

Two minutes after I talked to you on the phone yesterday, I thought of something I should have mentioned to you. I'll set it down now. Do you remember Hugh Wiley, who wrote the Wildcat (colored gent) stories for the *Saturday Evening Post* around the '20s? If not, he was a sensational success for a period of several years. Well, he put his savings in *Saturday Evening Post* stock. He bought it at two hundred forty dollars per share, under the advice of George Horace Lorimer. *Saturday Evening Post* stock went down to something like $0.62 1/2, and Wiley was wiped out. He took to the bottle, etc., and is in the inevitable situation of anyone who follows the rum path.

He was an enormously inventive guy, though, and might still be meat as a writer for the movies. I thought I ought to report him to you. If you should be interested, I can put you on his track. He's a much saner person than some I could name.

If you find that Winterich is the man who is holding up Shaw's play, let me know, and I will drop him a line requesting action.

Sincerely,

Ross

TO DOROTHY PARKER

*The New Yorker*
*April 12, 1944*

Dear Dottie:

It pains me to have to say so, but we think that this ["Epitaph for Lily-Colored Southerners"] is more propaganda than verse, and I think it contains a couple of flaws in fact, too. I think Negroes do pray beside the whites in Catholic churches in the South, and earth isn't black, or very little earth, especially down there, where red clay is the general surface. But aside from that, I don't believe any progress is made by printing violent and bitter things about this race business. This verse is truly dynamite; incitement to riot. I think the solution of the colored problem is something to be approached comprehensively and calmly.

I trust to God you will understand.

Sincerely,

Ross

*When John Hersey wrote the story of the wreck of John F. Kennedy's PT Boat-109, Joseph P. Kennedy tried to transplant it to the* Reader's Digest, *the broader exposure being helpful to young Kennedy's burgeoning political career.*

## TO JOSEPH P. KENNEDY

*THE NEW YORKER*
*MAY 18, 1944*

Dear Ambassador Kennedy:

I got busy at once in the matter of that story about your son. To begin with, I found that Shawn, the editor here who handles the fact, or journalistic, side of the magazine, had been trying for two years to get a story out of Hersey and was in a glow of satisfaction at having finally got one.... The story was morally ours, and I couldn't see how I could possibly be a party to its withdrawal from *The New Yorker.*

The day after I talked to you, Shawn talked to your son, who telephoned from Miami to report that Navy Public Relations wanted the story in a magazine of large national circulation because *New Yorker* readers didn't have to be convinced of the value of the navy, or of the PT boat section of the navy. The inference, if not the statement, was that the masses of the nation did have to be convinced of the value of the navy, or of the PT boats; or something like that. I am probably oversimplifying the viewpoint of Navy Public Relations, but at any rate I had no patience with it, believing firmly that the American public does have a sufficient appreciation of, and reliance in, the navy and its PT boats, and the story having been of our origination and not the navy's, and being palpably ours and not the navy's. Your son raised a second point: He said that the *Reader's Digest* had offered to pay two thousand dollars more for the story than we would pay, no matter what that was, and that he and his navy associates felt this money should go to the widow of one of the men in his crew.

All of these goings-on led us to believe that we were more or less being chivvied around by a bunch of heavyweights, and since we have long had a feeling here that we *are* kicked around a great deal by the big fellows, or in behalf of the big fellows, we were not disposed to lay down now.

It was finally decided that we would use the story as we had planned in this instance but that we would make an exception to our rule of not allowing reprints in the *Reader's Digest.* That decision seems fair to us. We run our story, the *Reader's Digest* gets it, you get your national circulation, the navy fulfills its ambition to get the story before the masses, and the sailor's widow gets her two thousand dollars, or whatever the *Digest* pays....

I earnestly hope that the decision is as satisfactory to all concerned as it seems to us, and especially that it is satisfactory to you.

Very sincerely yours,

H. W. Ross

P.S. We also decided that if the *Digest* should not reprint the story we will pay the sailor's widow the two thousand dollars she would have got from the *Digest,* so if the *Digest* doesn't come through, she and *The New Yorker,* the little people, will be satisfied. I think the author would be satisfied, too. I neglected to mention him in the above, but he is important, and I think that since he wrote the story for *The New Yorker* he would want it to appear here, initially at least.

## TO ALVA JOHNSTON

*MAY 19, 1944*

Dear Johnston:

I've read the three pieces and laughed all the way through them. You are still as wonderful as ever, probably more so. If Shawn and I get a vacation this summer it will probably be due to you and these pieces, which also ought to provide a lot of readers with a good escape from the current realities....

You had that story about Rickenback (I forget spelling) dropping nickels for Francis X. Bushman and causing a mob of followers. R. once told me about how he did this and he also once told me a wonderful story about Bushman's personal life that you might damned well use sometime. Stop me if you've heard it. Bushman was the greatest screen idol of his day, up to that point, and his employers always billed him as a single man, or let it be generally assumed that he was single, and virginal, too, I guess. Secretly he had a wife and five children, a situation that would have overwhelmed any star. The employers got along fine until he got stuck on Beverly Baines, his leading lady, and wanted to get a divorce and marry her. There was hell to pay. The employers tried to buy him off, and did for awhile, I think; they pointed out the advantages of illicit sin, etc. In the end Bushman got beyond them and they called in Rickenback, who was practically Bushman's founder. R. pulled all the arguments he could thing of— shattered career, big scandal, and so on, and got nowhere. Bushman completely bull-headed. Finally R. pointed out that he was a Catholic, his ace card, and that the Catholic Church would never stand for such a divorce. Bushman looked at him incredulously and asked, "Is the Catholic Church bigger than Francis X. Bushman?"

With admiration and best wishes,
Ross

TO PETER ARNO

*The New Yorker*
*May 22, 1944*

Dear Peter:

Herewith a report on the scheduling of your drawings in the past several months. You had sixteen drawings in twenty-one weeks, counting two covers, which seems to me an excellent showing by the layout department, considering the handicaps they were under, principally the almost complete absence of smaller-than-page drawings on the bank. With so many elements to take into consideration, especially at change-of-season times, you simply have to be left out from time to time if you don't have some small drawings around. As Forster says in his note, if we have small drawings we can use you practically every week. You will note from this report that there was a period when you had practically nothing on the bank, and that at this writing you have only four on the bank, which is not many. Personally, I am against going down to nothing with your bank, for several reasons, which I won't go into here. I will say that one of them is that we need a variety of drawings, God knows, to balance up the book and avoid conflicts in scene, wording, characters, etc., and that we really ought to carry eight or ten of your drawings on the bank to do the thing as it should be done.

Sincerely,

Ross

TO E. B. WHITE

*THE NEW YORKER*
*JUNE 6, 1944*

Dear White:

Herewith the form, which I had no difficulty in filling out, due to your brilliant instructions. If I had you at my elbow all the time I would get ahead in the world. More of my time goes into trying to find where to sign such documents as this than into my regular job....

I shall expect the piece entitled, "About Myself." Please do not arouse my hopes thus and then let me down. As to me, my eyes are hazel. People often ask me what color my eyes are, and I answer, "Hazel." I learned this from my army discharge, which detailed several of my more salient features in a rugged way. It says on the back:

BORN: Aspen, Colo.

EYES: Hazel.

HORSEMANSHIP: None.

MARKSMANSHIP: Never qualified.

That was about all.

The invasion has started and everyone is agog.

As ever,

Ross

*At Thurber's urging, Ross was attempting to hire De Vries, then editor of* Poetry *magazine, but money was an issue.*

## TO PETER DE VRIES

*[1944]*

Mr. De Vries:

There is to be a cost of living payment at the end of the year, and it will, it now occurs to me, considerably more than make up the difference in the pay set for you and the amount set by you as minimum, basic living costs. I didn't think of this at the time. It came to me while discussing finances the other evening. As a matter of fact, at the time we talked, there was no official word that the bonus would be paid, although it was in the bag. You will get a lump of money, and the thing to do is ration yourself out of it at a certain rate per week. Mentally, I mean.

Ross

## MEMO TO EDMUND WILSON

*JUNE 27, 1944*

Mr. Wilson:

I assume that the reference to Nero's wearing a monocle in the Italian film was written and edited in complete ignorance of the existence of the emerald monocle. There is a chance that either the reporter or the rewriter of the story, or both, knew it and left it out, elliptically. Satisfied with the fact, or the supposition, that the monocle Nero wore in the picture was a modern monocle merely. That is unlikely, though. I'll look into it if I have time, but this is war, and my mood is defeatist. Whatever happened it was a mistake and I thank you for letting me know about it.

I don't agree with you at all that the Newsbreak on the Russian grammar was lowbrow. I don't think the level of the brow can be brought into question at all. It certainly can't as I read it when I put it through, and as I reread it now. White, in the line he wrote, took a crack at the lady author of a book for her bland statement that an obviously difficult explanation of Russian word forms is "Quite understandable and easy to remember." White says, "You don't know us (me)." He thereby denies that it is "quite understandable," that it is "easy to remember," merely that. My belief is that only a question of memory is involved, or an aptitude for difficult languages, or of human temperament. His viewpoint may be provincial at worst. . . . I don't think at all that it would be sidesplitting to tell a Russian that *I went* is the past of *I go*, but I think it might be worthy of a light comment if he were told that it was quite understandable and easy to remember.

As to the Cummings quote, I disagree with you also as to the point involved. As I understand that item, White wasn't picking on Cummings's queer way of expressing himself, he was picking on what Cummings said, in his queer way. Translate that into straight non-queer English and you have a "thought" so trite and worn (i.e., "Art is a mystery") that it is astonishing that even an art dealer would use it to lend tone to a catalogue. The queerness of Cummings's expression is irrelevant. White has been running those "thoughts" for years, much of the time picking on aged windy statements.

Please do not let the fact that I argue deter you from making any other remarks that you care to make; I would appreciate getting them. I appreciate knowing about Nero's monocle, but what I'll do about it I don't know. . . .

H. W. Ross

*A heavy smoker from his teens, Ross sent in an order like this one every few weeks.*

TO THE ORDER DEPARTMENT, BENSON & HEDGES

*THE NEW YORKER*
*JUNE 29, 1944*

Gentlemen:

Will you please send three cartons of Parliament cigarettes to me at the above address, and charge them to my account.

Thank you.

Yours very truly,

H. W. Ross

*A* Stars and Stripes *colleague of Ross's, Early was a secretary to President Roosevelt.*

TO STEPHEN T. EARLY

*THE NEW YORKER*
*JULY 3, 1944*

Dear Lieutenant:

I send you the enclosed, knowing you will be interested if you've got time to read it. That I sent it to you should forever be held confidential. It is a sort of plea that some little thing ought to be done, from time to time, about General Pershing, as a humane matter. It is from a distinguished member of the old guard, to which you belong. Personally I get riled occasionally at the highly patronizing attitude of the present army bunch about the last war. The way they talk, you'd think it was the Spanish-American War.

Remember, I am the man who notified you some years ago about Bernard Baruch being on the verge of cutting his throat because he had been kept so long in the dog house, with the result that he was immediately let out, as nearly as I could figure, and since has risen to even greater heights as a leader in national affairs. I get into national affairs only once every seven years myself.

In the Pershing case, I think a lot of old vets of the last war feel as I do, that he might well be openly cherished a little. Possibly the President ought to call on him or something. Maybe his birthday comes up soon.

With respect and regards and the hope that you are not being worked to death.

Ross

P.S. I find that Pershing's birthday is September 13th, almost two full months before election, when two million old A.E.F. soldiers vote.

H.W.R.

MEMO TO TED COOK

*JULY 27, 1944*

Mr. Cook:

There are a great many good stories that cannot be told now, for security reasons. We will be able to use these after the war, when censorship ceases. I advocate that your office begin outlining now any such ideas for post-war use. We would do well to have a bank of ideas to start work on as soon as peace comes. Radar, for instance, is an obvious one, and I suggest you outline that. I am putting through an idea on the German radio station, Atlantique, which is certainly a good idea. I'd title these ideas "Now It Can Be Told"—as working title.

H. W. Ross

TO JOSEPH P. KENNEDY

*THE NEW YORKER*
*AUGUST 14, 1944*

Dear Mr. Ambassador:

Now it is I who have a problem. Some years ago I put up the money for a fellow to open a restaurant in Hollywood and to the astonishment of everybody it has been a big success. I recently had a conference with my partner out there (in regard to converting from a corporation to a partnership to see if we can save anything from taxes) and he told me that he sorely needs some Haig & Haig pinch bottle and could do with some St. James, too. If there is anything in the world you can do about this, will you please take action?

My man says it would improve his face in the Pacific Coast no end if you personally ordered Young's Market out there to deliver to him one hundred cases of Haig & Haig and fifty cases of St. James. He would, however, be happy to get twenty-five cases of each. Needless to say, the delivery of this whiskey would also improve my face on the Pacific Coast.

The place is Chasen's, 9039 Beverly Boulevard, Hollywood, California, and the boss's name is Dave Chasen. It is a well-known place out there. It is possible that you have eaten there. Anyhow, one or more of your sons have. It would be a good high spot for your brands, being patronized by many big shots, including the Roosevelts.

I will appreciate anything you can do.

Sincerely yours,

H. W. Ross

P.S. I have word that Dr. Jordan has gone to the state of Washington and I'm smoking like a locomotive.

H.W.R.


TO ROBERT FROST

*THE NEW YORKER*
*SEPTEMBER 4, 1944*

Dear Mr. Frost:

I have received a disturbing letter from E. J. Kahn, who worked in this office for several years and is now in the Army, stationed in Washington. It contained a paragraph which I quote below:

> "One other matter: Colonel Ulmer, of the *Infantry Journal,* was at the Breadloaf Writers Conference, and says that there was a fairy up there, by name of Truman Capoti or something like that, who claimed to write the Talk of the Town, and who created a scene by walking conspicuously out of an auditorium where Robert Frost was reading a poem. Capoti (the spelling is phonetic) had been loudly identifying himself as a *New Yorker* staff member (is he? I've never heard of him), and Frost was accordingly prompted to say that 'Well, if that's the way *The New Yorker* feels about my poetry, I'll just stop reading.' Whereupon he stopped. It was, says Colonel Ulmer, a highly embarrassing situation for all concerned, and did not improve *The New Yorker*'s standing at the conference one whit. Did you know anything about this? If you didn't, I think you should, because I know how sensitive you are about what people do as representatives of the magazine."

You will see why the letter distressed me. The facts are that this fellow, Truman Capote (not Capoti), was employed here for a while as an office boy. He wouldn't have been employed here ever as that probably, if it hadn't been for the man- and boy-power shortage. We have checked up and found that he did attend the Breadloaf Conference—so that much is true at least. I am told that he was sent there by some publisher for whom he has contracted to do a book. Amazing things are happening in publishing circles these days.

I will very much appreciate if you will tell me how much of Mr. Kahn's hearsay report is accurate, what did happen, and supply me with the name of some official of the conference to whom I might write in explanation. I was going to say apology, but the fact is I don't feel any responsibility for this youth. We get into something like this every once in a while, though, and when we can, we try to make a disavowal on behalf of the organization.

Sincerely yours,
Ross

## TO E. B. WHITE

*[SEPTEMBER 5, 1944]*

White:

I earnestly wish that you would be thinking about a peace editorial, and be prepared to say something when the day comes. It looks to me as if it might be tomorrow if the Germans can run fast enough. For all I know they're going to keep right on retreating until the kind Americans take Germany and protect the country from the Russians. If they've got that secret weapon they'd better use it quick, and it better be good.

Ross

*Sullivan was with Chadbourne, Wallace, Parke & Whiteside.*

## TO ROBERT SULLIVAN

*THE NEW YORKER*
*OCTOBER 3, 1944*

Dear Mr. Sullivan:

I have finally raised some money, or am on the verge of doing so, and I am disposed to take advantage of the proposition you make in your letter (third paragraph) to me on June 29th, i.e., I think I'd like to buy a thousand shares of F-R [*New Yorker*] stock on behalf of Miss Grant on the basis you outline. Will you please let me know if you people and your client are disposed to go through with this now?

This is a matter that should be handled fairly soon, for there will a kind of melon cutting at the end of the year and it would be to the best interests of all of us if Miss Grant got in on it, I think.

I am sorry I have delayed so. My personal finances have been extremely complicated, and my job has been the same all year. I've been hard pressed all around.

Sincerely yours,
H. W. Ross

*Since his return to the Comment page White had been propounding the controversial idea of a "world government." Ross found his argument eloquent if rather naive, but nonetheless felt White had earned the right to use the magazine's editorial platform any way he saw fit.*

MEMO TO E. B. WHITE

*SUNDAY [OCTOBER 1944]*

White:

Your new last sentence for the long Comment came through and we used that one, everyone agreeing that it was clearer and just what was needed. I was going to write you a couple of weeks ago about your new world line of Comments and then didn't because I thought you were coming down. All I was going to say, though, was that they seem to me to be the most eloquent things you have ever written and magnificent. My viewpoint is that if the people of the earth don't get a new set-up, they are being offered a very remarkable line of writing and thinking anyhow. You (collective) can't lose on that basis. And damned if I don't think you're having some effect. You've moved me, for one, and I'm a cynic from 1922, and I must be legion, and the President has released the Dumbarton Oaks proposals so that the people of the world can shoot at them and formulate an opinion, and I wouldn't be astonished if you have had an influence on some of the conference delegates and the President, too. Those boys are sensitive to the clearly and forcefully printed word.

I say dismiss any fear that you might make the magazine a crank publication. Probably that's what it ought to be, if the crankiness is sound. There is no question you are sound; the uncertain factor is how soon will such truths be effective. But aside from all that and from everything else, you made the Comment page what it is, God knows, and I have for long regarded it as yours to the extent that you want to use it. That is not only the right way to look at the matter, but very sound business, I am convinced. I say carry on without hesitation or qualm.

Ross

*James was managing editor of* The New York Times.

TO EDWIN JAMES

*THE NEW YORKER*
*NOVEMBER 6, 1944*

Dear James:

A man named James A. Coldwell (567 W. 133d Street, University 4-2498) called in to see me, wanting a job. He is an old San Francisco copy reader and pal of mine, although to tell you the truth I don't remember him very well. It has been more than twenty-five years since I was in San Francisco. He told me he wants to work on the *Times* above everything and that he'd seen you. I volunteered to drop you a line, why God knows, for every newspaperman I've ever got a job for during my whole life has immediately got drunk and kicked the city editor in the chin, etc. It is just possible that this man might not do that. He looks conservative and calm, and I'm entitled to one break in this respect before I die.

Sincerely yours,

Ross

*In October 1944, Ring Lardner's son David was killed while reporting for the magazine in Europe.*

## MEMO TO RAOUL FLEISCHMANN, LLOYD PAUL STRYKER, AND HAWLEY TRUAX

*NOVEMBER 9, 1944*

Mr. Fleischmann, Mr. Stryker, Mr. Truax:

It occurs to me that if you want a trustee with discretion for the money to be set aside for the Lardner children, that you might name John Lardner with his brother Ring, Jr., as a substitute in the event of his demise. The mother could be named if both die, I guess. The Lardners are a bad risk, I think. The one that was killed in Spain [James] was hell bent to get into the war, being not satisfied as a correspondent. David, we now learn, was oblivious to buzz bombs during his stay in London, and now John is going to the Jap war regardless. Maybe there's a compulsion in the family.

H. W. Ross

## MEMO TO A. J. LIEBLING

*NOVEMBER 27, 1944*

Mr. Liebling:

I quote below a paragraph from a letter from Robert Sherwood:

"I want to add a word of overwhelming appreciation of Liebling's stuff. Having seen something of the scenes on which he reports, it is my opinion that he has done a better job than any of the others—and I said so to the chief army public relations officer in London last spring when Liebling was having some difficulty getting to France."

I saw Sherwood in person subsequently, and he was more lavish than in the above. He thinks you are the best war correspondent there is, and apparently he gave army public relations quite a lecture—said our circulation was no indication of our importance, that every editor in the United States read *The New Yorker*, terrific influence, etc.

H. W. Ross

*True to his word, Ross was unyielding in his campaign to safeguard the rights of authors. Here he is writing his friends Crouse and F.P.A. as officers of the Authors League.*

TO RUSSEL CROUSE

THE NEW YORKER
NOVEMBER 27, 1944

Dear Mr. Crouse:

I call the attention of you gentlemen to the enclosed legal opinion from attorney Alexander Lindey, a copyright expert and the author of a book on copyright. He says, in effect, that all stories and drawings reprinted in anthologies should bear an individual copyright notice. Not only does Lindey say this, but he cites the concurring opinion of the Acting Register of Copyrights in Washington. And not only that, I have asked four or five other legal and technical authorities about this important copyright point and they all agree with Lindey and the Register of Copyrights.

The practice of the book publishers is not to put individual copyright notices on stories and drawings they reprint in anthologies, and the consequence of this seems to be that the copyright of practically every story and drawing printed in an anthology for many years (and they are legion these days, gentlemen) has been lost to the author. I have told a couple of publishers about this and have found them incredulous. When I insisted flatly on the facts they said breathlessly that there have been few cases of piracy in recent publishing history, that regardless of the technicalities of the law the authors are in little danger of losing their property because publishers are gentlemen, observe trade practices, etc. I am of the opinion that writers and artists should not depend on that flimsy status quo indefinitely. Some publisher, new or old in the business, is going to cut loose and have a hell of a time printing stories and pictures that authors and artists (and their publishers) blissfully think are protected by law, and aren't.

There should be widespread dissemination of the facts, and insistence upon protection by all authors and artists.

Yours sincerely,

H. W. Ross

cc: Mr. Franklin P. Adams

Mr. James Thurber

*While vacationing in Virginia, Thurber sustained a ruptured appendix and peritonitis, nearly killing him. Ross had sent money to help the Thurbers through the emergency.*

TO HELEN THURBER

*THE NEW YORKER*
*NOV. 30 [1944]*

Dear Helen:

I didn't break my neck. The way things are these days I either do a thing instantly or don't get it done for days or weeks, as it gets sidetracked. One hour's relaxation and my desk, couch, table, chair, and everything else is covered with papers.

Honest to God, I was scared to death when I heard "perotinitus" [*sic*]. I'm afraid of that, even with the modern drugs, especially in a railroad hospital in Virginia. I'm told, though, that surgeons are first class all over the country now, and I guess that's the case. Anyhow, I thought Jim might claw and bite. Give him my admiration, and ditto to you, and you have but to call if you want anything, of course. Keep him down there until he can walk. Wheeling him through town might have a permanent effect on him. Also, he might get cold and wet. The weather is lousy here.

Ross

*As part of his divorce agreement with Frances, Ross made all the decisions as to Patty's schooling. He knew his daughter was intelligent, but she was a slow learner. He had doctors examine her repeatedly and moved her from school to school trying to address the problem. It wasn't until she was an adult that Patty learned she was dyslexic.*

## TO VIRGINIA HIRST

THE NEW YORKER
DECEMBER 4, 1944

Dear Miss Hirst:

I enclose a check for Patty's tuition, and I expect that some one of these days I shall meet you. I am going to try to get up to that school early some afternoon and have a talk about Patty. I am glad that you think she has made progress, especially because of the fact that I got a telephone call from Miss Smith at the school (or my wife did) saying that Patty was evincing no sense of responsibility at all and hadn't bothered to get her lessons for a couple of weeks. There was a mistake in signals, or I would have seen that she got the lessons: I understood that she didn't have homework if she did the lessons at school and that I would be notified at once if she didn't. Patty doesn't like to study as much as I should hope, and she doesn't seem to have any pride to speak of so far as marks are concerned, which is annoying and baffling. I guess she's been getting away with murder. The most hopeful theory I have is that she missed so much schooling for two successive years, because of colds, whooping cough, etc., that she never got into the habit of studying and is going to find it very hard to do so now.

At any rate, my gratitude.

Sincerely,

H. W. Ross

## TO JAMES THURBER

*THE NEW YORKER*
*DECEMBER 13, 1944*

Mr. Thurber:

The checking of the names in your Natural History series has revealed that only one name is a real name, the one Rea Irvin happened to know about: there is an actual fish called the pout.

You have a bird called a shriek. In real life there is a bird called a shriker and also one called a shrike. I should think the approximation here does not matter.

There is a bee called a lapidary, but you have drawn an animal.

You have a clock tick. There is, of course, a tick. No matter, I say. There is a bird called a ragamuffin. You have drawn a ragamuffin plant. No real conflict.

H. W. Ross

## MEMO TO JAMES GERAGHTY

*DECEMBER 20, 1944*

Mr. Geraghty:

Lobrano and I decided that this was not so hot for a war year and to hold over for later use—next year, if conditions permit. (That is no reason for holding up the execution of it, however.) Also, Lobrano and I both think earnestly that there must be a lot more people in the scene. It must be a big party—fifteen or twenty people in sight one way or another and perhaps more suggested. A little bunch of three or four people wouldn't sit around this way and wait for noise-makers; only a party would do that. In other words, more of a picture. I think this idea with Taylor doing it is worth a full page, and I'd have him build it up on that scale.

H. W. Ross

encl. R. Taylor rough. Caption: "For God's sake get them on the phone again, Parker. The noise-makers should at least be on the way."

## TO RICHARD RODGERS

*THE NEW YORKER*
*JANUARY 29, 1945*

Dear Richard:

The status of that Walter Mitty story at the moment is that [Sam] Goldwyn has paid one thousand dollars for an option for sixty days and can come into possession of it by paying fourteen thousand dollars more at the end of that period. When he came through with the grand he is supposed to have expressed doubt that he would go through with the deal, having misgivings about getting it adapted properly, but since then Thurber has had two offers of thirty thousand dollars for the story, and I should think that might clinch things with Goldwyn. If he can't get the thing in shape for himself, I should think he would grab the fifteen-thousand-dollar profit, or try to.

On the other hand, one of the thirty-thousand-dollar offers came from Nunnally Johnson, who wanted the story for Jack Benny, and apparently the second offer came from a man who had Benny in mind. Now by a coincidence, I happened to see Jack Benny the other night and I asked him about it. He was very vague about the whole thing. He had been given the story to read, but apparently had got bewildered by it. I gathered that this might be due to overwork. In the course of the conversation, Benny said that he wanted to do a New York show, and it occurs to me now that you, Hammerstein, Benny, and Thurber could all get together—providing Goldwyn doesn't take up his option. You could do the show and then sell it to the movies afterward, and everybody would be intensely happy.

In any event, Goldwyn is only buying the movie rights, leaving the stage still wide open. I don't know whether you fellows would be interested in a story that has already been done in the movies. I shouldn't think it would matter, for, from my viewpoint, most stuff that goes into the movies might as well go into the wastebasket as far as the great public is concerned.

I am referring this whole business to Thurber, for it is getting beyond my depth. I only crashed into this business as a fan of the story and as an admirer of you and Hammerstein. I have always thought it had great stage and screen possibilities.

Let me know what you think, if anything, and I will do anything I can that is helpful, although the man this situation demands at this point is really Jake Shubert.

Sincerely,

Ross

cc: Mr. Thurber

TO ORSON WELLES

*THE NEW YORKER*
*JANUARY 31, 1945*

Dear Orson:

I was astonished at your column in yesterday's *Post*, in which you say *The New Yorker* sneers at you. You were brimful of prunes when you wrote that. Our piece was straightforward and sympathetic, and there wasn't a sneer in it, and it contained not one unfriendly or unkindly word. I read it carefully before it was published and I have just read it again. Several other people of sound judgment have read it, too, and they concur in my opinion.

Every once in a while such a thing as this comes up: someone misses the point of what we say about him and assumes that he is being spoofed. Almost invariably, this happens to people whose powers of discernment are blunted, either temporarily or permanently, by hypersensitivity or a sense of insecurity, or both. I don't know which of these states afflicted you the day before yesterday, but one or the other did, and as an old acquaintance and admirer, and one who earnestly has your welfare at heart, I advise you to beware of columning if it is going to continue to throw you off balance to this extent. Columning is a deadly occupation, leading frequently and successively to overzealousness, super-seriousmindedness, monomania, hysteria, and sometimes madness. When a columnist begins to take himself too seriously he is in grave danger. Look around. Look at what happened to Broun, Pegler, Winchell, and several others. Look at the states they got themselves in. But it took them years, whereas you got the heebee-jeebees in eight or ten days. If this condition continues, or recurs frequently, I urge that you wage your attack upon fascism, in which I sincerely wish you well, with some other weapon than the syndicated column. . . .

Sincerely yours,
Ross

TO CARL ROSE

*The New Yorker*
*January 31, 1945*

Dear Rose:

This check is unquestionably yours on the face of what you say, and damn it, you cash it and keep it. We make three different payments for this series, in addition to the payment to Williams for the drawing. Maloney is getting a small payment for each picture we run, no matter who thinks of the idea for the individual picture, for originating the series. (This is customary here; anyone who thinks of a series idea gets a royalty on each picture run, whether he has anything further to do with the series or not.) Then, second, whoever thinks of the idea for a picture gets paid our usual idea rate for the idea. Next, third, whoever writes the caption (if, as in this case, there is one) gets paid for that.

On your own say so, you are clearly entitled to payment or part payment for the idea since you "outlined roughly a few situations." Outlining roughly a situation constitutes providing an idea for a picture, so far as this series is concerned. You have been thinking that Maloney didn't get paid for writing the captions. He did. He didn't for a long, long time, because of the customary collapse of our bookkeeping system, but he finally did get paid and, in his opinion, got a few dollars that was coming to you. This, in his opinion, squares things, and I concur in his opinion, from what you both say.

Your home life sounds exactly like mine on a smaller scale. My wife's sister has been living in the place in the country with five children and her mother, the whole lot of them being more or less homeless for the moment because of the war, and the whole thing is very debilitating. The Russians are going to see us all through, and soon, however, and after that things will begin to get simpler—or more complicated; I don't know which.

As ever,
Ross

MEMO TO JOSEPH MITCHELL

*FEBRUARY 13, 1945*

Mr. Mitchell:

A writer named Lawton Mackall became the one thousandth man to speak to me in a laudatory manner about your Flood piece. He followed this by urging me to suggest to you that you do a story on the pigeons of New York. He thinks you are the only man to do this and says that it is as reasonable a subject as rats. I herewith pass the idea along for what it is worth, with some sympathy for the idea. I was in the Post Graduate hospital once for a week and all I could do was look out the window at East Side roofs and the pigeon activity was tremendous; gents were always waving fishing poles around scaring the pigeons into the air. I assume this was for exercise, for the pigeons returned as soon as the brandishing was over. Mackall says these fellows are mostly pigeon fanciers, rather than commercial raisers of pigeons, and that some New York pigeons are worth $1,200 for breeding purposes. The men have boxes that look like suitcases that they carry pigeons around in, to have them mate. I suspect that Mackall is getting homing pigeons mixed up with common eating pigeons, but it may be that all the privately owned pigeons in New York are homing pigeons (otherwise, why would they stay home all the time?). Maybe homing pigeons are as good eating pigeons as any others.

H. W. Ross

*Packard ran the magazine's fact-checking department.*

MEMO TO FRED PACKARD

*FEBRUARY 19, 1945*

Mr. Packard:
Does this item make any sense on fact—has a Boris of Bulgaria
been executed by the Russians, or has there been such a report that
anyone knows of?

H. W. Ross

*For nine unhappy months in 1931 Cain was Ross's managing editor. By
1945, however, he was the acclaimed creator of such novels as* The Postman
Always Rings Twice *and* Double Indemnity. *Cain had written his old
boss because the Optimist Joke hadn't appeared in the twentieth-anniversary
edition. The two-line joke, intentionally inverted, first appeared in the inau-
gural issue and was meant to send up the stale humor of the day. Ross had
reprinted the gag in every anniversary number since. It went like this:*
*Pop: A man who thinks he can make it in par.*
*Johnny: What is an optimist, Pop?*

TO JAMES M. CAIN

*THE NEW YORKER*
*MARCH 1, 1945*

Dear Jim:
The omission was intentional, and the decision fairly well considered. We ran that damned thing annually for nineteen years and finally weakened. Also, there is some talk of not running the
anniversary cover again. That won't be decided until ten minutes before schedule time next year. It always embarrasses me slightly and
we're the only magazine that celebrates an anniversary. Not even the
*Saturday Evening Post* does it.
I'm very glad to have heard from you and send good wishes on your
various successes, and my best regards. There was a hell of an argument the other night as to what movie star you were married to. It was

presumed that I should know, but I didn't. The general opinion was Myrna Loy, I believe, but I expressed a firm negative opinion on that.
    Sincerely,
    Ross


TO LYNN FONTANNE

*The New Yorker*
*March 13, 1945*

Dear Lynn:
    I got a big thrill out of hearing from you. I've heard *about* you considerably, and Alfred. I'll tell people nonchalantly that I've had a letter from you, and that may boost my social stock by a point or two. It's been sinking rapidly lately, one reason being that I have no social life to speak of. I'm working harder in this war than I did in the last one. And it isn't nearly so satisfying. I sit here while everybody else travels all around to strange quarters and does exciting things—or they sound exciting.
    Now these pieces won't do, I regret to say. They don't fit in anywhere. They're too slight to stand by themselves, particularly with paper the way it is. We haven't any space for secondary things. They have some merit. You can tell the author I said that, if you want, but I don't know where in the world they could be sold; an English publication might be better than an American one, but then the paper situation over there is far worse than here.
    I went to a party the other night given by Madeleine Sherwood and Marcia Davenport, the first large scale social affair in quite a while, and saw a number of old-timers. All seemed well, but a lot of the men folk weren't present. Bob Sherwood was, and is, in the Pacific somewhere, and a lot of other people are in various places. I see [S. N.] Behrman from time to time and he usually mentions you and Alfred and other people he saw on his recent trip to England, although whether he actually saw you then I don't know.
    Love to you both,
    Sincerely,
    Ross

TO H. L. MENCKEN

*THE NEW YORKER*
*MARCH 19, 1945*

Dear Mencken:

I duly received the reprint on American profanity and have read it with interest and profit. Damn it—if you'll pardon me—I wish I could be sure that none of the stuff you have been doing for the forthcoming book would have made pieces for us. . . .

Writing of the Holy Name Society you say that "numbers of those who are enrolled have apparently got wind of the fact that *hell* and *damn*, if unaccompanied by sacred names, are not . . . blasphemous . . .". That's correct. I've got wound stripes from my encounters with the Holy Name Society while engaged in getting out this home journal. The outfit as constituted locally—headed apparently by a monsignor, a police lieutenant, and a few other lay zealots—claims jurisdiction over all blasphemy, profanity, and all artificially opprobrious expressions. They regard *son of a bitch* and *bastard* as clearly within their sphere, and deplore *gosh* and all other euphemisms, I think. (I don't talk to them when the committee makes its periodical appearance in this office; we have a lad here who looks at them with a bleary eye and exudes a stale whiskey odor.) . . .

As ever,
H. W. Ross

TO JAMES THURBER

*THE NEW YORKER*
*MARCH 19, 1945*

Dear Thurber:

I will now wind up our present business negotiations by committing to paper the arrangement with you regarding your potential quantity bonus on writings and drawings:

*The New Yorker* has in effect a system whereby it pays all its fiction writers and all its artists on the following basis: If a writer in any twelve-month period turns in six acceptable stories he gets a bonus of 12-1/2% of the total payment for those stories, or if he turns in ten stories during the twelve-month period he gets a bonus of twenty-five percent; if an artist turns in twenty acceptable drawings he gets a bonus of ten percent, or if he turns in thirty-five drawings he gets a bonus of twenty percent.

*The New Yorker* recognizes you as a unique contributor in several respects. One—and the only one we need go into here—is that you are both an artist and writer. Considering this, *The New Yorker* deems that you should have a bonus cycle of two years instead of one, and that has been so ordered: If you turn in enough stories or enough drawings to qualify for any of our assorted bonuses in a twenty-four month cycle, you will be paid the bonuses.

This is effective forthwith, with the qualification that your bonus cycle cannot start earlier than February 25th (since a settlement has just been made as to your accrued bonuses).

Trusting that you know what I am talking about, I am, as ever,
Yours sincerely,
Ross

TO JAMES THURBER

*The New Yorker*
*March 23, 1945*

Dear Jim:

I can stand up against the reprint magazines all right. I'm in no position to say to authors, "Let us all refuse to give reprint rights," because I ain't part of the "us," but I can say to the management of this magazine "Let us refuse to allow other magazines to reprint our stuff because they are dirty competitors of ours" (although how far I would get with the management I cannot tell at the moment), nor have I a conviction of how far the management should go.

What I can't do is say to publishers that they are robbing authors, because I am not an author, and they can come right back at me and say I am robbing authors, too, or am a party to robbing them. It is true, at least, that I have been a party to robbing them, for I unquestionably sat around this joint for years and didn't see that authors were done right by.

I am having dinner Monday night with Russel Crouse, president of the Authors League, and Franklin P. Adams, director of same, and I will recommend to them a course of action. If they don't take it, I have other ideas, although I haven't time at the moment to do a great deal about them.

As ever,
Ross


## TO LILLIAN HELLMAN

*THE NEW YORKER*
*APRIL 2, 1945*

Dear Lillian:

I read the manuscript of that *Collier's* piece, and now I've also read it in print. I have nothing else to do but things like that these days. It gives me a good insight into the publication business; one can always learn. I was going to telephone you, and maybe I did and didn't get you; I forget. In any event, I will write this note and thereby get a rather large clump of paper off my table.

From our standpoint, you did a superficial piece, and it had on it the curse of every Russian piece I've read in years: you were personally conducted. The Russians are foolish and incompetent about their public relations to a weird degree, from where I sit. In your behalf, I will say that I don't think there is a journalist in the world who can do anything other than a rush superficial piece on Russia these days, because the Russians won't let them. I am honest to God hungry for information on Russia and I can't get it, and nobody else can get it either. If they change after the war and I last that long, I'm going to try to get some definitive stories out of the place. In the meantime, I'm not going to give it a second thought.

I'll take you to dinner any night next week you name. My wife is going to California to see her brother off to the Pacific and I can fit in to anything.

As ever,
Ross

TO FRANK SULLIVAN

*THE NEW YORKER*
*APRIL 4, 1945*

Dear Frank:

I will think over your problem. Meantime, I find a note on my desk that Miles Standish, Daniel Webster, Walter Raleigh, and Andrew Jackson are listed in the New York telephone book and that probably all other historical characters are also, including Julius Caesar. Why don't you do something about this? You might have them all in for cocktails, on paper.

As ever,

Ross

P.S. As to whether it was Pretty Boy Floyd or Baby Face Floyd— how can we be expected to know, being so cloistered? Maybe it was Baby Face Nelson.

TO FRANK SULLIVAN

*THE NEW YORKER*
*APRIL 5, 1945*

Dear Frank:

. . . I much appreciate your telling me of the discussion about the merits of various editors, and I regret deeply that I cannot reciprocate in kind. The fact is, since the subject has come up, I have heard nothing good of you in three years. Anyhow, I regard such discussions of editors as in a class with the debates I used to hear as a lad in Salt Lake City as to whether Fannie Brown or Helen Blazes was the best in the five-dollar bracket. . . .

As ever,

H. W. Ross

*Wallgren was governor of Washington.*

## TO MONRAD C. WALLGREN

*THE NEW YORKER*
*MAY 2, 1945*

Dear Mr. Governor:

Drop those state papers for a minute and read this.

I have a cousin, a first cousin, who was born in your fair city of Seattle about the time the L.C. Smith Building was put up and who is still nominally a resident of the state of Washington, I suppose, and therefore your responsibility. He is a victim of infantile paralysis and, as I understand it, has been disabled to about the extent of President Roosevelt. He has not, I regret to say, risen above this disability. I don't blame the poor bastard much; he had nothing to start with and nothing has ever happened to buoy him up. His mind seems to have got twisted up, too, to a certain extent: he has changed his name and, from a confidential report I got from a friend a year or so ago, has become a discouraged, embittered, and disagreeable customer. His name used to be Eastland. His father's name was Thomas Eastland and he was a soft-spoken insurance man around Seattle for many years, until his death, which I should say was twenty years ago.

I enclose a copy of a letter I have just received from the fellow, who is within a few years of being as old as I am. Please take time to read this, conscientiously, as a public official should. It will give you a line on how he thinks. For one thing, he thinks that I have a hell of a lot more money than I have. He asked me for one hundred fifty dollars, mostly to pay back taxes. I am not one to pay another's back taxes these days, by God, being just one jump and a half ahead of the jail-keeper myself, and I have sent him a small sum to buy a couple of clothes with and advised him what to tell the various federal and state tax people. I don't see how the hell they can put an invalid in jail, and if they do, he would seem to be as well off as he is now. He's been in Honolulu for some years and at one time was getting some help from some charitable outfit out there. They were giving him free medical services, or some such. He types and does office work, I am told, and is reasonably competent at that. Since the war started he has had some kind of job—which you will note he figures, perhaps soundly, he will lose when the war pressure is over.

Well, what I want to know is this: is there anything the state of Washington does for its invalided citizens in such a plight as this? Does it take any responsibility? Does it have any jobs it can give people like this, or any institution they can go to and get treatment and sustenance? What in God's name happens to all the millions that are raised for infantile paralysis victims by the President's Birthday Balls? Is any of that dough available for a fellow like this? Please give this matter your attention, and let me know, or have someone let me know. If Vierhus were alive I wouldn't be bothering you, but if you don't want to be bothered about such matters you shouldn't have gone into public office. Here is a common and forgotten man that some government agency ought to do something about, beyond question: the government must take care of its halt.

I happened to think of you in connection with this chap because I talked to Dave Chasen on the telephone the other day and he told me you had been around Los Angeles and threatened to invite the two of us to Washington to fish. Fishing is my dish, and if that is true, you can count on me with my last ounce of strength—if you can just get this damned war settled and let me get some manpower back so I don't have to work *every* day in the year. Please let me know when you get east again, or are going to get east. I will line up a band.

With very best wishes,

Ross

TO E. B. WHITE

*[JUNE 1, 1945]*

White:

The ultimate word on the weekend-mail-to-you business is that if a piece of mail makes the State of Maine Express at ten P.M. Saturday you get it Monday morning, unless there is a boggle. Please tell Katharine this, if you think of it, for she left a memo with me saying emphatically that things had to be mailed Friday here to reach you on Monday.

Miss Terry says, "Mrs. White knows nothing about the mails to Maine. I have been handling the mails for years." You can tell Katharine this or not, as your judgment dictates. What *I* think is that Miss Terry is right, and has been right, in theory but that Saturday mailings last year, and perhaps in earlier years, didn't go through as they theoretically should have because of the w[ar]. I suspect, for one thing, that mail we put in our mail chute here didn't get to the train for maybe twenty-four hours, although it's only a couple of blocks.

Ross

TO ERNEST BYFIELD

*THE NEW YORKER*
*JUNE 4, 1945*

Dear Ernie:

... The Chasen thing is a long story, most of which I hesitate to put on paper. The skeleton is this, however: A gent named Dan Silberberg, whom you may know, and I put up a little money for Dave to start with. We rigged it up so that we took notes for the cash we put in and took common stock in the joint as a bonus. Subsequently, I went out there and was convinced that Dave could go over big if given more capital, which Dan would not stand for. I took over Dan's interest (for cash) and gave Dave some more capital. It was only then that my investment in the place really amounted to anything, and by that time it looked like a cinch. This scheme of financing boomeranged badly when the government got stringent on taxes: there being no actual investment in the place, the government took eighty percent of all profits above $7,500. One year the place made about six times that, and the net to the business was under ten thousand dollars. I felt responsible for the set-up and figured I'd done Dave a dirty trick, which was true, though the act was inadvertent. ...

My sullen viewpoint is that any business that gets through the war whole is damned lucky, and that no money can be made with taxes as they are—or not by me. On *The New Yorker* here, millions pass under my nose, and right on into the government till. I've never worked so hard in my life as the last few years, and I've gone into the hole steadily. Nuts, is what I say. My how I have run on.

As ever,

H. W. Ross

## TO E. B. WHITE

Mr. White:

As to "compost" I only asked. An old man once worked for me in Connecticut and he made a ceremony of piling leaves in small, improvised circles of chicken wire all over the premises. He was sober and learned about it. He never told me he was composting the leaves, but I now know what he was doing.

I happened to have a dictionary at my elbow and I looked up that word. I had never seen it before, I think. I had the dictionary handy because I had been reading a Flanner piece. Whenever a Flanner piece shows up I grab the dictionary, knowing there will be five words, at least, I have never heard of. I usually, but not always, find her words, most of the time in the agate type at the bottom of the page. It has taken me years to realize how Flanner came about her odd and amazing vocabulary. She gives a reader the impression of knowing all the words in the languages, especially the unlikely ones. This isn't the case. Her girl friend with whom she lived for years in Paris, Solita Solano, studied medicine—specifically, I think, surgery. Flanner acquired a vast vocabulary of medical terms. And not only that, she acquired it in French. As a consequence of knowing these words, and having a vicarious medical education, her instinct is to use polysyllabic medical lingo whenever she hops into an explanation of anything. On top of this, she thinks as much in French as she does in English. She gets the French word and either imagines the English equivalent, or, just possibly, looks it up in an English medical dictionary. The result is amazing. If there is a remote, secondary word with a whiff of the meaning she is after, it gets into her copy. Never has a style, or at any rate a vocabulary, developed in such a peculiar way in my entire journalistic experience. . . .

Now as to "compost," having the dictionary handy, and being conscientious (and always looking up a new word when I have time—which isn't always), I looked this one up. I knew beforehand that a word with the syllable "compo" in it must relate to composition, or mixture. I didn't learn this at school, having learned only four Latin words in my formal education, but in my various experiences in the building business: "compo board," for instance, meaning a board composed of other boards. My dictionary did not give the meaning you quote. I have it before me at this moment. It doesn't say "to make into compost." It says "to treat with compost." The verb that is. "Compost," noun, is "a mixture ... of such substances as peat, leaf mold, manure, lime, etc." Nothing about any one of these substances alone and in itself being compost. The second definition of the verb in my dictionary is "To mingle, as different fertilizing substances, in a mass. ..." Mixing again, or composing. In other words, plainly no justification in my dictionary, and that was all I had to go on unless I checked further. If I had left this up to someone else that checking would have been done, all right; other dictionaries would have been consulted, or the *Rural New Yorker,* or some such, in an extremity. But the simplest thing to do was ask you. The fact is, I never really doubted you. Between you, a semi-practical farmer, and the dictionary, I would have bet on you. I have found my dictionary negligent in several respects lately; notably, in the case of the word "chisel," which damned near got me sued for libel by Marshall Field. ...

I had nothing to do with some of the minor changes marked above, and with one or two that are major, either. Problem No. 17 was presented to me late Thursday evening, messenger waiting to go to plant. Whitaker proof said sentence didn't parse. I didn't believe it until it was explained to me, patiently. Then I had to agree. ... It's all right for people to say that we are too fussy, that ten or twenty slightly ungrammatical sentences don't matter, but if (from where I sit) I break down on that the magazine would break down all along the line. If we find something wrong, it should be fixed, I claim, even if it is minute. We run Newsbreaks picking on everybody's frailties, and I think it's up to us to get out as clean a book, as to fact and grammar, as we can. ...

Ross

TO PAUL HYDE BONNER

*THE NEW YORKER*
*JUNE 13, 1945*

Dear Paul:

The boys have referred to me your letter of June 11th, because I was the guy that sponsored that canning-of-airplanes item and got the dope on it. I got it from a terrific industrialist, who mentioned it over the telephone, and it got into print at once, which probably will have astonished him no end. This fellow is one of the few big manufacturers I know. I'm going to send your letter to him and have some fun. We haven't enough space to run letters, anyhow, these days, vital or not. I'll let you know if I get a rise. I think this fellow is clutching at a straw.

I won't get you into any personal fuss; you needn't be concerned about that.

Love to Mrs. B.

As ever,

Ross

TELEGRAM TO EDMUND WILSON

*JUNE 25, 1945*

Shawn on vacation few days. We feel cannot now have another long piece London without changing the name of magazine and there is no space and your subjects would infringe on normal London Letters. Main consideration is space of which we have practically none. Your plans for Italy and Greece and return in August seem satisfactory. Have not read Malraux article yet. It seems brutal on length.

Regards,

H. W. Ross

*As the war neared an end, Ross, exhausted from his grueling workload and bitter about his desultory financial situation, quietly informed* The New Yorker's *officers of his intention to quit. They responded with a sweetened compensation offer. After looking it over, Ross sent a reply to*

*Wall Street attorney Stryker, head of* The New Yorker's *executive committee.*

## TO LLOYD PAUL STRYKER

*JULY 4, 1945*

Dear Lloyd:

I will remark as follows as to your proposal of the other evening. I still admire its ingenuity, but it seems to have the fatal defects of all the other arrangements I have made through the years, to my gradual and inevitable ruin. I think there are two fundamental flaws. One is that the major owner of *The New Yorker* is a fool and that the venture therefore is built on quicksand. Another is that you envisage another employment contract for me, and I feel that I would be an ass and a traitor to my vow if I signed any such thing. I have forsworn employment contracts.

I believe you when you say you want to see justice done me, but I don't think you want justice done *now*. I think you want, practically, to see justice done me at some date in the future, after I have been drained some more. You want to make another deal with me, contingent on the consideration of future service. That won't do. I will make no such deal. I am in no mood for justice for me. I don't expect justice. I can speak flatly on this and with some detachment, for I have long ago renounced the hope of justice. I don't think it is within your power, however well-intentioned you may be, or in any man's power, to give me justice. I'm frozen in injustice.

You airily brush aside my comments and warnings about the present set-up. You horrify me by saying "they're pretty good," etc. You are completely and terrifyingly deluded about this. I am not the creature of perverted and hysterical imagination you think I am. It is I who am sound; it is you who are not. I will not here go into details on this point. I mention it merely as a basis for making the statement that I could not contract to edit *The New Yorker* for two weeks, let alone three years, with the Fleischmann ring of stupid fumblers in the background, in a position to take over at will; and for making the statement that I don't think you have a chance in the world of getting a replacement for me with things as they are, for no man with enough sense to do the job would try to do it. I don't think you can hire a hopeful candidate of standing. This outfit is known as a leper spot throughout the industry.

As to your breathtaking proposal of financial security for me, my thought is that the amount you suggest is fantastic and impossible, and the expense part of it illegal anyhow. How could I collect expenses if I weren't working? I did a little wistful thinking about such a romantic arrangement over last weekend, and a little financial doodling. According to my hasty and unchecked figures, a fund of four hundred thousand dollars invested at three percent and drawn upon at a rate of forty thousand dollars a year would be exhausted in twelve and a fraction years. My result cannot be far from right. . . .

On top of everything is the tax deadlock resulting from the Jane Grant agreement. What with that, and all the other bewildering factors, I have no faith. I am rather definitely convinced that the only thing to do is laughingly and finally face the miserable facts openly, and then let certain others do the sweating for a while. I've done it for twenty years now, and maybe it's their turn. Justice can't be done me, but I'm in a position to do justice to them, in reverse. I think it is my duty to myself and to the men who have been associated with me here editorially for so long—and to the movement or whatever it is that *The New Yorker* spearpoints—to consider any proposition you want to make, and I will do so, but I am extremely dubious of there being a way out.

Sincerely yours,

Ross

P.S. I read the foregoing to Hawley [Truax], who happened into the office, and he said the thing to do was send it to you, regardless of my hopelessness, so I have got out the carbon paper and personally made a copy, for secrecy. Hawley seemed to think there was some hope. He told me, for one thing, that the present executive committee remains in power for three years. I didn't know that. I'll tell you one thing, though: I have a deep-seated hunch that any arrangement I make with the F-R Corp. is doomed by God. I've made five or six arrangements here and none of them has worked out to my advantage. This is partly through the trickery and stupidity of the management and partly due

to factors beyond their control. And I'm awfully, awfully tired of ne-
gotiating. If you want to go further with this thing, you will, I warn
you, find me very stern, and probably preposterous.

H.W.R.


TO E. B. WHITE

*July 5, 1945*

Mr. White:

I herewith report on the changes made in your Comment department for the issue of July 7th. . . .

Katharine has devoted a paragraph in a memo received today on
this and another change made, [saying] "White, for one, is up in arms
about it. . . ." We have not all gone crazy and blown the roof off the
building. If you are up in arms about this word, you are up in arms
against a mere typographical error. The printer set "her" for "hen" and
that is all there is to it. . . . The second change in this sentence concerned the phrase "full-grown squab." The checking room (which you
yourself said was good the night we sat down last week over these
changes) queried this. The checkers insisted that a full-grown squab
would not be fed by its mother. They still stand on that today, although
your wife writes convincingly as if she were an eyewitness to mother
pigeons feeding "full-grown squabs." This biological question on pigeons would undoubtedly have been tracked to the very last expert if
the fact had mattered. But the point was, what in God's world is a "full-
grown squab"? I don't think there is a satisfactory answer to that question. At what point in life does a squab become full grown? A squab is
the pigeon equivalent of a human baby. You can't say "full-grown" cub.
Please tell me if you think I'm wrong, but I'll put up an argument if
there is strength left in me to do it. We put in "new-born" with reser-
vations and later had killed it out entirely, leaving the sentence without an adjective, when your telegram came about the thing. . . .

Ross

*William O'Dwyer became mayor of New York the following January. He was such a close friend that Ross would spend many private evenings at Gracie Mansion.*

TO WESTBROOK PEGLER

*The New Yorker*
*August 1, 1945*

Dear Peg:

Now, when *I* was a lad out west, we used to call those five- and six-cornered brawls "battle royals." That was the plural I used, but my recollection is that the copy readers were usually stuffy and made it "battles royal." Over-exhilarated spectators among the gentry, with an hysterical urge to add to the general confusion, used to heave seat cushions into the ring, and occasionally beer bottles.

You heaved a beer bottle at Bill O'Dwyer in your column yesterday and hit him in what I believe the Hearst papers delicately call the groin. With a convenient rationalization characteristic of you majestic cosmic thinkers, you directly implied that O'Dwyer's army career was a political maneuver. I don't know what was in O'Dwyer's mind, God knows, but I do know the following facts: 1) He volunteered for the army immediately after Pearl Harbor, with no strings attached, and, anyhow, you don't volunteer for any particular line of work when you volunteer for the army, as you and everyone else knows. 2) Mr. Roosevelt (as you say) supported LaGuardia in the last local election, not O'Dwyer. 3) O'Dwyer joined the army very soon after the last election.

You say, "Mr. Roosevelt thought he (O'Dwyer) might become useful if Fiorello LaGuardia should become too preposterous, so Mr. O'Dwyer was bidden into the army for non-shooting duties ..." That is crap, self-evident crap, unfair and foul. It is not credible that Roosevelt, having just opposed O'Dwyer, should immediately have picked him up as a political pawn to frustrate LaGuardia, whom he had just supported. Nor is it credible, either, that the army could be used thus loosely as a political trapeze. O'Dwyer did what he was told in the army, as did everybody else, and he was in combat areas quite a bit, and I know that he did able work in the investigation of several very hot cases.

O'Dwyer isn't to blame for the present local battle royal. He ran on the Democratic ticket last time and damned near got elected with the President against him and he was the man who would inevitably run again. That is simple and obvious, and not a single commie in the shrubbery. What has happened beyond that isn't his doing, and from all I can see, he has stood up righteously throughout, having been, for instance, unprecedentedly highhanded in rejecting running mates, the selection of whom is usually regarded as none of the candidate's business.

You say, "Mr. Farley holds that no good can come of such promiscuity and has washed his hands with disinfectant." Again, I don't know much of anything, being by nature detached about political and other grim problems, but I gather that it is possible that somebody beat Mr. Farley to the hand-washing, that he got washed off somebody else's hands before he did any washing of his own. I wouldn't be a damned bit surprised if Jim Farley is passé, and, further, that he is as fevered and jumpy as you are, seeing a commie every time he looks up. Every time I've spotted him lately, he's been looking over both shoulders and seems taut. I've wondered if he isn't getting sour-balled.

Yours as usual, you ornery bastard,
Ross
P.S. O'Dwyer's brother is *not* counsel for the transport boys.
H.W.R.

*Married to Fleischmann's ex-wife, Ruth, a major* New Yorker *stockholder, Vischer played a strong behind-the-scenes role at the magazine and was trying to keep Ross from quitting.*

TO PETER VISCHER

*THE NEW YORKER*
*AUGUST 7, 1945*

Dear Peter:
I got your letter after it had kicked around town for a few days and finally got to my office. It was addressed to the Ritz and I haven't lived there in several years. My address is 375 Park Avenue.

I see no hope in the situation. The further I have gone into it, the more hopeless it seems. You speak of "playing fair with us." Good

God, I have leaned over backwards playing fair with this organization until my spine is like a horseshoe. That has gone on for twenty years, and I have been rooked and imposed upon throughout most of the entire period. I've kept this publication going singlehanded a lot of the time, saving it in crisis after crisis brought on by stupidity and neglect.

I don't know whether you know it or not, but you and Ruth added one dandy straw to the pile that finally broke my back when you lightly tossed out my plan for the Jane Grant refinancing, as I will euphemistically call it. The plan you and Stryker and Truax gave me to swallow hasn't worked, having blown up in the face of tax laws and regulations, landing me far, impossibly far, out on a limb. That was not the thing that caused me to cancel my contract, however; I didn't even know of the fix I was getting in until after I'd turned in my notice. But it does leave me more ruinously off than I had anticipated, even at my gloomiest. It is just one more fantastic rap I have taken around here.

You write under the misapprehension that my employment contract was signed two years ago. It is more like four years, I think, although my sense of time hasn't been good lately, because of preoccupation with minute-to-minute pressure. It seems to me that it is two years since I served notice terminating the contract, which I did in terror, after a year in which the management of this enterprise was completely inactive—somnolent, oblivious, and to all practical purposes nonexistent. I found myself in the horrible position of being signed up to get out a magazine that it was probably going to be impossible to get out. The staff was leaving for the services or to competitors, the government red tape was getting so thick you couldn't cut it with a sickle, and I was getting no help or support. My position was impossible and intolerable, and, on top of that, the deal I made wasn't working out for me, its purposes being defeated by laws subsequently discovered, or interpretations of them. That could be ignored or laughed off during the war, when I felt obliged to carry on if it was humanly possible to do so, but it cannot be anymore.

Pardon me if I seem heated, but I get bitter now whenever this thing comes up.... Please tell Ruth that I'm sorry about it, and that I have, all through, felt a sense of responsibility toward her, if no one else, but you can also tell her that this was diminished in my mind by the stand you and she took on the Jane Grant feature of the contract. You will gather that I'm a little sore all around, which is true.

If you write me again, please address me at 375 Park Avenue, for I do not want letters pertaining to this subject kicking around the office.

Sincerely yours,

Ross

## TO HOBART WEEKES

*AUGUST 23, 1945*

Dear Weekes:

I got your telegram and was heartened. I hope you come up, and I hope to Jesus that you are in a mood to go to work soon, because you are the only man around who would relieve Shawn appreciably and he has taken more than any other man I know of in this war, and that goes for General Marshall and a lot of others I can name. He has done two-and-a-half jobs for four years, working every night practically and every weekend, having been driven in a most inhuman manner. It is heart-rending.

I am in a position to swing a big lump of dough your way, and will do so, but I want to talk to you.

As ever,

H. W. Ross

*Ross's friend Beatrice Kaufman, wife of George S. Kaufman, died of a cerebral hemorrhage.*

## TO FRANK SULLIVAN

*THURS.*
*[OCTOBER 18, 1945]*

Dear Frank:

. . . I spent most of a week ago Sunday with George after Beatrice's death on Friday. That is, I was in and out of the house, as were a lot of others, it being obvious that George was better off with people around. George had no idea of the seriousness of the thing and he is convinced that Beatrice had no intimation at all as to what she was up against. The doctor undoubtedly knew a hell of a lot more than he told either of them. There is no question about that. George's sister knew a lot, too, but she never told George or Bea. After twenty words of monosyllables and three-word sentences widely spaced, George cut loose that Sunday and talked his head off. It was a very unusual thing.

Yes, there are few of us left, God damn it. I saw old Chauncey Depew once, years ago, in a dentist's office, having his last tooth out, I guess, and I thought, there goes a man who has undoubtedly survived every one of his contemporaries and hasn't an old pal left in the world, and I hope I don't wind up that way. I now seem to be, though.

More on the piece later. I am writing this in the middle of a very busy day.

As ever—even more fondly than ever,

Ross


TO FRANK SULLIVAN

*THE NEW YORKER*
*OCTOBER 22, 1945*

Dear Frank:

. . . I don't know how much Lobrano trimmed out, but I know it reads just dandy now. Lobrano cut a couple of editorial touches and he was unquestionably right in that because you don't want to stop a thing like this with extraneous matter. I know that's right, so help me.

You mention H. G. Wells, which reminds me that I got a letter of about a thousand words from Rebecca West the other day in which she enumerates a vast number of difficulties in connection with a marvelous story she did for us on the Lord Haw Haw trial a few weeks ago. One of the difficulties was that H. G. Wells, "who is very sick, maybe dying," kept calling for her, and for eggs (which, it seems, she has been able to provide from time to time because she has a farm in rural England). When she got to London to cover the trial, she couldn't get a place to stay some nights and on those occasions got a roof over her head by acting as night nurse to H. G. Miss West seemed very detached, and to take H. G. Wells as very much a matter of course. All English writers are inclined to do that, which amazes me, and the picture of H.G. Wells on his deathbed calling for a woman and some eggs, like an ordinary person, gave me pause. At the end, we all get the same, evidently.

You will get a check and the proof in due course.

As ever,

Ross

## MEMO TO WOLCOTT GIBBS

*OCTOBER 23, 1945*

Mr. Gibbs:

Until I read the last paragraph of your review of *Polonaise* I hadn't realized that we have a rule that the theater must be mentioned in the review of every show you cover. I talked to Mr. Weekes about it today and he says he recalls talk of the thing several years ago and of complaints from readers. I am not certain that it wasn't a foible of Benchley's, and that it has been carried on mysteriously through the years. Whatever it was, I suggest that you not feel obliged to mention the theater when you don't want to (which Mr. Weekes tells me was your apparent policy in your X-issue department) and see if all the subscribers cancel.

H. W. Ross

*Into the autumn of 1945 Ross was still trying to negotiate a new deal with* The New Yorker. *At the same time Jane Grant was conducting her own battle with Fleischmann. During the war she had conceived and overseen the magazine's "pony" edition—a miniature, ad-free version of* The New Yorker *that reached hundreds of thousands of American servicemen overseas. Jane felt that given the unqualified success of the pony edition—it fueled* The New Yorker's *rapid postwar growth—she had been underpaid. At that point an arrangement occurred to Ross that might satisfy everyone.*

## TO LLOYD PAUL STRYKER

*THE NEW YORKER*
*OCTOBER 29, 1945*

Dear Lloyd:

There follows an attempt to set down my ideas on the Jane Grant situation:

I want this cleaned up, got on a practical basis from the standpoint of Jane, the F-R Corporation, and myself. First, I think the corporation should recognize and admit its obligation to her, that she played a vital part in the promotion of this enterprise and that she has never in any degree whatever been compensated for it. She is the one who got Fleischmann interested in promoting the magazine. There would be no *New Yorker* today if it were not for her. She got a sucker where I failed, after a long hunt for suckers. Since Fleischmann has drawn a large salary from the business for twenty years, since he has drawn considerable sums for expenses, since he and his favored group walked off with practically the lion's share of the stock, and in view of the comparatively enormous success of the business, I propose that the corporation assume the responsibility of paying Jane five thousand dollars a year for the rest of her life. I set this amount arbitrarily, but whatever amount is set must be set arbitrarily. I think that this sum is small when you consider that the company has paid her nothing during the twenty years of its life, most of them exceedingly prosperous, and that it would be now making but a belated gesture toward justice.

I see no room for argument against this debt, except possibly that it is outlawed, and I do not intend to swallow that. Fleischmann and his group have made millions and Jane Grant has made not one cent. All she has ever got from *The New Yorker* she got from me personally, and I could ill afford it because I, too, had been robbed. Fleischmann et al. hogged everything they could hog, which was practically everything there was.

I propose that if the corporation recognizes this claim and meets it in a practical way, personally to arrange for some kind of a fund, in trust or escrow, whereby Jane gets another five thousand a year for life.

It is my thought that perhaps these two ends can be accomplished in one motion somehow, that that might be the best way to work it out in view of everything. I am naturally vague about how such a deal could be made, practically, but my thought is that perhaps the corporation could take a fraction of that money it proposes to escrow for me and instead of escrowing it for me, escrow it for Jane Grant; or that it could escrow it to me in such a way that I could give her a first lien on it, or transfer the escrow to her, or some such, so that she would be sure of the payments from me, or of my share of the payments.

... It certainly is to Jane's interest to make such an arrangement. It certainly is to my interest to do so, and rid my mind and nervous system of my terrifying obligation. And it would seem to me that it is just a dandy opportunity for the corporation to clear its conscience by recognition of this claim, however tardily, and thereby contribute to Jane's self-respect and to my peace of mind....

As ever,

H. W. Ross

## TO FRANK SULLIVAN

*FRIDAY*
*[AUTUMN 1945]*

Dear Frank:

I have your letter and am disappointed, because the least I expected from you was a couple of C notes as a small split in that thing. However, I have come to expect little from writers, including writings. How about that cliche piece on what to do with Germany after the war, Sullivan? Do not think that that Christmas poem (fine as it was, as usual) is going to influence me to lay off hounding you. The recent remittance to you, along with a considerable number of others that went out, has given me a Godlike feeling and I am going to act like God in his sternest mood for some time to come. I may put on a big flood, to get you people thinking.

Despite your colds and elusiveness, I will catch you next time you are in town and we will have social intercourse.

I was once told that [Stanley] Walker said of [Lucius] Beebe that he writes like an educated Negro and I quoted that line, crediting Walker, for years but I have recently heard that [James Gibbons] Huneker applied it to someone else before Beebe was born and, I guess, before Walker was either.

Ross

*Baer was Ross's personal attorney.*

TO JULIUS BAER

*THE NEW YORKER*
*NOVEMBER 12, 1945*

Dear Julius:

I enclose copies of the two documents I told you about Saturday, which I've been meaning to hand you personally sooner or later. I've been delaying, to see if there is enough hope of anything coming out of the situation to warrant your professional attention. You asked for it, however, and here the problem is.

The first document, the "proposal," was handed me by Stryker and Truax and debated briefly. I took it under advisement, where I still have it. The increase in salary it offers means very little, only about four thousand dollars net, as I figure it. The whole editor emeritus proposition, whereby I retire and live luxuriously for life, is worthless, because it assumes the continuity of *The New Yorker* pretty much and *The New Yorker* will blow up like a firecracker if I leave. I am so sure of that that I wouldn't gamble five cents against it, or an hour's time. Anyhow, their Clause a. of Paragraph 2 defeats anything they are offering because, as I understand it, they would have to be satisfied with my successor and that is impossible.

Paragraph 3 means that I can still buy at six dollars a share the stock I had under option under the employment contract I broke. If you or your tax man can figure out how I can gain possession of this stock, I can have it, but I am damned sure you can't. So this part of the offer is meaningless. The stock has gone from six dollars to forty-one dollars (as bid the other day, according to a postcard I got from a broker).

The second document [his letter outlining the Jane Grant proposal] explains itself. I am going to cram this down their throats or else, and I'll want you to stand by with your technical and fatherly advice when I do, of course.

As ever,

Ross

*Despite Ross's misgivings he soon signed a generous new contract that also gave him the right to retire anytime, on three months' notice, as "editor emeritus." In short order Jane won a consulting contract for $7,500 a year, renewable by her for life; Fleischmann got back some of the management control he lost in the 1942 shareholder revolt; and Jane absolved Ross of any further financial obligation to her.*

*West began writing for* The New Yorker *during the war, and Ross admired her as much as any contributor he ever worked with. Their friendship launched a prolific correspondence, and since West lived in England, Ross's letters to her were among the newsiest and most personal he would write.*

TO REBECCA WEST

*THE NEW YORKER*
*NOVEMBER 16, 1945*

Dear Miss West:

God forgive me, I haven't answered your letter of last month. I don't think I've ever been more thoroughly swamped or had more things on my mind than now, even in the last few months of the war, up to that time the most strenuous and difficult period of my life. Some of the members of the staff have finally come back and things are on the verge of getting simpler, but the reorganization and readjustment problems have been numerous, complicated, and maddening....

I shall answer your letter in portions, as I have several things to discuss. I will take up two of them now, as follows, the others later.

I am an old duodenal ulcer boy. They had me down bad and I was in and out of the hospital three or four times, and on a couple of occasions the surgeons were whetting their knives. I finally got tipped off to go to the Lahey Clinic in Boston, which is one of the top medical outfits in this country now (I think probably *the* top) and there I got cured medically. They have a wonderful doctor there, a woman. (I was as suspicious of a woman doctor as anyone else when I started out, but I'm thoroughly convinced now.) If your husband doesn't get cured over there I suggest that he come over here and get cured. I have to take a lot of pills and other remedies and have to spare myself considerably, or am supposed to, but I went through the war feeling fine and it was the most difficult thing I ever did. . . .

Second point: Do you want us to send you over any food? Your mention of your diet and of the pathetic shouts of H. G. Wells for eggs gave me the idea that we might do something. We are sending packages of food to two or three people overseas and we can send you some packages if it would help out; we could send them as a regular thing for a while. I am advised that bacon can be sent, for instance. If you think we can be helpful in this respect, please let me know without hesitation. There are several women in the office who apparently like to shop these things up.

Please give us notice by cable about the Amery trial, as you did on Joyce.

Sincerely yours,

H. W. Ross

## MEMO TO KATHARINE S. WHITE

*[UNDATED]*

Mrs. White:

There is nothing to be done about [Edmund] Wilson's editing that I know of. He is by far the biggest problem we ever had around here. Fights like a tiger, or holds the line like an elephant, rather. Only course is to let him peter out, I guess. If you have the strength and the opportunity, and the will, you might ask him about this point sometime, since you seem to have a special position with him. You won't get any satisfaction beyond satisfying your curiosity, though.

R.

*Mrs. Baskin was the writer Marjorie Kinnan Rawlings, who had submitted the story "Miriam's Houses."*

## TO MRS. NORTON BASKIN

*THE NEW YORKER*
*NOVEMBER 30, 1945*

Dear Mrs. Baskin:

Mr. Lobrano showed me that letter you wrote a month ago, when you sent back your proof, and I kept it to write you. I put it in my "slow" basket and then I didn't do anything about that basket, beyond retrieving occasionally something that had ceased to be "slow," because things have been coming at me so fast lately that I've been dizzy....

You are a little wrong in your idea of how we work here. I never actually decide on the details of a piece, or when I do it is extra routine business. I do what I call "query" things in a story, pass the queries on to Mr. Lobrano, and then he and the author decide on the details. And actually what I and the rest of us do is query, too, for in the long run the story is the author's and is run over the author's signature, and if the author wants to retain some bad grammar or some ambiguity, or even print two or three words upside down, we let them do it if the story is good enough to get by with the defects, or what we consider the defects. We've got to accept or reject what the author wants in the long run, in toto. We do put up a hell of an argument about details sometimes, though, and occasionally we have to hand back a story we think we have bought because the author won't yield on points we consider important. (The worse the writer is, the more argument; that is the rule. There are a vast number of writers around who can't write. They get by through diligence, application, and various other qualities that are not primarily literary.) I usually pass my query sheet along to Mr. Lobrano and he decides all the small points, he and the author. We also have a demon editor here who reads all proofs for style, spellings, wordings, grammar, usage, and everything else he can think of. He originates most of the little queries, from commas to usage. In the case of the proof of [your story], Mr. Lobrano took the buck on all the points I raised and, as is usual, I never paid any attention to them—or

I wouldn't have paid any attention to them if he hadn't passed along the letter you sent with the proof, as a matter of personal interest.

The only great argument I have against writers, generally speaking, is that many of them deny the function of an editor, and I claim editors are important. For one thing, an editor is a good trial horse; the writer can use him to see if a story and its various elements register as he or she thinks they register. An author is very likely to suffer a loss of viewpoint (due to nearness to the subject) before he gets through with a story and finish up with something more or less out of focus. For another thing, editors perform a technical function in small matters that I suspect writers shouldn't concern themselves with overmuch. I think writers, or most writers, ought to let editors backstop the small, more or less technical points. The trouble with our querying system is that it sometimes makes writers self-conscious; they get to thinking—oh, Christ, three or four people are going to pick flaws in this—and they freeze up and ponder every word they set down and every punctuation mark. My sage advice to them is to go ahead and write their story and then at the end (with the help of an editor) pick up the chips. This self-consciousness isn't really much of a problem, however; most of the writers think we are helpful at times, if a nuisance generally. We are unquestionably captious and careless frequently and occasionally we suggest changes for the mere sake of change, or for a peculiar personal feeling, but we try not to cram our theories, little or big, down writers' throats....

Sincerely yours,

H. W. Ross

TO REBECCA WEST

*The New Yorker*
*December 6, 1945*

Dear Miss West:

We didn't try to handle the Amery piece as rapidly as the Joyce piece. It came in at the end of the week again and we were in such difficulties at the printing plant and in our own office that we let it go over an issue. It will be just as good, for the papers here did no more than mention the trial, and is just as well that we did, for the radio copy had no punctuation whatever again and we had to puzzle everything out from paragraphing down to commas, and such a process takes time, and when you get through you know you've been in a fight. We punctuated the piece in copy tentatively and then had to figure out doubtful passages in the proof. There was one that had us down bad. One sentence read in the proof, "He left England under our law," which was palpably wrong, but it took three of us forty-eight hours to interpret that as "He left England. Under our law...." There were several others like that. I think we now have all but, say, two or three of your sentences set up as you wrote them. That is an offhand estimate, based on the laws of chance. I don't know what in the world the radio outfit was thinking of when it didn't send punctuation. Maybe over there they won't transmit punctuation unless it is spelled out in the copy. Over here they'll spell out the punctuation marks for you, or they will sometimes. On the whole, we have had a four-year nightmare in handling telegraphic copy.

One thing is certain: the piece is a wonder. You have again done what is certainly a dazzling feat of journalism. More about that later, when I catch my breath....

Sincerely yours,
H. W. Ross

TO REBECCA WEST

*THE NEW YORKER*
*DECEMBER 17, 1945*

Dear Miss West:

... I have a clump of things here marked "West" which has been accumulating for weeks. It includes your letter about your troubles preceding the Joyce trial, which ranged from an amorous bull to the sickbed of H. G. Wells, and reminded me of a remark that Robert Benchley once made about his sex life. He said it wasn't normal but it was interesting. The thing in your letter that wrung my heart most was the mention of your husband's ulcers. As I think I said in an earlier letter, I know probably the best place in the world to cure them, the

Lahey Clinic in Boston, and I urge that if he doesn't get completely cured soon he come over to this country and go there. They got me fixed up so that I was able to go through the war period, which meant 365 days and nights of work a year. I was also touched by the sickbed scene at H. G. Wells' house. I rate Wells higher than most of you British people do, I have found—not because of his fiction but because of his *Outline of History* and his *Science of Life* which, next to Herbert Spencer's *First Principles,* I regard as the most educational and helpful books I have ever read. . . . A woman I was having lunch with a couple of weeks ago told me about sending food packages to people abroad and I was fired with the intention of sending a bunch of food over for Christmas, to a number of people, including you. This lady drenched me with lists of dainty foods that can be shipped, with the result that I merely got bewildered and did nothing. I may do something yet, as a matter of fact, although it is too late for Christmas. I will say one thing: If there is anything you want specifically—food, medicine, or cutlery—I will send it to you if you will name it. The point is, I am not capable of selection. . . .

Gratefully and sincerely yours,

Ross

*Ross's wife was at her parents' home in Beverly Hills.*

TELEGRAM TO ARIANE ROSS

*DECEMBER 20, 1945*

Will unload Pasadena. Tell Chasen not to tell everybody date arrival for don't want to be jumped on by too many people at outset. I would as soon stay with your parents if there is room there but it matters little.

Love to all,

Harold

# VII

# "THESE ARE NOT HO HUM TIMES . . ."
## 1946-1948

Ross had hoped that peace would permit *The New Yorker* to return to "normal," meaning the way things were before the war, but that proved no more possible for the magazine than for anyone else. What the editor used to call his "fifteen-cent comic paper" had evolved into a respected world journal, and there was no going back. Indeed, Ross made sure of that himself when, a year after the dropping of the atomic bomb on Hiroshima, Japan, he filled an entire issue of *The New Yorker* with John Hersey's chilling reconstruction of that event. Ross was genuinely flummoxed by the Cold War mentality, and he was distressed by establishment sentiment that *The New Yorker,* if not downright "red," was certainly pink. Still, this naturally conservative man fought hard for the right of his journalists to say what their facts warranted. His two paramount correspondences of this period are those with Thurber, with whom the editor was reconnecting, and with Rebecca West, who received some of the most discursive letters Ross was to write.

———

MEMO TO E. B. WHITE

Mr. White:

I found your note about the BIDE-A-WEE HOME FOR VERBS idea two minutes after you left my office the other day, as expected. Hence I am reminded that you spoke of putting a notice on the bulletin board calling for nauseating verbs. I favor your doing this, and I hope the results will be successful.

While I am at it, I will say that you may feel at liberty at any time to make any use of the bulletin board you may see fit. Your service has been such that I have no misgiving in extending to you this sweeping privilege. The only trouble is that for the last several months the light on the bulletin board has not been working and nobody can read the notices on it. I have spoken to Miss Terry about this and she said she would speak to Mr. Gebert. The bulletin board ought to be working again within six months.

On a chance, I am putting Lang's memo about his Newsbreak idea on the bulletin board. Something might come of it. I'm always in there trying.

H. W. Ross

*Parker was headmistress at Patty's school in New York.*

TO RITA PARKER

*THE NEW YORKER*
*MARCH 12, 1946*

Dear Dr. Parker:

I should very much like to have your opinion as to whether Patty ought to go to a camp this summer. I think I will have to make camp arrangements soon if she is to go. Patty insists that she doesn't want to go. I have asked her several times. Her mother is under the impression that you said she should go to camp—whatever her feelings, apparently. I don't think you said this to me. I am writing this rather than bothering you on the telephone, but you can get me on the telephone more or less any time, if you should want to talk to me about this. I have no tangible alternative to camp for Patty so far. She says what she would like to do is spend the summer at my place in Stamford and at her mother's in East Hampton. She is very fond of both places, especially Stamford. There is a possibility that I can send her west to stay with my wife's sister's family, which includes five children, with whom Patty has always had a more or less thrilling time, but this family is homeless to date, being unable to get possession of a house the parents purchased months ago.

Patty is showing an amazing interest in her lessons. She has become practically studious. I think there is a great change, and she tells me that her teacher has complimented her on her progress. I have not confirmed this with the school yet, but I have no doubt it is true.

Sincerely yours,

H. W. Ross

MEMO TO WILLIAM SHAWN

*APRIL 3, 1946*

Mr. Shawn:

Mr. Ross's notes on Wilson's Books lead—THE STRANGER by Camus

Oh, God, Wilson will have to show a heart in dealing with O'Hara here, and he's got to realize that we are in a position whereby any discussion of *New Yorker* writers in the pages of *The New Yorker* is always embarrassing and frequently full of dynamite. (Both true in this case.) I don't know whether our viewpoint on this has ever been explained to Wilson or not (I'm quite certain I've never taken the subject up with him). Any mention, good or bad, of a writer prominently identified with the magazine is embarrassing. Who the hell are we to say in our pages that one of our men is a great, or a good, or a capable, or an important writer? Such things always look fishy to the reader, and are more embarrassing if the mention is favorable than if it isn't, as far as that goes, or that is my personal feeling. It so happens that Wilson's references here would probably raise hell with our relations with

O'Hara, but I'd be as much against the comparison in this piece if they were favorable, or more against them.

1. I think it is dangerous to say that O'Hara is derivative of Hemingway, and I think it unwise from the standpoint of the magazine and unfair from the standpoint of O'Hara to mention him in same breath with Cain. Is there any real comparison between these fellows on the basis of merit? Their names are linked again at (2), but I doubt if that is objectionable there.

3. Here Wilson seems (to my hypersensitive eye) to be going out of his way to take a shot at—or to review—a several-years-old book of O'Hara's. I am aware that my ear would have detected nothing unreasonable or objectionable here if a writer named John Jones had been mentioned. I'd have passed it over without a pause. But I'm only human, and I stopped at O'Hara, who is a very real proposition in this place. I wish Wilson would take O'Hara out entirely, solely because of our peculiar position with our own writers—any of our writers—but if that is too drastic for him, I think he must tone the thing down considerably, and cut that "review" at (3). I don't think we should run the piece as is.

H. W. Ross

At (a), just above (3), the statement that Cain set forth a conception of sex relations between the sexes in America seemed, at first reading, an amazing one. Cain wrote of sex relations in a very special, very unusual part of America, and sex there seemed very special. On the other hand, it seemed world-wide, for that class of people are the same the world over, I guess. This is none of my business. I see what Wilson is getting at all right. I am just explaining the blue mark there.


TO MAURICE SAETA

*THE NEW YORKER*
*APRIL 8, 1946*

Dear Mr. Saeta:

I am pleased to get endorsement of those Nuremberg pieces from members of the bar. The trouble with them is that they are inadequate in number. We didn't know the thing would last on and on like this and we split Genêt's work, and she doesn't like to stay in Nuremberg any-

how, because living there is tough—only one toilet per forty correspondents, she keeps reporting. I took considerable satisfaction in the
piece about Jackson. I happen to have had dealings with three men
now on the Supreme Court and I have a very low opinion of all of
them. The situation curdles my blood when I think about it. I'll tell
you about some of the august justices some day.

God knows when I'll get back to California. My last visit was highly
unsatisfactory. I didn't see anybody as much as I wanted to, largely because of transportational and geographical difficulties out there. I was
dependent on Chasen and my wife to drive me around, with the result
that I went where they wanted to go always and I couldn't go out on
my own because I would have got lost. I'm hoping to get out there this
summer and if so I'll see you.

Sincerely yours,

H. W. Ross


*The women were reporters for the* New Orleans Item.

TO MARJORIE ROEHL AND BARBARA SELBY

*THE NEW YORKER*
*APRIL 9, 1946*

Dear young ladies:

You have the wrong year for me. I went to work on the *Item* in 1913,
the winter of that year. I know I got into New Orleans from Panama
on Thanksgiving Day that year and I went to work on the *Item* soon afterward, at the lowest pay I ever got on a newspaper anywhere, before
or since. I left there the following spring. I don't know the date, but it
could be looked up, for after a day in Birmingham I got to Atlanta, arriving there the morning Mary Phagan's body was found in the pencil
factory. That started off the Leo Frank case, which the old-timers can
tell you about. Ask some of the old-time southern newspaper men
about Bill Ryan and Joe (I'm not sure of this first name) Crimmins.
They were colorful people, older itinerants, whose stay coincided
more or less with mine. Ask some of the old-timers about them. If
they can't do justice to this pair, I will.

If you do go ahead with this history, really, and don't go too fast at it, I'll try to recall some things, and get time to put them down, but I'm pretty busy and will be for a quite a while, I'm afraid.

Give my regards to Father Chapman, and tell him you couldn't print all I could tell about New Orleans. I was the police reporter in my day, and saw a lot. . . .

Sincerely yours,

H. W. Ross

*In the spring of 1946 John Hersey was in China, reporting for both* The New Yorker *and* Life. *Shawn had the idea of diverting him to Japan in order to investigate what really happened at Hiroshima, on the ground, when the atomic bomb was dropped.*

## MEMO TO WILLIAM SHAWN

*MAY 13, 1946*

Mr. Shawn:

I have just read the [Daniel] Lang piece on the atom bomb explosion—his talk with the scientist. I observe as follows: I don't think this will infringe on the projected Hersey piece, but I think Hersey ought to read it so as not to repeat.

Also, if Hersey can get into that piece a conjecture as to the potentialities of a *big* atom bomb, it would be well—if it doesn't scare everybody to death. In this Lang story the physicist speaks of this bomb doing as much damage as one thousand superfortresses and then calls it a "little bomb." Very effective, and alarming.

H. W. Ross

## TO IAN FLEMING

*THE NEW YORKER*
*JUNE 27, 1946*

Dear Mr. Fleming:

. . . Your brother's story was too British for us, in pattern. It was one of those pieces with a London club setting, and London clubs have been done to death for forty years by British authors who have been best sellers in America. They have a bad name with us and, moreover, have no real parallel here and, I think, are viewed with deep suspicion by Americans. I was sorry, but such things happen all the time. Publishing is eighty percent disappointment, as I figure it.

I am not familiar at first hand with the details of the British piracy of American stuff. I know it has gone on for a long time, and I know that it is going on intensely now because of the muttering I have heard lately about it. A lot of the artists are indignant. I think the business office is trying to do something about it through an agent. The fault, though, is primarily with this country. We didn't line up with most of the other nations behind a good international copyright agreement when we had a chance, and Congress has never done anything about it since. As nearly as I can make out, American publications have no actual legal protection abroad, and foreign publications none here.

Sincerely,

H. W. Ross

## TO ST. CLAIR MCKELWAY

*THE NEW YORKER*
*JULY 18, 1946*

Dear Mac:

I suspect you'd recognize the old follow-up, no matter how well disguised, so I guess I won't try to disguise it. How in the hell about some pieces?

As for news from here: there isn't much. Gibbs is on Fire Island for the summer (there's a rumor, surely unfounded, that he's working on a fact piece); Perelman is in Bucks County for the summer (his musical is now scheduled to open in New Haven this October); Kober is taking long weekends (Thursday to Tuesday approximately) at Pleasantville and Long Beach. And so it goes. Only vacationless man is Ross, who sweats here and grumbles about such things as not having seen a piece from you in a hell of a while. And that last item, I note, just about brings me full circle.

Yours,

Ross

## TO WOLCOTT GIBBS

*THE NEW YORKER*
*JULY 18, 1946*

Dear Gibbs:

Here is more money pouring in. Unless you have conjured up or do conjure up some objection, please sign this [first-read agreement] and return it and cash the check.

I objected to this document because it is only a fiction agreement and makes no provision for fact pieces you write. You should get a bonus on these and it should be so stated. You will undoubtedly get a bonus on fact pieces, but on some arrangement improvised hurriedly when the problem comes up. I am trying to get the Business Brains to work out an agreement for both fact and fiction that can be offered to bisexual writers like yourself, who are more or less equally adept at fact and fiction and do both, and who are fairly numerous. This is being worked on. Meantime, this inadequate document goes forward. My advice is to grab the dough. You are entitled to it beyond doubt in view of the reception of the Fire Island series, which seems to be arousing widespread acclaim. Several people have asked me how you came to write that piece for *Life,* one of them using the word "disloyal." ("Why was he disloyal like that?") I just pass these off. But people noticed that piece. . . .

As ever,
Ross

## TO H. L. MENCKEN

*THE NEW YORKER*
*JULY 27TH [CIRCA 1946]*

Dear Mencken:

It's a small world. The attached unanswerable question has reached my desk. I forget exactly when the Algonquin Round Table started, which I take it is what you innocently are getting at. Sam Adams has the right date in his book on Woollcott. I refer you to that. I am pretty certain it is the right date. That is about all he has right about that round table. I was there a lot and I never heard any literary discussion or any discussion of any other art—just the usual personalities of some people getting together, and a lot of wisecracks and quoting of further wisecracks. It was always about the same as a dinner with you, [George Jean] Nathan, and a couple of more—Grant Rice and Paul Patterson, say—at "21." No cosmic problems settled; merely laughs.

Come to think of it, I can more or less fix the date of the starting. As I recall, Woollcott always said the table started when he made a date with Murdock Pemberton and someone else to eat there and they agreed to eat there again the next day, and that must have been sometime in the summer of 1919, for Aleck and I got back from Europe and the war in June of that year. I trust I am useful.

Best regards,
Ross

*When S. N. Behrman submitted a humor piece that mentioned syphilis, Mrs. White wondered if it didn't upset Ross's famously delicate sensibilities.*

TO KATHARINE S. WHITE

*[JULY 30, 1946]*

Mrs. White:
Reference attached: I had not a trace of squeamishness. . . . [I]t never occurred to me that it would offend anyone, and I can't believe it would. It is the filthy excretions of the body that bother me; a matter of the stomach only. If we had a rule that we didn't print anything that a man with a tender stomach couldn't read at lunch it would be all right. . . .
Ross

TO E. B. WHITE

*[SUMMER 1946]*

Mr. White:
I have your learned remarks on "The Omnipotent Whom" heading. Lobrano joined me in my doubt about it—may have inspired my

doubt, in fact—and as he is away I will keep the question pending until he returns ... I think circumstances killed the Ho Hum Department. These are not Ho Hum times, or they are not in the present atmosphere of this office, which has become grim. Hersey has written thirty thousand words on the bombing of Hiroshima (which I can now pronounce in a new and fancy way), one hell of a story, and we are wondering what to do about it. Shawn has an idea we should print it all in one issue, and print nothing else that week. That would make the NYer a pamphlet for that week. He wants to wake people up and says we are the people with a chance to do it, and probably the only people that will do it, if it is done. ...

The foregoing ... is confidential and top-secret. We are keeping our mouths shut for fear someone will take the edge off the story, which is impossible, but something to worry about. ...

Ross

*Wigglesworth was one of those small but important cogs in* The New Yorker *machine: the man who took all the query sheets about a given story from various editors and pulled them into one master list. Ross's query sheets were legendary, for their quirks and humor as much as for their length; on the huge Hiroshima story he had several hundred questions and observations. Hersey was writing furiously, in secret, and Ross was reading the story in pieces.*

## MEMO TO JOSEPH WIGGLESWORTH

*AUGUST 8, 1946*

Mr. Ross's notes on "Reporter—Some Events at Hiroshima—Part II" by Hersey.

A very fine piece beyond any question; got practically everything. This will be ... the classic piece on what follows a bomb dropping for a long time to come. I read it very carefully, and have a lot of notes. I probably read it over-zealously, and more than the normal number of queries are to be discounted probably.

I am still dissatisfied with the series title.

There is, I think, one grave lack in this piece. It may be Hersey's intention that there be. If so, ask consideration for what I say anyhow. All the way through I wondered about what killed these people, the burns, falling debris, the concussion—what? For a year I've been wondering about this and I eagerly hoped this piece would tell me. It doesn't. Nearly a hundred thousand dead people are around but Hersey doesn't tell how they died. Would it be possible—if so, would be wise—to tell on Galley 7 where he gives the one hundred thousand people, how many were killed by being hit by hard objects, how many by burns, how many by concussion, or shock, or whatever it was? Or would this be getting ahead of his story? I haven't read third and fourth parts yet. At one place, away over on Galley 14, a woman with no visible injury dies. Were a lot of the corpses that day without visible burns or injury? How about all the dead that littered the pavement when the Catholics were migrating—what proportion of them unmarked? I think getting a little of this into the piece, fairly early, would be a good idea—unless, as I said, it conflicts with Hersey's basic plan.

One thing, though: I think he ought to mention the vomiting. He doesn't mention it at all until Galley 13, where it comes as a considerable surprise to the reader that, more or less generally, the ailing were vomiting. That pretty late in piece to be telling that; several scenes have been described in which there must have been general vomiting. . . .

I would suggest (I'm making this as an insert in these notes after completing annotating) that Hersey might do well to tuck up on the time—give the hour and minute, exactly or roughly, from time to time. The reader loses all sense of the passing of time in the episodes and never knows what time of day it is, whether ten A.M. or four P.M. I thought of this halfway through annotation and mentioned it several times. If I appear to be nagging on the subject, that's why. . . .

H. W. Ross

TO REBECCA WEST

*THE NEW YORKER*
*AUGUST 27, 1946*

Dear Miss West:

I was two or three days late getting off a message acknowledging receipt of your Nuremberg story as a consequence of a strange and unprecedented condition in the office, which I may as well tell you about to begin with. One of our writers—new writers—John Hersey, was in China and we suggested that he come back by Japan and do a definitive story on the bombing of Hiroshima. This was a revision of an idea we had had around before the war in Europe ended. We had a man doing a conclusive and final story on the bombing of Cologne, a piece that would tell in detail, from start to finish, what happens when a city is destroyed by bombing. He had got his data and was fairly well along with the writing when the atomic bomb dropped on Hiroshima, and that project was blown up. Hersey came back a few weeks ago and shortly thereafter turned in one of the most remarkable stories I have ever seen: thirty thousand words of description in detail of what happens when an atomic bomb drops. It wasn't a series of pieces, as our series go, and it couldn't be, by its nature, and we finally decided that it wouldn't work as a serial, so we decided to use it all at one time, although it would take most of an issue. After a couple of days more of reflection, we got into an evangelical mood and decided to throw out all the other text in the issue, and make a gesture that might impress people. We couldn't have used humorous drawings or anything frivolous with the story, anyhow, and all problems were solved at once in one sweeping decision. So next week's issue will be a very peculiar one. I don't know what people will think, but a lot of readers are going to be startled. . . .

Sincerely yours,

Ross

*Hersey's landmark story, entitled simply "Hiroshima," filled the August 31, 1946, issue of* The New Yorker.

*Forrestal, then secretary of the navy, was one of the few people in Washington close to Ross. The editor had not been above asking for personnel favors during the war.*

TO JAMES V. FORRESTAL

*The New Yorker*
*August 29, 1946*

Dear Jim:

I've got to bother you again, but I haven't been after you in months, and that is pretty good.

We have had a young man working here for the last three years who was a godsend during the war. With the lads coming back we don't need him anymore and we've been suggesting that he get another job, and he has been stalling about it, and finally it has come out that during service in the navy he got in what is called, I believe, a "scrape." He now has a chance to get a job, a good job, in the Public Information Department of the United Nations, and it seems to be contingent on his clearing his record with the navy, which, as I understand it, constitutes getting an honorable or a "white discharge" to replace a dishonorable discharge he now has. . . .

The so-called scandalous conduct involved homosexuality. I do not know the details, not having inquired. I doubt if they are significant.

I am told . . . that the navy changed its policy on homosexuality at a certain point in the war and didn't put the boys in the can anymore. Some of the afflicted were given medical discharges, I believe, and others were just accepted for what they were, the navy getting to a point at which it could take them in its stride. This man . . . is said to be one of the last men to have got it in the neck before the change of policy. . . .

If it is true that the navy is taking a more enlightened and liberal view of clean fun these days, I ask that you please see what can be done in this case. This man is in a serious fix. He hasn't been able to go out and get a job for a year, because he feared the question of his dishonorable discharge would come up, as it did in the case of this job he has landed. (The United Nations doesn't seem to be bothered but wants the record cleared.) As for me, if it hadn't been for the help of several such culls from the armed services during the armed service, my office wouldn't be in existence now. I feel that I should go to bat for at least one of the boys. They didn't convert me, quite, but they won my sympathy.

I will be grateful for anything you can do, and send my greetings and best wishes to yourself and wife.

As ever,

Ross


TO FRANK SULLIVAN

*THE NEW YORKER*
*SEPTEMBER 5, 1946*

Dear Frank:

Thanks for the letter [about "Hiroshima"], and I admire your generosity in wanting to buy a sewing machine for Mrs. Nakamura, and your brilliance in thinking of it. As I read that piece (two or three times), I had a feeling that something ought to be done for that woman, but I didn't have the wit to think of replacing her sewing machine. Nor has anybody else that I have heard of.

I don't know how you would get a sewing machine to a woman in Japan. I'll put the question up to Hersey, who will doubtless know how, but that will take a few days as he ducked out of town and has stayed out of town since.

The *Herald Tribune* is going to reprint the whole story in installments, and I think most of the papers in the United States would reprint it if they had the paper. There was never any magazine story in my life that went off like this one.

In the excitement, I didn't get to Saratoga as intended. It was this story that kept me from getting up there. You should never work for any publication that prints my picture. You should write for papers that I am on.

GOD DAMN IT, WRITE SOMETHING!

As ever,

Ross

MEMO TO HAWLEY TRUAX

Mr. Truax:

I have a note from Mr. Geraghty, as follows:

"Charles Addams isn't satisfied with the money we pay him. I told him I'd pass the word along to you."

I subsequently talked to Mr. Geraghty and said I would pass the word along to *you.*

Mr. Addams is a special problem, somewhat like Mr. Mitchell among the writers—excellent quality, low productivity. He has sold us only seventeen drawings this year. Ideas for him are scarce, by their nature. We have been able to give him twelve ideas only. If he could do forty or fifty drawings a year, he would be sitting pretty, and so would we.

Mr. Geraghty has tried to lead him into other kinds of work for us, but without much success to date. He doesn't get advertising work, etc., as do the other artists, because of the limitations of his style.

He's some kind of special proposition, beyond question, and I recommend consideration of him as such. I have no solution, no constructive thoughts at the moment.

H. W. Ross


TO EMILY HAHN

*THE NEW YORKER*
*SEPTEMBER 11, 1946*

Dear Emily:

. . . I have seen none of your Chinese friends. I went back to that Chinese restaurant the other night, and after shouting your name around ineffectually, I used that of Dr. Quo and got a bowl of shark fin soup. I took my daughter to dinner. She got back from camp saying she was in the mood for chop suey. Up to then she had always got her chop suey at Longchamps restaurant and I gave her a little touch of the world.

More in due course.

As ever,

Ross

TO IRWIN SHAW

*The New Yorker*
*September 16, 1946*

Dear Shaw:

Thanks for the note. That story is a wonder, all right, and I don't think I've ever got as much satisfaction out of anything else in my life, including what some of the boys write about.

As ever,

Ross

TO JOHN HERSEY

*The New Yorker*
*November 6, 1946*

Dear Hersey:

I got the autographed copy of the book, and I reiterate the comment made at the time I saw the dedication. Those fellows who said "Hiroshima" was the story of the year, etc., underestimated it. It is unquestionably the best journalistic story of my time, if not of all time. Nor have I heard of anything like it.

I got a laugh out of a clip last night (a British clip), on its way through to you, which asked, "Are governments to be less responsible than a satirical, sophisticated magazine?"

I expect that I shall see you Friday night, for I have now booked myself for the *Stars and Stripes* dinner. And I am going to organize a reunion with you and Shawn when this thing goes down a little more.

Sincerely,

Ross

*Crabbe was a British army officer and part of a Rossian circle that included Ernest Hemingway and Paul Hyde Bonner.*

## TO ARCHIBALD CRABBE

*THE NEW YORKER*
*NOVEMBER 6, 1946*

Dear Archie:

... I have nothing to report beyond the fact that Ernest has taken his new wife out to Sun Valley to teach her to shoot, just as he did with Martha [Gellhorn]. He has to go through that every time. I was invited by the Cunard Line to go over there and come back on the Queen Elizabeth, but I didn't go.

As ever,
Ross

## TO GUS LOBRANO

*NOVEMBER 20, 1946*

Mr. Lobrano:

I say reject both [poems]. The Poplar one is just another tree one to me and, so help me God, I'm for a moratorium on trees for two or three years. Didn't read the other, in view of the doubt. While I'm at it, this is the last time I consider things in clumps, also, so help me God. I'm asking De Vries to start all things through separately. This pairing began with him.

Ross

*Kober was in Hollywood.*

## TO ARTHUR KOBER

*THE NEW YORKER*
*DECEMBER 9, 1946*

Dear Kober:

... [S]everal of you writers [have] discussed the working of this office and several reviewers have had passing reference to me as dynamic, boisterous, mad, violent, impatient, and so on, when everybody whom I ever associated with knows that I am one of the longest-suffering and pleasantest and, at heart, quietest men alive today, a sort of gentile Christ. I had a straight flush the other night that gave me a momentary lift, but only momentary, because, aside from that, I didn't do so well. We had two tables last week.

No hard luck, but I hope you come back.

As ever,

Ross

## MEMO TO WILLIAM SHAWN AND JOHN HERSEY

*DECEMBER 16, 1946*

Mr. Shawn, Mr. Hersey:

Note handed to me by my wife's sister Sunday evening:

Louella Parsons listed on air tonight the ten Americans of the year and among them were General Eisenhowser (correct) and John Hersey. Miss Parsons did not attempt to pronounce "Hiroshima."

H. W. Ross

## TO FRANK SULLIVAN

*THE NEW YORKER*
*DECEMBER 17, 1946*

Dear Frank:

Herewith an enclosure from *my* statistician. You are just spreading another of your canards, like the one you spread last summer, when you went all around northern New York saying that your own sister smokes reefers.

The damned calamity of this whole situation is that only sixteen percent of your writings of the last two or three years, or whatever period of time is involved, were for *The New Yorker,* which makes me sadder than you can possibly imagine over your non-mention. My earnest hope is that this will be a lesson to you. How about that cliche piece on newsreels ("There is one in newsreels, Ross. I go to them constantly and I know.")?

How about the cliche piece on the post-war world ("I have been thinking about a cliche piece based on the post-war world, plans for same.")?

How about a cliché piece on newspaper headline words?

I wish you sixteen percent of a merry Christmas and send 184% to [Sullivan's sister] Kate, balancing things.

Your last letter was written on Cornell [Club] stationery and I thought you were in town and called up. When I was told that you weren't here, I got switched to the house committee and turned you in as a letterhead stealer. I have in mind that girl you wrote about, but I haven't had the nerve to do anything about it. We had an office full of girl assistants during the war, Frank, and I solemnly swore to God that if I lived through the war, that would end lady editorial assistants, with three or four exceptions. Nobody knows what war is unless he goes through a war in a magazine office with lady editorial assistants, some of them wearing pants after being rejected as 4-F for psychological reasons. (Ask me sometime to tell you about one case that came up in the office involving a former naval man.) I'll ask people about this young lady and see, though. The only way I can work in anyone here, male or female, is to have someone take her on as an assistant, and that usually isn't easy. Moreover, I have a very bad record as to the people I am instrumental in hiring. They all turn out bad. They always have, all my life. . . .

I must now go to lunch.

As ever,

H. W. Ross

*Held is best remembered as the artist who created the symbol of the Jazz Age, the flapper. He grew up in Salt Lake City several years behind Ross, and in* The New Yorker's *first years Held's bold woodcuts represented some of the most inventive new humor in the magazine.*

TO JOHN HELD JR.

*THE NEW YORKER*
*JANUARY 6, 1947*

Dear John:

After I wrote you about that story two or three weeks ago, I got to brooding about you and your not doing any drawings. What in God's name goes on? Aren't you ever going to do any more art? I have heard stories that you have renounced drawing and haven't done a drawing in years, and so on. We need pictures here more, even, than we need writings, I should say, and you're an artist. Is there any chance of getting you started up again? I'd like to know about this. I'd also like to take you to lunch or dinner or something when you are in New York. I haven't seen you for years and would like to.

Let me know about these things, please.

As ever,

Ross

P.S. Your note of January 4th came in after I wrote the foregoing. How the Christ I could get to New Jersey to see somebody is beyond me. You must get to New York *sometime.*

I think it's a dirty trick to plagiarize an artist's work in ads and always have. I'm the boy who helped artists to meet at least partially this menace years ago by suggesting that all artists sign their things. Drawings in ads now are generally signed, and at least other artists and other people closely concerned know a genuine drawing from an imitation. I don't think, alas, that the general public does, though. I don't know what can be done about the morals of advertisers and agencies beyond establishing the practice of letting artists sign their drawings. I think that is generally established now.

H.W.R.

TO AL FRUEH

THE NEW YORKER
JANUARY 12, 1947

Dear Al,

It's good to see your caricatures back in the issues this season, for distinction and various other desirable qualities. The recent one on the Cornell show caused general exclamations of admiration. It was a wonder. You're not only, as I am ready to argue at any moment, the best caricaturist alive, but the best that ever lived.

Don't give it a second thought.

As ever,

H. W. Ross

TO FRANK SULLIVAN

THE NEW YORKER
JANUARY 20, 1947

Dear Frank:

I've had around for weeks the letter you wrote about the young lady on Project X that wants a job, intending to speak to you about it when I saw you. Since the way things work I may never see you again, I will speak now as follows: There aren't any jobs for girls here now. We got too damned many girls around here during the war and still have too many, and we are striving now to get men. I'll keep your letter around to come up in three or four months and see what the situation is then. The idea of employing a pip appalls me, though. This office isn't the hot love hole it once was by a great deal, but I got a dose of trouble with pips around the office in the old days that still makes me shudder. Looks have been against women in this place so far as I am concerned. I kept the bars down for several years, but some good-looking ones have crept in lately. I'm too old to fight it, and I guess the boys are older and the pursuit is not so hot. And Arno almost never comes around the office. . . .

As ever,

Ross

*Molotov was the Soviet foreign minister and Gromyko the Soviet ambassador to the United States.*

## TELEGRAM TO VYACHESLAV MOLOTOV AND ANDREI GROMYKO

*MARCH 3, 1947*

*The New Yorker* magazine respectfully calls your attention to the fact that it is not being represented in the group of thirty-six American correspondents who have received visas to attend the Foreign Ministers Conference in Moscow. . . . We consider this a serious omission in terms of balanced American press representation and for the following reasons plead again that this magazine be represented. *The New Yorker's* total paid circulation is close to four hundred thousand per week, a unique circulation in U.S. publishing annals for the reason that it has never solicited circulation. All this growth in nearly twenty-five years has been through word of mouth among the most important opinion-forming group of people in America. These nearly four hundred thousand readers include a higher percentage of people with intellectual attainment such as lawyers, doctors, executives, artists than does the circulation of any other American magazine. Over the past year alone . . . more than 450,000 [words] were direct, on-the-scene reports from our small but highly select group of foreign correspondents. This wordage alone places the magazine higher in the dispensing of foreign news than many of the newspapers and periodicals that are being represented at the conference, but we wish it clearly understood that we are not asking representation at the expense of any of those. . . . This reporting is analytical and background reporting and is unique in that it is not concerned with spot news. It is, however, an extremely important kind of reporting that supplements the spot news reports read by this important opinion-forming group.

The reporter for whom we ask a visa is Janet Flanner, for twenty years our European representative who is well known to the American press and public for her fearless and independent reports on European affairs. . . .

We fully appreciate the reasons for limiting the number of correspondents in Moscow. The housing shortage is terrible in New York and we were never besieged, bombed or strafed, except of course by an incalculable number of words, and for that reason we feel thirty-six reporters is probably enough if not too many. And we are so cooperative that if you find after looking over your housing situation you can't squeeze in Miss Flanner, who takes up no more room than any other ordinary woman, we will abide peacefully if sorrowfully by your decision. We hope, however, that you will let her in now, but if you can't will you permit her to come in right after the conference and stay for a while? We should like very much to have her reports on the U.S.S.R. and we would be surprised if you didn't like to read them, too.

Harold Ross
Editor

*Ross's appeal failed; Flanner did not get into Moscow.*

TO JANET FLANNER

*THE NEW YORKER*
*MARCH 18, 1947*

Dear Janet:

. . . The Art series ["The Beautiful Spoils," about the Nazi plunder of European artworks] has now run. It has apparently created as much interest as anything since Pétain. Out in California (where I went—quickly—for my vacation) I found Albert Lasker, the advertising man, reading the series aloud to his wife and several others who made up an appreciative audience. Excellent reports all around, of course. It was another distinguished and monumental job. The second story was my favorite, Goering. That piece did more than anything I read during the war and since to show up what brigands the bastards were. Goering was just what Al Capone would have been in control of a continent. You will doubtless hear a lot about this series, even at your distance.

With admiration and love,
Ross

## TO JOHN CHEEVER

*THE NEW YORKER*
*APRIL 3, 1947*

Dear Cheever:

I've just read "The Enormous Radio," having gone away for a spell and got behind, and I send my respects and admiration. That piece is worth coming back to work for. It will turn out to be a memorable one, or I am a fish. Very wonderful, indeed.

As ever,

Ross

## MEMO TO ROGERS E. M. WHITAKER

*MAY 5, 1947*

Mr. Whitaker:

I had a session of considerable length and weight Friday with Messrs. Shawn and Weekes on ways and means of getting out of the horrible nightmare of hand-to-mouthness around here, of never getting anything through until the last minute. (Profile being finished at midnight Thursday last week, for instance.) You would have been asked in on the session if you'd been here.

The big point I made so far as I am concerned was that I'll go nuts if we don't catch up and the magazine will probably go out of business, and the big point I made so far as you are concerned was that your work had to be cut down to a point where you can reasonably be expected to get ahead on long pieces, and stay ahead. It was also agreed that other adjustments have to be made so that the whole office is ditto. The sense of the session was that we will quit guiding ourselves on the A-issue and would work to get on top of the job and stay on it. This from my viewpoint is running the magazine instead of being run *by* it. I've been run *by* it for seven years now....

I gained agreement to the following as concerns you:

You are hereafter to be expected to read long-fact pieces and Letters only twice (one of the long-fact readings to be the pre-me reading).

You are not to be responsible for reading long-fact page at all.

You are to read the BoB [back of the book] departments only once, either in galley or page, as the case may be, except Feminine Fashions and About the House, which, it is proposed, you continue with as usual.

It will not be necessary for you to edit any book leads, if you are willing to give them up.

You can give up the editing of the Art Gallery column if you want to.

You are not to have to read captions on drawings in proof (since you already give them a once-over in copy and they are presumably watched competently after that).

You are to proceed with Talk, verse, Newsbreaks, and so on, as now, but any suggestions for relief as to these you may have will be welcomed.

The three of us agreed that with the editing power we now have there was no reason (theoretically, at least) that we cannot soon get back to a pre-war basis, or at any rate to a good bank of overmatter, and it was realized that with the mass vacations coming we had better damned well do so. There was, of course, concern over spreading you thinner (for everyone realizes the spectacular late catches you make from time to time, and so on) but we felt—or anyhow I felt—that it is best to do so, let the chips fall where they may. There will be chips, and no question about it. These we shall try to pick up somehow. . . .

H. W. Ross


MEMO TO *THE NEW YORKER* STAFF

*THE NEW YORKER*
*MAY 14, 1947*

To whomever it may concern:

The following figures, which fell into my lap, may be of interest:

In the first sixteen weeks of this year, we ran a total of 2,049 columns of editorial matter, consisting of the following:

| | |
|---|---|
| Fact | 1200 cols. (including Goings On—260 cols.) |
| Art | 414 cols. (including spots, caricatures, etc.) |

Fiction       347 cols.
Newsbreaks    63 cols. (including a lot of long ones.)
Verse         25 cols.

Figuring four hundred words to the column (no allowance for heads or for smaller type in Goings On) we put through 628,800 words, of which 480,000 was fact, 138,800 was fiction, and ten thousand was verse (figuring prose wordage displacement). This is an average of thirty thousand words of fact stuff per issue, and of 9,300 words of fiction and verse, which is almost forty thousand words of total text per issue, or around two million words per year.

Don't give it a second thought.

H. W. Ross

## TO FRANK SULLIVAN

*THE NEW YORKER*
*JUNE 5, 1947*

Dear Frank:

Here is a check, delayed. This piece has been on my mind all week. I have had complications. I was going to edit this and put it through, but Rebecca West came up to my place for the weekend, and I didn't get my work done. It wasn't that I had to entertain her—for she worked most of the time herself—but she had been to Greenville [South Carolina] for the lynching trial and turned in a terrifically long piece, and I had to read that and talk to her about it and didn't have time for little driblets like yours. She wrote sixteen thousand words, all in a few days, and all good, in my judgment, by God, and I don't know another person, male or female, on any continent, that can do that. She is about the brightest thing I have ever encountered. I wasn't so concerned because Lobrano was due back Monday. He came back all right, took your piece over (he's handled all yours recently and I would much rather have had him do it), but he's working slow, recovering from the heart flutters he had. As nearly as I can make out, he's got the same thing [Heywood] Broun had when he used to have to beat it out of theatres with palpitation years ago: nothing organic, but it beats wild from time to time. . . .

As ever,
Ross

## TO NUNNALLY JOHNSON

*JUNE 17, 1947*

Dear Nunnally:

You are the second or third person to tell me that Dudley Malone gets tearful at the thought of our Joe Mitchell on the grounds that Mitchell is married to Doris Stevens, and after your mention of this odd and colorful fact I decided by Jesus to find out, because I was interested, and it didn't sound plausible to me. I began by asking several people around the office. They all thought not. I could have asked Joe Mitchell himself, of course, but I am a trained newspaperman and don't get my dope in any such half-baked way as that. After going as far as I could with my office inquiries, I then referred to *Who's Who.* There I find that Doris Stevens is married (2nd) to Jonathan Mitchell, not Joseph, and I find that Jonathan was b. Portland, Maine, 1895, worked on the *New York World,* and wrote a book, *Goosesteps to Peace,* 1931. Not only is the first name different, but it would be contrary to the nature of our Mitchell to write a book called *Goosesteps to Peace.* . . .

Rebecca West thought you were charming. I think you're beautiful.

As ever,
Ross

*Botsford was an important* New Yorker *editor for more than four decades.*

## MEMO TO GARDNER BOTSFORD

*JULY 2, 1947*

Mr. Botsford:

This story is a big disappointment to me, and not what I outlined, or intended to outline (I now reread the outline and find it wasn't very good). What I had in mind was the thrilling and gruesome story of the depletion of the rat population of many millions, or several millions, to a few, the story of famine and starvation or of the orgy of cannibalism, or both, which I assumed and which I wrote into the earlier Riker's [Island] story. This is a story of rat control on a small scale, of how Hirschhorn handles the few remaining rats. It's not the story of the death of them by the millions. The piece dwells on this small-scale, peanut business for three pages and finally on P. 4 there is one scant paragraph on the subject (A), and that is that. I've been through the notes and find a little more, but not enough to get hold of and elaborate. All it says is that Mr. H. is *convinced* that the rats ate each other, that he knows of an instance or two of it, etc. Christ, that is not the story I wanted. I want the whole story of the decline, how the population dropped off year by year. The theory of it, if not the fact. Can't the reporter go into this phase of the thing?

When the first story went through it said the city stopped dumping garbage on Riker's nine years ago. The present notes say this happened two years ago. I have gone back to the first story as it came out in the magazine and find out that the nine years there was changed to two. That means that from five to ten million rats died off in a very short time—unless the city gradually stopped dumping garbage on the island, ending finally two years ago, and the dying off was slow.

I suspect that the modest, small-scale rat control dwelt on in the first three pages of this piece can be got in an Agricultural Department bulletin for fifteen cents any time. It has a certain interest, because of the way it's told, but it's not the story of the great famine on Riker's, or the great cannibalistic orgy.

Ross

*Bemelmans was in Paris.*

TO LUDWIG BEMELMANS

*The New Yorker*
*July 22, 1947*

Dear Ludwig:

Yes, but how about those stories? Let me know. The summer is half over.

Bureaucrats are going to be the ruin of the world. They are more of a menace than insects, or fascism, or even than lawyers, to whom they are first cousins. Don't try to do anything in this country, such as sell an automobile, or you'll get submerged in pieces of paper. Your mention of Benchley in a French film came just after I was thinking of him. I went up to "21" to have dinner the other night, late and alone. I didn't know a damned soul in the place, and felt terribly alone—no Benchley, no anybody. Most of my contemporaries are gone and the world is getting lonesome. Send the French film over here and I will run it off from time to time for the half-dozen survivors. This reminds me that I have something interesting for you. You once spoke of "21" as proprietor-ridden, which bright remark I have remembered since. Well, Charlie Byrns sat down with me for a few minutes and I learned that he is not a proprietor, which astonished me. He just acts like one, out of habit. He gave his interest away to his brother and to a couple of Jack Kriendler's brothers when Prohibition came. That is a funny thing, and it explains why there are so many proprietors. Charlie couldn't be both a wholesaler and retailer of liquor under the New York state law, and this was his way out. He didn't even give me a drink, for early and good attendance. Love to all.

As ever,
Ross

## TO REBECCA WEST

*THE NEW YORKER*
*JULY 24, 1947*

Dear Rebecca:

The attached clears up the Ben Hecht beard matter. I don't know where [Nunnally] Johnson could have got that. People in California live in a world of rumors, dreams, and superstitions, because newspapers out there don't print much news.

As ever,
Ross

## TO JOHN COLLIER

*THE NEW YORKER*
*AUGUST 8, 1947*

Dear Collier:

A peculiar thing has come up. We believe that Billy Rose, the theatrical producer who has become a columnist, has plagiarized recently one of your stories, "Back for Christmas," which ran in *The New Yorker* in 1939 (and has appeared widely in anthologies since then). See the enclosed photostat of his column that appeared locally in *PM* on July 28th.

If you concur with others in the opinion that your plot has been lifted and want to make something of it, you might collect some damages from *PM* and the other papers that published the Rose column. At any rate, we got hooked a while back on what seems to me the same sort of thing, although we established that we were entirely innocent in intent. I don't think that an innocent intent could be shown in this case, because once before Rose (we allege) lifted some stuff from *The New Yorker* and we protested it, in the case of *PM*, at least. We wrote to Marshall Field, the owner of *PM*, about it and got kissed off.

I have a kind of personal interest in the matter, aside from the official one that I don't like to see our authors' stuff lifted, because one of Marshall Field's minions threatened to sue me some time back for a remark I made about one of his publishing outfits and I had to more or less eat some words.

I'd like to know how you feel about this thing. If you should be disposed to take some action, I think maybe we could do something about it here for you, with our lawyers, if you want us to, for, technically, you are the copyright holder on the piece since we assigned the copyright on it to you in 1943.

It might be interesting. Please let me know.

I wish to God you would write some stuff for us. I feel dismal when I think of the pieces you used to do and realize that you haven't done any more in years. Maybe I ought to be suing you.

With best wishes,

Ross

## MEMO TO WOLCOTT GIBBS, JAMES THURBER, AND E. B. WHITE

*AUGUST 11, 1947*

To the Messrs. Gibbs, Thurber, White:

Greetings. A writer named Allen Churchill, heretofore unknown to me, is doing a piece on *The New Yorker* for *Cosmopolitan* and has the idea that he wants to quote some interoffice memos in it, being under the impression that these are interesting as hell. He seems to have been told so. The fact is that certain notes written at various times by you gentlemen, among others, *would* be interesting, I believe, and also entertaining, and doubtless many of them are around. How do you stand about letting him have some of yours? They could be dug up and shown to you first.

I deplore such projects as this story, but don't know what to do about them, other than to be decently cooperative. This organization has been bothering everybody in New York for twenty years and I'm ashamed to do otherwise.

Please let me know.

There is always Gibbs's note on the proofs of Max Eastman's book, that ". . . he got American humor down and broke its arm."

H.W. Ross

TO REBECCA WEST

*THE NEW YORKER*
*AUGUST 12, 1947*

Dear Rebecca:

... God, I wish you would get a break and get to Palestine. That, next to Russia—everything journalistically is next to Russia, to my mind—is the most interesting spot there is now, from a news standpoint, and I have never seen anything other than an unsatisfactory fragment from there. And your conclusion that there is something behind it more sinister than meets the eye arouses my sense of news and mystery....

Now, I've got to get to work on a couple of pieces that, at first glance, seem to have been written by educated Negroes.

I earnestly hope that your jaw infection has disappeared by the time you get this. As for my mouth condition, the dentist has all my bridges for remodeling, and I won't get them until I get back. I've been going around looking, to use an old line of Alec Woollcott's, like an English theatrical company. My condition is not threatening world letters, or world journalism, as yours is, however.

As ever,
Ross

*One afternoon while he was on a writing sabbatical from the magazine, fiction editor William Maxwell bumped into Ross on the street and told him he was in town to see a show. Ross assumed, mistakenly, that Maxwell meant a matinee, and was relieved when he was later set straight.*

TO WILLIAM MAXWELL

*THE NEW YORKER*
*SEPTEMBER 3, 1947*

Dear Maxwell:

... Mason seems undaunted. He has given me a note reading as follows: "I will flag you when Maxwell has been away six months and nine months so he can be warned that he needs to sell us something to protect his [pension] rights." There I leave the thing lay. The plan will have merit, from my standpoint, if it forces some pieces in from various writers. . . .

I am enormously relieved to learn that you didn't go to a matinee of those shows. I don't like the feeling that I know men who go to shows in the afternoon. It's worse than smoking reefers and, I believe, practically the same as subsisting on the fruits of fallen women.

As ever, and for not longer than six months, I am

Sincerely,

Ross

---

*Thurber and Samuel Goldwyn had a public contretemps over the movie adaptation of Thurber's story "The Secret Life of Walter Mitty." In an exchange of letters in* Life, *Goldwyn patronized* The New Yorker *as a "little magazine"; Thurber replied that " 'the little magazine,' so much bigger than Goldwyn, Inc., except in physical size, needs no other defense than the revealing slur itself."*

MEMO TO JAMES THURBER

SEPTEMBER 8, 1947

Mr. Thurber:

. . . I am confronted with a roomful of things on paper, and will answer the rest of your letter with the terseness of a busy man.

I got a great deal of satisfaction from your answer to Goldwyn. Selznick pulled that "little magazine" stuff on me, too. I think several of them may have that phrase in their bean. It's a funny coincidence, anyhow. I'd like to know who wrote Goldwyn's letter, or how it was got together, but I'm not enough interested to devote any time to finding out. There's something funny there, though—the idea of Sam Goldwyn writing a letter. I'll buy you a meal for coming back at him on behalf of the organization. . . .

H. W. Ross

---

*Ross was forever dubious about the place of serious poetry in the magazine, as much as anything because he couldn't figure out a logical compen-*

sation scheme for it. When at one point he decided payment should take into account how wide a poem was set, Mrs. White, who had cultivated The New Yorker's poetry, ridiculed the idea.

## MEMO TO KATHARINE S. WHITE

*SEPTEMBER 9, 1947*

Mrs. White:

The new poetry payment scheme is in to stay, or the principle of it is. It's the only way I, for one, can operate, with any idea of what I'm doing. We pay for everything else by space—or at any rate we measure everything, and space is one factor—and we should unquestionably pay for poetry that way, too.

I think it is a mistake to explain the rates to poets, unless some one of them asks for an explanation, which is unlikely. All through this payment thing one factor sticks out to me: Prose writers, artists, poets, are appalled at the thought of space entering into the appraisal of their, and other people's, work, but space is certainly a factor in the value of a contribution to the New Yorker Publishing Company, Inc. If we measure poems by their length (which we have always done, and which practically everyone else does), it seems to me absurd not to take into consideration also the width.

H. W. Ross

## TO JAMES THURBER

*THE NEW YORKER*
*SEPTEMBER 10, 1947*

Dear Jim:

... I had dinner last night with [Thurber's old friend, Elliott] Nugent, who had had some drinks following an actors' meeting, and he swayed and swung and was very expansive. It started out as my dinner, as I understood it, but he bought champagne and other fancy and high-priced items and kept doubling up as we went along and I let him have the check. In fact, I insisted upon it. Morris Ernst was there, having been found friendless and alone in the place ("21"). Nugent told about a dispute with you arising from your spurning of a financial proposition he had put up to you to work on a play. I never understood the deal. It was more complex than *New Yorker* finances, which I grew up with. Ernst nodded wisely throughout and then interjected an anecdote about your throwing twenty-eight thousand dollars in Goldwyn's face. They both agreed you were an odd character, and unworldly and impractical beyond human credence. When it was all over, I said I thought you were right throughout. You should have seen them. Instantly, I retreated to a corner and unsheathed my rapier. I stood them off for about thirty minutes, at the end of which time they were worn down. I told them businessmen would never understand artists, many many other things—thrust after thrust. Remind me of this and I will tell you more when I see you. Nugent was affectionate toward you throughout, of course, and also toward me as far as that goes. I had a good time.

As ever,
Ross

## TO CHARLES ADDAMS

*THE NEW YORKER*
*OCTOBER 16, 1947*

Dear Addams:
We went over that caption on the cannibal drawing today—Geraghty, Lobrano, and I—and we concluded that you absolutely have to use "missionary." If you use "people," it will have two definite meanings and the wrong one most likely to register instead of the right one. "He likes people" is a very common expression, meaning just what it says. Moreover, you've got to have a singular verb in the last clause, and that is a final clincher, and you can't have one with "people," which is plural, and that is all there is to it.

If you still have anything to say, though, say it. Tell Geraghty.

As ever,
Ross

## TO H. L. MENCKEN

Dear Mencken:

Have you any drag with Johns Hopkins by which I could get an appointment for a four-year-old girl with some kind of heart irregularity with those doctors who do their stuff on blue babies? One of them, a woman, is named Taussig and she has a male teammate whose name I do not recall. The situation is this: My wife has a sister who had two children who a year ago were aged five and four, respectively. The older one died of leukemia last winter and now the doctors are in a state of alarm about the younger one, who was born with a heart skip, or some such. She threatened to be a blue baby, as I understand it—although I understand nothing about this condition—and then wasn't a blue baby, quite. The medical sages in Los Angeles, where the family lives, have had their say, which is that complications have developed, the little girl's heart is enlarged, and so on. The parents want to go to the top place about it, and consider the Something-Taussig clinic at Johns Hopkins the top place.

I dislike bothering you about a personal matter, but this is in a good cause. If you haven't the proper influence, would Paul Patterson have it? I could line him up, I suppose. The parents can get here and can deliver the little girl in Baltimore any time an appointment can be got.

Best regards,

As ever,

Ross

## MEMO TO KATHARINE S. WHITE

Mrs. White:

. . . I'd like to know which authors are saying it's too much trouble to fix their stuff to suit us. O'Hara doesn't count, although I don't know whether he has ever gone to the trouble of making such a remark as this. For years, I've been getting complaints about the obscurity of O'Hara's stories, and, if anything, it's he who is getting away with something, and not us. Nor do the vast number of semi-literates who write three-fourths of our stuff count—that Eaton woman, for instance [fiction contributor Evelyn Eaton]. You don't know what she's talking about a third of the time, and that goes for a lot of others. Those people aren't writers. Their stuff has to be rendered into English and can't rise above the plane of straightaway English because that's as high as editing will raise it. But it ought to be edited to that plane.

H. W. Ross


*Hughes was with* Advertising Age.

TO L. M. HUGHES

*THE NEW YORKER*
*NOVEMBER 7, 1947*

Dear Mr. Hughes:

I looked for you yesterday in Mr. Forster's office soon after we parted at the elevator, but you had gone off with him some place. Mr. Forster tells me that you asked him about the old times around here, and I will tell you a little about them here that may clarify the situation to some extent. It is touchy, as are all such, but it is especially touchy here because we don't have many titles. This is probably an inadequacy in our organization, but we never have bothered much. As I told you, Mr. Shawn is in charge of fact things—all long fact articles, all long departments, the Talk of the Town Department, etc.; Mr. Lobrano is responsible for all non-departmental text, and, in addition, sits in on the selection of the drawings we use; and Mr. Geraghty is responsible for drawings. Mr. Shawn has been here about twenty years. Mr. Lobrano and Mr. Geraghty have been here around ten years. Mrs. E. B. White, another old-timer, has been here more than twenty years. She used to be responsible for the fiction and humor pieces, with Wolcott Gibbs who has been here seventeen or eighteen years and used to spend most of his time editing. He quit editing eight or ten years ago and since then has been a writer, devoting practically all of his time to writing for *The New Yorker.* In addition to the foregoing editors, there are several old-timers who do not deal with the contributors and are hardly known on the outside at all but are people of exceeding importance from my standpoint. These include Sanderson Vanderbilt, who assists Shawn as an editor of manuscript; Hobart G. Weekes, who is in command of getting the text and drawings organized and in shape to go to press (he has no concern for anything until it is bought, when he more or less takes charge of it); Rogers E. M. Whitaker, who devotes practically all of his time to editing of a very high order, who reads almost everything that goes into the magazine, and who works on getting it right as to English, style, sense, etc.; and Carmine Peppe, who is in charge of what we call the make-up room and who actually lays the magazine out, sizing the drawings, making a first choice on which ones will go in each issue, and does all of our dealings with the printer and the engraver. Those are the most important old-timers.

In addition to these, there are about an equal number of newer people, most of whom have been around several years. When you come down to it, we've got quite a number of capable people here. There aren't quite enough, but there are quite a number of them at that.

Mrs. White works practically full time but spends part of the year in Maine. She and Gibbs carried the fiction load for a long time, before Lobrano took over.

E. B. White, who has been around the office for twenty years or more (as I told you, I'm a little foggy about these time periods), has always been a writer but has nevertheless been important in an ex officio editorial capacity. So has James Thurber, in a like role, and so have a number of others. There are, of course, many old-timers among the contributors. The list of them would be long.

I trust the foregoing will be helpful. Please don't quote me on any of this. I'm writing this hastily and have undoubtedly left out a couple of people who should be mentioned.

Sincerely yours,

H. W. Ross

*When Hellman left* The New Yorker *for a better-paying job at* Life *magazine, he sent Ross some of Time Inc.'s distinctive powder blue memo pads. Ross often used these to correspond with Hellman, a small but satisfying joke at Luce's expense.*

## MEMO TO GEOFFREY HELLMAN

*TIME INCORPORATED*
*11/13/47*

To: Mr. Hellman
From: Mr. Ross
What is the temperature over there?
Do you need any pencils?

*The DuBarry ads, which ran regularly in the magazine, featured before-and-after pictures of dowdy women miraculously turned thin and glamorous.*

## MEMO TO HAWLEY TRUAX

*NOVEMBER 24, 1947*

Mr. Truax:
That DuBarry Success School ad on Page 93 of the Nov. 15th issue is another insult to our readers and a reflection on everyone working for the magazine—cheap, quack stuff of the most palpable kind. Why in God's name we keep on using this stinking copy is beyond me.
H. W. Ross

## TO REBECCA WEST

*THE NEW YORKER*
*NOVEMBER 25, 1947*

Dear Rebecca:
... I didn't know anything about the dedication [in *The Meaning of Treason*] until I was looking through the book and saw it cold. After getting my breath, I went out in the kitchen and found Ariane and her brother and told them I had just received the most notable honor of

my life. I regard it as that still, and am much flattered, and just over-flowing with gratitude and goodwill to you. I can't wait until people begin to notice the dedication, notably my lawyer, who, as I think I told you, regards you as the greatest living writer and has read your Yugoslavia book over several times. And there are many others. I consider that I have now crashed American letters, which gives me much amusement. I'm planning to get about a hundred copies of the book and send them out for Christmas under an alias. God bless you for doing this.

The book came by messenger from Viking Press—which may have been [Harold] Guinzburg's doing—and I had had no intimation, although when I mentioned it to Shawn I found that he had known it two weeks earlier, a review copy of the book having come in. He said he didn't bother to tell me because he thought I knew it. Shawn himself was acting hangdog because Mollie Panter-Downes had dedicated her novel to him. It's a big year in this office. I was glad for Shawn. I don't give a hoot about any kind of mention for me any more, having had enough, and so much that I am sheepish about it around the office, which contains quite number of other people who have given their lives and talents to this venture and have got practically no credit at all. One of the most notable of these is Shawn—who is the hardest-working and most self-sacrificing man I have ever done business with. I was glad for him....

An odd thing: Your friend Elsa Maxwell called me up on the day of the wedding [of Princess Elizabeth and Philip Mountbatten, duke of Edinburgh] and invited me to dinner with the Duchess of Windsor (and the Duke, too, I guess, although he was not mentioned in the message Elsa left). She says the Duchess wants to meet me. I think there is some truth in this, for shortly after the abdication over there I got a letter from the Duchess thanking us for something we had said about the business. It was something Flanner wrote. I forget now what it is, but Flanner is around, and I'm going to get her to refresh my memory before the dinner, which is tomorrow evening; black tie. This is not my only British contact of the week. I am invited to a cocktail party this afternoon for the proprietor of *Punch* and am going to get there if I can. I've always been curious about *Punch* and how it is run, and I may learn something, if nothing more than how the proprietor of a magazine ought to dress and act, looking toward instituting reforms in those regards here. . . .

As ever,

R

*West got the invasive* Time *treatment in a cover story.*

TO REBECCA WEST

THE NEW YORKER
DECEMBER 2, 1947

Dear Rebecca:

I doubt (in reference to your recent wireless) that *Time* was motivated by a desire to discredit a *New Yorker* writer. If so, it was a secondary motive. They're just naturally that way and always have been. We have a rule on this magazine that a man (or woman) is entitled to his private life. Thus, we never print scandal. It is a good rule, and a magazine can go on forever and hold its head up with such a rule as that. *Time* loves to dig up skeletons. Recently, a congressman named Thomas headed an investigating committee and earned a considerable degree of unpopularity. He is a stupid and a dangerous man, and considerable of a heel. Everyone knew that Thomas isn't his real name, or his original name—that his mother had left Thomas's father, taking her son with her, when the son was very young, and resumed her maiden name and given that name to the son; nobody printed it but *Time,* which was unfair. *Time* made a career of referring to Ramsay MacDonald as a bastard when MacDonald was prime minister. A while back, someone remarked that all the *Time* outfit were sons of bitches, but he didn't know whether they were that way when *Time* hired them or got that way after they went to work there. They're just naturally that way and that's that, although envious of *The New Yorker* along with it, for we print well-written things and they don't. The reason they don't is that they don't know when a thing is well-written and when it isn't, but they don't know that they don't, and have no idea what the trouble is. . . .

As ever,
Ross


*Taussig was a renowned pediatric cardiologist.*

TO DR. HELEN B. TAUSSIG

*THE NEW YORKER*
*DECEMBER 2, 1947*

Dear Dr. Taussig:

I am the uncle of the little girl in California, the four-year-old daughter of Mrs. Gordon N. Scott, of Beverly Hills, on whose behalf Mr. H. L. Mencken called on you yesterday. Mr. Mencken is an old friend of mine, and in the extremity I drafted him into this case. He advised me yesterday by telephone of your very kind offer to fit the little girl into your engagements on December 18th—at nine A.M.—but he told me further that you would have no hope of continuing the examination then and that you regarded the case as presenting no emergency and demanding no great haste. I talked to Mrs. Scott in California today, and in view of this assurance, Mrs. Scott decided not to bring the child east at this time. She has three other children and decided that it would be best to stay with them until after Christmas. Will you please, therefore, cancel the date for nine A.M. on December 18th, but retain the appointment for Mrs. Scott you specified in the letter you wrote to her direct some days ago? This was for some date near the end of January.

The fact is that Mrs. Scott would, of course, like to get the little girl to you as soon after the first of the year as possible, and I herewith ask that if some shift in your schedule should make it possible for you to see the child at some date earlier in January than the one set, that you let me know by wire, telephone, or in any other expeditious way, at my expense. I can get Mrs. Scott started east from California on very short notice. The waiting is going to be agonizing for all concerned, naturally, and I earnestly hope that something will happen that will leave a hole in your schedule. Mr. Mencken has told me that you are under terrific pressure, although that was unnecessary, for I was certain of this before.

I thank you, on behalf of the parents of this girl and myself, for your generous consideration to date, and we shall all hope for the best.

Gratefully yours,

H. W. Ross

## TO JAMES THURBER

*THE NEW YORKER*
*DECEMBER 11, 1947*

Dear Thurber:

Sure (referring to your recent note to Shawn about tag lines for anecdotes) you can put them on, but you are you. Other people, I regret to say, cannot, or cannot a lot of the time. A few months ago, I read in Herbert Spencer's autobiography about his having dinner with Thomas Carlyle. Carlyle was testy on the subject of genius, said there was no such thing, was impatient with people who couldn't do certain things, such as put tag lines on anecdotes: he said *anybody* could put them on. Spencer gets testy in his autobiography about this; Carlyle's intolerance [was] wrong, he said, and adds a definition of a genius, which is the best definition I've ever come upon: "A genius is a man who can do readily what other people cannot do at all."

Don't give it a second thought.

As ever,

Ross

## MEMO TO HOBART WEEKES

*DECEMBER 17, 1947*

Mr. Weekes:

I don't think the last issue was Christmassey enough—or pre-Christmassey enough. The number of idea drawings used was right, I think, but not enough Christmassey spots were used. There were only a few of them, and at least one, while Christmas all right, didn't look Christmassey. Spots are the thing to tone up the book on such occasions as the pre-Christmas season. As I recall, we were deficient last year, too. This arguable, maybe, but I'll get it down thus while I think of it.

H. W. Ross

TO CLIFFORD REEVES

*THE NEW YORKER*
*DECEMBER 17, 1947*

Dear Mr. Reeves:

I have your letter of December 11th. The question of whether the people on the free list have the right to object to our opinions has never, to my knowledge, come up before, but I believe they should be accorded full privileges.

You say it is arrant nonsense that the ten Hollywood men were fired "for refusing to reveal their politics," and that "the man who wrote that [Talk of the Town] piece knows it." The man who wrote the piece doesn't know it, or he wouldn't have written it, and I don't know it, or I wouldn't have allowed it to be run. You accuse us of complete lack of integrity, and that piece was written and run with complete integrity.

You say "communism . . . is an international revolutionary movement pledged to the violent overthrow in the United States and elsewhere. You don't have to take my word for this. It is a matter of established record that is beyond dispute. . . ." What communism is outside the United States has no bearing on the issue dealt with in our piece, which was concerned purely with what communism is in the United States. One thing it is is a political party. There car be no doubt of that, for under federal law and most state laws it is allowed to appear on ballots as such and to run candidates as such, and to act in all ways like any other political party. As long as it has that legal status, there is no question in my mind that those ten Hollywood men were being asked what their politics were, and there is no question in my mind that that was unconstitutional.

In the issue of December 13th, we ran a piece with the intent of setting down coldly some of the facts on communism in the United

States, which includes what I have just said. It also points out that while it is legal for a Communist to be a congressman, and there may be a Communist congressman, a congressman as much as told the movie people to fire their employees suspected of being Communists. I can imagine few things more terrifying to an American than such dictatorial governmental bludgeoning.

The Communist Party may be out to overthrow the government by force and violence. If so, the orderly and legal and democratic procedure would be to prove that and outlaw the party, but nobody has proved that—not Edgar Hoover, not any element of our police power, not you. It is not a matter of "record that is beyond dispute." It is not a matter of record at all. This fact may prove to be exceedingly unfortunate and lamentable, but even if I thought it were going to be fatal I wouldn't want to see the Constitution of the United States scrapped. That piece was defending the Constitution, not communism.

I enclose that later piece I spoke about, marked in blue.

Sincerely yours,

H. W. Ross

*When Ariane traveled to England in the summer of 1947, one of the people she met up with was the scion of a family that had amassed a fortune in cotton, Sir John Leigh. Seven years after Ross's death, she would marry him.*

TO REBECCA WEST

*THE NEW YORKER*
*DEC. 21ST, 1947*

Dear Rebecca:

. . . I knocked off work a while ago (I'm in the country) to see a showing of the pictures Ariane took of you, Henry, and your place last summer. They are fine. The likenesses of you and Henry are rather thrilling. The only trouble is that Ariane had the camera geared wrong and you both appear in slow motion, as though walking around under water. So does Sir John What's-his-name (that lord of Ariane's) and he doesn't do under water as well as you and Henry.

This will be your Christmas letter. Love to you and Henry and merry Christmas and all that.

As ever,
Wembley

MEMO TO WILLIAM SHAWN

*JANUARY 2, 1948*

Mr. Shawn:

I notice that an idea of Mr. Botsford's has been put through for Talk on the song *Happy Birthday to You.* In this connection, I herewith report that I favor such a piece and have ideas as to how it should be reported and written. . . .

We ran a story on this song in 1941. I have reread it and find it disgracefully deficient. The song was written by Dr. Patty Smith Hill, professor emeritus of education at Columbia, not the lady Mr. Botsford names in his outline. I propose that this second story get right down to brass tacks on the finances of the copyright—the money Miss Hill has raked in as royalties and the money the publisher has raked in. What are total earnings? What average earnings per year? The reporter of the facts for the first story didn't get these facts, nor did he get to Miss Hill but only to her former secretary, who said that Miss Hill didn't care anything about making money out of the song. Nevertheless, she has undoubtedly made a lot of it. Or her publisher has. Maybe it's the publisher who is so hard-boiled about it. Who are the personalities behind the publishing firm, the Clayton F. Summy Company? How much they make out of *Happy Birthday?* Our first story said that the producers of a revue called *The Band Wagon* got hooked when they innocently used the song in a skit, but the story didn't say how much they got hooked for. We could find this out from Max Gordon, who produced *The Band Wagon.* I think we ought to get at the guts of the story this time, and maybe see Miss Hill herself. I presume she's still alive, and living right in New York.

H. W. Ross

TO EMILY HAHN

*THE NEW YORKER*
*JANUARY 5, 1948*

Dear Emily:

... I am not enthusiastic about any story about a Negro guest. That damned colored question would come up in every other story, verse, etc., if we didn't watch it, and I'm suspicious of the whole proposition. I meet many modern Abraham Lincolns these days, who have freed the colored race all over again. Their activities consist mostly of entertaining the Negroes in their homes. That doesn't convince me at all. The test comes when Negroes entertain the white folks in their homes, and the white folks go. Most of the activity seems to me straight, self-conscious patronization of the colored folk—or dangerously close to being simply that—and, moreover, I think the colored folk feel it. I intend nothing personal in this. Your situation is different over there [in England], the colored gent being probably a stranger in a strange land. That is something else again. The colored problem goes much deeper than superficial social intercourse, which is about as far as my pals, and our writers, have gone.

I suppose you know about Noel Coward's remark about the Negro troops in England during the war. I heard about it long ago, but a few weeks ago I got it straight from Coward himself. It was a crack made to Adolph Menjou, and made to shock Menjou. Menjou was in England and was wringing his hands to Coward about what might happen to English womanhood with all the colored American troops about and Coward said, "Thank God. Maybe it will give us some good teeth." Or something like that. I don't seem to have straightened out much at that. Maybe you better ask Coward to get the exact facts....

As ever,

H. W. Ross

*In 1947* The New Yorker *published West's startling dispatch from Greenville, South Carolina, about a group of whites being tried for lynching a black man. Ross had edited the piece himself and was enduringly proud of it.*

TO REBECCA WEST

*THE NEW YORKER*
*JANUARY 7, 1948*

Dear Rebecca:

... I enclose a clipping revealing that there was only one lynching in our South all last year, that of Willie Earle. This must be a new low, although the story doesn't say so. I will say we made the best of that one. I think probably your piece was a strong influence against lynchings. I think the South has got self-conscious about them and that it has gained a certain amount of enlightenment—or anyhow, restraint.

As ever,

Ross

MEMO TO GUS LOBRANO

*JANUARY 26, 1948*

Mr. Lobrano:

I suppose the following is obvious and would have been picked up otherwise, but I'll get it off my mind. The Eisenhower announcement that he won't run seems final and contravenes the line in the Thurber story "... until Eisenhower starts Eisenhowering ..." or whatever it is (I quote from memory). I think it contains a good verb, though, and suggest that it be saved in some form or other, if feasible: "... now that Eisenhower isn't going to Eisenhower ..." or some such. This particular variant doesn't sound so good on paper, though, maybe.

H. W. Ross

## TO GEOFFREY HELLMAN

*THURSDAY*
*[EARLY 1948]*

Hellman:

That concern of yours over taxes and over finances in general worries me, too, or it has since Shawn mentioned to me the other day that you have turned back [the] Baedecker pieces to him, saying you can't afford to write them because of taxes. In my judgment, you are carrying the concern with taxes beyond a point of reasonableness. A writer's career should come first, I think, ahead of little details. And I think that on rewrite you ought to take the hard with the easy, as an averaging-out proposition. The prices for rewrite were set with that in mind, although I don't recall that this peculiar possibility was foreseen, i.e., the influences of the income tax on a difficult piece. That would have seemed too far-fetched.

Ross

## TO JOSEPH ALSOP

*THE NEW YORKER*
*FEBRUARY 24, 1948*

Dear Alsop:

I regret that after considerable hemming and hawing here we decided against this. It would be suitable material for us if it weren't for the fact that we are heavily banked up with reminiscent pieces, but we are a year ahead on these, or thereabouts, and we have resolved not to load up further at present unless something pretty damned compelling comes along. This, frankly, wasn't considered compelling enough to warrant an exception. Its slightness militated against it here. During the next year you will see a number of reminiscent stories in the issues that, unfortunately, won't be nearly as well written as this, but they will have more substance—except for some already bought that won't.

I'm sorry to be writing thus, as we had hoped for further pieces from you, although not reminiscent ones, and we hope that you won't be discouraged.

I heard a great deal about that last piece, but it got mixed up with politics and emotions to such an astonishing degree that I fear it was approved by many for reasons other than its merit as a story, which is what I saw in it principally, although I knew right along, of course, that it was a topical and an informative story involving matters that people get emotional about, as indeed, what timely things do not these days.

Sincerely,

Ross

TO H. L. MENCKEN

*THE NEW YORKER*
*MARCH 3, 1948*

Dear Mencken:

I'll write this now, although I know you are in Florida—or anyhow, I trust to God that you are and getting a rest. I enclose the official copy on Susan Scott from Dr. Taussig (as written out by one of her young assistants, a very nice fellow named Lambert). The girl has a bad heart; there is no question about that, but they told me orally when I was down there that they thought she was good for twenty or twenty-five years with it and that long before then there probably will be a corrective operation. This, I think, has been confirmed by the later examination.

It is notable that Dr. Taussig expressed the opinion outlined in the enclosed shortly after looking at the little girl through the fluoroscope and that all the subsequent tests bore out what she said. She is a wonderful woman and we had her personal interest throughout, which was regal. . . .

I assume you will read this on your return and that you will come back thoroughly invigorated and good for another twenty or twenty-five years yourself.

As ever,

Ross

## MEMO TO LILLIAN ROSS

Miss Ross:
I have received the following telegram from Hollywood:

"Dear Harold
Lillian Ross superb job only serves to support my belief that that rag of yours is the best magazine ever published.
                              Regards—John Huston"

This kind of thing is no more than I expected.
H. W. Ross

*Lovett was undersecretary of defense.*

## TELEGRAM TO ROBERT LOVETT

*APRIL 1, 1948*

Am instructed by Adele to call you and see if you can have lunch with me and my wife and Rebecca West in Washington Sunday. I will be there Saturday and will telephone you about this then. Anxious to discuss state of roadbed Union Pacific Railroad west of Winnemucca, Nevada.
Regards,
H. W. Ross

## MEMO TO WILLIAM SHAWN

*APRIL 5, 1948*

Mr. Shawn:
Forrestal in Washington told me a couple of odd things: I told him I was astonished at a sentence in a recent story ([Daniel] Lang) that the principal activity of the atomic commission is the manufacture of weapons; that I'd thought it would develop the atom for peace use. He says that the weapon use is all there is to it at present—that the peactime use is visionary and very far off.

He also said that when Roosevelt and the rest of them were debating whether to drop the bomb on Hiroshima or not (which was flatly unnecessary militarily) one of the powerful groups in favor of dropping the bomb were the scientists, and exactly the same scientists who, after the bomb was dropped, started wringing their hands. They had made the bomb and they wanted it to be dropped. Also, Forrestal says, there would have been one hell of a congressional investigation if the bomb hadn't been dropped, to find out what happened to the two million [*sic*] dollars.

H. W. Ross

TO JEAN STAFFORD

*The New Yorker*
*April 22, 1948*

Dear Miss Stafford:

How about Clyde Barrows (or it may be Barrow) for the outlaw in "A Summer Day"? In case you don't know, he was an outlaw of the Pretty Boy Floyd era and, I am advised, committed two murders in Oklahoma. He traveled with a girlfriend, Bonnie Parker, who, it is my recollection, died with him.

I think a real name would help if we can get it in there. Mrs. White is in the hospital, which is why I am writing this—aside from the fact that I said I would undertake to dig up an outlaw.

Sincerely yours,

Ross

*After deciding to publish in a single issue a portfolio of Williams drawings about a lavish wedding, Ross gleefully endeavored to keep the project a secret.*

TO GLUYAS WILLIAMS

*375 Park Avenue*
*May 20 [1948]*

Dear Gluyas:

... Operative KX12 didn't slip up in mailing those proofs from the office. I said nothing whatever in my note that would reveal our fell plan. I assumed that my secretary (whom I recently acquired and, to tell the truth, do not trust completely) and whoever else saw the communication would think I was just lining up a normal series—if they thought anything. . . . Anyhow, I couldn't bring the batch of proofs home here and mail them, for lack of facilities. The strain of finding a stamp in the rat-nest of my wife's top dressing-table drawer, addressing an ordinary envelope, and slipping out through the kitchen to the mail chute, propping the kitchen door open so that I am not locked out on the landing, is as much as I can take. I would never make a spy. I'd tip over the invisible ink.

From here on I will be completely underground and you won't hear from me unless there is a crisis of some kind, in which case I will probably endeavor to telephone you. If you get a call from Ulysses S. Grant, talking in a low, husky voice, you will know who it is.

As ever,
Ross

*Ross was troubled when the Algonquin was sold to Ben Bodne, who made his fortune as an oil distributor.*

TO ELMER DAVIS

*THE NEW YORKER*
*JUNE 1, 1948*

Dear Elmer:

I got your letter about Johnny Martin and the Algonquin. I didn't know what had happened and I don't yet, although, stimulated by your expression of interest, I sounded out a couple of waiter pals. One said he'd seen it coming for a long time and seemed to be pro the new management, although he was cagey and didn't go beyond that observation. The other was just plain cagey; I got nothing out of it either way.

I got suspicious some time ago, and was prepared to blacklist the place or something, when I found that my old waiter captain, John, wasn't on evenings any more, but he told me later that that was his doing, not the new management's. Prior to that I had got sore because they fired the two old hatcheck girls, long pals of mine, and put in a couple of brassy Broadway-basement figures (since slightly improved on). I inquired around about that and learned that for a long time the hatcheck girls had been on salary and had had to turn in the take to the management, and that under the new management the hatcheck concession had been sold to a professional and the new girls were his. I didn't find out who instituted the scheme of appropriating the girls' take, whether it went back to Frank Case's day (which I suspect) or had been put in by Martin or by the new owner. In any event, the deal made a very unfavorable impression on me and I went back to a dime or a fifteen-cent tip. I'm God damned if I'm going to give much charity to a millionaire oil man from the South who blows in and buys a hotel, although I know that hatcheck concessions are big business and that that isn't the modern way to look at it.

I've taken the thing with considerable detachment, which probably was wrong, because Martin was a most obliging man to me for years. I've been sort of thinking I'd see him and learn the facts, or his side of it, but I haven't. But when Case died, I assumed the place was a goner and let it go at that. It is damned important to me, however, for I work right across the street and that is the only decent place to eat within blocks, and, aside from my good will toward Martin, I would be available to do anything I could for the old place if you can think of anything and will provide the leadership.

As ever,

Ross

*When failing eyesight forced Thurber to stop drawing, Ross was determined to keep his cartoons in the magazine—even if it meant recycling them.*

TO JAMES THURBER

*THE NEW YORKER*
*JUNE 17, 1948*

Dear Thurber:

The following question comes up: How do you stand on putting captions that may come from the outside, or materialize here and there, on some of your old drawings? For instance, there is a caption here on a sketch by an idea man that it is thought might do for a reused drawing of yours, as follows: (two women talking) "Every time she tells a lie about *me*, I'm going to tell the truth about *her*."

Now that I've got it on paper, it may not sound so hot, but it might do. The women in your drawings used to say some pretty batty things. Anyhow, what do you think about the principle involved and, if you are willing to accept outside lines, what about this one?

It is quite possible that we can get some lines for the drawings here. They would be sent you for approval, of course, which is what I assume you would want.

There is great acclaim of the Mrs. Forrester story. Truax, for example, says it's the finest thing you have ever done, or something to that effect.

As ever,
Ross

## TO JOSEPH WECHSBERG

*THE NEW YORKER*
*JUNE 28, 1948*

Dear Wechsberg:
I hadn't read your piece on Stradivari when I wrote you on the sordid subject of money. I have since read it, over the weekend, and will say that it is a lulu. You outdid yourself on this one. It's the first time the author of a Reporter piece has ever confessed in print to getting drunk on the job, but I think that even the members of clergy among our readers will overlook that under the circumstances.

Every once in a while I get a pleasant surprise like this, and it encourages me to carry on.

As ever,
Ross

MEMO TO GEOFFREY HELLMAN

*TIME INCORPORATED*
*7/20/48*

To: Mr. Hellman

From: Mr. Ross

Would be delighted to have you up next weekend. You don't know a girl or boy of around thirteen you could bring up for my daughter, do you? It is understood that you will expect little of me in the host line (and, come to think of it, that I will be away for lunch one day— to see the British ambassador) but the place will be yours—comfort and peace.

Please confirm receipt of this.

*A proposed Comment from White that made reference to "one of those large boxes that you see by the railroad, six feet long and three feet wide" prompted this query from railroad buff Ross—a note longer than the original item.*

TO KATHARINE S. WHITE

*[LATE JULY 1948]*

1. I don't know what boxes White means here. The first thing I thought of was packing boxes on station platform, but they are of wide variety of sizes. Next thing thought of was those little houses beside the track (from which trainmen telephone in emergencies) about the size and shape of the old out-houses. But probably it's the tool boxes where the section hands store their equipment, the low-lying ones. He might say *tool boxes* instead of just boxes. But the main thing that slowed me, I think, is the use of *wide*. If he'd said *high* I'd probably have had no trouble. A box inevitably has three dimensions, and when you read length and width you wonder about the other. This wouldn't come up with *high*. And would "track" help, inserted as marked? No matter.

H.W.R.

*Hyman, a* New Yorker *staff writer, was married to Shirley Jackson, whose short story "The Lottery" shocked readers when it appeared in the magazine in 1948. In it, Jackson describes how the residents of an un- named but pleasant small town gather every year to decide, by drawing lots, which of them will be stoned to death. In an attached note to an aide, Ross had suggested that the many letters* The New Yorker *had received about the story be sent to Jackson for later promotional use.*

MEMO TO STANLEY EDGAR HYMAN

*AUGUST 9, 1948*

Mr. Hyman:

Please see attached, especially the third sentence of the second paragraph. Maybe there's an idea here, and that you ought to tell your wife. And, while at it, tell her that the story has certainly been a great success from our standpoint, as it was a certainty to be. Gluyas Williams said it is the best American horror story. I don't know whether it's that or not, or quite what it is, but it was a terrifically ef- fective thing, and will become a classic in some category.

H. W. Ross

*After divorcing Ross, Frances had married a British oil executive, Harold "Tim" Wilkinson.*

TO REBECCA WEST

*THE NEW YORKER*
*AUGUST 24, 1948*

Dear Rebecca:

. . . I regret that your association with the magazine and with me got you tangled up for fifty minutes with the lady who had read the Greenville piece, and let you into social intercourse with the Wilkin- sons. Boats make strange bedfellows, and the coincidence of your crossing twice with the Wilkinsons and my daughter is almost too much. I'm damned if I know about Wilkinson. He's always been in- clined to be matey with me. When he and my ex-wife were living in Washington during the war and I went down there to see Patty, he always warmly invited me to stay with them, which I regarded as odd conduct, and certainly nothing that I would have done. I have been thankful, though, that Frances married him, for he is a man of substance, and it was one thousand to one that she would marry a bum. I don't give a hoot, of course, except for my daughter, and she is important. Ordinarily, he's as cordial as can be to me and my friends. He's a terrific corporation man, I suspect, and it is just possible that he disapproves of your politics, but that is rather farfetched. The fact is I have no theory. I never understand businessmen very well, and I think I understand British businessmen less than American ones—the higher-up businessmen, that is. The simple fellows I understand. Wilkinson is the head of a big subsidiary—the president, I think—of the Shell company....

As ever,

Ross


TO JAMES THURBER

*THE NEW YORKER*
*AUGUST 25, 1948*

Dear Jim:

That letter from the [*Reader's*] *Digest* is indeed entertaining, or something. I tell you there is a circuitousness and oiliness and evasiveness about them that is baffling; I never know whether they do things through straight simplemindedness or with the considered advice of sixteen of the best corporation lawyers in Wall Street.

That "one other complicating factor"—the nonreceipt of a release from *The New Yorker*—is pure horseradish. They're crawling, and they just threw that in there to build the letter up in wordage.

I'm firmly decided now, by God; I'll never again be a party to an attempt to violate, or abrogate, or make an exception to, our rule against periodical republication. Somehow I thought this would come out as it did. Do a play about the *Digest* office. They've got thirty-six editors up there.

I haven't got time to discuss your *New Yorker* play. I'll have to reread your letter in a more relaxed mood and give my emotions time to organize themselves.

Do those casuals. ...

As ever,

Ross

## TO FRANK SULLIVAN

*THE NEW YORKER*
*SEPTEMBER 13, 1948*

Dear Frank:

... I'll get at this proof again fairly soon, but not at once, probably, because now I'm going to try to take a week or so off, and the hell with it. Did you hear that Shawn's wife had twins, six weeks prematurely and very much underweight, that they had to be kept in some kind of super-incubator for weeks, and are still in an ordinary incubator, doing well? Shawn was sick for a week, then recovered, then was told that his wife was to have twins. He went right back to bed. I damned near went to bed, too.

If any woman was talking about me at Saratoga it was in a purely reminiscent vein.

Pardon the brevity of this letter. I didn't have time to write a long one.

As ever,

Ross

## TO ERNEST HEMINGWAY

*THE NEW YORKER*
*SEPTEMBER 14, 1948*

Dear Ernest:

I hope that by the time you get this you will have had a good and interesting time on the Polish boat and will be enjoying the return to Paris. As it happens, I got a letter from Archie simultaneously with yours, and it now reposes just below yours on my desk. When I get done with this, I'll answer him, and tell him you're coming, which will be big news to him if you haven't already notified him. Every time I write him, which is about once every six months, I try to get him to come over here, offering my house in the country, etc., but no bite so far. He's been subdued by the war, labor government, and so on, I guess, and maybe age.

Damned if I know what you could write for us, or what you will want to write. If you are going to revisit the old Paris hangouts, there might be a story in that, and in the change, or lack of change, in Paris and its people and atmosphere. An obvious idea that, of course, but it might be good if you should be in the humor. Every place I've ever revisited has been a heartbreaking disappointment to me, or used to be until I got old enough not to expect anything. The people are gone, or have changed.

Our prices depend on various things, including length, but a piece would come to around a thousand or twelve hundred dollars, more or less, and maybe more.

Are you ever going to write any short stories again? My God.

If you should have any ideas for pieces, you might let *me* know. I don't have much faith in doping out anything for you. How am I to know how you're feeling?

Anyhow, God bless you.

As ever,

Ross

TO REBECCA WEST

*THE NEW YORKER*
*SEPTEMBER 14, 1948*

Dear Rebecca:

... I can give you some advice about your teeth. Let the crater from which the extraction was made lay until you get here and then have the major repairs done. I am a one-hundred-percent American as far as dentists are concerned. They are comparatively wonderful here, and since you're coming over, this is the place for reconstruction. I've lost a lot of teeth in my day—on occasion two at a time—and I have a man who keeps abreast with replacements. I've got two bridges in my mouth at present, one of them large enough to be taken out in emergency for use as a brass-knuckle, but they fit and give perfect service. My dentist is no better than thousands of others, and an old pirate as to rates, but he's certainly capable, and comforting. I'll line you up with him if you'll wait till you get here. . . .

As ever,

Ross

*Flanner had notified Ross of her intention to quit, then changed her mind.*

TO JANET FLANNER

THE NEW YORKER
SEPTEMBER 15, 1948

Dear Janet:

I didn't get your letter until yesterday, because it came in over a weekend. I immediately sent a wireless, intended to get you off the tenter hooks as soon as possible and to express our great satisfaction at your decision, and our relief, for we haven't got a replacement and, in fact, haven't done anything seriously about trying to get one, for you couldn't be replaced. We were just going to do the foreign stuff some other way, and what that way was I haven't any clear idea.

Every time I've read the proof of a [Paris] Letter from you, I've groaned at the idea of their not continuing after the first of the year. I had vaguely hoped that you would decide as you did, and I think you are being wise, although God forbid that I should give anyone advice in such matters as this. The housing situation here is practically hell, and the difficulties of life are many, and are going to continue to be, and from here Paris seems simpler and better.

I'll hold a post-mortem over that change in the price of *bifteck,* which was probably read literally here and shouldn't have been. Sometimes we have to guess what you're getting at, and I've been arguing that, rather than depending on checking and theories we might cable you and ask what you are getting at, when we're puzzled. I'm going to take that up further. Sirloin isn't so very expensive, as things go.

No more for the present, because I'm trying to get off for a few days at the end of the week, and also I want to get this right off.

Just know that we're all breathing easier in the knowledge that you are staying put.

As ever,

Ross

TO JAMES THURBER

*THE NEW YORKER*
*SEPTEMBER 15, 1948*

Dear Jim:

I've got several points to raise on "Six for the Road" and after some mulling around have decided to put them up to you at this point, the principal reason being that I want to get them on paper while they are fresh and clear in my mind. Herewith a proof of the piece with certain marks on it—a Varitype proof. We are using these now to cut down corrections at the printers and (as in this instance) to get things measured up, and paid for quick. I can help Lobrano out by handling direct; he's been away and work is banked up, and Mrs. White is now away.

1. Inasmuch as you have an introduction to the answer below, would it not be well to have one here, as marked. Or it might be just: "The Question:" Seems to me would be consistent, and also work for quick clarity.

1a. Suggest moving phrase marked from here, where not essential, down to 1b, where it seems to me it is essential, or anyhow more useful. It isn't a typical party you're talking about here—doesn't include the kind of mild parties you've enumerated in preceding paragraph, but a party typical of this particular circle, the Spencer-Thurber circle. Also, suggest that these people here be pegged as suburban, as I have marked, or some such, for later in the piece, much later, it turns out that they live in places with stairs, which means houses, not apartments. You start a story like this off without a suburban plant and a reader assumes you're talking about metropolitan apartment house life, and is unfairly surprised when he comes to a passage about someone going upstairs.

2. You might, if you want, clinch the suburban atmosphere by putting in here the name of some town in the region—Rye, or a Connecticut town.

3. Above you twice call this function an *evening party,* in one instance saying it begins in afternoon. Here you say the Spencers were asked to dinner. Now, even in the Spencer circle the dinner guests can't be asked to come in the afternoon, certainly. This mixing up of a dinner party and an evening party that begins in the afternoon baffled me for quite a while, and I have come up with the suggestion that the party be made a cocktail party with buffet dinner. I think this is a brilliant suggestion. You never later have the people sitting down to dinner, nor do you take any notice whatever of dinner. If you make cocktails and buffet dinner, there is no question in readers' minds at all, and it seems to me the kind of a function the Spencers would give—as I did in my younger days. This the real reason I'm writing these notes direct. I think such a fix would help considerably.

4. It seems to me that the *however* isn't right in this sentence, and that some such phrase as marked might be better. Please consider.

5. This sentence won't parse as is. Needs insert such as marked, or *points out that* or some such.

6. *June* will probably sound stale by time we get out. Can be changed later, I assume. (Am noting here so query will be carried.)

7. There hasn't been more than one phase of this ailment, has there? (The second phase—itching knees—isn't mentioned until later.) Also, please give this point a thought: You tell the story of the party in the present tense, but you have this paragraph in the past tense. Shouldn't this paragraph be in the present tense? I suspect so, and with initial, to help with the switchover. Also, suggest that there might be more definite wording here to indicate this is the evening of the party. The transition here may not be quite right.

8. If you don't make a buffet dinner, or do *something,* it seems to me that these people are leaving awfully quick. I thought maybe all this happened before dinner, because you have *early in the evening* a paragraph and a half above (7) and you've accounted for very little time lapse; not much has happened.

9. The sentence at (a) differs in nature from sentence at (b). In the (a) sentence you are writing from the viewpoint of the Bloodgoods, in the (b) sentence you're the omnipotent author, knowing all about it. Seems to me wrong.

10. The *over their shoulders* phrase here give the right picture? Suggests to me *on their shoulders*, like a Greek maiden holding a vase. (Small matter.)

11. Very unexpected to learn at this late date that there's a bar in this place. Not mentioned before, and the definite pronoun has no antecedent.

12. Is it consistent that Mrs. Bloodgood would be the repository for this confidence in view of the fact that she and her husband met the Spencers only two weeks before and have only seen them that once? And is it as clear as it should be *what* Dora whispered?

13. And same question here. Remember, Mrs. Bloodgood has only met the Spencers that one time, when she asked them to the party. How could she know?

14. A timid suggestion: Would phrase written in help point it, or would it over-diagram it?

Pardon me for being fussy. Most of the foregoing not important, but I think that buffet dinner business is, and the locating of the story out of New York City. You'll see another proof of this, set in regular type. Some of the incidentals may be untimely by time this can be used. Can check on these later.

As ever,

Ross

P.S. The only other complication I can think of is that the very next story we bought after this one was titled "One for the Road." My tentative stand is that you have seniority around here and the junior man will have to get another title.

TO FRANK SULLIVAN

*THE NEW YORKER*
*OCTOBER 18, 1948*

Dear Frank:

... I can't vote for Truman or Dewey. I have been in the same position in earlier presidential elections, but never up against such a stone wall. I don't know what I'm going to do, but I'm not wasting time thinking of it, or I would get desperate. Certainly FDR is responsible.

He never let any Democrat at all come through. For Christ's sake, he had [Henry] Wallace before he had Truman, and it's only by the grace of God that he didn't become president. The system is wrong, as I have long known; it doesn't train able men. I jumped Elliott Roosevelt about Wallace and Truman once and he made a good answer—or rather, an explanatory answer. He said, "You don't think my father thought he was ever going to die, do you?" The hell with it all. Do some pieces. The country can stand a little humor.

As ever,
Ross

TO JAMES THURBER

*THE NEW YORKER*
*OCTOBER 21, 1948*

Dear Jim:
You (or rather, Helen) sent in a caption to go with drawing #0143, reading "You're *you*, but I'm only me." We want to know if you will agree to this going: "But you're *you*, and I'm only me."

We think the but would help, as indicating that the man has said something to cause the woman to say the above, that this is a continuance of a conversation.

Let me know. If you are agreeable, through it goes.

As ever,
Ross

*The actress had suggested a cartoon idea: A very pregnant woman says anxiously to her doctor, "Are there any other symptoms I should have?"*

TO LAUREN BACALL

*THE NEW YORKER*
*NOVEMBER 5, 1948*

Dear Miss Bacall:
We have received the idea for the picture. I think it is funny, but I have misgivings, because of the difficulty of doing pregnant women in drawings. I don't think we've ever made one work yet. I'm passing it

along to the art department, though, and if we can make anything out of it, you'll hear later.

My regards to you both, and tell Humphrey I'm praying every night that the baby doesn't look like him.

Sincerely and gratefully,

H. W. Ross

## TO JANET FLANNER

*THE NEW YORKER*
*NOVEMBER 9, 1948*

Dear Janet:

I got a letter from Kay Boyle the other day saying you looked tired, "probably because of the headaches." So help me, that was the first word I'd heard about your neck. I later found out, *something*, but not a great deal, from Shawn and Truax.

I'm sorry about this, and most earnestly hope that the headaches have passed by now, and that your neck is all right.

Since I'm at it, I'll say again that it is an enormous relief to know that you're going to stay on the job over there. We'd have been very much concerned by this time if you hadn't changed your mind, and it is hard enough to get sleep as it is.

God bless you.

As ever,

Ross

## TO H. L. MENCKEN

*THE NEW YORKER*
*NOVEMBER 10, 1948*

Dear Mencken:

The latest proof has arrived back, and I am gratified to note that you are still patient. We have carried editing to a very high degree of fussiness here, probably to a point approaching the ultimate. I don't know how to get it under control. I think it all started because we pick on everybody else all along the line, and especially in those newspaper misprints and *faux pas* we use. If we make a bull we take a heavy rap.

The election gave me more laughs than anything in fifteen years, maybe twenty, and the returns are still coming in. The best laugh was provided by myself: my conception of Westbrook Pegler's face as the developments came. My lawyer, of Wall Street, revived an old line of Al Smith's to explain Truman's success: "Nobody ever shoots Santa Claus."

We have only two language pieces on hand now, so please get some more in when you can. I recall that you told me you thought you would exhaust the subject with four or five more. I hope you've thought of others in the meantime. They are fairly wonderful, I think, and we certainly can use all that come to your mind.

As ever,
Ross

TO E. B. WHITE

*November 13 [1948]*

White:
Very good Comment, I thought, and very acceptable. I am encouraged to go on.

Ross

MEMO TO PHILIP HAMBURGER

*December 6, 1948*

Mr. Hamburger:
I have heard much astonished and enthusiastic comment on the Argentine piece, even from people who realized the length of it first and suffered shock. E. B. White read it at lunch at the Algonquin, he tells me, and was halfway through the piece when he finished his lunch, and finished reading the piece in the lobby. Several such reports, but none from a man who started to read it while getting a haircut.

I hear your music department is good, too. I will read it in the issue; too bleary Friday night to do it justice.

H. W. Ross

## TO FRANK SULLIVAN

*THE NEW YORKER*
*DECEMBER 10, 1948*

Dear Frank:

In connection with yours of December 8th, I will report at once (having been supplied with the facts) that your Trappist, [Thomas] Merton, had a couple of poems in the magazine in the early forties, and that [Robert] Lax is a real man—or a real name—and that he worked here some years ago, is pleasantly remembered, and sold us ten poems. I sometimes wish I had become a Trappist monk, but the places monks live in always seem cold to me. Merton seems to have shown judgment in picking Kentucky, where the winters are not severe. Strange people come around this place....

Merry Christmas to you, and that is the first time I have written that phrase this year. I use it with reluctance, for I am always cynical and bitter at this season, which, with large issues, year-end finances, etc., is an annual outrage.

As ever,

Ross

*At Ross's urging* The New Yorker *had banned ads for "restricted" hotels and resorts—those not open to Jews—in 1942.*

## MEMO TO PHILIP W. WRENN

*DECEMBER 15, 1948*

Mr. Wrenn:

*Cue* [magazine] is ballyhooing its hotel, resort, and travel coverage. The December 11th issue printed the attached pieces, evidently as a start off. I'm curious as to what they've done in these about the restricted hotel business that we ran up against so sharply. I'd appreciate your reading these articles and letting me know what they have done about it, if anything. I suspect they've done nothing. I've read these only hurriedly, but I notice that they've got a Palm Beach hotel or two in there, and I suspect that all or nearly all Palm Beach hotels are restricted. Isn't the Breakers restricted, for instance? If you've got time, please let me know, for this [is] a hot problem for any New York publication that takes hold of it.

There is, or used to be, oddly, a kosher hotel in Palm Beach, which I suspect was restricted in reverse. I don't know whether it is still doing business or not, and no matter.

H. W. Ross

*Typical of the kind of complaints Ross routinely fielded was a protest from the League of New York Theatres that the capsule reviews in* The New Yorker's *theater guide were unduly negative and amounted to "continued carping." Reilly was executive director of the league.*

TO JAMES F. REILLY

THE NEW YORKER
DECEMBER 22, 1948

Dear Mr. Reilly:

I have your letter of December 17th about the theatre listings in our Goings on About Town Department. The view of the gentlemen who have spoken to you about this matter seems to me myopic. In the long run, our listing, which is headed conspicuously "A CONSCIENTIOUS CALENDAR OF EVENTS OF INTEREST," must send a lot of people to the theatre, and if it were denatured as your associates propose it would lose the confidence of the public and sell no tickets for them at all. By your count, thirteen out of twenty-five shows listed got rosy, unqualified notices, which would seem to me cause for jubilation, or at least deep, quiet satisfaction, and most of the twelve others are unfairly represented by the phrases you quote.

These entries are, as you aptly call them, "ratings," and I think they will remain "ratings." . . .

Sincerely yours,
H. W. Ross

VIII

# "NEARLY ALL WORRY IS ABOUT THE WRONG THING . . ."

## 1949-1951

These years should have been Ross's season in the sun—a phrase, as it happens, that Wolcott Gibbs used for the title of a comic play that he wrote with his longtime editor very much in mind. The central character, Gibbs said in the stage directions, "should really be played by Harold Ross of *The New Yorker* but, failing that, by an actor who could play Caliban or Mr. Hyde almost without the assistance of makeup." As it turned twenty-five *The New Yorker* had never been fatter or more influential, and Ross basked in the acclaim and affection that arrived from every quarter. But on the personal side his life was becoming a shambles. His marriage to Ariane was acrimonious. Patty was at school in New England. Friends and acquaintances were ailing, dying, or, in the case of former Mayor William O'Dwyer, heading off to Mexico. In the spring of 1951 Ross's own health took a bad turn. And just when he thought he would recover, he didn't.

—

*Charles G. Ross, secretary to President Truman, wrote to Harold Ross (no relation) saying that he wanted to purchase a* New Yorker *subscription for his boss.*

MEMO TO E. B. WHITE

*THE NEW YORKER*
*JANUARY 14, 1949*

Mr. White:

I was completely without suspicion in the matter of the President's subscription, but I'm forewarned now and will watch to see what form the payment takes, especially as I have just read in the *Times* that Truman is to get a tax-free fifty-thousand-dollar annual expense allowance and apparently isn't going to have to account it. With Truman getting that amount, it seems heroic of Ross (salary ten thousand dollars, I believe) to pay the bill.

There is another side to this business. The public paid the bill for all those miniature *New Yorkers* that went out to men in the services during the war—God knows what the amount was—and that distribution was all, from our standpoint, straight promotion. The government send out millions of introductory issues to alert young readers, with the result that our circulation is more than twice what it was before the war (or something like that) and we have since been in an era of prosperity. I often think of this, with amazement, when I am getting to sleep at nights. We were handed a terrific platterful. Whatever the circumstances surrounding this subscription, the least we can do is keep our mouths shut.

H. W. Ross

TO ROBERT SHERWOOD

*THE NEW YORKER*
*JANUARY 18, 1949*

Dear Bob:

I've sent the letter along to Thurber, after reading it, pursuant to what I took to be a hint in the note to me. I glowed at your every sentence, except the one in which you indicate your age as fifty-two. Jesus

Christ! Everybody is younger than I am. I was doing all right until I read a piece the other day in which it was set forth that man reaches his peak at fifty-five and then starts downhill. Inasmuch as I had become fifty-six a couple of weeks before that, the piece discouraged me. After thinking it over, I am willing to concede, but I'm still discouraged.

Thurber is in New York.

My regards to the little woman.

As ever,

Ross

## TO ERNEST BYFIELD

*THE NEW YORKER*
*JANUARY 18, 1949*

Dear Ernie:

Later and fuller report:

I personally talked to [Joseph] Mitchell (whom I happened to find in the office) and he cringed and said he wasn't the man for that sort of thing. I gave him a mild selling talk along the line that you were a fine fellow and that he'd have a good time [in Chicago], but he just winced more and said he couldn't get mixed up in autographing. Inasmuch as I have been sneering at autographing authors for thirty years, that ended me. Also, Mitchell has a living to make, and he is doing some stories that we want done. It is almost inevitable that when a writer has a book come out he has to drop all regular work for several weeks or months and become an *author*, with public appearances, fan letters to answer, further projects to talk about, etc., and in some cases I think it takes up so much time that the profit from the book is gone. I am sorry for you, but I uphold and applaud Mitchell's conservatism.

I think it's Sloan that died. At any rate, I am certain that Pearce is alive. He used to work around this office, even after the firm started out, and sometimes he d-r-a-n-k. He got drafted, learned judo, and then when he got back to New York on leave turned up here and damned near broke several people's backs, including mine.

I will get *Theatre Arts* when it comes out, and admire that picture.

I report that I think I have transferred Beebe and his pal Clegg and their private car from Carson City to Aspen, Colorado for next summer. Anyhow, I've got the Aspen gang putting heat on the Denver and Rio Grande Railroad. The Virginia City railroad, which has harbored their private car to date, is being torn up. This is my good deed for my hometown this year.

I'm still working like a bastard. Love to Mrs. B.

As ever,

Ross

MEMO TO RICHARD ROVERE

*FEBRUARY 22, 1949*

Mr. Rovere:

While I think of it (I forgot it once), I found the last Washington Letter engrossing. I think the idea of having one every month is working out fine, and I say this as one who has for twenty years been skeptical of anyone ever doing a satisfactory Washington Letter for us. Nobody ever did over that period, and a lot of people tried.

I'm for your going on with these and that is the official viewpoint, settled between Shawn and me. We thought maybe summer would be dull down there, though.

H. W. Ross

*Goodman was editor in chief of Simon and Schuster.*

TO JACK GOODMAN

*THE NEW YORKER*
*MARCH 8, 1949*

Dear Jack:

Here is a million-dollar idea for a book, I think. I hear you have been after Fred Allen for writings, after he quits the radio. This has given me the idea that you don't have to wait for Allen stuff, that you could get up a book from the scripts of his radio programs of the last seventeen years—skits, sketches, parodies, lines, etc. There must be millions of words there, from which a lot of gold could be mined.

... I am not entirely altruistic in making this suggestion. I herewith impose the stipulation that if you should make a deal with Allen and start out getting up such a book, we would have a shot at some of the material, which might possibly be fixed up by Allen for magazine use ahead of book publication. I haven't much faith in our being able to use any of it, but I think that possibility should be considered.

I have already spoken to Allen about this idea. He didn't say no and didn't say anything that indicated he would discourage such a project. He just blinked and kept quiet.

As ever,
Ross

*Ross was interceding on behalf of Philip Hamburger, who did get the adjacent space.*

TO VINCENT ASTOR

*The New Yorker*
*April 14, 1949*

Dear Captain Astor:

A writing member of the staff of *The New Yorker* (among other things our music critic) has happily occupied an apartment in the building at 188 East End Avenue for six years, but not so happily recently as formerly, because of an increase in his family, which crowds him up badly. He has been living in the hope of getting additional space through taking over an adjoining apartment which he learned might become available, through the departure of the present tenant. The tenant is now on the verge of moving out, he learns, and he is very anxious to take over.

If you can see your way clear to his getting this additional space, you will be doing him a great kindness, and me a great favor. Not only has he a child, but he needs a place to work at home, where he does some of his writing.

Sincerely yours,
H. W. Ross

## TO BERNARD BARUCH

Dear Mr. Baruch:

I got your message the other day about my not being asked to the Churchill dinner. I regard it as extremely thoughtful of you to have thought of me and then to call afterward, after you forgot. I didn't give a hoot. I don't go to many dinners, as a matter of fact, and I understand that, anyhow, the office was represented. It was *not* represented at a dinner Luce gave to which he is reputed to have announced that he was inviting the two hundred most important men in the United States, although eighteen of the guests were Time-Life employees. That is a high score for one publication. I'm mildly troubled by that and by a headline I read in a paper a few days ago. I attach it hereto. Now, editors have a more or less closed association and it's hard to crash. If you've lost your mind and want to become an editor, however, I'll do my best to fix it.

Greetings and best wishes.

As ever,

H. W. Ross

## MEMO TO ROBERT COATES

Mr. Coates:

I have an idea, got under stress the other day. I was calling a Canadian railroad to find out when the fishing season opens in Canada and learned later that I'd missed an important call: the caller got tired of waiting for me, hung up, and disappeared. The notion is that you might do a story on the telephone system getting completely tangled up as traffic got tangled up in that story of yours about the law of averages breaking down: A fellow calls up a friend to learn about fishing conditions, a lawyer calls him to tell him his wife has sued him for divorce, a friend of the lawyer is holding the phone to tell him his house is on fire, Bernard Baruch has to get hold of the lawyer on important international business, while he waits Gromyko tries to get him to tell him Russia will be friends with us if we do so and so, the Kremlin can't get Gromyko, thinks he has been kidnapped and starts off a plane with a bomb. That off-hand buildup, I believe, will convey the idea. The fact is, I don't know why, some day, everybody in town isn't hanging on the telephone waiting to talk to somebody who is talking to somebody else.

This for what it is worth, but I wanted to get it out of my system. Come to think of it, I guess having Russia start a plane off would be war-mongering, and I wouldn't want to be quoted on it.

H. W. Ross

The Hollywood Reporter *had run an item saying the reason* The New Yorker *was so hard on movies was that "the mag's Harold Ross ain't what you'd exactly call a socially accepted local personality when he hits town." Johnson wrote Ross to say he was immediately setting out "to get a total of at least five homes here in which you would be accepted socially. All right, laugh, but I'll bet you dough I can do it."*

TO NUNNALLY JOHNSON

*THE NEW YORKER*
*MAY 19, 1949*

Dear Nunnally:

My first sensation upon reading the item was, of course, one of complete, black hopelessness. Thank God, I gained sufficient control over myself to read your letter, and instead of heading for ʰe East River, decided to *fight this thing through* under your splendid leadership. I have spent most of the intervening time consulting with friends, and, as a matter of fact, with, possibly, some non-friends. One cannot be particular in a crisis of this sort. What I did head for was "21". I was frank about it. I showed people the item and then showed them your letter. The general feeling seems to be that you are doing one of the finest things ever done for a white man. Those are almost the exact words of Irving Netcher, whom I encountered immediately. I *think* we can count on Netcher, and possibly on his brother, Townsend, too. I'd like to see the crooked grin on that Rambling Reporter's face if I can swing them. The only hitch here is that Mrs. Netcher asked what muff is. I handled that by referring her to last week's *Life*.

And MacArthur. I think he can be counted on, too. The only reason I am not positive of it is that, frankly, he didn't commit himself clearly. It isn't that he wouldn't talk. I had no difficulty whatever in drawing him out to the extent of fifteen, twenty thousand words over a period of half an hour or so, but he seemed to be afflicted with a temporary impediment of speech of some kind and I am by no means absolutely certain as to what he said. I'll catch him another time.

But now hold onto your chair. The big news is that Elsa Maxwell is lined up on our side. I can unquestionably fix it for her to give a party for me that the *Hollywood Reporter* cannot possibly ignore. We have already been over the preliminary ground. We will take the Rose Bowl, arrange with Ringling Brothers-Barnum and Bailey (I'm just like that with Johnny North) to borrow a tent to cover it, book the Philadelphia Philharmonic, and invite a select seventy-five thousand of the cream of all Southern California, *including Pasadena.* Chasen is our ace in the hole here. He's been talking for months about the possibility of catering a dinner for sixty-five hundred people. Sixty-five hundred people hell! Here I'm laying seventy-five thousand on the line for him, providing him with an opportunity to do his stuff unhampered, unhindered, on a memorable scale. I only hope his knee holds out. We'll invite the Rambling Reporter, of course. I wouldn't miss the look on his face for a million dollars.

It turns out that Harpo Marx is in town, and I'm leaving in a few minutes to consult him. You can regard Harpo as definite. I've got certain facts as to what went on between him and a cigarette girl in Detroit in 1934 that wouldn't look so well in print.

I will report further later, and I won't attempt at this writing to tell you how boundlessly gallant I consider your stand, how grateful I am personally.

As ever,
Ross

*White had submitted a casual, but upon rereading it he was dissatisfied and asked Ross not to publish it.*

TO E. B. WHITE

*THE NEW YORKER*
*MAY 24, 1949*

Dear White:

I have your note and am rather overwhelmed by your decision, especially as I was on the verge of reporting that several people in the office have now read it and raved about it. There is no argument, however, and I am having the amount paid for it charged against your account, to be worked off as you suggest, and God be with you. My sympathy with creative people is extensive. It's a tough life.

As ever,

Ross


TO LELAND HAYWARD

*THE NEW YORKER*
*MAY 26, 1949*

Dear Leland:

The drama editor of the *San Francisco Call-Bulletin*, who happens to be a pal of mine of thirty-odd years standing, is in town and can't get into your damned *South Pacific*. He got word to your press agent before he left the coast and has heard nothing from him, although he advises me that he hasn't called him up and put any heat on, out of natural reluctance and modesty.

I thought maybe I ought to tell you about this, for it seems to me that a producer ought to be laying his groundwork for national publicity while the sun is shining. Anyhow, I *do* tell you. This man's name is Fred Johnson, and he is staying at the Algonquin.

I never can understand why you producers don't hold out some tickets for the press but you never seem to. Drunk with success, I guess.

As ever,

Ross

*In May 1949, Ross's friend James Forrestal, former secretary of defense, leaped to his death from a window of the Bethesda Naval Hospital.*

TO REBECCA WEST

*THE NEW YORKER*
*JUNE 7, 1949*

Dear Rebecca:

... It so happened that I was in Washington on the night he jumped out of the hospital window and at the very moment he killed himself was talking to a couple of Washington people who knew about Forrestal, who damned well went out of his mind. He got to a point where, under the nagging of Drew Pearson and Walter Winchell, he believed that he had failed in everything. It is an example of how brutal and destructive free speech, as practiced in this country, can be. It can be murder.

What took me to Washington was the Gridiron Club dinner, which was much like the dinner I went to with you a year ago. Everything about it was reminiscent of that affair: I sat in about the same place, below left of Truman, and had to look over my shoulder to see how he was taking things. I learned that these dinners, in the aggregate, are brutal, too. Charles Ross, the president's secretary, whose guest I was, told me that Truman has to attend eight a year, at which he and his administration are ragged quite broadly, and he doesn't like it much. One thing that makes him uncomfortable is that he knows four or five hundred pairs of eyes are turned toward him every time he's ragged, to see how he's taking it, and he has to pretend to take it in a spirit of high good humor. He's as chipper as can be, though, as blithesome a sixty-five-year-old I know.

I will raise some money to make your fortnight in France more carefree. This will be charged as expense money. I'm minded to arrange for five hundred dollars, inasmuch as you spoke of being over there only two weeks. On the other hand, I can double that if you want me to. Let me know, since there is time for you to get an answer back. Name the amount, and don't be bashful, for even if nothing productive comes of this jaunt, it is a good speculation for us. As you say, you've been absent from our pages for a long time. It is too long, and no question about it. . . .

As ever,
Ross

MEMO TO WILLIAM SHAWN

*JUNE 21, 1949*

Mr. Shawn:

You said you would consider adding a thing or two to the Talk piece being prepared on the whisk broom that umpires use. At a ball game at the Yankee Stadium the other night, I noticed that the umpire seems to have a page boy at his call, a lad in a red coat (with some gilt on it, as I recall) who seemed to deliver messages to him and accept messages from him. These were oral, I believe, except in one instance possibly; I thought I saw the umpire write out a message. Nobody around me could explain the page boy; he is an innovation, evidently. Also, I think we could have something about how many baseballs an umpire's pockets will hold. They are apparently capacious. I have heard criticism of the fact that umpires are required to wear a coat all through the hot weather. Maybe they wear coats because they wouldn't have any place to keep the balls otherwise. Come to think of it, maybe that page boy delivered the new balls to the umpire, although I'm not sure; maybe was the batboy. How many baseballs are used in a game, on the average? Is a ball ever used more than once, or, to state the question more comprehensively: When a ball is hit foul, another ball is immediately put in play by the umpire; the ball that went foul, if retrieved (as opposed to going over or into the stands) seems to go to the home team's dugout. Then, later, a quantity of balls are delivered to the umpire, who puts them in his pocket. Are these brand new balls, or are they balls that have been played with some, and been knocked foul?

H. W. Ross

TO JOHN LARDNER

*THE NEW YORKER*
*JUNE 29, 1949*

Dear John:

I wish to get on record early as saying that that is a brilliant piece you have written on Mencken. It was positively thrilling to me, and it also gave me much personal satisfaction, for I have a foreboding that, despite the tense, it is in the nature of an obituary. Anyhow, in pessimism over his condition, I, for one, read it that way. He has been in pitifully bad shape for months—can't read, memory erratic, etc.—and I am becoming hopeless. A hell of a note.

As ever,
Ross

TO JAMES THURBER

*THE NEW YORKER*
*JULY 18, 1949*

Dear Jim:

This is an answer, head on, to your letter to Lobrano about the sixty dollar overpayment, so called, on "Daguerreotype of a Lady."

To begin with, Lobrano was in no wise responsible for that, nor was the accounting department. I am the boy, throughout, entirely, and in toto.

I can understand an author's dismay at being thus docked, especially on a piece he has put in years on, and is especially fond of, but at the same time I have sympathy with myself, for the financial side of such an undertaking as this is a most brutal thing to be up against. It damned near killed both me and the magazine in the early days and why I remained and still remain up against it, I don't know. I must be crazy to go on in the spot I am in. The only editing job I ever had that I have really liked was on the *Stars and Stripes* in the Army, where nobody got paid anything, and no financial factor came in at all; this misled me into the financial hell-hole I got myself into thirty years ago, and still am in.

I say as follows in my behalf: We worked out a payment system which, I think, is magnificent in its adaptability to a very peculiar situation. Having worked it out, it must be administered, and administered fairly. One thing the system calls for is prompt payment. God knows, we get checks through quick—quicker, I believe, than any other magazine ever did or ever does. This means that all pieces go through on a somewhat tentative basis and are paid for on that basis. Almost certainly the piece isn't going to end up the exact length it was when it was set.

You say "Cuts and additions balance out in the end." For the office to take this viewpoint would be unfair to the authors, for experience shows that the tendency of stories is to grow between the time of their arrival here and the time of use—the author thinks of something he wants to get in, or we want explanations of things, and the wordage goes up. It was early found that it would be unfair to the author to assume that cuts and additions balance. They do in the case of you, within a reasonable limit, I admit, for there is no record of an adjustment of pay on a piece of yours in the last several years, at least.

The system of rechecking the length of a proof when it reaches the final proof stage has been in effect for many years. We rarely find, as I indicated, an overpayment. At the moment, I recall only one other, a long piece by Cheever, which he cut a couple of galleys out of. But all the time we find underpayments, and make good. We do not make adjustments for $2.85 or other small sums. The amount has to be considerable, usually fifty dollars, although I think in some cases we have made smaller payments than that, when we thought it was right to send an author (with a somewhat lower rate than yours, say) an amount that would matter to him.

You say the elimination of the rechecking would "save at least a hundred dollars a week on the salary of whoever does this unnecessary and degrading work." You have the wrong picture. No actual word counting is done. Our stuff is set in galleys twelve inches long. The girl who does the check-count multiplies the number of full galleys by twelve (in her head; my daughter could do it), adds to that the inches of type on the last galley, thereby getting the total number of inches the piece runs. She then multiplies the number of inches by the word-bogey per inch (forty-three, as I recall it) and that's that, except that doubtless she doesn't actually perform the last multiplication because she has a chart with the total right before her. Total time elapsed in the whole calculation: fifty-four seconds. Total time spent per week at this work (we run an average of 3.6 non-department pieces per week): three minutes, fourteen seconds. Cost: a trace. (Don't think the girl gets anything like one hundred dollars per week.)

I am willing to put you on a give and take basis—everything comes out even in the course of a lifetime—and I am having a check sent you, but want to improve any impression that I am a damned fool— although I am one, or I wouldn't be mixed up in this kind of goings on when I might be out in the open air or cultivating my mind with a good book. I'm crazy, all right, but you can't say that most of my mad acts haven't been in behalf of writers.

The check will be along later.

As ever,

Ross

*Mitchell had written about a local tribe of Mohawks who put up the steel for the city's skyscrapers.*

MEMO TO JOSEPH MITCHELL

*July 26, 1949*

Mr. Mitchell:

I would report that I've read the story on the Indians, and that I consider it wonderful. Not only am I gratified at being a party to the publication of such a distinguished piece of writing, but, personally, it takes a great load off my mind: I've been nagged about those Indians in Brooklyn for ten years, and have been lobbying for a story on them most of that time. I never expected one as brilliant as this, but you cast your bread on the waters and sometimes a miracle occurs.

H. W. Ross

TO A. J. LIEBLING

*THE NEW YORKER*
*JULY 26, 1949*

Dear Joe:

I didn't know you'd gone [to Nevada] until the end of last week, although I expected it. That damned Reno is unique and one of the crazy places of the world, and stories are lying in the street there, unquestionably. I was told, for instance, that that Harold's Club, which is nationally advertised by billboards—you see the damned billboards in New Jersey, etc.—set up a nursery when it opened its second floor a few years back, where mothers could leave infants in competent hands, while they gambled. . . .

If Lew Wertheimer is around there, tell him you're a pal of mine, and he can give you some streets. He's on the inside of the gambling there, and knows the racket. He was running the gambling place in the Mapes Hotel last year—as a concessionaire, I think. He can tell you a lot; what you believe is something else. He told me the percentage on the slot machines in Reno is six-plus, which I didn't believe on general principles.

One item that has always stuck in my mind: Even the drug stores out there have slot machines—you go in to buy some suppositories and stop at the door on the way out to gamble a couple of quarters. Well, Lucius Beebe told me that he called a surgeon's office to have some wound taken care of, and found a slot machine in the surgeon's waiting room.

Another fellow that knows the ropes out there is a gent named Standerwick, who I looked up while in Reno last summer. I worked with him on a newspaper in Sacramento thirty years ago, or maybe it's forty. He's been practicing law there for years; that is, he's been getting divorces for people. He told me that marriages run away ahead of divorces in Reno and that the weekend line-up of couples getting married is an amazing sight: The marrying is done by the judges (two in number, as I recall it) who do the divorcing. They get seven or eight thousand a year for being judges, but they have a monopoly on the marriage business and that brings in thirty or forty thousand a year.

I'm full of things like that, but I was only there two days and you are a better reporter than I am (like hell) and have more time.

Good luck and God bless you.

As ever,

Ross

MEMO TO GUS LOBRANO

*July 27, 1949*

Mr. Lobrano:

A reminder that you said you would ask Mr. Henderson to suggest, over the telephone, to Miss Ives, Truman Capote's agent, that we would like to see any Capote stories that aren't too psychopathic.

H. W. Ross

TO EDWARD NEWHOUSE

*The New Yorker*
*August 2, 1949*

Dear Newhouse:

I think that story, "My Brother's Second Funeral," which I've just read in proof, is quite a moving one. That scene of the mother praying would wring tears out of the banker in East Lynn, and the whole thing seems wonderfully sustained and real to me, and very fine.

As ever,

Ross

P.S. You whippersnappers of World War II are kicking us W.W. I boys around harshly. There were practically no generals in Paris in the First W.W. Pershing wouldn't stand for it—just an old bastard nominally in charge of the area, who had forty-five dog robbers, and a band, by God, to play for him every afternoon, and a couple of quartermaster generals, but let it go, let it go.

H.W.R.

MEMO TO WILLIAM SHAWN

*AUGUST 9, 1949*

Mr. Shawn:

While you were away, Mr. Botsford and I agreed to use that Liebling piece on coon hunting in Connecticut, and Mr. Botsford had Liebling fix up the time references so it would run in mid-summer. Then the piece got crowded out. (Or we thought it best to leave it out; I will not here go into the wisdom of that decision.)

I suggest that now the timely references could be stetted and the piece run in the fall, when the temperature will be about the same as of the time of writing, which was spring, and the coon hunters will be wearing cool weather clothes.

So far so good, but Liebling didn't want to retain the real name of the town in which the coon trial was held when he converted the piece to summer, and put in a fictional name. The story would be considerably better with a real name, to my mind, and I advocate using the real name if the piece [is] used this fall. It will be belated then, but not wrong—i.e., the characters will be using the right clothes, and if Liebling's coon hunting friends ask him how come he can merely say that he wrote the piece on time but that it was held over by the editors. My conscience is always clear in such cases as this. We have a right to be naive.

H. W. Ross

*Oscar Hammerstein had written Ross that this Price drawing—it showed a boy sliding into home plate on an empty ball diamond at dusk—was the best* New Yorker *cover he'd ever seen.*

TO GARRETT PRICE

*THE NEW YORKER*
*SEPTEMBER 12, 1949*

Dear Price:

I return herewith the letter from Hammerstein, which Miss Terry sent me, and now that he has brought up the subject, I'll get on the bandwagon by saying that I thought that cover was one of the very best we have ever run. Perhaps I should have said so sooner, but my position is peculiar. By the time a cover materializes, it's an old story to me and I feel that I've probably suffered lack of viewpoint and other disqualifications, including the fact that I am helping sponsor it, and who am I to say anything. An imaginative person can certainly get a lot out of a picture, and so can an artist.

Someone said that *New Yorker* covers will be the Currier and Ives prints of their day, which in my judgment is right, but for the fact that they aren't issued as prints, but as something attached to a magazine. I've always thought that some outfit would come along and issue them as prints, but none has. It would be expensive. Maybe someone will, someday, and the heirs will profit. You've done two of my recent-year favorites: the one of the boat moving away from the artist who was drawing it was a wonderful piece of work to my mind, too. I'm having copies of Hammerstein's letter displayed on the bulletin boards. I regard it as important recognition.

Here is the letter back, and God bless you.

As ever,

Ross

*Ross was appalled at the idea of Aspen, the rough silver-mining town of his birth, becoming a center of culture.*

TO ELMER DAVIS

THE NEW YORKER
SEPTEMBER 13, 1949

Dear Elmer:

I got a laugh and grim satisfaction out of your letter to *Harper's*. I was told about it earlier and knew it was coming, and have been exuding dirty chuckles every time I've thought about it since.

My attitude has in no wise been governed by personal feelings, however, or only very slightly and subconsciously so. I had dinner last spring with [Walter] Paepcke, the promoter of Aspen, and [Robert Maynard] Hutchins, of the University of Chicago, when they were in

New York raising money for that Goethe celebration. They were buoyantly going around to foundations and individuals who are known to promote culture and putting the bee on them. Their gay plans curled my hair into small ringlets. I knew they were going to stink up the old place. Making Aspen cultural is one of the greatest profanities of modern times. There are five or six old-timers left out there, men of the original generation, and they are not fools (not college men, but wise) and I could visualize the expression on their faces and imagine their remarks. My malice was augmented by the fact that I didn't pronounce *Goethe* right when I first used it in the presence of the Messrs. Paepcke and Hutchins—or at any rate didn't pronounce it the way Hutchins did. I am not a college man. I stuck to my pronunciation throughout, however, as Hutchins did to his. (Paepcke dodged the point, as well as I could recall.) I was advised later by the office Rhodes scholar that Hutchins was wrong, too, but he may have been making a concession to my version—going as far as he could.

Well, as a semi-disinterested observer, I applaud you. I don't know anything I've done for the human race, except possibly entertain a minute segment of it from time to time, and I can't compare myself with Goethe, because I don't know what he did for the race, either, despite the spouting at Aspen, of which I faithfully read in the *Times,* which duly had a man out there. He missed a bet when he didn't interview the old-timers. I'd like to find out what Paepcke and Hutchins say about your letter, and I will if I can figure a way to get a rise out of them.

As ever,

R

P.S. That time I saw you in Washington, at the Gridiron dinner: I intended to stay over the next day and take advantage of that invitation to call you up, but when I got up in the morning the bellboy in the hotel told me about Forrestal killing himself and after fidgeting around the lobby of the Willard for half an hour I got a train back to New York. Forrestal was an old friend of mine and I felt low and bitter.

Ross

TO REBECCA WEST

*THE NEW YORKER*
*OCTOBER 4, 1949*

Dear Rebecca:

I am finally writing you. I have been carrying that last letter of yours around for the last three weeks, which is the length of time I have been back from my vacation, with the idea of writing you more than perfunctorily, but not only have I been more hard pressed with work than usual, because of being away, but I have got into a state in which I don't relish things that happen to me enough to be interested, or interesting, in the retelling. I suppose that it is a matter of being too heavily occupied, too, and, come to think of it, it is not entirely true, for I have relished a few adventures I had on my western trip, such as playing no-limit stud poker with the old-timers in a gambling hell in Reno, Nevada, which is an occupation that gives me more fundamental enjoyment than anything else I know. The players are all mostly authentically fascinating characters, including the one-armed men, who seem to be numerous. I played in the Reno game last year and there was always a one-armed man in the game, and the same was true this year. In fact, both years, there was a one-armed *Chinaman* in the game, and the one-armed Chinaman who was in the game last year was not the one who was in the game this year. I have been considerably preoccupied with the problem of why there are so many one-armed poker players in Reno (all of them had learned to shuffle the cards with one hand, efficiently) and I think I finally worked out an explanation: Reno is a railroad town and the one-armed men are probably injured and retired railroad men. That is only a partial explanation, though; it can't include the Chinamen, for Chinamen don't work on railroads. I'm still baffled by that one. However, poker stories aren't good fare for a female member of the British upper classes full of experience with Gilbert Miller and the Duke of Windsor on the Riviera. I met the Duke here last winter, incidentally, and I will say that I saw no Americans bobbing at him here, and I will say that I left (a dinner party) when I damned well had to catch a train, although it was pointed out later that that was a ruinous social act. . . .

As ever,
Ross

TO JAMES THURBER

*THE NEW YORKER*
*OCTOBER 12, 1949*

Dear Jim:

As to McNulty's Irish story, you understand wrong throughout; you understand as wrong as a man can understand. Whoever told you that McNulty "had a terrible struggle for survival" is a liar or a spreader of outrageous slander. There was never a flicker of struggle. McNulty got some help, and seemed grateful for it, as he always does, and I'll bet you a hundred to one that he would tell you so. The help he got was considerable when you consider that, after he decided with Shawn to write a story on his Irish trip, he then backed out of it several times, declared his efforts a failure, and only wrote it because of Shawn's patient and persistent encouragement. The fact is that, beginning with a five-hundred-word nugget, he fed it to Shawn in fragments and shreds, which Shawn assembled. He never turned it in as the entity it became. He finally got it done, triumphantly, but Shawn was the obstetrician, the midwife, and the godfather of that piece, and it never would have been done without him. No one ever called his piece noncreative around here. I never heard anyone call it journalistic, either, although I don't know quite what the word means in this connection.

I will now change the subject. Grantland Rice took me to a World Series game, and for a couple of innings talked about your baseball story, going over with great relish the scene of the midget at bat. He thinks the story would make a movie, and, by God, I do, too, although it has been a long time since I've read or thought of that story. Do you want me to start selling it? Remember I'd have made a better deal on the Mitty story if you had let my plan run its course. The thing to do is stir up interest and sit tight until the ferment gets well along. Give me a signal and I'll start.

As ever,

Ross

## MEMO TO SALLY BENSON

*OCTOBER 24, 1949*

Miss Benson:

If you'll pardon my mentioning it, I thought "The Comeback" came out just fine. Seems a very good and trim story to me, and it has been a pleasure to read it in proof.

Twenty-six stories in the next twenty-six weeks is what I expect from you, young lady, and come to think of it no more suicides during that period. Our characters have been bumping themselves off so often lately that our readers think they're reading *Official Detective* half the time.

H. W. Ross

## MEMO TO E. B. WHITE

*OCTOBER 25, 1949*

Mr. White:

Mr. Lobrano mentioned that you were interested in an item he spotted in the paper about the invention of a small watermelon by some professors at a northern college. You are advised that I sent this through for investigation and that it now is being investigated. Progress is slow, because dealings are by mail. Only two men in the world know about the small watermelon, the professors who invented it.

Mr. Shawn is going to turn the facts over to you. The reason I wanted facts is that I have a notion that the small watermelon may become a big economic proposition. I planted some watermelons in Connecticut one summer and they grew fine but hadn't completed their growth until they were knocked off by frost, in the fall. If the small watermelon grows quicker than the normal one (and why not, because it hasn't got so far to go), then it can be grown in the northern season and the South's monopoly on watermelons will be broken.

H. W. Ross

TO JAMES THURBER

*THE NEW YORKER*
*OCTOBER 31, 1949*

Dear Jim:

. . . While I think of it, I have just gone through the new Rand McNally Atlas (finding a mistake right off—they've got Snowmass Mountain in California instead of Colorado) and I find that there are about fifteen Columbuses in the United States. Two of these are pretty well known: the Columbuses in Georgia and Kansas. Inasmuch as our pieces are signed at the end and the reader doesn't know who is writing them until he gets there, I think that in the Album series the Columbus you refer to ought to be pegged as in Ohio. This would involve writing *Ohio* into them, after the first use of *Columbus.* I intended to propose this when the proof on the last piece went through, but forgot it, and I now find that two of the Album pieces on the bank aren't pegged. May we peg them? Please answer this in due course.

As ever,

Ross

P.S. Further: Just read *The White Rabbit Caper* with great pleasure. You go better & better as you get older. If you were twins, there would be no trouble at all about getting out a magazine.

R


TO KAY BOYLE

*THE NEW YORKER*
*NOVEMBER 4, 1949*

Dear Kay:

. . . We've had a terrible tragedy here, as I suppose you know, the death of our artist Helen Hokinson in a damned airplane accident at Washington. This has distressed everybody all week. I've got to go now and see Helen's mother, who is leaving this afternoon for her hometown in Illinois, for the funeral. Hawley Truax went down to Washington to identify the body and get it sent west, etc.

I wouldn't be a bit surprised if anxiety is causing all your trouble. I know that anxiety *can* cause a lot of complications, if, for instance, you start a weekly magazine. I once batted around to half a dozen doctors and clinics until a doctor told me that there was nothing wrong with me but worry, and immediately recovered. I remained recovered for a long time, but I finally did get duodenal ulcers. I'm going to a hospital for a week to be looked over later this month, at the insistence of my doctor, although I feel fine. The doctor says this is a precautionary step "for one of my age."

Get that story done when you get a chance. Don't become too engrossed in your crass mothership.

As ever,

Ross

## TO S. N. BEHRMAN

*THE NEW YORKER*
*NOVEMBER 7, 1949*

Dear Sam:

I am enormously grateful for the tickets to the show [*I Know My Love*], and enormously pleased with the reviews. I read only Atkinson's review the morning after the opening, and didn't learn for a couple of days that all the other critics had been pleased—the daily critics, that is. I had a fine time, but what with being at an opening, which I always find distracting, and sitting in the Hope Hampton seats, I was hardly in the mood of a true lover of the drama. The only time I ever had those seats before—middle of the first row—was once a number of years ago when I called up Ed Wynn's box office two hours before his (and Ethel Merman's) opening, and found Ed himself in the box office. To my astonishment, he said yes, he had two good seats and he'd leave them for me. They were right in the middle of the front row, and I thought that that was social success unparalleled by anyone born in Aspen, Colorado, or, in fact, in the whole state of Colorado. I went to sleep on that reassuring note and then read in the *Times* the next morning that at five o'clock the previous afternoon, Hope Hampton had shot Jules Broulatour in the head.

Anyhow, deep thanks, and best wishes. I will see you sooner or later, so help me God.

As ever,

Ross

TO JANET FLANNER

*THE NEW YORKER*
*NOVEMBER 14, 1949*

Dear Janet:

... I went over your earning figures the other day (it was on my conscience) and learned as follows: You have done eighteen Letters so far this year (as of the date of the calculation), for which you have been paid $7,545, and you've received $3,960 in expenses, making a total of $11,505. In addition you are to get payment for further special expenses Truax has written you about, and, also in addition, you will eventually get paid for the time you have put in on the series you are working on. ... You are not doing bad and, personally and as an old pal, I will say that I think you're worrying more about finances than necessary, although I am not one to say that finances are not important—savings, I mean, especially. But you've got a terrific break there, because of your peculiar and enviable tax situation. No one in this country, generally speaking, is saving *anything*. I don't know what is going to become of most of this generation eventually, and all of the next generation. They won't have any savings.

I will now close this subject, with wishes for a merry Christmas.

As ever,

H. W. Ross

TO OGDEN NASH

*THE NEW YORKER*
*NOVEMBER 14, 1949*

Dear Nash:

Yes, where are the young writers? The success, so-called, of this magazine is primarily a straight matter of luck. Within a year after we started we had White, Thurber, Hokinson, Arno, and within a few years more we had a lot more good people, humorists with pen, pencil, and typewriter. Now, by God, a whole generation has gone by and very few more have appeared—a couple of artists, and not one (or not more than one or two at the outside) humorous writers. I don't know whether it's the New Deal or Communist infiltration or the law of averages, or what, but I do know that if I'd known how little talent was going to develop I'd have got in some other line of work years ago.

As ever,
Ross

TO WILLIAM MAXWELL

*THE NEW YORKER*
*NOVEMBER 14, 1949*

Dear Maxwell:

I've just read in proof your topical light tragedy, as I've decided it should be classified, and will report that I think it's just fine, and that it was a great relief to me to go over something written by a professional writer after having been through five or six very ragged things.

I still have some argument on your well business. I'm a well expert. In Utah, where I spent my adolescence, they used to drill down twenty or thirty feet and get what was called a flowing well, or artesian well. The water would rise, through a pipe, about four feet above the ground and overflow. In Connecticut I dug a surface well, or the man who remodelled a house I bought did. He just put a laborer to work—a pick and shovel man—and in a couple of days he was down about fifteen or eighteen feet, and had three or four feet of water. I bought another place and had to drill a well. It went down just under two hundred feet. The man who drilled it referred to it as an artesian well, as did everybody in Connecticut who spoke of it. He didn't expect water to flow up from it of its own volition, though. That led me to the dictionary, where I found that the word comes from Artesia, in Greece, where they drilled and got flowing wells, as the Mormons did later in Utah. Originally an artesian well was a flowing well, and that is still the first meaning. A secondary meaning is a drilled well (I suppose of considerable depth) that doesn't produce flowing water, but from which the water has to be pumped. Or that is how I remember the dictionary. I haven't looked it up again.

Anyhow, I think the piece fine. As you know it's going in the back of the book, because of the sharp time element, which, from our standpoint is good, for it runs around five thousand words and will provide a high spot in a big pre-Christmas issue.

As ever,
Ross

*Harriman was in Paris, helping oversee the Marshall Plan.*

TO W. AVERELL HARRIMAN

*THE NEW YORKER*
*NOVEMBER 15, 1949*

Dear Averell:

Very good as to my pal Henderson. (He got me a divorce once.)

By God, *The New Yorker* had five foreign stories in the last issue, of one kind or another. We may sound provincial to you but we seem like the International Gazette to me. We got started on the wide world during the war and can't quit. Also, the writers got in the habit of traveling. They can always see a story far away, although they can't see one here.

One thing you didn't start [was] a weekly magazine. If you had, you wouldn't be where you are today. You'd just be back home in the office. Come to think of it, by God, you did start a weekly, but as an owner. I'll amend that to: never edit a weekly magazine. Owning one is all right, though.

My very best regards to you and Marie.

As ever,
Ross

*In the early years of the Cold War* The New Yorker *was considered so liberal that some referred to it as "The New Worker." One reason why was contributors like Boyer, who was a talented reporter but whose politics were openly leftist.*

## TO RICHARD O. BOYER

*THE NEW YORKER*
*NOVEMBER 18, 1949*

Dear Boyer:

I've read your letter again, and carefully, and there is one point I want to clear up right away. You speak of the possibility of *resigning* under certain circumstances. Damn it, you can't resign, because you're in the status of a free-lance writer. You can quit writing (which would be a state of mind, I guess), but you can't resign, because you have nothing to resign from. Likewise you can't be fired (you use the word *firing*). Our relationship with a free-lance writer is that we buy his stuff when it's done, if we like it, and that's that. A couple of letters have come into the office using the word *fired* in your connection, and I now, by God, find *you* using it.

Sincerely,
Ross

*A Cornell student and the son of Ross's* New Yorker *colleague, McKelway had written an article about the editor.*

## TO ST. CLAIR MCKELWAY, JR.

*THE NEW YORKER*
*DECEMBER 6, 1949*

Dear Son:

When you get to be my age, you finally concede and call everybody son who was born in this century. I got that piece and finally read it, with only a minimum of embarrassment. That pair of suspenders you mentioned was the last *wide* pair I had. They were pre-war, and manufacture hasn't been resumed, which is unfortunate, because they were the best suspenders made, to my mind. I use the past tense, because they have given way since you saw them, and my pants look more like gunny sacks then ever, I guess.

Don't grow too much, now.

Sincerely yours,

H. W. Ross

## TO REBECCA WEST

*THE NEW YORKER*
*DECEMBER 27, 1949*

Dear Rebecca:

. . . That Hokinson thing was an outrage by fate. The poor little girl never did a bit of harm to anyone in her life, and she brought a great deal of pleasure to many people. The only close relative she had was her mother, whom you met at that party we had that time. Within a few hours after the death, the mother was talking about taking Helen "home" for burial, and returning "home" herself, although both of them had lived here for twenty-five years. The old lady, who, I learned to my amazement, was eighty-five, didn't have a single root here, not one. She's now gone back west to live with some cousins. . . .

I saw John Gunther at the theatre the other evening and he asked me if I'd heard from you, and I had to say no. I then ventured the theory that you must be working on your novel, or maybe some short stories. Then, the very next day, I think it was, your story dropped in my lap. Get the second one under way.

Happy New Year to you and Henry.

As ever,

Ross

P.S. Don't forget to send the cuttings.

*A former personal secretary to Ross, William Walden, wrote a play entitled* Metropole *with a Ross-like figure at its center. Ross hated the play, which was directed by George S. Kaufman, and was happy to see it fold after a few days.*

## TO GEORGE JEAN NATHAN

*THE NEW YORKER*
*DECEMBER 27, 1949*

Dear George:

I read that piece on *Metropole* when it came out, and then the clipping of it got under something. I had intended to write a learned acknowledgment at considerable length, but now forget what I was going to say, beyond this: I'm much obliged. And your statement that most magazine successes have been helped largely by pure editorial accidents is a knowing and sagacious one. If it is off at all, it is off on the side of understatement. Look at *Life,* a recent example. It is wholly an accident. That zealot Ingersoll crammed the idea down Luce's throat, bullied him into getting it out. Luce himself told me (on the occasion when he spoke to me for the last time) that he would give a million dollars if he didn't have to come out with *Life.* (The first issue was then on the presses.) *The New Yorker* is pure accident from start to finish. I was the luckiest son of a bitch alive when I started it. Within a year White, Thurber, Arno, and Hokinson had shown up out of nowhere. I guess they had shown up within six months. And Gibbs came along very soon, and Clarence Day, and a number of other pathfinders I could name if I spent a little time in review. It just so happened, accidentally, that all that talent was around, waiting. No other single year has produced anything like as much, not, probably, any five-year period. There hasn't, as a matter of fact, been a new humorist since then.

And Benchley was alive, for instance.

Magazines are about eighty-five per cent luck. All an editor can do is have a net handy, to grab any talent that comes along, and maybe cast a little bread on the waters.

Anyhow, many thanks.

As ever,

Ross

*Throughout late 1949* The New Yorker *campaigned vigorously against the broadcasting of commercials in Grand Central Station. In a public hearing on the matter, the crowd-conscious Ross, who regularly commuted through Grand Central and considered the broadcasts an affront, agreed to testify. Describing himself as the "editor of an adult comic book," he entertained the audience and made headlines. The campaign was stopped soon after.*

## TO FRANK SULLIVAN

*THE NEW YORKER*
*DECEMBER 28, 1949*

Dear Frank:

... I had promised the Public Utilities Commission lawyer that I'd go to the hearing. He said that usually only six people show up for such things and put it up to me to appear. Later he told me I wouldn't have to testify, because it was obvious that a good showing was going to be made anyhow (which it damned well was, it seemed to me). But I went down anyhow, and then when that adult comic [book] business came up I got sore and took a few shots at them. I wish I'd done some preparing, though, instead of ad libbing. Within four hours, I'd thought of a dozen swell cracks, including one reviving that motto of the founder of the N.Y.C. [New York Central], the Public be damned. It's peculiar that nobody thought of that. It would have been better than all the other points made, put together.

I'll see you sooner or later. Love to Kate.

As ever,

Ross

## TO MARY HOKINSON

*THE NEW YORKER*
*JANUARY 3, 1950*

Dear Mrs. Hokinson:

I am very glad to learn that you have got settled out there [in Illinois]. I hope things go well, and I think they certainly will go better than in such a crowded place as New York. I will convey your thanks to Mr.

Truax, Miss Terry, and the others, but what we did was really in fulfillment of duty to one who had been a member of the family here so long.

I, too, hope that Helen knows all that has happened, and how the value of her work has been recognized in print and otherwise. Her passing has left a great hole in our lives and in the lives of hundreds of thousands of people. If she knows, she has the satisfaction of realizing that she left such an extensive record behind her that she probably never will be forgotten.

We have saved all the newspaper clippings, letters, and so on that came in, and our intention is to get them in some kind of preservable form and send them to you....

I send you best wishes from all of us here, and the hope that you will keep in touch with us. We stand ready at any time to do anything we can, of course.

Sincerely yours,
H. W. Ross


TO ELMER DAVIS

*THE NEW YORKER*
*JANUARY 12, 1950*

Dear Elmer:

I got the remarks. Apparently you have a hell of an audience [on the radio], for a dozen people spoke to me or wrote to me about the mention.

As I have always known, it is a journalistic mishap to win a campaign, or to win one too soon, for it leaves you with nothing to talk about, which is our present fix, and we had to scrap a number of good ideas, one of which I am reminded of by your mention of the Pathfinder project. We had blocked out a panorama of the Grand Central concourse filled with honky-tonk items, such as a crystal gazer to tell when trains were arriving, a dime-a-dance area, and a locomotive with a sign "Toot the whistle for 25¢." This was real funny, and had to be scrapped.

As ever,
Ross

*Sefrit was the Salt Lake City newspaper editor Ross always credited with sparking his interest in journalism.*

TO FRANK SEFRIT

*THE NEW YORKER*
*JANUARY 16, 1950*

Dear Mr. Sefrit:

I've just had a note from Miss Norma Abrams, of the *New York Daily News,* relating that she saw you out there recently and that you mentioned me, Harold Ross, and remembered me. Having this assurance, and your address, I herewith report in.

I've just been trying to figure out when in God's name I nosed into the newspaper business as a Tribune League Reporter (complete with badge). I was still going to grammar school when you recruited the student body of your practical school of journalism. That I remember clearly. And I also remember that I entered high school in Salt Lake City in 1904 (being able to date this because I was of the class of '08). I was born in 1892, which means that I was either ten or eleven when you started me off. I got into high school early because my mother, who had been a school teacher for twelve years before her marriage, coached me intensively at home and also took advantage of two or three moves we made to slyly advance me a grade, and I guess I got to be a Tribune League Reporter because I was big for my age, or lied about my age, if the question ever came up. I don't recall that the age question ever came up with you, but it did come up when I got to batting around town on assignments a few years later, and I lied plenty then. I was getting into saloons when I was fifteen, pretending to be twenty-one, and on one occasion I ran into my father, which was embarrassing, but not fatal, for I told him (lying again, perhaps) that I was there on journalistic business. This explained everything satisfactorily to my father, who was always enormously proud of my connection with the *Tribune,* for he was an ardent and violent anti-Mormon and thought you were the greatest man in the world for exposing Mormonism. Years later, I came to admire and approve of the Mormons— as a social organization, at least—but at that time they were all black. I never did finish high school. With your name behind me, they used to let me hang out around the local room and would give me assignments, and I was soon too heady for any academic life. The end of my high school career came, as I recall it, when I was reported for being seen in Commercial Street in my High School Cadet Battalion pants (I used to keep a civilian coat in the office and would put it on when engaged in journalistic works, but kept the pants on). Being on Commercial Street in uniform, or in part of a uniform, was a high crime, and general hell was raised. The story that I was making a dash from the Tribune Building to the police station, and that the shortest way was out through the *Tribune* press room, up Commercial Street, and out Orpheum Avenue, wasn't fully accepted. I was never so pleased in my life as when I talked my father into letting me quit school and work full time on the *Tribune*. I used to find it embarrassing, especially when my mother was still alive, to admit that not only hadn't I been to college but that I hadn't finished high school, but I long ago got over that and adopted a reverse attitude. I got a good practical education around the fellows on the *Tribune*—and later the [Salt Lake] *Telegram*—and though I miss an academic education I wouldn't trade what I learned then for one.

I was in Salt Lake a couple of years ago—spent an afternoon there between trains—and walked down Main Street to the Tribune Building. I didn't have nerve enough to go in, for I knew I wouldn't know anyone there. Later, at the Hotel Utah, a young lady from the *Tribune* was interviewing Lowell Thomas, with whom I was having dinner. I asked her if she'd ever heard of Harold Ross around Salt Lake City and she said no, and I let it go at that.

I was thrilled to get track of you, and if I ever get out west again, as far as Washington, I shall look you up. And I'm enormously grateful for what you did. You may not recall it, but you gave me personal encouragement. I remember seeing you several times, and the fact that I had contact with you directly, come to think of it, undoubtedly impressed the city staff, upstairs. Miss Abrams says you saw promise in me. What I think you saw was zeal, for that I certainly had. The newspaper business was made for me, and I was fascinated. I recall that covering the police beat from midnight until four A.M. was one thing that interfered with my high school work. The morning paper police reporters—of whom there were three—used to let me cover for them while they went off and played poker. That is probably the most appreciated responsibility of my life.

Gratefully and sincerely,

H. W. Ross

TO REBECCA WEST

*[Winter 1950]*

Dear Rebecca:

I can write quicker with this paper, and I can't find any other, for the house in the country, where I am writing this, is a mess. I don't know whether I told you or not, but the roof caught fire last fall, and things have been in confusion ever since, and especially since the painters came in to go over the place, which they have done, finishing as of Friday (this is Monday, but what day of the month it is I don't know, because I haven't a calendar). But nothing is in place yet. I came up for two weekends alone and slept on the porch, where it was very cold, encouraging a man and his wife I had previously engaged for the summer. They are Finns, and so far have been fine. They're moving things and getting the place cleaned slowly, room by room. I suppose they'll get drunk and wreck everything in a week or so, but they haven't yet....

I'm coiled up in my den with proofs around me like snakes, wistful and motherless.

To tell the truth, I suppose I've been delaying seeing [West's son] Anthony because the last time I did see him I ran into a slight embarrassment. Ariane drank too much from a rare bottle of brandy somebody sent over to the table—a press agent who does things in a lavish way—and had to be led out of the joint, after pouring out most of the brandy, which, as I understand it, rated at three dollars a sip. I guess the press agent got stuck heavily, which will teach him a lesson....

As ever,

Ross

*Kahn had approached Ross about doing a Wayward Press piece critical of columnist Westbrook Pegler, a neighbor and onetime friend of Ross's.*

TO E. J. KAHN, JR.

*[MARCH 1950]*

Mr. Kahn:

I have no objection, professionally or personally. Professionally, we must pursue our course and let the chips fall where they will. Personally, my creed is that a journalist is entitled to no friends, and I have never (so I claim) let personal considerations interfere with this undertaking. I don't give a hoot in this case, anyhow, and am for teasing Pegler a little now and then. . . .

Ross

The New Yorker *celebrated its twenty-fifth anniversary with a gala party at the old Ritz-Carlton Hotel.*

TO REBECCA WEST

*THE NEW YORKER*
*MARCH 21, 1950*

Dear Rebecca:

. . . A week ago today, Ariane went to bed with what we thought was a cold. I got a doctor and he gave her a shot of some one of the new remedies. By the next noon she was in great misery and had a heavy fever and, when the doctor finally came (he was being run ragged with numerous flu cases) he ordered her hauled off to a hospital by ambulance, fearing, it turned out later, some complication or other that didn't materialize. Her fever was gone in twenty-four hours (on just docine and aspirin). I went up to see her, feeling ragged, and the doctor happened in and stuck his thermometer in my mouth. I turned out to have a degree of fever, so I came home and went to bed, and stayed there—or at any rate in the house—for a couple of days, during which time Ariane came back. We both got to the *New Yorker* anniversary party—which will be the last one, thank God, for there never will be sufficient provocation for another in my day—and got through with the business. Seven hundred people turned up, and I have never been pulled and hauled around so much in my life. Everybody, or most everybody, is reported to have had a good time, though, and I am still alive. My worst trouble was that I was persuaded to drink a highball, or part of one, during the stress, and that threw my stomach into a well-tied knot. It was too much, after years of abstinence. I've had slight headaches and traces of exhaustion since, which, I trust, are psychological.

I saw Anthony at the party, but only briefly, the way I saw everyone else—like a movie film running at five times its normal speed—and have had no contact with him since then other than by telephone yesterday, to read him a paragraph from your last letter, which I thought would be good for his morale. . . .

As ever,

H. W. Ross

TO PATRICIA ROSS

*The New Yorker*
*April 4, 1950*

Dear Pat:

Here are autographed copies of the anniversary cover of *The New Yorker*, which Miss Asher said the girls might want for their scrapbooks. Pass them out, if there is a demand for them, and if you've got the nerve to do it. Me, I'm slightly embarrassed about this.

As ever,

Dad

TO ST. CLAIR MCKELWAY

*The New Yorker*
*May 17, 1950*

Dear Mac:

You got the prevailing rate for that last piece, for all those pieces. My recollection was wrong. I thought you had done part of the last story while on salary, and that there had been a deduction. My life is full of more details than I can remember, and I shouldn't try to remember.

You'll get the prevailing rates for whatever else you write, and what that is at the moment is what it has been for the last couple of years, but I'm trying to get the rates put up a notch, and think maybe I will. I can make no commitments, though.

I haven't time for long letters, so I will terminate this with the suggestion I frequently make to writers: Don't waste your time and words on letters; you don't get paid for them.

As ever,
Ross

*E. B. White later said about the Comment item in question: "[It] ran exactly as I wrote it. I simply told Ross he was crazy—which satisfied him completely."*

TO WILLIAM SHAWN

*[1950]*

Mr. Shawn:
I now make the alarming discovery, seeing Comment in proof, that the sentence at (a) contains a phallic figure. Oh, my. I didn't pick this up when I read the copy, although I wondered what in the world *erect* [was] doing in there. I probably got distracted by the following sentence, which [refers to] sex. I see no objection to that sentence, but I don't think we can print this erection business. I know we can't. And see (b) *penetrate* and *rubbers*, which makes it really fancy.

Ross
Wording at (b) may be unintentional, and certainly harmless without the antecedent of (a).

R.

*Cain had complimented the editor on Lillian Ross's controversial Profile of Ernest Hemingway.*

TO JAMES M. CAIN

THE NEW YORKER
MAY 31, 1950

Dear Jim:

Thanks for that letter, on behalf of Miss Ross and the magazine. It has kicked up many expressions of admiration from writers, at least; God knows what readers think of things, ever, but writers recognize good work.

I'll tell Miss Ross, to whom I can claim no relationship, although I'm thinking of adopting her.

Glad to have heard from you. Carry on.

As ever,

Ross


TO FRANK CAPRA

THE NEW YORKER
JUNE 5, 1950

Dear Frank:

Your telegram received with great joy and pleasure.

I have a letter from my Colorado detachment, Art Quaintance, proposing a general rendezvous, or marshalling, at the Conoco Gas Station in Dillon, Colorado, at twelve noon on June 27th, from which point we will descend the Blue River twenty-two miles to the mouth of a canyon, where a man will be waiting to open a gate for us. They keep this canyon locked up. We will proceed by car and go up the canyon by car. They seem to have built a road into Black Lake, which is where we will have headquarters.

Now, if I should go into the ditch, or over a cliff, out there, and therefore not be in Aspen when you arrive, you are to proceed on to Dillon, meeting Quaintance, Chasen, et al. there. The chance of my not making the tryst in Aspen is extremely remote, but we will be out of telephonic touch at that stage of the game, and should have an alternate plan, I guess. But, unless disaster pursues me, I shall be in Aspen as advertised, and come to think of it, even in the event of disaster, I can telephone the Jerome Hotel and leave word. If anything should happen to you on the road, you telephone the Jerome and leave word—if I'm not there.

When you get to Utah, head for Grand Junction, Colo., and from there go up the Colorado River to Glenwood Springs, where you might want to stop off for a meal and to look around. The biggest outdoor swimming pool in the world is there, a hell of a thing.

You turn off at Glenwood for Aspen, which is forty-five miles up Roaring Fork. From Aspen to Dillon is over the Continental Divide, on the highest road in the United States that doesn't go up to the top of a mountain and go right down again. It goes above the timber line.

My watch now reads 1:06:18. We must have precision in this undertaking.

As ever,
Ross

*Flanner had spent months on what was to be a four-part Profile of the venerable French socialist Léon Blum. When Ross wanted to kill the piece, Flanner was angry because she thought they had an agreement to run the series whether the aged Blum was still alive or not.*

TO JANET FLANNER

*THE NEW YORKER*
*JUNE 9, 1950*

Dear Janet:

You said your last letter to Bill Shawn would be brief. This one will be a real example of brevity, for I'm rushed to death. I'm leaving on a vacation at the end of next week and this weekend . . . I'm going to Boston to get my daughter out of school and, incidentally, into New Hampshire to—by God—accept a degree from a college, about which I'm sheepish, having sneered at colleges all my life.

I don't at all deny that I said O.K. to Blum dead or alive. I don't remember the talk but I nearly always say dead or alive on such projects as this, for a policy or a psychological reason: I think a writer must believe that his (or her) piece is going to be printed, and that if they don't think so they are working under a terrible handicap. So, on occasion at least, my answer in such cases is routine and may be tarnished with insincerity. Suppose I'd said we couldn't have used Blum dead; you'd have been stopped, probably, or at least would have lived with a serious mental hazard all the time.

I always figure that financially we take the buck in such cases, to a considerable extent, however, inasmuch as we encourage writers to go into pieces about ancient people with our eyes open.

Frankly and truthfully, our suggestion that you come back here is no reflection on your letters. It is merely, and simply, that we want you to re-sense the temper of the country here, which is rather outlandish: witch hunts, *The New Yorker* accused of being red, etc. etc. That degree I'm taking, I'm taking really as a defensive demonstration: I thought recognition by a fairly conservative college (Dartmouth) would be impressive, within its limits.

No time for more now. Shawn is taking a week in Chicago, to show the twins to his parents. He left feeling dizzy; overwork, I guess.

As ever,

Ross

## MEMO TO WILLIAM SHAWN

*JUNE 14, 1950*

Mr. Shawn:

Hold up on the story of the redecoration of Gracie Mansion for a while, until I get a chance to tell you about it. The fact is there are no redecorations to speak of there—none at all aside from the changing of a painting or two—except on the second floor, the personal quarters of the O'Dwyers. I doubt that there is really a story in the thing, and if there is a story Mrs. O'Dwyer is committed to one or more newspaper writers who got after her before we did.

There is a lot more to tell about this—fairly amusing—that I will go into orally if we get around to it.

H. W. Ross

TO REBECCA WEST

*THE NEW YORKER*
*JULY 18, 1950*

Dear Rebecca Lou:

Instead of a month of mysterious pains from an antrum (yours of July 5th), with which I sympathize, as I had an operation on one once, I spent three weeks out west, traveling around and fishing, and had a very good time, and came back invigorated. I took my daughter along and, wisely, a companion of hers, and they had a wonderful time, too. I'd always figured that I'd show her something of the country at this age, and I've done it. In that respect, the trip was also heartening to me. The United States is quite a place, which most easterns don't realize.

Now for a report on several matters.

Anthony is still engaged in *Time*. He lives in Stonington and comes to New York on Thursdays and Fridays. I met a *Time* man the other evening and got his address, which I didn't have. The *Time* man anticipated me, and had Anthony call me up. I talked to him on Friday and made a date to have a meal with him on Thursday or Friday of this week. I will report what I learn after that meeting.

When I got back, Shawn was wringing his hands because he had again sidetracked your crime stories. He had to because of the Korean thing breaking, and he may have to again. I told him to take the viewpoint that these pieces are non-rush ones—historic, or whatever— and that war takes precedence. I am therefore relieved to note the broadminded attitude expressed in your letter. Incidentally, you have two or three thousand dollars more coming on these, I think, awaiting your order. I'll get the exact sum and let you know....

The Korean business isn't a war, and it won't be unless some Russians show up at the front. When they do, there will be a war, all right. I'm pinning my main hope for peace on what I have regarded as a first principle: you don't have a world war oftener than once a generation, because the people don't want to fight. I can't believe the Russians want to fight. But maybe the world is getting so crowded now that the rule won't hold.

Let the French press story come when you get it done. The big issues will start up again in the fall and will be eating up text fast. The bottleneck is a temporary one.

As ever,
Ross


TO S. J. PERELMAN

*THE NEW YORKER*
*AUGUST 7, 1950*

Dear Sid:

I think the piece on "Wife of the Centaur," which I have just reread quickly in proof, is a lulu, very funny, quite distinguished. I was going to write you to this effect a week ago when I read it in manuscript, but got sidetracked. The circumstances are these. I was working in the country and got word that Mr. Perelman had called me and wanted me to call him back. Something about a Mr. Schindler was mentioned, and the only Mr. Schindler I know is a private detective of great caliber. I lost no time in calling back the number given me, long distance. Damn the expense; I was prepared to stand by whatever happened and to supply bail for any crime less than sedition. I got Mr. Perelman after getting a couple of other gentlemen on the phone first, presumably a police captain and an F.B.I. man, and said reassuringly, "Hello, Sid." "Well, my name isn't Sid," said Mr. Perelman, and went on to say that Mr. Schindler had promised to speak to me about having his restaurant, somewhere in Westchester, listed in our Goings On About Town department, and to drop in anytime if I happened to be going "across Westchester." I'll probably get a free meal out of it if I ever cross that county.

Anyhow, the new piece is very good, and no argument.

And, not to waste a postage stamp, I'll propose that maybe a Tarzan book would make a Cloudland piece. I know nothing of Tarzan, except that [early *New Yorker* writer] James Kevin McGuinness once wrote Tarzan scripts for the movies and that Johnny Weismuller married a young lady whose figure I admired enormously, but it might be a possibility.

Don't bother to answer this. I'll ask you sometime, or have you asked.

As ever,
Ross

TO REBECCA WEST

*THE NEW YORKER*
*AUGUST 8, 1950*

Dear Rebecca:

. . . I will here confine myself mostly to two points, upon which I feel I have something to say.

The Korean thing is awful when you personalize those lads dying and getting pounded over there. It's almost incredible that such a thing could have come about. It's incredible for Americans, that is; the English are used to it. British soldiers have been banging around the world for centuries. But we haven't taken over management in far-off places much. There's the Philippines, of course, but that was different—or we'll say it was different. But from the hard-boiled military standpoint, the Korean thing won't be serious unless the Russians go in there personally. . . .

So much for that. I will now discuss Hiss, fairly learnedly. That law officer of the crown who read the verbatim report of the Hiss hearings may very well be right in his conclusions that Hiss convicted himself. Nobody here ever read the verbatim report. They based their opinions on the newspaper accounts, which were, of course, very fragmentary, and on the surrounding circumstances, which were peculiar. The Un-American Committee was thoroughly discredited because of its wild-eyed goings on over the years, especially during the latter years under the leadership of [J. Parnell] Thomas, who is now serving time for padding his office expenses. The people that testified against Hiss were unbelievable characters—Chambers, that woman spy revealer, etc. They were a very shady lot. Certain Americans in the know also were aware that homosexuality was mixed up in the thing (and that provided a possible explanation for Chambers' attitude). And, finally,

I'm not at all sure that most Americans thought Hiss guilty, although maybe they did. Acheson, our secretary of state, for instance, certainly did not. He said so, and that carried weight with many people, including me. I couldn't figure out how a man in Acheson's advantageous position, in possession of all the facts, could reach a false conclusion. Personally, I was open-minded about Hiss. I thought the homosexuality stuff would come out in the trial, but it never did. One hears one reason as to why it didn't, and one hears another. I still have a lingering doubt that Hiss is guilty (I've seen one or two innocent men convicted) and certainly the trial didn't have comfortable finality.

The funny thing is that I probably could find out the whole truth if I had—or took—the time for it. [Undersecretary of Defense] Bob Lovett (whom you will remember) knows much, of course, but I haven't seen him in a year. When I saw him once before that, he said that the people concerned were all "very, very peculiar." Also, Lloyd Paul Stryker, who defended Hiss, is an old pal of mine. As a matter of fact, he married Hawley Truax's sister. I've never seen him to ask him about the thing, either. That shows how busy I am, or else dilatory....

As ever,
Ross

## TO THE STAMFORD POLICE DEPARTMENT

*STAMFORD, CONNECTICUT*
*AUGUST 11, 1950*

Gentlemen:

I herewith report the theft of a number of things from my house on Wire Mill Road. The circumstances are these: There was a fire in the house last fall, and it wasn't occupied all winter. During the winter and spring workmen were in the house making repairs and painting not only the damaged part of the house but the undamaged part. We didn't get reorganized until early this summer and since then Mrs. Ross has compiled a list of articles she is certain are missing, as follows:

3 all-wool imported English gabardine slack suits, tailor-made in California.

1 completely fitted Elizabeth Arden overnight bag, alligator, initialled "AA," never used.

<u>Sheets</u>
| | |
|---|---|
| 12 | 72 × 108 |
| 4 | 90 × 108 |
| 4 | 108 × 122 |
| 18 | 72 × 108 scalloped |
| 8 | 90 × 108 scalloped |
| 6 | 108 × 122 hemstitched |
| 30 | pillow cases, scalloped |

The contractor who supervised the repairs is Robert Young, 5 Station Drive, Hartsdale, New York, in case you should want his name, but in giving it to you I don't want to seem to be casting any aspersions on the people who worked on the house. God knows who took the missing things. We tried to keep them locked up in rooms not being worked on, and did this to a large extent.

Sincerely yours,
H. W. Ross

TO LILLIAN ROSS

*THE NEW YORKER*
*AUGUST 11, 1950*

Dear Lillian:

The trouble with that photograph may lie with the subject. Neither my coat nor my pants seem to be hanging right. Even discounting the wind that was blowing against me, my appearance is shocking. One in my calling should, of course, look hard-pressed, harassed, and careless, but not that disorderly. I'll get my suits pressed up. The basic trouble is, though, that I'm sort of warped.

You seem to be getting organized on a firm basis out there [in California], and I can think of nothing else to do, but if there is anything you think I can be helpful in, let me know.

I've passed on to Mr. Shawn the non-personal part of your letter and have advised Mason that the car has come through; he arranged that. Give Huston my regards. Tell him to ask Capra about Black Lake. Give Reinhardt my regards, too, if you see him again. Give everybody my regards, and don't let those high-powered boys steam-roll you.

As ever,
Ross

TO HARRY S TRUMAN

*THE NEW YORKER*
*OCTOBER 24, 1950*

My dear Mr. President:
Charles Ross advises me that you have remarked to him that you are not receiving copies of *The New Yorker.* In the face of your *wanting* to see the magazine, it is humiliating that it isn't being delivered to you, for we thought in the editorial department that it was being sent. That it isn't is the fault of the business office, which operates rather bureaucratically. We've put you down as an honorary subscriber (the first and only such) and will try to get the copies to you on that basis. We are flattered by your interest, I assure you.

Yours respectfully,
Harold W. Ross

*Hahn was in India.*

TO EMILY HAHN

*THE NEW YORKER*
*OCTOBER 25, 1950*

Dear Emily:
Gus Lobrano has passed on that letter of yours about the Commie papers that printed the wild stories on MacArthur—the girl put to bed with her brother and the other one. If you have the clips of those available and clips of any others, I wish you'd send them to me. I think we could make use of them one way or another. I won't go into just how in this note, but I have at least half an idea.

We just put through a story of yours, the one about a trip to India, second class. I'll hope for more pieces, and I send my best wishes. I hope you've been having a good and an enlightening trip.

As ever,

Ross

P.S. If you could subscribe to a Commie paper or two for me, I'd be interested. Apparently *Daily Worker*s are starting up in various parts of the world, and I'd like to keep track to a certain extent.

H.W.R.

*Gibbs had written a well-received Broadway comedy,* Season in the Sun, *whose central character was explicitly based on Ross.*

MEMO TO WOLCOTT GIBBS

*OCTOBER 31, 1950*

Mr. Gibbs:

You've fixed me up fine. I had a toothache the other morning and headed for the dentist and got in the chair, and the dentist grabbed a couple of sharp instruments and brandished them, and inquired, "What's this about that line in the show where you say 'You talk like my dentist?'" Christ! I denied everything, from the presence of the line on up, but the first claim will hold up only until the dentist gets to the show. You may have to make an affidavit that the line is yours, or, at any rate, not mine. My dentist, who takes the theater seriously, and, in fact, takes Fire Island seriously, too, being one of the colony down there, is not going to take this thing lightly.

I hear you were in the office yesterday morning to handle your proofs. If you could make it a routine to come in on Monday mornings to handle your proofs, it would be a fine thing for the office, for Monday morning is the period of greatest pressure in the whole week, and sending proofs back and forth takes time and is really dangerous. I had a reminder to propose this to you when things quieted down, and I herewith do put it to you.

H. W. Ross

*Burrows's "little show" was the smash hit* Guys and Dolls, *which was directed by George S. Kaufman.*

## TO ABE BURROWS

THE NEW YORKER
DECEMBER 20, 1950

Dear Abe:

We used, or are going to use (I've lost track) that item you sent in about the plastic cowboys and Indians, and here is the usual check [for ten dollars], which you can regard as net, nontaxable income.

We appreciate your thoughtfulness in sending this item in, and I congratulate you on the success of your little show, which, I gather, is a worthy effort generally, but which I haven't seen, although I've nagged Kaufman for seats a couple of times while sitting directly across the table from him in a poker game.

As ever,
Ross

## TO VLADIMIR NABOKOV

THE NEW YORKER
JANUARY 3, 1951

Dear Mr. Nabokov:

It has been decided that I am to write you about the Russian piece you proposed—or pieces: we note that you use the plural, and suggest a series. We had been thinking of a one-article project. I will say at once, though, that our conception is readily subject to amendment and that if the subject would stand up for several pieces we would be for several pieces. By "we" I mean Mr. Shawn, who handles the fact articles here, and I. We have just had a discussion.

What we propose is that you try one article, a self-contained one, and let us consider that and that then, afterward, the three of us discuss further articles. This assumes that you could so divide the general subject and that a self-contained single article would be feasible. It is our experience that this nearly always is the case. We cannot, unfortunately, make any guarantee in advance that would protect you against loss in case you tackle the matter and we then do not accept the piece. We never have found how to do business that way and with fact stories as with fiction stories (the term "fiction" loosely includes reminiscence of the sort you have done for us) our method is to buy them when completed. You speak of the possibility of "some unexpected circumstance" preventing publication. I can conceive of no circumstance extraneous to the piece itself (or the pieces) precluding their publication, except the dropping of an atom bomb that would put us out of business, and in that event it is possible that the management would recognize pending undertakings. . . .

I have been somewhat reluctant to write you personally, because I've never met you, having missed you on several occasions, and have never had an opportunity to express in person my admiration for the stories you have done for us. I will be able to tell you that in person sooner or later, I trust; in the meantime, I will simply say that I admired them enormously, as did a great many other people.

Please let me hear from you.

Sincerely yours,

H. W. Ross

TO REBECCA WEST

*The New Yorker*
*January 9, 1951*

Dear Rebecca:

. . . All we've done about organizing against a bombing of New York so far is talk about it a little. Presumably, the printing plant, which is at Stamford (four or five miles from where I live) won't be a target area and won't be aimed at. If bombs drop and it survives, it is assumed that we can print something or other there, and can use it as a trysting place for the staff, which can get up from the city one way or another, as best they can. If the plant should go, God knows. I have a deep mine spotted in the mountains of Colorado, but I suppose that would be taken over thoroughly by the time I could get there, and one couldn't live in a mine forever, anyhow. . . .

One thing more in this compendium: There was a horrible typo in one of your pieces: *liveried angels* got changed to *livered angels.* We don't have one of those a year, and when we do have them it is usually in the pre-Christmas rush season when the issues are exceedingly large. What happened was that something happened to the line in the print shop and it was reset. That is the only way a typographical error can get into print, and it wouldn't get into print even then if the print shop had told us the line had been reset, which, under the rules, they are obliged to do. But one well-planted bomb would fix all those things.

Best wishes for 1951.

As ever,

Ross

*From the magazine's beginnings in 1925, Brubaker had contributed "Of All Things," a column of light observations, or "paragraphs," in a format borrowed from the newspapers of the day.*

TO HOWARD BRUBAKER

*THE NEW YORKER*
*JANUARY 22, 1951*

Dear Howard:

What happened is this: We've been having more and more doubts about light-hearted josh items, and realizing more and more that it is difficult to be light-hearted and carefree these days, as things continue to get tougher, and, as a matter of fact, we've been picked up two or three times for allegedly fiddling while Rome burns, or while *something* is happening. We had a session Friday afternoon and made a number of decisions, one of which was to suspend Of All Things for a while. We thought we might as well act at once, and finding that it was as simple to make up the issue without your column, I called you to head you off.

I don't know whether you've felt any self-consciousness or not in writing the paragraphs these days, or have had any difficulty with them, because of the current atmosphere, but I know that we've been puzzled by various items from time to time lately, and have thought that we ought to pull in our horns. I hope we are not being too hyper-sensitive and that we are not taking ourselves too seriously. I've never been up against a proposition such as the present one. War doesn't buffalo me professionally, everything being black and white in war-time, and peace doesn't, although journalistically it's not as simple as war, but I'm baffled by this in-between business. I started to get out a light magazine that wouldn't concern itself with the weighty prob-lems of the universe, and now look at me....

You've got a rest coming, anyhow, so take it easy for a while. And, come to think of it, you said you could use the time well. We'll give you due notice about starting up.

As ever,

Ross

*In August Hellman had written a droll Profile of a renowned ornitholo-gist who had been a spy during the war, and how the man had used each career to advance the other. Hellman discussed how on two occasions the scientist had used his acquaintanceship with Nehru to get access to study birds in previously restricted regions of the subcontinent. Nehru, appar-ently, was unamused.*

## TO JAWAHARLAL NEHRU

*THE NEW YORKER*
*JANUARY 30, 1951*

Dear Sir:

It has come to our attention that you and your government were disturbed by an article on Dr. Sidney Dillon Ripley II, by Geoffrey T. Hellman, published in the August 26, 1950, issue of *The New Yorker.* We wish to explain several things about this article. First, *The New Yorker* is a magazine of entertainment and information (it is, to some extent, a "humorous" magazine), and we prepared this article with no purpose beyond entertaining and informing our readers; the idea for writing such an article originated in our own office, and did not come from Dr. Ripley; we regarded Dr. Ripley as an interesting man and we asked Mr. Hellman, one of our staff writers, to write a biographical article on him. Although Dr. Ripley was kind enough to grant Mr. Hellman some interviews and to serve as one of Mr. Hellman's numerous sources of information, he in no sense "authorized" the article; nor was it submitted to him for his "approval," for that would have been against our editorial policy: therefore *The New Yorker,* and not Dr. Ripley, must be held entirely responsible for all the facts and interpretations—and errors—in the article. (As it happens, Dr. Ripley was not even in the country when the article was finished and published.) As for the references to yourself and to India, we wish to assure you that we made them with the utmost respect, but we can understand how, possibly considered out of context and read in an atmosphere of seriousness not attuned to our characteristically "humorous" and "ironic" style, these references might have been misinterpreted. If we could be thought to have pictured Dr. Ripley as a bounder who took your name in vain, we owe a profound apology to both you and Dr. Ripley. And if we gave the false impression that Dr. Ripley was a secret agent at the time of his visits to Nepal, we must again apologize. Certainly we should be greatly distressed if Dr. Ripley, who is in no way responsible, should suffer for our own seeming frivolousness.

*The New Yorker* wishes to take this opportunity to express its affection for India and its unlimited admiration for yourself.

Sincerely,

H. W. Ross, The Editor

*When Ross came under the care of Dr. Jordan for his ulcers, he was pleasantly surprised that the diet she prescribed permitted him to eat such favorite foods as lobster, as long as they were prepared properly. He urged her to collaborate with Sheila Hibben, the magazine's food editor, on a cookbook and promised to provide an introduction.* Good Food for Bad Stomachs *was published that summer. Meanwhile, though his ulcers were under control, Ross was intending to get up to the Lahey Clinic in Boston for an examination because he had been having chest pains and a bad cough.*

## TO DR. SARA JORDAN

*THE NEW YORKER*
*MARCH 13, 1951*

Dear Sara:

By the dope I have you are back in Boston about now after a month off. I hope it worked out that way, and I trust that you had a pleasant month (wherever you were). As for me, I've been plugging along as usual, and, in fact, in more hot water than usual, because of sickness in the office and several other things. These now make it impossible for me to get up to Boston for that surgical matter this month, as I had tentatively planned, and I want to figure to go next month—say, sometime around the middle of the month, although I haven't figured things out yet. Would that be all right? My recollection is that when I was up there it was agreed that I could return any time over a period of several months for the surgical tinkering, although I am not completely clear on that. In any event, I have until April, haven't I?

I spent part of last weekend working on the note I'm supposed to write for the cookbook. I'm behind with this, and somewhat worried about it, for I can't get it in shape by the deadline I now have. I'm appealing for a little more time. I think I'll get it. I got into this jam, really, because the publishers didn't handle the thing right: I was told by someone at Doubleday that I would be given a month's notice and they never did give me a month's notice. The first draft of the note I wrote out had to be scrapped. I realized that I spoke so unfavorably of doctors I have had in the past (as compared to you and your Lahey associates) that I would probably be offending whole segments of the medical profession. I've got to work the piece over and take out the sarcasm and the comparisons.

I was in Washington on a quick trip a couple of weeks ago and had lunch with Robert Lovett, the undersecretary of defense, who told me that Dr. Lahey had been called in to advise in some sort of medical reorganization and that his advice had been regarded as being very helpful to the defense department.

As ever,
Ross

*Patty, who turned sixteen, was at the Tenacre School in Wellesley, Massachusetts.*

TELEGRAM TO PATRICIA ROSS

*[MARCH 17, 1951]*

Dear Pat,
Best wishes on your birthday and please know that I am proud of you. Have got seats for *Green Pastures* for Thursday night so don't make any other date.

Love,
Dad

*Ross's illness turned out to be serious enough that he was ordered to bed for several months of rest. As the next several letters indicate, it was almost summer before he could catch up with personal correspondence. Mrs. Bacon was Ross's cousin. The Vicious Circle was a book about the Algonquin Round Table by Margaret Case Harriman, a* New Yorker *contributor and daughter of the Algonquin's former owner, Frank Case.*

TO SALLIE BACON

*THE NEW YORKER*
*JUNE 20, 1951*

Dear Sallie:
I'm two letters behind on you. The reason is that I've been laid up for a few weeks with pleurisy. I had a pain in my lung and it went away

after a few days but the doctors took an x-ray and told me to spend most of my time on my back for a while and that I have been doing. I have been in no pain whatever and, in fact, have never felt better in my life. It's all quite weird. The doctors think an old calcified area in my lung that dates back to childhood opened up. Things worked out fine, for it was spring and this place in the country is beautiful and as restful a place as I know. I'll be about after next week, apparently, and none too pleased about it at that for I've got accustomed to luxurious leisure.

I read only a few chapters of *Vicious Circle* and then gave it up on the grounds of practically complete inaccuracy. I don't read those things anyhow. They embarrass me, and I find I'm not so annoyed if I don't read them.

Give Bill and Doris and all the children my regards, wherever they are. I supposed they've moved again.

I'm taking care of *The New Yorker* subscription. I'm glad you are well enough to typewrite. Me, I write out things longhand and then have them copied.

Love,
Harold

TO REBECCA WEST

*STAMFORD*
*JUNE 20, 1951*

Dear Rebecca:

... The fellows come up and talk things over with me and I do a little in the way of reading copy or proofs, and occasionally get off a letter, but I have put off most correspondence as being secondary to work on contents of the magazine. ...

I read your observations on Eleanor Roosevelt to the widow of a favorite nephew of hers who was up here, a lady who, although she has lived more or less with the Roosevelts since the death of her husband, during the war, has a viewpoint of detachment toward them. She agreed that the lady is showing her age, and this reminded me that a couple of years ago I spent three or four hours in an automobile with

Mrs. Roosevelt and that one of many beliefs she expressed in her conversation was that old people ought to be bumped off when their usefulness is done. I mildly raised the question of who would make the decision as to when the moment had come and she didn't have a ready answer for that. At that time she was quite vigorous, but I've seen her on television lately and she does unquestionably look old. All in all, she's had a stiff life, what with her husband and children, all, I should say, more or less difficult.

Whatever is wrong with [me] is "minimal." That's the word two or three of the doctors employed, and I'll almost certainly be restored to an erect position when I go back to the clinic for a big once-over next week. . . .

As ever,
Ross

TO GINGER ROGERS

*THE NEW YORKER*
*JUNE 20, 1951*

Dear young lady:

I should have written earlier, after your first note, but I've been dilatory in my correspondence. . . .

I think they're going to tell me to get up and go to work soon, just as I'm getting accustomed to leisure. Oh, I do a little work and consult and so forth. Pleurisy is what I've got. My ailment was discovered at the Lahey Clinic in Boston and I was on my way from there to here by train and ran into Jerome Zerbe, who was bound for that party for you at the Stork Club. As I unloaded from the train here, I told him to ask you to call me up. That's how that happened.

If you do get to these parts again, let me know, damn it.

As ever,
Harold

MEMO TO LOUIS FORSTER

*JUNE 26, 1951*

Mr. Forster:

The following, regarding editing matter, is to be routed pursuant to our talk on Friday afternoon.

I earnestly recommend that we abandon the word *understandably*, which has been a fad word with us for a good many months and creeps into all sorts of pieces. I saw it in *Life* the other day and when *Life* takes up a word it is time for us to unload, I think.

[E. J.] Kahn started this word, I think, and it is still a sort of Kahn trademark. At any rate, it was in one of his recent Letters from Korea. It isn't a very good word, anyhow, I have always thought, being an editorial one.

In a recent Kahn Letter from Korea the terms *EUSAK* and *FUNA* were printed in large caps, whereas, I am quite certain, the style should be small caps. This capping business should be watched carefully, for our caps are so big that when a cluster of letters get capped, it becomes highly conspicuous. There are problems here, of course, and I don't see how to write a comprehensive style rule governing capping at the moment. For instance, *U.N.* looks all right and should be our style. We use periods there which makes a difference.

*A little* is still being used too frequently. I have read several issues through at one sitting—more or less—lately, and the *a little* phrase hits you right between the eyes, and you come across it in Theater, and Cinema, and four or five other places. The variant *a trifle* does not alleviate the situation at all in my opinion. It looks just as bad.

I think a lot of paragraphs, especially in fact stuff, are running too long. In the issue of June 23rd, there were three paragraphs of over five hundred words, i.e., over a column, and two paragraphs of over four hundred words. I strongly suspect that a lot more long paragraphs in fact stuff should be broken up and that nearly all four-hundred- and five-hundred-word paragraphs should be divided somehow.

H. W. Ross

TO E. B. WHITE

*[JULY 1951]*

White:

Maybe you saw this, maybe not. *Life* does story on the placid and historic Thames and finds nude sunbathers on its banks. This must be the *fifty-eighth* way of working in naked women.

I had an X-ray taken and the doctor in preliminary telephone report says good news, but no details yet.

Ross

*O'Dwyer had resigned as mayor of New York just ahead of allegations that he had taken political payoffs, and he was now ambassador to Mexico. Ross's medical condition, meanwhile, was considerably more serious than he lets on here to his old friend. Back in June Ross really did think his chest pains were due to pleurisy. When he didn't recuperate fully his doctors ran more extensive tests and found that what Ross, a lifelong smoker, really had was cancer of the windpipe. He seems to have kept this news from everyone except his confidant Hawley Truax and attorney Julius Baer. The treatments Ross alludes to were radiation therapy, which he began July 10 and would endure five more weeks.*

TO WILLIAM O'DWYER

*THE NEW YORKER*
*JULY 30, 1951*

Dear Bill:

I have given a letter of introduction to you to Dr. William H. Resnik, of Stamford, my principal personal physician as well as my friend, who is headed your way with his family for his vacation, and I've asked him to call by and tell you the recent news of me, which is nine-tenths medical, and to which he is one of the few who are privy. It is, I assure you, a most amazing yarn, with a happy ending. It is one too complicated to go into on paper. One factor is that I was on my tail in bed, either in a hospital or at home (in Connecticut) for three months. I'm on my feet now and feeling no pain (in fact I've never felt any to speak of) but I've got to be in Boston on Mondays, Tuesdays, Wednesdays, Thursdays, and Fridays for treatments, which can be given only in Boston. This leaves me weekends at home. It is a very peculiar life.

Boston is the only place where they have the apparatus for the treatments. I tried to get one installed in New York and, failing that, in Mexico City, but have so far failed. I have a few more weeks of this kind of thing to go through, at the end of which time I will be restored to duty. As I will not have been in the office for four months at the end of that time, I will probably be ruined. In that event, I intend to become a beachcomber at Acapulco, claiming the protection of the American embassy.

If this letter sounds self-centered it is because I know little of what has been happening in the outer world lately, especially New York. I read about the municipal officeholders from time to time and smile smugly. They are up against a losing game at best, and you are well out of it all.

Love to Sloan.

As ever,

Ross

P.S. Come to think of it, you'd better let Resnik listen to your glands. He might hear something. He is a man in whom I have great confidence, and if you aren't feeling just perfect, ask him about yourself. You had better do it anyhow.

H.W.R.

P.P.S. The old Stamford place, from which this is written, is really a peaceful place to come, and it is looking fine this year.

H.W.R.


TO E. B. WHITE

*[SEPTEMBER 1951]*

Mr. White:

I am back at work on a break-in, gradual basis. I am reading Newsbreaks and Talk anecdotes and doing a couple of other small things.

The Newsbreaks are a pleasure. Through the years, they have remained my only weekly pleasure.

Pls. note Packard's note below this and decide how you want the item headed. Packard's first two sentences seem to contradict each other flatly, but you'll get what he means.

I marked English quote marks into this, instead of stetting the French quotes. For one thing, I doubt if Nast has French quotes on hand for the Linotype machines, and if he hasn't he would have to borrow them from a French printer here. I was in the reverse of this situation once and know how tough it can be. I undertook to get out a black market publication in Paris during the First World War and made a deal with an American Army printing company (soldiers) to do the composition. They were glad to earn some money and worked cheap. The only thing was, there weren't any English quote marks in the French print shop in which they were stationed and did their work, and my copy was full of quotes. I had to provide English quotes. I had drag with the foreman of the composing room of the *Daily Mail*, which printed the *Stars and Stripes*, upon which I was then employed, and he would lend me, for the daylight hours, the quote marks from the *Daily Mail*'s machines. I had to have them back by dusk for use at the *Daily Mail* plant, or the *Daily Mail* wouldn't get to press. The French print shop was in the outskirts of Paris, twelve miles about from the *Daily Mail* plant, and for ten days I had to make two trips a day between the two places, delivering and recovering twelve small slivers of metal. I have never been the same since.

I don't know why I pause to tell you this. I should be writing my life, which is full of such oddities.

Ross

TO REBECCA WEST

*THE NEW YORKER*
*OCTOBER 11, 1951*

Dear Rebecca:

Hawley Truax told me about that letter you wrote him, and I am responding more or less at once, sheepishly, because I should have written you three or four weeks ago, when I got back in circulation, on a limited basis, at least. The reason you haven't heard from me is this: I put in a folder, on my desk up in the country, a rather vast accumulation of personal letters, intending to answer them soon, and I have put off doing so because of giving office work precedence when I've been at my desk in the country.

I have taken back about one-third of the work I used to do at the office, but that has kept me busy, partly because, I suspect, I just got out of the habit of working and partly because I am only about fifty percent efficient yet, although I am pronounced and seem to be eighty-five percent recovered. It isn't that I have been conspicuously racked by sickness. I look fine, everyone says, and I haven't looked bad all the way through, I take it, but for ten weeks or thereabouts I have had (to be frankly clinical) a running abscess in my lung. I have had spells of coughing up this discharge, one or two spells of an hour's duration during the night and some during the day, and that has prolonged my periods of rest in bed, or of staying in bed, and so on, and cut seriously into my time. An infection has been, of course, the cause of it all, and I have been taking antibiotics of one kind or another by the handfuls to kill off the bugs. For most of the period three types of bugs were going at me, but the number had been reduced to two at the time of my last check-up, and these survivors were getting the worst of it. But the antibiotics didn't do the job as quick as the doctors thought they would; that is a cinch. It has taken a long time. The infection was accompanied by an off-and-on fever. I had and still have, as a matter of fact, a male nurse with me, to keep track of my medications, take my pulse, temperature, etc., and over a long period he would stick a thermometer in my mouth and, half the time, order me to bed, on the grounds that my temperature was over a hundred. The fever, and the discharge, are greatly reduced at the present time. As a matter of fact, I haven't run any temperature in a week or ten days. I'm beginning to feel pretty good, although, as I estimated, I'm not yet as efficient as I was.

I've had the damndest summer of my life, the damndest period of my life, but I won't take time to go into that now. The recollection is pretty much of a blur, anyhow. I was in and out of the hospital, and for seven or eight weeks lived with my male nurse, eating with him three times a day, sleeping in adjoining rooms at an old-lady's-home sort of a hotel in the suburbs of Boston, a city I have come to hate with a bitterness that is unholy. This is largely because of the restaurant situation there; the poor quality of the food is unbelievable. You were better off in England at the height of the food shortage than the people of Boston are today; take my word for it. . . .

What I was doing during my hotel stay in Boston was taking a series of treatments administered by an apparatus so new that it was available only in Boston. I don't know what was the matter with the King of England [George VI], but his summer's experiences parallel mine (except that he was ordered to Scotland to walk the moors and I was ordered to bed at home in Connecticut for a spell), but I have wound up without surgery, and I suspect it was the way the thing was handled. It is either one of two things: He was worse off than I was or else I had better doctoring, and I suspect the latter. These lung things take time always, it seems. They take an X-ray (during the diagnostic period) and say, "Well, that didn't show anything conclusive—no change to speak of over the last X-ray, so we'll wait a week and take another," and there you are for another week, flat in bed.

I was touched by the suggestion, mentioned by Hawley Truax, that you could come over and see me if it would be helpful. I was tempted to put on a long face and ask you to come, but I'm really on the road now (barring, of course, complications). As a matter of fact, I'm back at work half time or better. More later. God bless you.

As ever,
Ross

TELEGRAM TO JOE E. LEWIS

*OCTOBER 15, 1951*

Am again on my feet and if you will kindly let me know how I can reach you by telephone I'll make advances. Looking forward to social intercourse.

H.W. Ross

TO J. D. SALINGER

THE NEW YORKER
OCTOBER 23, 1951

Dear Jerry Salinger:

I got your note about not coming to the country on time, but I can't keep up with my personal correspondence, it seems, so please forgive me for not acknowledging it. I'll put you down for the spring. If you should want to come earlier than that, let me know, for my present plan is to keep the joint open weekends for the winter.

As ever,
H. W. Ross

*During their visit Ross told his daughter, now at the Woodstock Country School in Vermont, that he was returning to Boston for more medical tests. But he never told her about the cancer.*

TO PATRICIA ROSS

THE NEW YORKER
OCTOBER 30, 1951

Dear Pat:

I arrived home with the toothpaste you bought at the drugstore and whatever else is in the package. It was in my overcoat pocket. I'm mailing it up to you. I left your hat at the hotel and told them you would call for it. We are both rattle-brained.

I got back to town late yesterday and haven't been able to get your mother on the phone this morning. She went out. I'll get her soon, though, and tell her about your plans.

I very much enjoyed my stay at Woodstock and am more proud of you than ever.

With much love,
Dad

P.S. I just talked to your mother. She is calling Mr. Bailey to see if you can come down right away, because the doctor has ordered her to go away and rest for a couple of weeks and she won't be here after the

15th. There is nothing serious but she isn't regaining weight fast enough. She took a trip to Easthampton and it exhausted her; no chance of her making the trip to Woodstock this fall. So you've been worrying unnecessarily, as usual. Nearly all worry is about the wrong thing.

*Ross had named attorneys Baer and Greenstein as the executors of his estate. The radiation hadn't arrested the cancer, and he typed out this statement two days before undergoing exploratory surgery in Boston.*

TO JULIUS BAER AND MILTON GREENSTEIN

*DECEMBER 4, 1951*

To My Executors:

Upon my death, I desire that my remains be cremated and that my ashes be held until my daughter Patricia attains the age of twenty-one. Unless Patricia wishes to do otherwise with my ashes, they are to be strewn from a plane on the mountains around Aspen, Colorado.

I request that one or more of my friends at *The New Yorker* magazine take charge of my funeral services and suggest that they be held at Frank Campbell's Funeral Parlor, where things are made about as simple as possible.

Harold W. Ross

*During an operation on December 6 at New England Baptist Hospital, doctors discovered that Ross's cancer had spread to his lungs. He died before coming out of the anesthetic.*

*Harold W. Ross was fifty-nine years old.*

# INDEX